Religious Thought
and the Modern Psychologies

Religious Thought
and the Modern Psychologies

Second Edition

Don S. Browning and Terry D. Cooper

Fortress Press
Minneapolis

RELIGIOUS THOUGHT AND THE MODERN PSYCHOLOGIES
Second Edition

Cover art © Photodisc, Inc.
Cover design: Ann Delgehausen
Interior design: Beth Wright

ISBN 0-8006-3659-7

The paper used in this publication meets the minimum requirements of American National Standard for Information Sciences—Permanence of Paper for Printed Library Materials, ANSI Z329.48-1984.

Manufactured in the U.S.A.
08   07   06   05   04   1   2   3   4   5   6   7   8   9   10

Contents

Preface to the Second Edition

Many new trends have touched the fields of psychology and psychotherapy since *Religious Thought and the Modern Psychologies* was published in 1987. Furthermore, there have been several scholarly responses to its central thesis, i.e., that the modern psychotherapeutic psychologies are not strictly scientific. They should be viewed, instead, as mixed disciplines blending psychological insights with both ethical and quasi-religious assumptions. Some of these responses agreed with this point of view and applied it to the analysis of schools of psychology and psychotherapy that were not reviewed in the first edition.

In this second edition, we will examine some new schools of psychotherapeutic psychology. We will do this in part with the help of other scholars who have extended in their writing our original thesis to additional schools of psychology. At the same time, we will be in critical dialogue with these same scholars; even though they make use of *Religious Thought and the Modern Psychologies*, they invariably have their own philosophical and methodological twists to add. Hence, we have interesting differences even with those who have used our insights.

The reader will have noticed that the pronoun "we" is being used in this preface. This is to inform you of something that is clear enough on the cover of the book: the second edition is the product of two authors, not just one. The first edition was written by Don Browning. In this second edition, Browning is joined by Professor Terry Cooper. While finishing his second doctorate, Cooper did extensive work with *Religious Thought and the Modern Psychologies* and began consulting with Browning about how to develop the second edition. Michael West of Fortress Press had encouraged a second edition as well. Hence, a partnership between Browning and Cooper was formed.

Here is how we have decided to sort the various uses of "I" and "we" throughout the revised text. In this preface, it is "we"; the plan for revision is a product of our joint deliberations and needs to be represented as such from the beginning. Throughout the original chapters of the first edition, i.e., the preface through chapters 1 to 9, Browning still speaks with the pronoun "I" even though the many revisions are a result of joint consultations between the two of us. Chapters 10 and 11 are entirely new. Although first drafted by Cooper, they subsequently have been so jointly revised that now the editorial "we" seems both appropriate and efficient.

Since 1987, there have been several new commentaries attempting to define what kind of discipline psychotherapeutic psychology actually is. *Religious Thought and the Modern Psychologies* was one of the first books arguing that psychotherapy was not only an ethical process but a quasi-religious one as well. Since then, several other books have advanced at least part of this argument. By this, we mean they have taken up the moral side of the argument and claimed that the modern psychotherapeutic psychologies are value-laden and moral through and through. In effect, they are agreeing with our argument that these psychologies are expressions of what the ancient Greeks called *phronesis* or practical reason. Many of these new works also agree that the ethical slant of much of modern psychotherapy is individualistic, i.e., a form of what moral philosophers call ethical egoism. This is certainly the core argument of William Doherty's excellent *Soul Searching: Why Psychotherapy Must Promote Moral Responsibility* (1995).[1] This is also the argument of Ellen Herman's *The Romance of American Psychology* (1995).[2] From our perspective, these welcome new commentaries are still a little unnuanced in their moral analysis of the modern therapies. But they shun even more any analysis of the religious and metaphysical horizon of these psychotherapeutic psychologies.

We will enter into extensive dialogue with two new books on the modern psychologies and psychotherapies. The first is Philip Cushman's 1995 book titled *Constructing the Self, Constructing America: A Cultural History of Psychotherapy*.[3] The second is *Re-envisioning Psychology: Moral Dimensions of Theory and Practice* (1999) by Frank Richardson, Blaine Fowers, and Charles Guignon.[4] These books share a very important feature that our revision must address. They both develop a hermeneutic perspective on modern psychology and psychotherapy. What does this mean? Hermeneutics deals with the rules of interpreting a text. But in the case of these two books, they not only see psychotherapy as a kind of text to be interpreted, they also are making use of hermeneutic philosophy—a school that is associated with such European thinkers as Martin Heidegger, Hans-Georg Gadamer, and Paul Ricoeur. In short, this school sees all interpretation as a kind of dialogue between historically situated persons and their respective utterances, texts, and monuments. In this school of thought, dialogue becomes a key to the very nature of human existence—the key to human *ontology* or what it means *to be* a human. This school would say that all psychology and all psychotherapy are forms of dialogue. This means that whatever objective science they contain, it should be seen as situated within theories that are themselves largely products of historical forces. Hermeneutic perspectives on psychology and psychotherapy also see these disciplines as helping clients with historically situated problems and furthermore finding answers that largely make sense within particular historical contexts.

We gradually will unfold throughout this second edition the central ideas of these two hermeneutic analyses of modern psychology and psychotherapy. We will then bring them into dialogue with *Religious Thought and the Modern Psychologies*. It should be pointed out, however, that the first edition did not explicitly take a hermeneutic approach to the relation of theology and the modern psychologies. To be frank, Browning at that time had not yet read—at least not read seriously— Gadamer's great *Truth and Method* (1982).[5] Ricoeur was very important for the first edition, but mainly in terms of his philosophical anthropology and his interpretation of Freud. The relevance of Ricoeur as a hermeneutic philosopher was only lightly touched. Almost immediately after the first edition was published, Browning did give a fresh reading to the hermeneutic philosophies of Gadamer, Ricoeur, and Richard Bernstein and began to understand their relevance to a reconceptualization of psychology, sociology, and the other human sciences. A hermeneutic view of the social and human sciences, including psychology, was extensively developed in Browning's *A Fundamental Practical Theology* (1991).[6] In part, this second edition is an attempt to bring *Religious Thought and the Modern Psychologies* in line with the hermeneutic turn taken in *A Fundamental Practical Theology*.

This second edition will reflect the fruitfulness of a hermeneutic perspective on the modern psychologies and psychotherapies. *Hermeneutic philosophy helps us understand why the modern psychologies cannot avoid either a moral or theological horizon.* Hermeneutic philosophy reinforces the original argument of *Religious Thought and the Modern Psychologies*. But there are at least two major differences between the argument of the first edition and the views reflected in *Constructing the Self, Constructing America* and *Re-envisioning Psychology*. Both of these books do not understand why the hermeneutic perspective also requires uncovering the religious or visional levels of the various modern psychologies. These books, for the most part, ignore the role of religion. Or to say it differently, they abstract the modern psychologies from the religious dimensions of their "effective history," i.e., the effects of the past that continue to influence the thinking of the present, even the thinking of psychologists and therapists as researchers. In addition, these two pathbreaking books are simultaneously insightful yet limited in what they have to say about the moral dimension of the modern psychologies.

And finally, these books fail to address adequately the question of relativism. If psychotherapeutic psychology is invariably freighted with historical, moral, and even religious assumptions, how does one make judgments about the relative adequacy of these assumptions? It is not enough to demonstrate that these judgments are present in psychotherapeutic theories and practice. It is not enough to acknowledge that they play an important role. We must go further and discuss the difference between good and bad moral judgments and uplifting and damaging religious assumptions. One cannot speak about morality and religion after the post-9/11 catastrophe without introducing an element of *critique*. *Religious Thought and the Modern Psychologies* discussed the questions of relativism and criticism in the first edition. It will extend those remarks in the second edition, now in conversation with those theorists who are urging a hermeneutic perspective on the modern psychologies. The position that we will develop goes beyond hermeneutics as it is often conceived. We will advocate a brand of *critical hermeneutics* or *hermeneutic realism*.

By engaging the new hermeneutic perspectives on the human sciences, we are in effect taking a step into the muddy waters of postmodernism. Hermeneutic philosophy can be seen as a form of postmodernism when that term is thought to refer to the historical and linguistic conditionedness of all thought, including allegedly scientific thought and theories. Addressing the impact of this particular form of postmodernism will make setting forth the central themes of our book both easier and harder to accomplish. It is easier in that postmodern thinkers readily admit that a horizon of assumptions, implicit values, and theoretical commitments is a part of even our more rigorous scientific efforts. No one begins their theorizing from a neutral place, and a pretense to pure objectivity must be exposed as hubris. In view of this new mindset, there may be less resistance to our conviction that the clinical psychologies contain "metaphors of ultimacy" derived from what Gadamer called "effective history," even the effective history of much older theological and religious views of the most determinative context of experience.

Postmoderns are a little more comfortable admitting that they base their "official" thinking on a cluster of culturally inherited assumptions. The realization that psychology is a hermeneutical enterprise may not be as shocking today as it was to the inheritors of the Enlightenment. After all, isn't this the age of postpositivistic science? Consequently, our job should be easier.

On the other hand, many postmodern themes also have made our work more difficult. Our goal is to tease out the implicit philosophical assumptions, ethical principles, and metaphysical visions of contemporary psychological and psychotherapeutic theories. Yet we do not stop with a simple recognition of the many occasions when allegedly scientific psychologies lapse over into ethics and quasi-religious visions of life. Instead, we wish to bring selected alternative moral and religious visions together into what we call a "critical correlational" analysis—a concept and method we explain at various points in the main chapters. With the help of a multidimensional model of practical reason that we use to analyze the full reality of the modern psychologies, we also will enter into critical dialogue with the new hermeneutic interpretations of psychology and psychotherapy. In short, we go beyond most hermeneutic perspectives; we aspire to compare and contrast implicit images of the human with an eye toward discovering those perspectives that more adequately describe the human condition. This is what makes our view a form of critical hermeneutics.

Some postmodern voices believe this effort is a waste of time. After all, all perspectives are historically given, socially located, and completely relative to particular communities of discourse. They contend that we cannot step outside of our own perspectives long enough to evaluate anyone else's point of view on life, morality, and ultimate things. Even if we could, say many postmoderns, there is absolutely no standard by which we could assess alternative views. Thus for many postmoderns, critical dialogue is not possible. We have only two options open to us. One is to point to the multiplicity of interpretations and describe them the best that we can. The other is to describe our own perspective and assert its truth and authority as an act of faith.

We agree with postmoderns that no one can completely step outside a cultural tradition and start thinking from a neutral, totally objective space. In fact, it is precisely this point that we will spend much time trying to delineate in this book. Yet we also believe along with Paul Ricoeur that even though pure objectivity is impossible, acts of "distanciation" from one's inherited assumptions are possible and important functions for every thoughtful person and, indeed, for every psychology.[7] We agree that philosophical foundationalism—the idea that human thought must rest on indubitable, rock-bottom, objective facts or *a priori* assumptions—is impossible. Yet, even though we cannot totally detach our descriptions and concepts from our pre-theoretical life world, this does not mean that we cannot gain levels or degrees of critical distance from it. Although a critical analysis of alternative images of the human in our various psychotherapeutic psychologies will never reach pure objectivity, it can be conducted with a degree of success. If this is not the case, then all intellectual discussions would be reduced to something like comparing our favorite foods; they would be largely a clash of differing personal tastes. While we respect the richness of a variety of perspectives, we think it is still important to examine issues of comprehensiveness, moral and metaphysical adequacy, and empirical plausibility when investigating alternative psychological theories. Just because we cannot know Absolute Reality as it is In-itself does not mean that we cannot come close to it as we explore our own and others' assumptive worlds. Stated bluntly, some views are indeed better than others.

A number of persons were thanked in the preface of the first edition. Those expressions of gratitude still stand. But new names should be added. In addition to the helpful guidance of Michael West of Fortress Press, we want to express our appreciation to our new dialogue partners to be discussed in the chapters to follow—principally Stanton Jones; his partner, Richard Butnam; Paul Watson; and Stephen Evans. Their insights have extended our own grasp of the argument of this book.

Don S. Browning
Terry D. Cooper

Preface to the First Edition

This book attempts to uncover the ethical and metaphysical horizon of some of the major contemporary psychotherapeutic psychologies. It does this by analyzing the implicit principles of obligation and the deep metaphors embedded in and around the conceptual systems of these psychologies. But the book not only analyzes these psychologies' deep metaphors and implicit principles of obligation, it also advances a critique of these dimensions of the modern psychologies. This critique is informed by the ethical and metaphysical resources of the Jewish and Christian religious traditions.

Such a venture can give rise to several misunderstandings, and it is appropriate to use this preface to anticipate and correct some of the more obvious ones that might arise in the minds of this book's potential readers. First, it is important to announce at the beginning that this book should be seen as basically an illustrative exercise. I hope to illustrate a kind of cultural conversation that I believe is important to have with the social and psychological sciences. Increasingly these disciplines are helping to shape the self-understanding of modern individuals.

There is little doubt in my mind that these disciplines deserve to play a role in influencing the view that modern individuals have of themselves. But it may be healthier for these sciences to play a limited role in shaping our self-interpretations, even though this role might still be very important. It is essential that the sciences of the human remain sciences and not become, in addition, our functional religions, worldviews, or ethics. Yet, there are times when the social and psychological sciences begin to occupy just these larger roles in our lives. When they do this, they rightly become subjects for religious and ethical criticism. In this book, I want to illustrate what this critical conversation might look like and how it might be conducted. I will not cover all the issues nor solve all the problems. I hope only to do a sufficiently serious job of conducting this conversation to demonstrate that critical discussion is possible and to encourage others to conduct it further.

Some will believe that it is too narrow and parochial to limit this critical conversation to the Judeo-Christian tradition. Some will insist it is necessary to bring into the discussion other non-Western religious and ethical views. Such an objection would be a good one, but if the reader keeps in mind the illustrative purpose of this volume, that complaint loses some of its force. My decision to confine myself to the West is motivated by three factors. First, I hope to show that a critical conversation is indeed possible between an established religious tradition and the normative horizons of the modern psychologies. Second, since the Judeo-Christian tradition is the tradition which has most substantially and most decisively informed Western cultures, it does seem to make sense to engage that tradition first. And third, my argument is that there are good reasons, although possibly not definitive ones, to continue to see that tradition as a major source for the interpretation of life and that we should not too quickly permit the implicit religious and ethical horizon of the social sciences to replace the explicit religion and ethics of the Jewish and Christian traditions.

Some may be concerned that I have limited the representatives of the Christian tradition principally to Reinhold Niebuhr, William James, and Paul Ricoeur. Other figures are referred to and employed, but these are the main sources. Once again, the reader should bear the illustrative character of this volume in mind. Other important contemporary theologians could be used to exemplify the kind of cultural conversation that I believe is important to pursue. Certainly the works of Paul Tillich, Karl Rahner, Bernard Lonergan, or David Tracy could be substantially used. But I have found it more productive to illustrate this conversation by pursuing the implications of the thought of a cluster of closely related thinkers and then gradually move outward from there. The reader will see how this happens in my discussion of the concept of neighbor-love; I start the conversation with the typically Protestant view of Reinhold Niebuhr and conclude with a *caritas* interpretation of the principle generally associated with Catholicism.

In critiquing the normative horizon of the modern psychologies, some may think that I do not value these disciplines. Nothing could be further from the truth. It is precisely because I feel that the modern psychologies are, in their different ways, indispensable for modern life that I believe it worthwhile to understand and evaluate the subtle ways in which they transcend themselves and play roles that they are not designed nor well equipped to fulfill. In each chapter I make a few remarks about the importance, as psychology, of each of the schools I review. But gradually as the book develops, and especially in the chapters on Jung and Erikson and Kohut, I will argue the view that the modern psychologies primarily offer modern culture theories of the "nonmoral good," which tell us what human beings naturally and regularly want and need. These psychobiological theories of the nonmoral (or premoral) good (a concept to be explained in detail later) function as basic frameworks for the definition of health and illness. The healthy person is the person who has free access to these premoral goods or wants, tendencies, and needs. The healthy person is also one who has significant, although limited, amounts of control over these basic wants, tendencies, and needs. The modern psychologies, and other disciplines as well, promise to give advanced cultures clearer knowledge than ever before about the range and development schedule of these tendencies and needs and also about how these tendencies and needs function psychodynamically with the outside social world and with each other. But knowledge about the range, hierarchy, and development schedule of basic tendencies and needs should not dictate how these needs are organized morally to fit or harmonize with the needs of others. These natural dispositions are relevant to but not exhaustive of the question of their moral organization. The modern clinical psychologies are not very clear about the relation of basic human tendencies and needs to their moral elaboration, and, as we will see, they frequently blur the conceptual boundaries between the healthy appropriation of these needs and their moral patterning.

The reader will notice two models of psychology emerging in the pages that follow. One model envisions psychology as a relatively objective and scientific discipline dedicated to the development of a body of knowledge about the patterns in human symbolic and behavioral activity. This view of psychology will be distinguished from another view that conceives psychology as a practical discipline based on a critical ethic and a critical theory of society. Although there is no absolute distinction between the two sciences, the second tries self-consciously and critically to ground itself in an ethic and a metaphysic, while the first focuses primarily on the generation of new descriptive knowledge about the way humans think and behave. On the one hand, it will appear that in this book I am criticizing the psychologies for their unwitting ethics and metaphysics. But the reader should keep in mind that gradually I will develop the argument that the clinical psychologies, especially, cannot avoid a metaphysical and ethical horizon and, for this reason, they should critically ground these features of their systems rather than unwittingly lapse into them.

I am aware that parts of this book have similarities to contemporary deconstructionist movements in philosophy and literary criticism. Both my efforts here and the deconstructionists' project attend to the analysis of metaphorical language and the way these metaphors form systems of meaning sometimes quite independently of, or differently from, the official preoccupations of the texts being studied. But I have resisted the temptation to attempt a full encounter with deconstructionism and to press it into the service of my project. I have commitments to the possibility of making reasonably valid rational arguments in metaphysics and ethics, which the deconstructionists believe to be impossible. Hence, I have resolved to delay until later a more careful review of the potential contribution of deconstructionism.

Unfortunately, Richard Fox's important biography entitled *Reinhold Niebuhr* (New York: Pantheon, 1985) was released after this book was already in the hands of the publisher and therefore too late to inform my discussion of Niebuhr. Although Niebuhr's relation to psychology and psychoanalysis is not a central concern of his book, there are within it significant discussions of Niebuhr's relation to Tillich and the way their different approaches to psychology constituted a troublesome issue between them. Fox's discussion of the Tillich-Niebuhr relationship on the issue of psychology (pages 256–59) gives some insight as to why Niebuhr, rather than Tillich, is the principal theologian used in this book.

A few people will be tempted to read this book from the perspective of their experience as a client or therapist within the context of their favorite psychotherapy. Their experience within the context of Freudian, humanistic, or Jungian therapy, for instance, will be used to measure what I say about these psychologies. But such an interpretive perspective may lead to misunderstandings. I am not speaking of these psychologies from the perspective of the experience of therapy; I am writing about them as cultural documents that are read by and therefore influence wide sectors of our society. We know enough about therapeutic practice to admit that what individual followers of Carl Jung or Carl Rogers do in their therapy may be something quite independent of the key literature that allegedly undergirds the theory of their work. But these psychologies as cultural documents and not the idiosyncratic activities of various therapists constitute the vantage point of my investigation.

Portions of this book were first delivered as the Sprunt Lectures at Union Theological Seminary in Richmond, Virginia in late January of 1984. I want to thank the administration and faculty of Union, especially President T. Hartley Hall III, Dean William Arnold, and Professors Charles Sweezy, Sarah Little, and William Oglesby for their generous hospitality during these lectures. Portions of this book were also given for the 1984 Colliver Lectures at the University of the Pacific, the 1984 Scott Lectures at Christian Theological Seminary, and the 1985 Stewart Lectures at Seabury-Western Theological Seminary.

I want to thank Peter Mehl, my research assistant, for his energy and dedication to the typing and editing of this book during a time when he had his own important research agenda. I also want to thank Professor Robert Fuller of Bradley University for giving the complete manuscript a thorough reading prior to my final revisions and additions. His comments helped me both broaden the scope of the manuscript and clarify many of the points I was trying to make. Professor Wallace Clift of the University of Denver read the chapter on Jung and gave me both encouragement and constructive criticism. Dr. Tom Jobe of the Department of Psychiatry at the University of Illinois Medical Center, Chicago, Illinois, both discussed some of the ideas in this book and gave it a critical reading. I profited a great deal from these conversations. I want to thank Dr. Edwin Wallace IV of the Department of Psychiatry of the Georgia Medical College for our fruitful conversations over the last year and his generous reading and criticism of this manuscript. And finally, my gratitude must go to Professor Bernie Lyon of the Christian Theological Seminary for sharing his thoughts about the manuscript and helping me, as he has done so many times before, come to understand more deeply what I am really trying to do. Of course, none of these colleagues must bear any responsibility for the shortcomings of my efforts on these pages.

And finally, I would like to dedicate this book to my wife Carol. Carol shared the dedication of an earlier book with my daughter Elizabeth, but she has never received an entire dedication herself. In addition to her generous review of this book, after twenty-seven years of marriage it needs to be said publicly that not only is she a great mother, wife, organist, pianist, knitter, and woman, but she also knows how to provide space and support for the flourishing of those around her.

Don S. Browning

Faith and the Modern Psychologies

I have a colleague who is fond of saying that modern individuals "live on scraps." By this he seems to mean that all modern individuals, whether they know it or not, live on bits and pieces, yes, scraps of *meaning*. They really have no encompassing faith, no ultimate concern, no real unity to their lives. They draw together their scraps of meaning like skid-row bums foraging for food in the trash bins of supermarkets and restaurants. They take what they can find and they use what they have on the basis of the exigencies of the situations in which they find themselves. Their self-understandings and identities change from crisis to crisis or from moment to moment as they move through their individual life cycles.

Such is his portrait of the life of people in modern societies. There is a great deal of truth in his point of view. And what truth there may be in his view applies not only to roller-skating counter-cultural types that still roam the beachfront communities in California and Florida. Nor does it apply only to the hordes of aimless tourists prowling Times Square. This picture of the identity structure of modern individuals may be true, to varying degrees, of us all—philosopher or minister, agnostic or faithful member of the church, laborer or educated professional.

In agreeing to some extent with my colleague, I acknowledge that all of us who inhabit pluralistic and rapidly changing modern societies construct our identities out of a wide variety of resources. But I am more optimistic than my colleague that some of us moderns can and do achieve a rather high degree of coherence, focus, and purpose out of the various bits and pieces that go into our identities. Some of the scraps can and do become master scraps, organizing and synthesizing the other fragments into a more or less working whole.

Those of us who call ourselves Christians or Jews or Protestants or Catholics must face the fact that we are never purely that. At best our Christian or Jewish identities can qualify or shape all of the other partial identities that make up our sense of self. Ministers, rabbis, and priests who have it as their special vocations to help fashion coherent religious identities in their people must face the truth that the most they can hope for is to deepen their followers' Christian or Jewish identities until they become central to their more limited identities as small town or urban, poor or wealthy, seductive or repulsive, worker or intellectual.

In this book, I will investigate the potential relationships between two sources of modern individual identity—religious faith as it has been formed by the Judeo-Christian tradition of the West and the disciplines of psychology as these have developed in the twentieth century. But why give such special attention to these two

1

sources and why together? My answer is this: *traditional religion and modern psychology stand in a special relation to one another because both of them provide concepts and technologies for the ordering of the interior life.*

The Influence of Psychology on Religion

In these pages I will address all those individuals who are interested in the contemporary interaction between traditional religion and the modern psychologies. Many of us who are concerned with this interaction have been influenced by the religious thought (the theologies) of our own religious tradition. But more and more, some of us also have been shaped by the interpretive perspectives of the social sciences and, especially, psychology in its various forms. But the question this book addresses is not simply a parochial matter; it is a cultural problematic of great general significance. Will our culture be oriented and directed by our inherited religious traditions or will it increasingly gain its orientation, especially with regard to the inner life, from the modern psychologies? Or is there a way to state the appropriate relationship between these two perspectives, thereby giving each its proper space?

Although this is an issue facing the entire culture, we see concrete symptoms of it everywhere. The religious leaders of our culture—our ministers, priests, and rabbis—all receive large doses of psychotherapeutic psychology, personality theory, and developmental psychology in their professional education, often without much careful reflection on how this knowledge squares with what they have learned about humans from a religious and theological perspective. These same ministers sit on boards of education, are trustees for institutions of mental health, refer individuals to psychologists and psychiatrists, and work with a variety of professionals in hospitals, jails, and other social service institutions. By their involvement with these various institutions and through their contact with secular professionals, clergy are constantly confronting the social sciences in general and psychology in particular as basic orienting disciplines for these institutions and their staffs. How do they order their religious and social science orientations in such a way as to communicate their convictions to a public world that is increasingly more pluralistic?

The tension that the clergy faces on this issue is really only symbolic of the conflict faced by most people in Western cultures, and it is on this broader cultural level that I want to move in this book. How do individuals who have been taught to orient their lives around the wisdom of Judeo-Christian religious thought handle the social sciences, especially the psychologies? How do they read these psychologies, understand what knowledge they give us, comprehend their boundaries, and most importantly of all, discern both their limits and what they cannot, do not, or should not tell us or claim to tell us?

I do not only address the "confirmed believer." Such a phrase does not describe with accuracy the situation of very many of us. Instead, I address all those who acknowledge that they have been touched, shaped, and influenced *in some way* by the Jewish and Christian traditions. I am writing for those individuals who are still wrestling with what these traditions and their claims may mean for modern persons. Although I will speak primarily about Christian thought, it is my conviction that Christianity cannot be understood without reference to its background in Judaism. In addition, the theistic metaphor that we will discuss and evaluate is fundamental to both of these religious traditions. But furthermore, I address all those who also acknowledge that they have been touched, shaped, and influenced by the modern psychologies and who are actively asking about the place they should occupy among the resources for modern living. It is not only the professional religious leader who is trying to muddle through to some understanding about the relation of inherited faiths to the modern social sciences; it is a problem for him or her because, in one way or another, it is a problem for most everyone in modern culture.

What Are the Modern Psychologies?

By the modern psychologies, I mean primarily those psychologies that have originated in the twentieth century. In this book I will certainly not discuss them all. In fact, I will limit myself to a few of the more prominent schools and systems that have dominated the twentieth-century cultural landscape. With the help of Terry Cooper and a few scholars who have extended my argument, this second edition will review several additional psychologies. There will be a preference in my discussion for the psychotherapeutic psychologies or, at least, those with psychotherapeutic implications. These have been the ones most influential on culture in general and religious institutions in particular. I will concentrate primarily on Sigmund Freud, some humanistic psychologies, B. F. Skinner, and, after a brief theoretical interlude, on C. G. Jung, Heinz Kohut, and Erik Erikson. In the new last chapters of the book, Albert Ellis, Aaron Beck, and Murray Bowen will be reviewed. I will not give exhaustive analyses of these psychological schools and traditions; the goal is far more modest. I want to illustrate a variety of issues and a particular approach to understanding the appropriate relation between Christian thought and these new psychologies.

I refer to these psychologies as modern psychologies in order to drive home an often forgotten truth—*psychology was not born in the twentieth century.* There are a variety of ancient psychologies, and many of these have affected religious traditions in the West. It is entirely appropriate to speak of the psychologies implicit in various manifestations of ancient Judaism or in different strands of early Christianity. Christianity has been variously affected by Stoic, neo-Platonic, Aristotelian, Thomistic, Hegelian, Kierkegaardian, Heideggerian, and Whiteheadian psychologies. These psychologies are properly understood to be philosophical psychologies in contrast to scientific or clinical psychologies. By philosophical, I do not mean that they were simply hatched up, or imagined, or mere products of speculative reason. Rather, they are philosophical in that they are meant to account for rather wide ranges of human experience—so wide, in fact, that they do not easily fit within the confines of rigorous experimental procedures or the narrow focus of behavioral or affective problems associated with the clinic.

The new twentieth-century psychologies aspire to go beyond philosophical psychology and become scientific in either the clinical or experimental senses of that term. Scientific psychologies claim to have a more rigorous relation to highly specifiable orders of concrete data than is the case with the philosophical psychologies. The clinical psychologies want their concepts to "fit" or "account" for certain observations they make in the clinical settings, but they do not achieve prediction or repeatability as do the experimentalists.[1] The experimental psychologies aspire to derive their concepts from controlled observations so that variables can be isolated, causes or correlations statistically stated, and publicly repeatable verification achieved.[2] Freud, Jung, Erikson, Kohut, Bowen, and the humanistic psychologists Carl Rogers, Abraham Maslow, and Fritz Perls are largely clinical psychologists, whereas B. F. Skinner is clearly an experimental psychologist. Ellis and Beck are clinical but imagine their work to be based on more explicitly experimental psychological concepts.

The Cultures of Modern Psychology

These expressions of modern psychology can be organized rather conveniently into what I have elsewhere referred to as "cultures" of contemporary psychology.[3] The psychologies that I will examine in these chapters can be seen as belonging to one of four cultures of contemporary psychology—the culture of detachment, the culture of joy, the culture of control, or the culture of care. There may indeed be other cultures of psychology just as there are other major modern psychologies besides the ones that I will review. For instance, I have made no effort to review the widely appreciated school of object-relations associated with the names of W. R. D. Fairbairn, D. W. Winnicott, and Harry Guntrip.[4] The marriage and family therapies are mostly omitted with the exception of the examination of Murray Bowen in chapter 10. My goal is to illustrate the possibility of discerning the cultures of a psychology and not to accomplish within these pages a definitive job of handling all conceivable schools. Nor am I trying to determine whether I have associated the various psychologies I am studying with the right culture. But I am trying to argue that the modern psychologies have some of the features of a positive culture and that the psychologies we are studying here can illustrate this point.

By *culture* I mean a system of symbols and norms that guides a society or group by providing general images of the nature of the world, the purpose of life, and at least some of the basic principles by which life should be lived. It is often thought that the modern psychologies are basically scientific and to this extent do not provide answers to life's meaning. But it is my argument that most of the more prominent modern psychologies, in addition to whatever scientific value that they may have, do indeed cross over into what must be recognized as types of positive cultures—cultures, indeed, that possess religio-ethical dimensions.

I will associate Freud most distinctively with the culture of detachment. The humanistic psychologies, Jung, and Marry are variations of the culture of joy. Skinner is the greatest example of the culture of control, but Ellis, to a degree, fits there as well. Erikson and Kohut are interesting examples of the culture of care, although Erikson more so than Kohut.

The culture of detachment is controlled by deep metaphors and views of human nature that push people toward pessimism about the range of beneficence that can be reasonably expected from one another. The culture of detachment sees the world as basically hostile and humans as largely self-absorbed creatures with only small amounts of energy for larger altruistic ventures. The culture of joy, on the other hand, sees the world as basically harmonious. It also sees human wants and needs as easily reconciled and coordinated in almost frictionless compatibility. This state is especially realized by people who are true to their own most basic natures. The culture of control has deep metaphors and images of human nature that lead it to see humans as primarily controlled and controllable by the manipulative power of their various environments. The culture of care, although sharing some of the metaphors of harmony of the humanistic psychologies, has a better grasp of the pervasive tensions and anxieties of life and gravitates toward an ethic that finds a place for both self-love and self-transcending love for the other.

Christian thought has points of contact and sympathy with all of these different cultures, although it has criticisms as well. If these different psychologies were strictly psychologies, Christian thought would have little to say about them. But insofar as these psychologies give rise to cultures with genuine religio-ethical dimensions, Christian thought is entitled to engage them in critical conversation.

We will find the most affinity between Christian thought and the culture of care. This does not mean, however, that because of this affinity the psychologies of Erikson and Kohut are the best psychologies, although it is my conviction that they are powerful indeed. But it does mean that if one is to conclude that all psychologies must finally function within some larger cultural context, then it can be argued that from the perspective of Christian thought the implicit culture in these psychologies may have much to commend it.

Can Psychology and Theology Conflict?

Insofar as the modern psychologies achieve the status of scientific knowledge (either clinical or experimental), logically they should not conflict with the claims of theology. On this issue I agree with a host of contemporary philosophies influenced by Ludwig Wittgenstein, such as the school of ordinary language analysis he inspired. Regardless of some of the limitations of this school, it has helped us to understand that there are many different forms of language and that it is both illogical and impoverishing to think about all the various forms of language in analogy to scientific language.[5] Ian Barbour states this point of view well when he writes, "This is an attractive solution to issues between science and religion; the two fields cannot possibly conflict if they serve totally different functions. The function of scientific language is the prediction and control of nature; that of religious language is the expression of self-commitment, ethical dedication, and existential life-orientation."[6] Although neither Barbour nor I take a strictly Wittgensteinian approach to the relation of religion to science or the relation of theology to psychology, there is still great wisdom in this position—at least up to a point. It is clearly the task of theology to orient the believer to the broadest ranges of human experience, to describe and represent what experience testifies to be its ultimate context, and to induce the appropriate existential and ethical response. The function of scientific psychological language, by contrast, properly should be far more modest. If theology tries to interpret the widest possible field of human experience, experimental psychology, as does any rigorous science, narrows its task and tries to test its propositions "against the data."[7] By *data* I mean a particular set or collection of sense data that are clear and distinct enough to be managed, controlled, isolated, and counted. The clinical psychologies, on the other hand, stand somewhere between experimental psychology and theology; rather than prediction and control based on the manipulation of discrete facts of sense experience, the clinical psychologies—or at least some of them—are thought to be concerned with the interpretation of basic patterns, modalities, themes, and narratives that give lives their underlying cohesion. To do this, they often proceed by correlating internally perceived introspective knowledge with externally observed patterns, themes, and modalities.[8] To characterize the clinical psychologies this way is consistent with a wide range of modern psychologies such as Henry Murray, Erik Erikson, Robert Lifton, Heinz Kohut, and Donald Spence, and with philosophers of psychology such as Paul Ricoeur, William Barrett, Daniel Yankelovich, Rom Harré, and P. F. Secord.[9]

Theology and the Clinical Psychologies

The reader will not have failed to notice the similarities between my brief initial description of both theology and the clinical psychologies. I used the word *interpretation* to describe the central task of both in order to suggest that they are more properly *interpretive* than *explanatory* disciplines. By using these two terms, I am introducing the classical distinction between what William Dilthey called *Geisteswissenschaften* (sciences of the human spirit in its quest for meaning—a meaning that must be interpreted) and *Naturwissenschaften* (sciences of nature that seek causal explanation, prediction, and control).[10] To say that both theology and the clinical psychologies are interpretive disciplines or *Geisteswissenschaften* is to identify another underlying commonality between them. The clinical psychologies try to interpret *individual lives;* theology tries to interpret *life*—life as a whole, in its entirety. And if this is so, both disciplines must face the question of the framework of meaning from which they make their interpretive judgments.

It is my thesis that significant portions of the modern psychologies, and especially the clinical psychologies, are actually instances of religio-ethical thinking.

They are, in fact, mixed disciplines that contain examples of religious, ethical, and scientific language. To state this about the modern psychologies is certainly to go against their own self-understanding. They see themselves as sciences, and some certainly do achieve this status more completely than others. But when many of these psychologies are submitted to careful analysis one discovers that they have religious and moral horizons about which both they and the general public are unclear. Frequently, the leaders of our religious institutions are also unaware of the religious and moral dimensions in the psychologies that they use (as well as in other social sciences that I cannot analyze in this book).

Within these pages I will be treating these psychologies more like practical moral philosophies than as scientific psychologies, whether either experimentally or clinically conceived. This approach may give the impression that I plan to treat these psychologies unfairly, contrary to their own self-understanding. That I will indeed treat them contrary to their own self-understanding I fully acknowledge. But that I will treat them unfairly is something I hope not to do. I intend to bring out of these psychologies something that is truly there and something that many readers of the modern psychologies have sensed for a long time but have had difficulty putting into words. But I do not intend to overlook what is scientific about these psychologies. In fact, it is precisely my intention to distinguish what is scientific from what is moral and quasi-religious and to make some evaluation of what sense can be made of each of these levels.

Since the publication of the first edition of *Religious Thought and the Modern Psychologies*, a hermeneutic view of the social sciences has been given more serious attention. The English translation in 1975 of Hans-Georg Gadamer's great *Truth and Method* (1975, 1982) set the stage for the hermeneutic point of view.[11] As we indicated in the preface, Paul Ricoeur's collection of essays in *Hermeneutics and the Human Sciences* further supported this trend. Richard Bernstein interpreted this emerging tradition to a wider philosophical audience in his illuminating *Beyond Objectivism and Relativism* (1983).[12] Robert Bellah and his team brought hermeneutic theory into sociology in *Habits of the Heart* (1985).[13] In 1995, Philip Cushman developed a very informative reinterpretation of the modern psychologies from a hermeneutic point of view in his *Constructing the Self, Constructing America*. A few years later, an even more systematic hermeneutic interpretation of the modern psychologies and psychotherapies was present by Frank Richardson, Blaine Fowers, and Charles Guignon in *Re-envisioning Psychology: Moral Dimensions of Theory and Practice* (1999).

Religious Thought and the Modern Psychologies had not officially taken the hermeneutic turn in the first edition, although in reality it did so implicitly in every respect except actually using the terminology and quoting from the new theorists who were beginning to be noticed by the American social-science community. Theology already had been influenced by hermeneutic theory from Germany and France; this was especially true in the writing of the American Roman Catholic theologian David Tracy. During the 1980s, Paul Ricoeur was my colleague at the

Divinity School of the University of Chicago and helped to bring hermeneutic philosophy to our consciousness. Gradually the relevance of hermeneutic philosophy to the social sciences as well as ethics and theology began to dawn on me. Ricoeur's philosophical anthropology had been very important for the first edition of *Religious Thought and the Modern Psychologies,* but hermeneutic theory, although already in my bones, had not yet crept upward into my brain—my full reflective consciousness. Part of what this second edition hopes to accomplish is to make the implicit hermeneutic philosophy of the first edition more explicit and then bring it into conversation with other contemporary hermeneutic interpretations of psychology and psychotherapy. I want to do this in order to better conceptualize what psychology is really all about; but I also want to do this to develop a better model for understanding the relation of theology to psychology and psychotherapy.

There are four core ideas in hermeneutic philosophy that are affirmed in this second edition and held in common with Cushman and Richardson and his colleagues. What follows is a highly condensed primer on hermeneutic theory—too condensed, I'm sure, but necessary to get us started. The first concept is Gadamer's important theory of "effective history." This idea points to the situated character of all thinking. History is not simply something that lingers in the past—something that is over and done with and hence has no effect on us today. History becomes a part of our experience today, shaping us in a myriad of ways that we often cannot name or readily bring to consciousness.[14] Second, this effective history shapes what Gadamer called our "pre-understanding," i.e., the inherited interpretative frameworks we rely on when attempting to understand our experiences of the world.[15] We would not understand anything if we did not have these inherited funds of interpretive perspectives built up by repeated successful understandings from past generations. From one perspective, these pre-understandings can be considered biases or prejudices, but from another, they are the comparative references against which we make sense out of our experience. The pre-understandings may need to be tested, but they should not be denied. To suppress them is to act as though they are not there, thus depriving us of our ability to test their adequacy in the ongoing understanding process.

The third concept is about the process of understanding. It holds that all understanding is like a dialogue, in fact, *is* a dialogue.[16] Understanding anything—an event today, an occurrence of the past, a bit of human behavior, a conversation, a therapeutic exchange—is first of all a matter of dialogue; it is not basically an objective process. We enter into the process of understanding something with our own pre-understandings and they, in turn, help us get oriented to what is happening. Without our pre-conceptions, we would be lost. This means that understanding anything—even a psychological or psychotherapeutic process—is more like a dialogue where people bring their historically conditioned perspectives directly into the understanding process. Understanding anything has something of the "question and answer" features of any conversation.[17] The fourth concept follows directly from the third and makes the connection between all attempts to understand and the nature of moral thinking. Gadamer believes that moral interests—interests about how to apply our understanding to the moral concerns of daily life—shape the understanding process from the beginning.[18] This says, in effect, that there is an unshakable link between understanding and practical moral reason. Understanding something is never just a neutral or objective act; no matter how hard we try to be objective, our practical interests and pre-understandings will always enter into the picture and enter so early as to be directing understanding from the very beginning.

What does all this mean for the fields of psychology and psychotherapy? First, it means that all efforts to conceive of them as totally objective sciences completely disconnected from the effective history and pre-understandings of the past are not only fruitless but positively destructive, both for psychology as an academic discipline and also for the efficacy of its contributions to culture and society. Psychology and psychotherapy must be conceived as a process of refining our effective histories and pre-understandings about human nature, thinking, and motivation, as well as the processes of individual and social change. These disciplines cannot properly be conceived as totally objective sciences completely disconnected or alienated from the accomplishments of the past and therefore determined to invent anew our guiding concepts about human nature and human change. Insofar as psychology conceives of itself as taking a completely fresh start on these matters and trying to find some indubitable foundation in sense experience, experimentation, empirically verifiable facts, or *a priori* first principles, it will end in functioning to alienate both individuals and the wider society from the cultural wisdom of the past.[19] In short, these disciplines will become nihilistic, i.e., function to disconnect people from the cultural accomplishments of earlier generations and undermine the very socialization process itself. Or, in the name of objectivity, they will become unwitting conspirators with and reinforcements of the dominant social and cultural ethos of our age, i.e., the rational-choice processes of the market and the individualistic and consumerist ethic that it encourages. This is in fact what Cushman and Richardson, et al., think is happening.[20] And this is close to much of the diagnosis of the cultural impact of these disciplines presented in the first edition of *Religious Thought and the Modern Psychologies*.

I have set out this overly condensed summary of hermeneutic philosophy at this early stage of the book to make one simple point: our interlocutors Cushman and Richardson, et al., agree with Gadamer and Ricoeur on these four points. Glimpses of these points also pervaded the first edition of *Religious Thought and the Modern Psychologies*, but now this revision is designed to explicitly agree with and develop these same points. But, as a matter of fact, *Religious Thought and the Modern Psychologies* will not go all the way with these authors. In short, Cushman and Richardson, et al., are more thoroughly and uncomplicatedly hermeneutic than we are. They tend to neglect two aspects of hermeneutic philosophy that are present in Gadamer but even more highly developed in the work of Paul Ricoeur. These two concepts are the idea of "distanciation" and the idea of the "classical." One finds little if anything about either of these concepts in these otherwise quite admirable pieces of scholarship. As a result, we miss learning from them how a hermeneutic psychology also can have an objective or "distanciated" submoment and why psychology must not totally ignore the classics of its culture, including its own religious classics.

We should start with the concept of the classical. Gadamer does not use this word to refer to a particular historical period, such as classical Greece or Rome. Instead, it refers to events, texts, and ideals that are so "enduring," so "timeless" in their meaning, and contain so much "historical validity" in themselves, that humans who live in the cultures fed by them cannot forget them, continue to refer to them, and constantly struggle to orient their lives to them.[21] They constitute the ideals that form the consciousness of a culture even though people seldom live up to their standards. What is the relevance of the idea of the classical to the social sciences, to psychology, and to psychotherapy? These ideals shape the consciousness of the people these disciplines study and shape the consciousness, no matter how vaguely, of the researchers in these disciplines. Bellah and his team made excellent use of the idea of the classical in their *Habits of the Heart*. They were using this concept when they demonstrated the importance of the "biblical tradition" and the "republican tradition" in the formation of the American ideals of individual responsibility and community.[22] I demonstrated in the first edition of *Religious Thought and the Modern Psychologies*, and we extend the argument in this edition, that the modern psychologies exhibit shadows of such classics themselves, sometimes more Greek than Christian or Jewish, and certainly more implicit than explicit. It is not clear that the modern psychologies either can or should completely suppress these classics in either their attempts to understand people or their attempt to define human health and fulfillment. In fact, it might be that these disciplines should conceive of themselves as helping the populations they serve to critically appropriate these classics. Because Cushman and Richardson, et al., ignore the classical in the shaping of historical consciousness, they also ignore the role of religion. Yet, this is difficult for hermeneutic philosophy to do. Bellah captured this in his appendix to *Habits of the Heart* when he wrote,

> Social science is not a disembodied cognitive enterprise. It is a tradition, or set of traditions, deeply rooted in the philosophical and humanistic (and to more than a small extent, the religious) history of the West. Social science makes assumptions about the nature of persons, the nature of society, and the relation between persons and society. It also, whether it admits it or not, makes assumptions about good persons and a good society and considers how far these conceptions are embodied in our actual society. Becoming conscious of the cultural roots of these assumptions would remind the social scientist that these assumptions are contestable and that the choice of assumption involves controversies that lie deep in the history of Western thought.[23]

This brings us to the last difference between *Religious Thought and the Modern Psychologies* and the Cushman and Richardson, et al., books. This has to do with the importance of what Ricoeur calls "distanciation" in the hermeneutically conceived social sciences. Both Cushman and the Richardson team reject the goal of simple-minded objectivity in psychology and psychotherapy. In fact, they claim that the very pursuit of absolute objectivity obscures the importance of the historical frameworks that make our questions and investigations meaningful.[24] But, from the perspective of this book, they do not make enough of the kind of partial or relative objectivity that is achievable in psychology and psychotherapy. It is, in passing, somewhat acknowledged by Richardson and his group when they write, "In studying human phenomena, the distance or detachment we achieve in order to examine critically our way of life is always partial and provisional, in contrast to the scientific aspiration to complete objectivity that has informed so much of the modern social sciences."[25] But neither Cushman nor Richardson make enough out of the concept of this "distance."

This concept is implicit in Gadamer but best developed by Ricoeur. It refers to the human capacity for reflectivity that makes it possible to both be conscious of one's historically conditioned beginning point but also partially distance or detach oneself from it, not in any absolute way but to some degree. Objectivity suggests absolute detachment; distanciation points to the simultaneous use of one's historical horizon and yet partial detachment from it to examine and test that very horizon.[26] To illustrate the meaning of the idea of distanciation, it is useful to point out the difference between speaking and writing. When we speak, we are immediately in the full context and our audience is directly before us. When we write something, what we put down with pen and ink can be read a hundred years later in a distant land and by an audience we never imagined. In fact, we gain a little distance from what we are saying as soon as we write it down and look at it a second time. The text takes on a meaning that is distanciated from the original situation of saying. Our various scientific methods help us gain that distanciation in more controlled ways. It makes it possible for us to think about and test our assumptions, but that process would not be meaningful if those assumptions—those pre-understandings and the effective history that delivers them to us—were not there from the beginning of the understanding process.

Implicitly in the first edition and explicitly in the second, *Religious Thought and the Modern Psychologies* assumes the hermeneutic perspective on psychology and psychotherapy. But because it makes more out of the concept of distanciation than Cushman and Richardson, et al., it does more to bring a critical perspective to hermeneutic theory. Tradition may be the source of our wisdom, but tradition is often conflicting, confused, and sometimes distorted. Hence, additional critical perspectives must be brought to our inherited traditions so we will not become blind perpetrators of not only its wisdom but also its errors. The distanciating moments of psychology as science helps us critique and correct some of the errors of the past when it comes to our cognitive emotional constitutions. The past is not all distortion; in fact, there is in it more wisdom than error. But there is error. Psychology as an act of distanciation can help us discover some of these distortions and errors.

But our capacities for distanciation help us to discover even more. In prior works, I have argued that all examples of practical moral thinking have implicitly or explicitly five different dimensions.[27] If many of our psychologies have affinities with systems of practical moral thinking, as our hermeneutically oriented friends and I are arguing, then these same psychologies, implicitly or explicitly, contain these five dimensions or levels ("dimensions" is the preferable term, but for variety, I use the word "levels" as well). I will first list these five dimensions, and then I will tell the reader how I have derived them. The very process of derivation helps to illustrate further what is meant by the concept of distanciation.

All instances of practical thinking contain (1) assumptions about a visional or metaphorical background, (2) assumptions about a principle of obligation that provides general moral guidance, (3) assumptions about our enduring human needs and tendencies that humans generally want to fulfill, (4) assumptions about the permissions and constraints of our social and natural environment, and (5) assumptions about recommended rules and roles that it would be good to follow. How do we know or intuit this thick web of assumptions when we think morally? I follow Jürgen Habermas in deriving these dimensions or levels through an empirical reconstructive process. Every act of moral thinking that I reflect upon, even if shaped by the effective history and pre-understandings of the past, abstractly contain assumptions about these five dimensions.[28] Careful reflection on examples of practical moral thinking always unearths them sooner or later. They seem to be invariable presuppositions of moral thought.

I have argued that these dimensions are, on the one hand, hierarchically related, with the visional and obligatory dimensions qualifying and influencing all the lower levels. On the other hand, reflection on our moral experience reveals that these five dimensions are relatively independent of each other. While each conditions or shapes the meaning of each of the other levels, fresh and partially independent judgments are made at each of the five levels. Or to say it differently, the content of no single level can be deduced from the content of any other level, even the higher levels. Genuine and fully practical judgments are only consummated at the last level when we actually decide what rules to follow and what roles to enact.

In the chapters to follow, I will deal primarily with the first three levels—the visional or metaphorical, the obligational, and the tendency-need levels. It will be enough of a task to demonstrate that each of these levels can be found in many of the contemporary clinical psychologies. The other levels can also often be found, but to establish that the first three levels can be uncovered is sufficient to make the point that at least the psychologies discussed here are *on the way* to being systems of practical moral thinking. In addition, I limit myself to the first three levels of practical thinking because I am primarily interested in the ideas and ideals of both the modern psychologies and Christian thought. I acknowledge that the social context of these psychologies influences to some extent the shape of these ideas and ideals. But in contrast to certain popular contemporary views in the sociology of knowledge, I do not believe that these psychologies are simply epiphenomena of social processes, such as the social forces of advanced capitalism. My approach owes more to the view of culture found in the work of the great European sociologist Max Weber. Hence, I see the modern psychologies as responding to and coping with the forces of advanced capitalism but indeed not shaped by these forces in all respects. I will open the question of the context of the modern psychologies in chapter 9 as part of a broader, albeit brief, discussion on the relation of psychology to society.

The five levels are derived from five basic questions that we generally ask ourselves silently and sometimes unconsciously when we try to determine *what we should do*. We ask first, "What kind of world do we live in and what is its most ultimate (in the sense of most determinative) context?" In answering this question, we always resort to metaphorical language—deep metaphors that are themselves frequently embellished into myths, stories, or narratives. This is the visional or metaphorical level of practical moral thinking. With regard to the psychologies reviewed in this book, I will be uncovering their implicit and explicit metaphors that function to give the consumers of these psychologies a sense of the meaning and foundation of life. In this regard, I will investigate metaphors of mechanism and the metaphors of life (eros) and death (thanatos) in the psychology of Freud, the metaphors of the coincidence of opposites (*coincidentia oppositorium*) in Jung, the metaphors of harmony in humanistic psychology (and to a lesser extent in Erikson and Kohut), and the metaphors of free variation and natural selection and what I teasingly call the "barnyard" metaphors in B. F. Skinner. In chapter 10, the most striking deep metaphors can be found in the more or less mechanistic images of the interacting and self-perpetuating systems world in the psychology of Murray Bowen, but there is evidence of background visions in Ellis and Beck as well. All of these will be compared and contrasted with the theistic metaphors of ultimacy that have been central to the Judeo-Christian tradition. What is at stake in these different metaphors and how do they affect the lower levels of practical moral thinking?

The second or obligational level derives from our attempt to answer the question "What are we obligated to do?" In answering this question, we are generally guided by some consciously or unconsciously held general principle about how our actions should be ordered. This principle may be beyond immediate articulation by particular persons or groups, but it is still functioning in their moral thinking. Moral philosophers study the various theories of obligation, order them, compare them, and critique them. For this reason, I will use the thinking of some contemporary moral philosophers such as William Frankena, John Rawls, Stephen Toulmin, and others to guide my efforts to analyze and critique the theory of obligation found in various examples of Christian thought (which, of course, can vary rather widely) as well as the implicit theories of obligation to be found in some contemporary psychologies.[29] The basic Christian theories of obligation center around the principle of neighbor-love that instructs us to "Love your neighbor as yourself" (Matt. 19:19; Mark 12:31), and the older and even more universal golden rule that says to "Do unto others as you would have them do unto you." Just what these principles actually mean is a matter of great dispute. The principle of neighbor-love is often associated with the idea of agape or self-sacrificial love. But it too has many different interpretations.

Several of the new psychologies have or suggest theories of obligation, and these theories are implicit in their images of human fulfillment. From the perspective of the categories of moral philosophy, most of the modern psychologies are quiet purveyors of what moral philosophers call ethical-egoist images of obligation. The word *egoist* should not be construed to mean something automatically crude, ruthless, and crassly selfish. Ethical egoism can take highly civilized, considerate, orderly, and even charitable forms. But in spite of these necessary qualifications, ethical egoism in all of its forms does mean something different from, for instance, agapism. Hence, the implicit theories of obligation in much of contemporary psychology may be in tension with leading interpretations of the image of obligation in the Christian tradition. But not all the psychologies we will investigate lean toward an implicit ethical egoism. Freud probably does not, although the issue is a matter of debate. Kohut and Erikson do not, although Kohut is closer to ethical egoism than Erikson. Skinner is furthest from an implicit ethical egoism and, in fact, gravitates toward a rigid form of justice as the major moral principle by which he judges human character. At the obligational level, Ellis and Beck are rife with moral assumptions of an ethical egoist kind, and Murray strangely blends his systems ontology with a harmonistic individualism not unlike what will be found in the humanistic psychologies. Yet, none of these psychologists is very clear about the practical moral implications of what he is doing, and none seems to know when he wanders past the boundaries of scientific statements about mental health and moves into the foreign land of normative and ethical speech about what humans are obligated to do.

Moral philosophers tend to divide the domain of normative ethics into two broad approaches: aretaic ethics and deontic ethics. An aretaic approach to ethics, on the one hand, deals with the ethics of character and the various ways of speaking about the good or virtuous person.[30] A deontic approach to ethics, on the other hand, is an ethics of principle. The latter goes about the ethical task by first trying to establish some general principle that can be used to guide ethical thinking.[31] The two approaches are not necessarily opposed to one another; some systems of ethics state relatively clearly both their fundamental principles and their visions of good character or the good person. But there are positions that split these approaches apart and try to do ethics only with basic principles or only with images of good character and virtue.

Since I will be examining various psychological views of human fulfillment for their ethical implications, it might be argued that I am approaching these psychologies as unwitting systems of aretaic ethics. To some extent that is the case. Many psychological views of the healthy personality are not stated in morally neutral terms; they are, in fact, subtle statements about the nature of the good or virtuous person in the moral sense of the word *good*. But even though in many ways I will be involved in an exercise in aretaic ethics, I will use the categories of deontic approaches to spot the ethical styles implicit in the different psychologies. For I take the view stated by William Frankena, Alan Gewirth, and others: we only know the virtuous person in light of some general principle of obligation that the good person exhibits in his or her response to the moral situations of life.[32] In contrast to the widespread popularity of ethics of virtue in the philosophy of Alasdair Mac-Intyre and the theological ethics of Stanley Hauerwas, I will enter the discussion of normative character through the gateway of more deontic approaches, knowing full well that no principle can ever exhaust what is meant by virtue, character, or the good person.[33] So I will use the language of obligation and the language of moral principles even though I will very much be in search of the various aretaic images of the good person to be found in both Christian thought and the modern psychologies.

And finally, at the third or tendency-need level we ask the question "What are the various fundamental needs and tendencies that should be morally and justly satisfied?" To answer this, we examine theories of psychological tendencies and needs, such as those contained in the respective theological and psychological systems that I will review. To do this is to study the image of the natural constitution of human beings as this is pictured in Christian thought and the new psychologies. In many ways, this is the psychological level of analysis par excellence. This is psychology's proper realm, as such concepts as Freud's theory of the id, Jung's archetypes, the self-actualization tendency in humanistic psychology, and Erikson's epigenetic timetable show. But as will be seen, it is a realm that theology occupies as well. It is precisely the task of our metaphors of ultimacy and our theories of obligation to put these psychobiological tendencies and needs into a metaphysical and moral context. Furthermore, it is also the crucial task of our moral principles to guide us in mediating among the great myriad of complementary as well as conflicting needs that we have in ourselves—needs that simultaneously weld us together in communities of mutuality and yet head us into conflict with one another in moments of scarcity and anxiety.

It is my conviction that a critical conversation between Christian thought and the modern psychologies will be more precise if it is guided by the levels I have identified as the structure of practical moral thinking, at least the first three of them. In reality a critical conversation between two disciplines logically can only proceed on the same level. By this I mean that the visional or metaphorical level of theology justifiably can be critically compared to the visional or metaphorical level of psychology. The same is true for their respective obligational and tendency-need levels. But it leads to utter confusion to compare critically the visional levels of theology to, for example, the theory of psychobiological needs of a psychological system. To do this is simply to mix apples and oranges; that is, these levels are categorically distinguishable and therefore cannot properly be compared.

But it can still be more complicated than this. It is possible to compare the visional level of theology to the tendency-need level of psychology, if in doing so

one is actually pushing behind a particular psychology's theory of our psychobiological tendencies and plumbing for the deeper metaphysical meanings that undergird it. When one does this, one is pushing beyond the superficial dissimilarities of
two different levels of thinking to deeper common metaphysical levels, which can
indeed be compared. I will frequently indulge in such a business of "pushing
behind" in this study.

Most of the theological approaches for relating theology and psychology have
used a variation of what I earlier identified as the position of Ludwig Wittgenstein.
This was true even though many of these positions were formulated before his
views were widely known by theological scholars. Most theologians simply have
argued that theology and psychology are disciplines that pose and answer different
kinds of questions. It is not that they deal with different kinds of reality, for
instance, the psychological and the spiritual. In spite of language in theologians
such as Paul Tillich and Reinhold Niebuhr that might lead one to think they were
proposing this solution, such a Platonic or idealistic view of the relation of theology
to psychology has been out of favor with most responsible modern theologians.
Tillich took the view that both theology and philosophy deal with what he called
the nature of being. But theology, he thought, asks the question of the "meaning of
being" and philosophy (and its subdisciplines such as psychology) deals with the
question of the "structure of being."[34] Tillich was fully aware that many philosophers and many psychologists often make statements beyond the boundaries of
their disciplines and deal with the question of the significance and meaning of
being and life. But when they do this, they make certain faith assumptions that the
data of their specific disciplines do not necessarily entail. Niebuhr, as will be seen in
more detail, took a similar position. He did not use the language of being and its
structure and meaning, but he did make a distinction between discrete and controlled empirical data handled by the human sciences and larger networks of
human experience that make up the ongoing flow of human life. While psychology,
he argued, deals with empirical data that can be limited, controlled, and manipulated, it is the task of theology to order and clarify these broader sectors of human
experience.[35] The interpretations of the modern psychologies and theology simply
deal with different ranges of human experience.

Even more conservative writers, such as Malcolm Jeeves and David Myers, take
much the same point of view. The tone of what they write is more defensive, but the
substance is very much the same. Jeeves, an established experimental psychologist,
argues in *Psychology and Christianity* (1976) that psychology and theology deal
with "different levels of explanation."[36] Jeeves takes a rigorous experimental view of
the science of psychology. To him psychology is a humble science that works with
limited ranges of facts established primarily through the hypothetico-deductive
method. To him, the facts and explanations of psychology can say nothing one way
or another about the truth or value of theological interpretations of experience.
The well-respected social psychologist David Myers also makes use of the "levels of
explanation" approach in his *The Human Puzzle* (1978).[37]

The conservatives such as Jeeves and Myers, more than the liberal-neoorthodox figures such as Tillich and Niebuhr, think of psychology in terms of its most rigorously experimental forms. As we will see in chapter 11, such psychologists tend to look down on the more clinical and interpretive psychologies. Tillich and Niebuhr, on the other hand, are primarily interested in the clinical psychologies, particularly Freud and the neo-Freudians. But all of them agree that psychology can only conflict with theology when psychology in some way ceases to be properly scientific (however this is defined) and drifts over into normative language of either an ethical or metaphysical kind.

The theological view that at first glance might seem to be an exception to these positions is that associated with the empirical theologies of Seward Hiltner and Daniel Day Williams. Both of these perspectives were influenced by the philosophy of Alfred North Whitehead. Hiltner and Williams speak of how as two different perspectives on experience psychology and theology can both throw light on religious truth.[38] But when they make this claim, they almost constitute the exception that proves the position that, one way or the other, Tillich, Niebuhr, Jeeves, and Myers all finally seem to hold. For when Hiltner and Williams speak of psychology's perspective on experience, they are speaking neither of the discrete and controlled data of experimental psychology nor of the highly selected and sometimes reductively explained experience of clinical psychologies. They are speaking of an almost phenomenological description of experience in that broad radical-empirical sense of the word associated with the philosophies of William James and Alfred North Whitehead.[39] In this sense, then, their doctrine of experience has gone beyond what most psychologies, clinical or experimental, claim to be able to describe. They too finally would agree that the more narrowly conceived clinical or experimental psychologies simply work at a different level of explanation and, for this reason, cannot finally conflict with theological or religious interpretations.

This consensus among writers who are favorably inclined toward religious and theological claims is basically sound. But its difficulty is finally that it writes off too quickly the implicit ethical and metaphysical claims that frequently accompany the modern psychologies. It may be true that when a psychology unwittingly lapses into ethical or metaphysical judgments it is no longer strictly science. But to say this is not to prove that a particular psychology's unknowing metaphysical and ethical visions are wrong. The metaphysical and ethical judgments may not be strictly psychological nor strictly scientific, but they may still be correct. In other words, a particular psychology may unconsciously project a very good ethical vision and a very commanding metaphysics even though it did not explicitly intend to do either.

The major theological consensus that we have been reviewing has had the defect of being unwilling to engage in a genuine revised critical correlational dialogue with the modern psychologies. This is the difficulty with the evangelical scholars reviewed in chapter 11. They believe that once the fringe, horizon, deep metaphors, or background assumptions of the modern psychologies are identified, this aspect of them can be immediately rejected as unscientific. The view of this book is different.

It is true that the background assumptions and metaphors of these psychologies have a quasi-religious character and are, in this sense, competitive with the theistic metaphors of the Christian faith. But just because these assumptions go beyond the empirical in the strict sense and conflict with Christian assumptions does not immediately make them automatically wrong. They cannot be trumped just because they deviate from Christian visions of the ultimate context of experience. A critical correlational perspective takes on the burden of demonstrating the relative moral and metaphysical inadequacy of the metaphorical horizons of these psychologies and, as well, the higher moral and metaphysical adequacy of the Christian vision. The various visions of the modern psychologies may be strong, powerful, and viable even though they go beyond the precincts of what can properly be called psychology. Hence, the full voice of the modern psychologies needs to be heard. In this study, using the critical correlational approach, I intend both to uncover and to evaluate critically the full normative horizon of the modern psychologies. But what is the "critical correlational" view of theology that should prove so helpful in pursuing our task?

A New Perspective on the Theology of Culture

In certain quarters of contemporary theology it is fashionable to call the kind of conversation I am proposing a "critical correlation" between theology and some aspect of the cultural world, in this case modern psychotherapeutic psychology. David Tracy adds a word and calls the method a "revised" critical correlational approach to the theology of culture.[40] By using "revised" in connection with "correlational," he wishes to distinguish his approach to the theology of culture from the powerful method of correlation developed by the late German-American theologian Paul Tillich. For Tillich the task of systematic theology and the task of a theology of culture were almost identical. Both enterprises were correlational in the hands of Tillich, but correlational in the specific sense of taking basic questions about the meaning of human existence that each cultural expression characteristically asks and correlating them with the answer provided by Christian revelation.[41] The form of the question comes from cultural experience, Tillich thought, but the substance of the answers to the problems of existence always must come from beyond existence—from Christian revelation. From this perspective, psychotherapeutic psychology (as is the case with any cultural discipline) can do nothing more than describe the tensions and ambiguities of existence in the language, symbols, and forms of a particular era and a particular region of experience; psychotherapeutic psychology can give no answers to the basic problems of existence and, to this extent, can provide no fundamental competition with theology. For instance, Tillich thought that psychoanalysis was capable of giving excellent descriptions of the nature of estranged or fallen human existence but was totally incapable of giving an account of what he called "essential" human nature.[42]

But the revised critical correlational approach to the theology of culture admits that cultural expressions not only ask questions about existence, they often project answers as well. Some of these answers are commanding and attract the imaginations of society. Some of the answers that the culture expresses have similarities with the answers of the Christian faith and, of course, some are vastly different from Christian answers. In fact, Tracy identifies three logically possible relations between the Christian interpretation of life and various cultural interpretations, including, of course, those interpretations implicit within the psychotherapeutic psychologies. There are possibilities of *identity* when the Christian claim and the cultural expression may be saying the same, or nearly the same, thing. There are possibilities of *analogy* when interpretations of the Christian fact or event and the cultural expression are very similar although yet still different. And then there are situations of complete *nonidentity* between the Christian witness and the cultural expression.[43] But agreement or nonagreement in and of itself does not settle the matter. If there is apparent agreement between the Christian claim and a cultural expression, that does not necessarily make either of them true. The conversation must be critical; the inner testimony of faith counts in the discussion, but additional reasons must be given in support of faith's claims. Similarly, nonagreement between the Christian view and a cultural expression does not necessarily make the cultural expression wrong or inadequate; additional reasons must be given to support the claims of both.

A mutually critical conversation must occur if we are to develop a critical theology of culture. And the mutually critical conversation must occur between the questions and the answers of the Christian view, on the one hand, and the questions and answer of the cultural option, on the other. Such a critical conversation necessarily will have to shift into a philosophical mode. Faith does indeed, here and everywhere, precede reason; this is the nature of life as well as the nature of the Christian religion. By this I mean that the powerful wheels of socialization leave us all with inherited assumptive worlds that exist prior to our capacity and will to reflect on them critically. But in the approach to the theology of culture that I am proposing, reason in the form of philosophical reflection must in the end be given a central role. This is necessary in order to convert the theology of culture into a critical theology of culture—one that conducts a mutually critical conversation between various interpretations of Christian claims and various cultural interpretations of human existence. In the pages that follow (and especially in chapter 6), I will try to illustrate what such a critical conversation would look like, although I doubt seriously if I will be able satisfactorily to conduct such a conversation in all respects. My goal is to portray and model such a mutually critical conversation and hope that by so doing we will gradually learn how to do this difficult task better than it will doubtless be done here. But it is precisely through such a critical conversation that modern individuals can begin to achieve some coherence amidst the scraps of identity that make up the pluralism of modern societies.

The mutually critical correlation between theology and the modern psychologies will be built around the first three levels of practical moral thinking: the visional or metaphorical, the obligational, and the tendency-need levels. After working hard to demonstrate that there are deep metaphors and implicit principles of obligation in the modern psychologies—which in itself is a task and will be a surprise to some—I will carry forward as far as space and my powers permit a critical conversation, one that will especially center on the respective deep metaphors and principles of obligation in Christian theology and the modern psychologies. Through it all, the discussion of the respective views of humans' fundamental tendencies and needs of these two sources of modern individual identity will be ever present. But the horizons of metaphysical and moral meaning that surround this properly psychological level of discourse will be what is basically at stake in the critical conversation that follows.

There is a close relation between a critical theology of culture and what I elsewhere have called a critical practical theology. A critical practical theology builds on a critical theology of culture but carries the conversation to an even lower level of abstraction. Practical theology becomes genuinely practical when it adds to the visional, obligational, and tendency-need levels the contextual level and the level of concrete concern with rules and roles. Practical theology in our time too must be revised correlational and build on a critical theology of culture.[44]

Vision and Obligation
in Christian Anthropology

There is a metaphorical foundation to Christian thought, but there is a metaphorical foundation to the modern psychologies as well. The two types of metaphors at times overlap, but on the whole they are distinguishable. A comparison of the grounding metaphors of the two disciplines should be the first and most important point of discussion between them.

Metaphor in Science and Theology

To assert boldly that there are metaphorical underpinnings to both disciplines sounds less startling in light of some of the recent claims put forth in both linguistics and philosophy of science. Lakoff and Johnson in their *Metaphors We Live By* (1980) contend that metaphorical language is not just a quaintly specialized language used for poetry and other fancy talk. It is, instead, fundamental to all our language, thought, and action. They write,

> We have found, on the contrary, that metaphor is pervasive in everyday life, not just in language, but in thought and action. Our ordinary conceptual system, in terms of which we both think and act, is fundamentally metaphorical in nature. . . . If we are right in suggesting that our conceptual system is largely metaphorical, then the way we think, what we experience, and what we do every day is very much a matter of metaphor![1]

If Lakoff and Johnson are correct, then it appears that poetry is the primordial language for both communication and discovery. All other more specialized languages—artistic, religious, legal, medical, and scientific—are grounded in poetry and metaphor. And so are both theology and psychology.

But what is a metaphor? This is a subject of much debate, which fortunately does not have to be solved here. But it will serve my purposes to set down some of the most common definitions advanced. Lakoff and Johnson write that the "essence of metaphor is understanding and experiencing one kind of thing in terms of another."[2] Examples might be "argument is war" or "time is money." Lakoff and Johnson characterize such statements as structural metaphors, where one concept such as "argument" or "time" is understood in terms of some of the selected features of another concept such as "war" or "money."

Ian Barbour, on the other hand, presents a definition of metaphor that points to the way it links the known with the unknown: "A metaphor proposes *analogies* between the normal context of a word and a new context into which it is introduced."[3] But Barbour wants to say that it is a selective analogical process. In this, he follows Max Black's *Models and Metaphors* (1962), which argues that in metaphorical language there is always a highly selective transfer of the familiar associations of a word to the new context.[4]

Sometimes this transfer seems customary and ordinary. But at other times, this transfer of the families to the unfamiliar is surprising—possibly even revolutionary. Paul Ricoeur likes to emphasize the surprising quality of metaphors, in part, one suspects, because of his study of the way metaphorical language functions in the parables of Jesus. Metaphors entail bringing two fields of meaning together in a single word in such a way that a collision occurs. We are surprised and a new meaning emerges.[5] These fields of meaning are shaped, as Paul Ricoeur reminds us, by the narrative context within which they function. This brings metaphor theory into the new considerations of the importance of narratives and stories for shaping the gestalt of meanings surrounding a metaphor, as this is discussed in philosophical hermeneutics. Metaphors do not stand alone."[6]

But whether upsetting or revolutionary or more ordinary and settled, metaphors do guide us as we investigate the unknown. They help us talk about the unfamiliar by employing experiences with which we are familiar. *This is the common element in all metaphors that makes them fundamental to both religious discernment and scientific discovery.* We represent our sense of the holy in terms of metaphors, but through metaphors we also probe with our imaginations the unknown realms of nature in our effort scientifically to represent its otherwise unfathomable reaches. Sallie McFague helps us understand the importance of metaphors for scientific discovery when she quotes Jacob Bronowski as once saying, "In this sense, the whole of science is shot through and through with metaphors, which transfer and link one part of experience to another, and find likeness between the parts. All our ideas derive from and embody such metaphorical likenesses."[7] McFague herself then concludes, "metaphor is not just the possession of poetry or the burden of religion as has often been supposed, but is evident in all fields and at the most basic level of their understanding and conceptuality."[8]

But few of the philosophers of metaphor have investigated one of the questions I am vitally concerned with in this book. And that is, what is the relation between metaphors that we use to represent the ultimate context of experience and our principles of obligation? This is really an old question that is discussed under a variety of rubrics, for instance, the question of the relation of religion to morality or the relation of worldview to ethics. For the purposes of this book, I want to broaden the discussion. I plan to investigate in selected theologies and modern psychologies the relation between their respective "metaphors of ultimacy" (whether they are recognized as explicitly religious or not) and the implicit or explicit ethics with which they are associated. I want to pursue the study under these rubrics because it will make it easier to establish one of the primary points of this book; that is, *it is not only in theology but, to a surprising extent, in the modern psychologies as well that the way we metaphorically represent the world in its most durable and ultimate respects influences (although not necessarily determines in all respects) what we think we are obligated to do.*

Metaphor and Obligation in Reinhold Niebuhr and Some Congenial Philosophical Theologies

To establish my theological argument, I will rely to a considerable extent upon the thought of the great twentieth-century American theologian Reinhold Niebuhr. But I will supplement Niebuhr's contributions with the thought of a number of other religious thinkers, especially the thought of the American philosopher and psychologist of religion William James and the complex and intriguing writings of the contemporary hermeneutic philosopher of religion Paul Ricoeur. Although there are some important differences among these three thinkers, there are amazing areas of congeniality among them as well. For example, I will use the work of James to fill out Niebuhr's own understanding of what is natural in human nature. James will be especially helpful in amplifying Niebuhr's implicit psychology and his suggestive yet cursory discussion of human instinctuality. In addition, James will be of considerable use in deepening Niebuhr's typically American appeal to experience as a test for theological judgments and truth. Ricoeur's concept of distanciation as a way of uncovering elements of experience slightly below our linguistic beginning points will also be useful. On the other hand, Ricoeur will be helpful in amplifying and balancing Niebuhr's critique of psychoanalysis. Ricoeur is also important for his general philosophy of the social sciences and for his penetrating hermeneutics of human fallibility and fault, a view of human brokenness that has resonances with Niebuhr's own understanding of original sin. But Niebuhr will be my primary theological beacon lighting the way for this theological encounter with the modern psychologies.

It is commonly conceded that Reinhold Niebuhr managed to develop one of the most powerful and well-balanced theological anthropologies available to modern theology. It is basically a biblical anthropology that strongly relies on the letters of Paul. But it also amplifies the Pauline anthropology with insights on the ambiguity of human self-transcendence that one can find in the writings of Augustine, Luther, and Kierkegaard. He gives this anthropology philosophical status by employing the support of Freud and Darwin on the nature of human instinctuality, Kierkegaard on the nature of anxiety, and Marx on the nature of ideology. In addition, he is a prototypical American theologian, in continuity with the thought of Jonathan Edwards and sympathetic to the broad-based empirical methodologies of American pragmatism. His thought was, of course, grounded in Scripture and biblical revelation, but he was also empirically oriented and tried to demonstrate how the biblical view of the human condition fit the facts of human nature and history.

Finally, Niebuhr was profoundly interested in both modern psychology and the social sciences and is seldom given the credit he deserves for his critical and appreciative appropriation of their insights.

It is difficult for harried and future-oriented modern individuals to take history as seriously as Niebuhr would urge. The daily problems seem so immediate and history seems so distant and irrelevant. But for Niebuhr the major problems facing humans have ancient and historic precedents. According to him, the central problem facing modern civilizations is their "lack of a principle of interpretation which can do justice to both the height of human self-transcendence and the organic unity between the spirit of man and his physical life."[9] In another place, I have called the problem Niebuhr is pointing to as an issue of the proper relation between the high in humans (their spirit, imaginations, and freedom) and the low in humans (their conditionedness by nature and instinctuality).[10] But what are the practical results of this lack of a proper interpretive perspective? Niebuhr's answer is that it dissipates our "sense of individuality."[11] In other words, it is subversive to our capacity for seeing human beings as the responsible, relatively free, self-reflective, and self-transcending individuals that they potentially and, to some degree, actually are. The problem of modernity for Niebuhr is that *although a high degree of responsible individuality is one of the presuppositions behind the possibility of healthy modern cultures, various forces within such cultures are now in the process of undermining this responsible individuality.* Furthermore, for Niebuhr the forces undermining the possibility of responsible individuality are primarily intellectual and cultural rather than sociological, although it is true that they have decisive sociological consequences and that social movements are themselves often carriers of these ideas. Various forms of naturalism, romanticism, and rationalism, some of which have their roots in Greek, biblical, and Renaissance intellectual movements, are the main cultural forces silently gnawing away at the roots of genuine responsible individuality (not to be confused with individualism) in modern culture.

Many of the popular contemporary intellectual movements obscure a fundamental truth about humans—that they are a synthesis or compound of nature and spirit. But what does Niebuhr mean by *nature* and *spirit?* He writes, "The obvious fact is that man is a child of nature, subject to its vicissitudes, compelled by its necessities, driven by its impulses, and confined within the brevity of the years which nature permits its varied organic forms, allowing them some, but not too much, latitude. The other less obvious fact is that man is a spirit who stands outside of nature, life, himself, his reason and the world."[12] If the reader can forgive Niebuhr for using "man" in contexts in which we are more likely today to use words such as "humans," we will discover that there is a gold mine buried in this paragraph. The problem of human self-understanding in modern cultures is precisely that this total view of human nature is not widely understood. The various naturalisms, romanticisms, and rationalisms see part, but by no means all, of the total picture.

The ancient Hebrews' concept of *ruach* and the Pauline use of the Greek word *pneuma* represent this subtle synthesis of nature and spirit. Both terms include the psychological dimensions called soul (*nephesh* and *psyche*) but preserve an understanding of spirit that is distinguishable from soul; spirit (*ruach* and *pneuma*) is capable of both relating to God and relating back to oneself in self-reflection and self-objectification. Soul and spirit can be distinguished but not separated, and the spirit is the principle of the soul. In addition, both soul and spirit can be distinguished but not separated from the body (*soma*). These well-known and elementary points of biblical anthropology are reemphasized by Niebuhr to assert that authentic Christian anthropology avoids both the dualistic separation of body and spirit and the over-identification of reason (*nous*) with the divine typical of most Greek thought and of much of later Christian thought influenced by Aristotle and neo-Platonism.[13]

As influential as neo-Platonism was on Augustine, Niebuhr still sees him as remaining basically true to the biblical insight into the human capacity for self-transcendence. Although Augustine did indeed sometimes appear to be associating human rational capacities with the image of God in man, one cannot fail to read the following passage from the *Confessions* without realizing that it was rather the human capacity for self-transcendence, closely associated with memory, that Augustine had in mind. It is the capacity for self-knowledge and introspection that Augustine believed was the image of God rather than the simple capacity to handle abstract and general concepts. He writes about it under the rubric of memory. What Augustine has to say about the self-transcending capacities of memory in chapter 10 of his *Confessions* points to what Niebuhr had in mind more than any other classical text that he can summon.

> All this I do inside me, in the huge court of my memory. There I have by me the sky, the earth, the sea, and all things in them which I have been able to perceive—apart from what I have forgotten. There, too, I encounter myself; I recall myself—what I have done, when and where I did it, and what state of mind I was in at the time. There are all the things I remember to have experienced myself or to have heard from others. . . . I can myself weave them into the context of the past, and from them I can infer future actions, events, hopes, and then I can contemplate all these as though they were in the present. "I shall do this," or "I shall do that," I say to myself in this deep process of my mind, full of the images of so many and such great things, "and this or that follows." "Oh if only this or that could happen!"[14]

"There, too, I encounter myself; I recall myself"—these words point to the essence of the meaning of self-transcendence. But such a capacity for self-transcendence is also a rooted, grounded, conditioned, contingent self-transcendence limited by the rhythms and patterns of nature.

But Niebuhr makes a further very subtle but extremely important point for the purposes of our critical conversation with the modern psychologies. This has to do with the relation of nature and spirit in human beings. Nature and spirit are distinguishable but never separate; for Niebuhr, they interpenetrate and mutually qualify one another. All of our natural impulses are qualified by spirit, by which he means the capacity for freedom, imagination, and self-transcendence. We never experience our sexuality or our hunger, our procreative impulses or our drive to survive, our fear or our natural aggressivity, as raw, mechanistic, and totally determined natural forces. They are always in humans qualified by freedom and imagination. We have alternatives and latitudes in expressing all of our natural tendencies and needs in ways that animals do not. On the other hand, none of our expressions of freedom, imagination, and self-transcendence is disconnected from our biological life. Our freedom is only a freedom to orient our biology one way or the other but never to disconnect ourselves from it, totally repress it, or act forgetfully of it. This truth makes our human creativity quite complex indeed.

But Niebuhr puts forth a further claim of even greater subtlety. He insists that we must not think that spirit is the exclusive source of everything that orders life and gives it form and coherence. Nor should we think that nature is the exclusive source of the energies and vitalities that exuberantly motivate us in our various activities. Niebuhr argues—and here his appreciation for the Hebrew foundations of Christianity begin to show—that both nature and spirit contain, in different ways, both vitality and form. "Nature and spirit," Niebuhr tells us, "both possess resources of vitality and form."[15]

What do these abstractions (or better, metaphors) of vitality and form as applied to nature and spirit really mean? What is at stake? The answer is rather simple but very crucial; there is hardly any single point in Niebuhr that is any more important and yet so easy to overlook. It means first that when we speak of our animal natures (our bodies and their instinctual tendencies), we should not think of them totally as energy, impulse, urge, appetite, and formless wants and wishes without any boundaries, order, or self-limitations. Instead, Niebuhr believes that both Judaism and early Christianity want us to think that in its created and undistorted condition, our animal and instinctual nature does have some internal regulating capacities and is not ordered simply by impositions from reason and culture. In addition, Niebuhr believes that this religious tradition does not understand spirit simply as order, rationality, and the container of abstract possibility. Instead, this tradition wants us to see spirit as both infused with the vitalities of nature and having its own intrinsic vitalities, imaginal yearnings, and higher spontaneities. Hence, human beings are *motivated* by both nature and spirit and *ordered* by both. Spirit does indeed add refinements to the ordering capacities of nature, but it can also, when distorted, add wild and chaotic embellishments—greed, pride, and the most hideous and uncontrollable disorders, crimes, and destructions. Such is the ambiguity of human creativity.

Vitality and form are both metaphors applied to the abstractions of nature and spirit. We speak of vital—in the sense of alive—dogs, cats, and people. But to attribute vitality to the abstract words *nature* and *spirit* is to speak metaphorically. In the same way, we speak of blocks, triangles, and statues as having forms, but to apply the word *form* to the abstractions of nature and spirit is to speak metaphorically.

Yet Niebuhr not only spoke metaphorically about the subject of anthropology, he talked metaphorically about God. Niebuhr believed that humans are fundamentally and essentially a union of vitality and form because he had the faith, trust, and *vision* that this was the nature and the character of the creator and sustainer of all reality—God. Niebuhr states these convictions in the following highly metaphysical and metaphorical passage: "The God of the Christian faith is the creator of the world. His wisdom is the principle of form, the logos. But creation is not merely the subjection of a primitive chaos to the order of logos. God is the source of vitality as well as of order. Order and vitality are a unity in Him."[16] So Niebuhr's anthropology is derived, in part, from this wider metaphysical tradition that is carried in the Judeo-Christian tradition. But I say "in part" because it is clear that Niebuhr believes that the facts of human nature also witness to and reflect this deeper reality. But in both cases—the mystery of human beings and the mystery of God—it is only through the exploratory power of metaphor that Niebuhr can discern and communicate his convictions.

In spite of the fact that we are originally, and at the deepest level of our beings, a union of vitality and form, distortion and sin do creep into our lives. But this distortion does not come into our existence because of some basic or ontological flaw in our biological structure; it is a result of our freedom. Through his insightful use of Kierkegaard's description of anxiety Niebuhr was able to locate human fallibility in our freedom rather than in our ignorance, our finitude, or our bodies.[17] More than for any other single contribution, Niebuhr is known for his creative retrieval of the so-called doctrine of original sin. And it was this recognition of original sin in human freedom that injected the realism into both his view of human nature and his understanding of the character of all political activity.

Christianity's belief—in contrast to the widespread modern perception to the contrary—in the essential unity of vitality and form gives it a positive appreciation for all dimensions of the created world. This is true in spite of its awareness of the actuality of sin. The belief in the goodness of creation includes, according to Niebuhr, all aspects of nature, animal and human instinctuality, natural human strivings for survival, primal attachments, sexual relatedness, material acquisition, and group relatedness. In other words, Niebuhr's interpretation of the primary metaphors of the Judeo-Christian tradition leads him to place a positive evaluation on all aspects of natural human striving, which he summarizes under the Greek word *eros*. Natural human self-regard in pursuing these goods of our wants is not the major source of evil from the perspective of the Christian myth. It is rather the reality of anxiety and sin that distorts natural self-regard (eros) into inordinate self-regard and a concupiscent striving to have more than we need or, as we moderns sometimes say, to "have it all."

Niebuhr's belief that our natural strivings have some form, some self-regulation, and even some capacity for justice, has consequences for his theory of obligation. Niebuhr's ethics and theory of moral obligation see Christian morality as building on and directing, without necessarily repressing, natural human needs and tendencies. Agape, or self-sacrificial love, is the primary moral obligation of the Christian, according to Niebuhr. But agape does not repress eros nor work against it; rather it builds on the natural unifying forces of eros and extends them, transforms them, and neutralizes the distorting effects upon them of human sin and unfaithfulness.[18] Because of the realities of sinfulness, Niebuhr argues that at the level of historic existence humans are only capable of the reciprocities of mutual love and justice.[19] This is the most, he contends, that humans can realistically aspire for and expect of one another in this poor and morally broken world. I will discuss Niebuhr's concept of mutuality extensively in later chapters on Freud, Skinner, and the humanistic psychologies, and demonstrate how it relates to the implicit ethical positions found in these psychologies. But I will also show how Niebuhr believes agape or self-sacrificial love is for the Christian a higher calling than simple mutuality and how, at the same time, it is the very presupposition of the possibility of fulfilling the demands of mutual love and justice—an idea that few of our psychologists acknowledge and some, in fact, have actively resisted.[20]

I will affirm yet to some extent criticize Niebuhr's specific understanding of agape, arguing instead that the truth is probably somewhere between Niebuhr's understanding of the highest ethics as self-sacrificial love and the implicit moral commitments of the modern psychologists. The issue will center around the nature and appropriate relations of love, self-love, mutual love, and sacrificial love. In the midst of this discussion, however, we will discover how Niebuhr's understanding of the deep metaphors of his faith and what they implied for the relation of vitality and form colored his final vision of the way humans should live to fulfill their moral obligation. Similarly I will show how the deep metaphors of the psychologists studied here color their implicit moral ideas. We will see how the function of deep metaphors in theology and psychology tends to put both on an equal footing: both disciplines rest their conceptual worlds on assumptions that fundamentally have the logical status of faith.

I lead with a discussion of Niebuhr, not because he is the greatest of modern theologians but because his concepts are widely known yet have never been satisfactorily exploited for the conversation between theology and the modern psychologies. I also rely heavily upon Niebuhr because of his particularly powerful appropriation of the idea of original sin—a doctrine, however, also prominent in the thought of Paul Ricoeur who, along with William James, also will be generously referred to in the pages to follow. It may seem strange at first glance to use in such close proximity the thought of Niebuhr, James, and Ricoeur. The public perception of these three modern religious thinkers frequently functions to put them in different camps. Niebuhr is often referred to as neo-orthodox and thought to have affinities with the European existential theologians of crisis such as Karl Barth or Rudolf Bultmann. James is seen as a founder of American pragmatism and the holder of a view of both religion and life that neo-orthodoxy was reacting against. Ricoeur is seen as one of the world's great philosophers working on the border line of the European traditions of existentialism, phenomenology, and hermeneutics. But such rapid first impressions overlook deeper affinities. For instance, it overlooks such things as Niebuhr's reliance on American pragmatism for the foundation of much of his own epistemology. It overlooks James's complex anthropology, which could lead him to have great affinities with Reformation views on the ambiguity of the will. And it obscures both the similarities between James's form of pragmatism and the existential and phenomenological strands in Ricoeur. Let us look more carefully at some of their broad similarities.

First, each has a view of human nature that sees it primarily as a *mélange* or duplex. Broadly speaking, each of them understands human nature as essentially a mixture of self-transcending freedom and natural finite conditionedness. All three have different ways of articulating this insight and use different sources for its development. Niebuhr, as we have seen, speaks of humans as a dialectic between nature and spirit and uses for his sources a combination of scriptural interpretation and philosophical analysis, with great indebtedness as well to Augustine and Kierkegaard. James understands human nature as a combination of different selves—the material self, the social self, and the spiritual self—all anchored around an ever-changing pure ego.[21] Although James had highly unique ways of accounting for human self-transcendence, from his early *Principles of Psychology* (1890) to his late *The Varieties of Religious Experience* (1903) his depictions of human nature constantly provide for this insight. At the same time, James drank deeply at the waters of Darwinism, and although he always relativized this modern view of the human animal by never permitting it to obscure human freedom and individuality, he clearly accepted what it implied for human biological and social conditionedness. His anthropology was based on an early, and largely self-discovered, form of phenomenology that was combined with, yet subsumed, his appropriation of Darwinistically oriented biology and psychology.[22]

Ricoeur, on the other hand, speaks of this *mélange* of the human with a variety of terms, depending upon which of the many points of view he employs in a particular writing. For instance, in his *Freedom and Nature* (1950) he refers to this mixture as the tension between "nature" and "freedom,"[23] while in his *Fallible Man* (1960) he calls it a dialectic between the finite and the infinite.[24] In the first book he grasps this dialectic through a phenomenological analysis of the human act of knowing. On the one hand, human perception is always perspectival, always from a certain angle of vision, and hence always finite in this respect. On the other hand, humans, in an effort to name and signify what they perceive, always go beyond what they have received in their perceptions. It is a part of our very essence to move toward totality and completeness (toward the infinite) in our effort to symbolize our world. In doing this, we expose the *mélange*, the disproportion, and the fundamental "pathétique of misery" of human nature; in other words, we exhibit the fundamental ambiguity between our finitude and our drive toward totality. Such themes follow into Ricoeur's later writings in *The Symbolism of Evil* (1960) and *Freud and Philosophy* (1965).[25] His methods range from the use of pure phenomenology in his early *Freedom and Nature* to increasingly more complex concerns with what he calls in *The Symbolism of Evil* a "hermeneutic phenomenology" of the classical religious and philosophical texts of the Western world. Ricoeur's complex analysis of the dominant narratives and metaphors of the Western religious tradition opens up not only the question of human fallibility but also the question of sin and finally the issue of deliverance from sin. These themes, from the standpoint of Ricoeur's hermeneutic philosophy, should inform the human sciences, even the psychologies, in Western societies. This is an insight that the hermeneutic perspectives of Cushman and Richardson, Fowers, and Guignon fail to acknowledge. These themes constitute part of the enduring classics that convey the deep philosophical anthropology out of which the human sciences should do their more detailed empirical work.

The second similarity among these three thinkers is even more striking than the first. All three of them hold parallel understandings about the reciprocal relations that exist between the voluntary and the involuntary aspects of human nature. In contrast to existentialists such as Sartre, who see the voluntary or decisional aspects of life as totally independent of the involuntary, the instinctual, or the passional,[26] or in contrast to the naturalists, who tend to collapse the voluntary into the involuntary, Niebuhr, James, and Ricoeur take the middle path and argue for a more reciprocal relation between these poles of human action. As we have seen already, Niebuhr does this in speaking about the dialectical relation between nature and spirit and by assigning various degrees of vitality and form to both dimensions of human life. James does this when he argues that the higher levels of will involved in deliberation and decision grow out of and refine our more instinctual and passional tendencies.[27] Ricoeur makes much the same point in his earliest writings when he advances such formulas as "the voluntary is by reason of the involuntary while the involuntary is for the voluntary"[28] or when he writes that "while nature makes freedom actual, freedom makes nature meaningful, and neither can ultimately be separated from the other."[29]

And finally, while all three of these thinkers appreciate the contributions of the modern psychologies, they all fought to keep them from impoverishing our view of the human. They all were fearful that these psychologies could serve to naturalize, mechanize, or biologize our image of human nature as well as function to obscure the intentional, the meaningful, and the relatively free aspects of human consciousness and action. Niebuhr did this in his critique of naturalism and its modern romantic transformations. James did it through his critique of scientism and his discovery in *Principles of Psychology* of an early American form of phenomenology that later matured into his radical empiricism.[30] Ricoeur does much the same in his use of both phenomenology and hermeneutics to critique the naturalizing tendencies of not only Freud but of many other examples of the modern social and psychological sciences. None of these thinkers was in any way trying to remove humans from nature or in any way trying to play down the role of nature in human existence. Rather they were simply trying to protect the human from being reduced to the natural, especially when nature was modeled after some of the more mechanistic and deterministic images of it found within the physical sciences—views of nature that, as we will see, frequently show up in the modern psychologies.

Looking at the Horizon of the Psychologies

A psychological system not only works, or seems to work, by virtue of its core psychological concepts, but also by virtue of its horizon. Richardson et al., building on

Gadamer, say that a horizon is a framework of pre-judgments that "first makes it possible for us to think and act in intelligible ways."[31] The horizon of a psychology is its larger, often vague and incomplete, view of the world that surrounds the more central key psychological concepts. This horizon is revealed in a psychology's deep metaphors and implicit narratives of obligation. Even if it is argued that these metaphors and implicit ethics do not represent the truly scientific core of a Freudian, Jungian, or Skinnerian system, they are still important because they tend to reveal the larger view of life that a particular psychologist carries around in his head and into which his psychology is seen to fit. This larger view of the world is silently conveyed to the user of the psychology.

Let me outline the map we will follow in uncovering and criticizing these horizons. Freud's early use of mechanistic metaphors and his later use of the metaphors of life and death imply a particular view of life. In addition, they set the stage for what he thought was ethically possible for humans to achieve, that is, a modest and cautious degree of reciprocity that would not overtax our limited libidinal investments or arouse our ready hostilities. Civilized *detachment* is the culture called for in the writings of Freud.

On the other hand, it is humanistic psychology's implicit metaphors of harmony that depict an image of the world where conflict can occur only if humans are somehow untrue to their own deepest selves. If they are true to their own inner plan for self-actualization—if they truly act to actualize their own potentialities first—then their own self-fulfillment will be complementary to the self-fulfillment of other people. In effect, philosophical ethical egoism can rule the day, but because of the underlying harmony of life, no strife, hostility, or dissension will ensue. A culture of expressive *joy* is the implicit horizon of the humanistic psychologies. Ellis, Beck, and Murray, for very different reasons and from quite different starting points, may also lapse into an ethical egoism, not so much because they assume a hidden harmony, but because of their close association of mental health with a particular brand of autonomy and individuality that becomes indistinguishable from individualism.

In the case of Skinner, an entirely new set of overextended and frozen metaphors of ultimacy appear. These are metaphors built around the Darwinian doctrine of natural selection and what it implies for the selective and reinforcing power of the environment. Content with the metaphysical assumption that natural selection is the sole agent shaping life and human destiny, Skinner tries to conceive a world in which humans would be reinforced to act in totally just and fair ways. Total justice, not self-actualization, was Skinner's implicit ethic, and the selecting, reinforcing, and controlling powers of the environment should be enlisted to bring such a justice into reality.

The situation is complex for Jung, but it is basically a variation of the culture of *joy* found in the humanistic psychologies. Life has so many possibilities (archetypes) and they develop at such different rates and mature at such different times that tensions, imbalances, and one-sidedness can occur in the psychic equilibrium. But one's task in life is still to be faithful to one's own unique set of archetypal possibilities, that is, to practice a kind of sacred egoism. Such an egoism will lead to a deeper harmony because of the final complementarity between each person's archetypal possibilities and the structure of the world.

And finally, Erikson and Kohut diverge from the ethic of self-actualization typical of the humanistic psychologists Maslow, Rogers, and Perls. They develop instead a generative ethics—an ethic and culture of *care* built around a model that sees health as the capacity for generative care for succeeding generations. Both of them retain the self-actualization motif of the humanistic psychologies but transform it by seeing the generative care of others as also an avenue for the actualization of each human's own deepest inclinations. This easy transition between self-regard and love for the other is made possible because even Erikson and Kohut have healthy doses of a harmonistic metaphysic not unlike what is found in the humanistic psychologies.

The comparison of these psychologies—their metaphors of ultimacy and their implicit ethics—with a Christian anthropology such as Niebuhr's is an exercise in the interpretation and evaluation of culture. It follows from a presupposition that gains its authority from Max Weber. More than any other intellectual of the modern era, Weber taught us the importance of ideas and ideals for the formation of a culture.[32] I have little doubt that the modern psychologies play the role they do in contemporary life because of a whole host of sociological forces—structural differentiation, the speed of social change, the widening gulf between home and work, and the demise of shared religious symbols that help in the organization of the interior life. People are desperate to find workable technologies to organize the new vacuums in their interior psychological lives that these social changes have inflicted upon them. To this extent it can be argued—or it frequently has been—that the social situation of modern societies has given the modern psychologies the power that they enjoy. Although there is truth in this view, the cultural point of view is just as true and probably more so. Since that great Weberian Philip Rieff wrote *Freud: The Mind of the Moralist* (1961) and *The Triumph of the Therapeutic* (1966),[33] we have been sensitive to the cultural power of psychological ideas—powerful not only because we have socially induced needs that they address, but powerful because they address these needs in particular ways typical of their own genius. This book takes the modern psychologies, their ideas and wider horizons, seriously as an independent source of culture, and this source deserves appreciative and critical evaluation from another source of culture—traditional anthropologies shaped by elements of the Jewish and Christian religious traditions.

Metaphors, Models, and Morality
in Freud

Some people with religious commitments believe psychoanalysis is an atheistic and mechanistic pretense that can be dismissed as irrelevant to the real problems of life. Such a view is surely wrong and will not serve well either the religious or social well-being of contemporary society. To write off psychoanalysis as atheistic and mechanistic is to fail to see both its religious and human significance. The characterization of psychoanalysis as irrelevant flies in the face of sociological evidence.

On sociological grounds alone, Freud's psychoanalytic thinking can be seen as a fundamental aspect of Western culture. It has been absorbed into our ways of thinking and feeling about the world. Philip Rieff has advanced the powerful hypothesis that through a worldwide corps of psychoanalytically trained psychiatrists and psychotherapists who function to pass on to their patients the wisdom of Freud a new character type that he calls "psychological man" has emerged and become dominant in modern Western societies. "Psychological man" is brooding, interior, introspective, interested primarily in his own internal well-being, and keeps a critical and suspicious distance from both the demands of community life and the anticipated pleasures of his own instinctuality.[1] Although Rieff's understanding, as we will see, of the moral and sociological implications of psychoanalysis is subject to debate, less arguable is the fact that Freud's psychoanalytic models are still a major influence on the mental health fields, especially with regard to their understanding of the nature and function of religion.[2] In addition, psychoanalysis in the popular mind is the basic model of what happens in psychotherapy, although many of the therapies are in fact not based on psychoanalytic theories.

The speed with which the theories of Freud made an impact upon our popular culture is one of the amazing stories of American life in the twentieth century. Almost immediately after Freud received an honorary degree from Clark University in 1909, James Jackson Putnam, a highly respected member of the Boston medical establishment, began introducing his ideas to American medicine. William James, although never himself a follower of Freud, predicted that the future of psychology would be dominated by psychoanalysis. About the same time, A. A. Brill of Columbia University began spreading the news of psychoanalysis throughout the eastern part of the United States. By 1915, Walter Lippmann was writing favorably about psychoanalysis in the *New Republic,* and widely read magazines such as *Good Housekeeping* were publishing articles with titles such as the "Diagnosis of Dreams."

The religious establishment was also being influenced by psychoanalysis. Many ministers responded favorably to Brill's efforts to evangelize on behalf of the Freudian gospel. Harrison Elliott, a respected professor of religious education at Union Theological Seminary in New York, used Freud in his courses. Although some of the biggest founding names of the clinical pastoral education movement in the United States such as Richard Cabot, Russell Dicks, and Anton Boisen tended to keep their distance from Freudian theory, especially its realistic theory of the unconscious and some of its clinical implications, their general emphasis upon the clinical situation certainly helped prepare the way for the reception of psycho-analysis among the ministers attracted to the clinical training movement. Later, Flanders Dunbar and Robert Brinkman directly introduced psychoanalytic ideas into the powerful Council for Clinical Training and in the process helped aggravate a growing division between the more conservative and idealistic New England wing of the council and the more Freudian group clustered around New York.

Psychoanalysis, in one form or another, is the dominant psychological influence on the American Association of Pastoral Counselors, a group organized in the mid-1960s for the burgeoning cadre of professional pastoral counselors and pastoral psychotherapists. This organization and the large number of counseling centers throughout the country that it accredits are significant resources to the American churches for the referral of troubled church members needing counseling. In turn, the members of this organization are through their writing and speaking influen-tial on the general pastoral care of both the Protestant and the Catholic churches. Hence, psychoanalysis, directly or indirectly, is a highly significant cultural force in the general secular society and in established religion that must be taken seriously, thought about, and evaluated.[3]

Philosophical Notes on Metaphors and Models

In our review of psychoanalysis we will confine our analysis to the psychoanalytic theories of Sigmund Freud (1856–1939). Psychoanalytic thinking is far more com-plex today than it was when it left the hands of Freud, with many schools such as psychoanalytic ego psychology, object relations, and self-psychology that now dot the landscape. Our purpose is not to be exhaustive but, instead, to illustrate the way a clinical psychology can gradually and silently drift into the area of religio-ethical judgments—judgments that invite a critical conversation with a discipline that has normative ambitions such as theology.

To understand Freud's theories one must be sensitive to the different kinds of models that make up the conceptualization of his system. Scientific thinking, including psychological thinking, is packed with such models. And the models themselves must be seen to have a strong metaphorical foundation. Ian Barbour, following the lead of Max Black, says that scientific models are "*systematically devel-oped metaphors.*"[4] Sallie McFague seems to agree when she writes that ". . . a model is, in essence, a sustained and systematic metaphor."[5] A model, even in the area of science, performs all the functions of a metaphor, but in less dramatic, less transient, and more settled and systematic ways. A metaphor is an analogy between something familiar and something unfamiliar; it highlights similarities and suppresses differences between the known and the unknown. In addition, a metaphor is sufficiently concrete to capture actual details of the unknown phenomenon.

Freud's writings are full of models. There is the early topographical model of the mind that divides it into unconscious, conscious, and preconscious. There is the much later structural or tripartite model of the mind that divides psychological life into the structures of the ego, id, and superego. Then there are the early hydraulic theories of psychic energy, the later models of life (eros) and death (thanatos) as symbols of the two great forces of biological life, and finally the use of myths such as the Oedipus myth, which functions as a model standing for the childhood conflict between a son and his father or a daughter and her mother. The questions that intrigue me are these: What are some of the different kinds of models in psychoanalysis? Do some of these models function more like religious metaphors (what I call metaphors of ultimacy) than they do limited scientific models? And finally, how do these models influence any explicit or implicit theories of obligation that may be lurking in the shadows of psychoanalytic theories of health and human fulfillment?

Even though they both have a metaphorical foundation, there are important differences between religious and scientific models. A religious model is like a scientific model, at least in the sense that it is more sustained and systematic than a simple metaphor. Our religious models, such as the theistic model for God, evolve out of the dramatic myths and narratives and more transient metaphors and parables. We might say that "God is love" or bears or supports us on "eagle wings." When we speak this way, the words "love" and "eagle wings" become metaphors for certain qualities that our religious experience leads us to attribute to God. But when we speak of the theistic idea of God, or even about monistic or pantheistic ideas of God, we are speaking about relatively more systematic models that order a wide range of experiences that humans feel they have about how God relates to the world.

Even though religious and scientific models are surprisingly alike, in that they are both analogical and used to organize and discover aspects of experience on the basis of more known and familiar aspects, scientific models are more strictly cognitive and aspire to develop theories that order discrete sets of observed data, such as a neurotic's repetitious handwashing, the voting behavior of blacks in Detroit, or our tendency to get drowsy after the ingestion of a particular medicine. Religious models, as suggested earlier, correlate not just discrete and limited observations of sense data but broad patterns of "human experience," such as the accrued sense that life has meaning, that our acts have lasting significance, or that life is sustained by forces beyond ourselves.[6] But in addition, religious models inspire us and induce commitment as well as give us some allegedly cognitive knowledge of the ultimate context of experience. We do not expect our scientific models to inspire us and induce commitment, but it is one of the major points of this book that they indeed sometimes perform these functions anyway and, to the extent that they do, lapse into quasi-religious attitudes and language.

Models of Instinct in Freudian Psychology

Freud used a variety of models to depict his understanding of human instinctive tendencies and needs. But there were two that were predominant—models of constancy and tension-reduction drawn from electronics and hydraulics and more organic models drawn from evolutionary theory. He tried to use both of the models in ways consistent with his understanding of the scientific *Weltanschauung*. Freud denied that psychoanalysis itself had a *Weltanschauung*. And here Freud may be correct, if we grant him his inflated understanding of *Weltanschauung* as an "intellectual construction, which gives a unified solution of all the problems of our existence."[7] Of course, on that score, nothing short of a full-scale, institutionally embodied religion can be said to have a worldview, a conclusion that Freud basically wants us to reach. But he does admit that science has a *Weltanschauung*, although an "incomplete" one, and that psychoanalysis need only to partake of it.[8] Basically this worldview insists that there is no other knowledge save that which can be achieved through the "manipulation of carefully verified observations."[9] Note that Freud did not say that among all the various forms of knowledge that exist, scientific knowledge is based on the manipulation of observation. He took the far more positivistic stance that there is no other knowledge except scientific knowledge. Neither "revelation, intuition [n]or inspiration" can be a source of knowledge for Freud. It is within this narrow understanding of knowledge that he tried to establish his theory of human instinctual tendencies and needs. Yet we will soon see how the human need to think holistically and religiously about the world appears so strong that even Freud, in and through his theory of instinctuality, projected a new *Weltanschauung* not unlike, in its formal dimensions, the religious worldviews that he saw himself so severely criticizing.

The Mechanistic Freud

Freud's early and more mechanistic theory of instincts was developed in close connection with his work on hysteria. It evolved out of a scientific ethos characterized by the mechanistic and positivistic scientific worldview held by his four teachers in medical school: Ernest Brück, Emil du Bois-Reymond, Hermann Helmholtz, and Carl Ludwig. These four men revolutionized the vitalistically oriented character of German physiology by entering into a solemn oath "to put into power this truth: no other forces than the common physical-chemical ones are active within the organism."[10] It was in this scientific context that Freud and Breuer devised their theory that hysteria was caused by a traumatic event, which Freud thought was always sexual, that dammed up the flow of instinctual energy, thereby converting it into a physical symptom. Freud called this dammed-up flow of energy "a quota of affect of a sum of excitation" and likened it to a "flow of electric fluid."[11] This flow of energy was marked by the constancy principle that meant, for Freud, that the organism reacts against any external stimulus that upsets its equilibrium by attempting to return to a state of quiescence.[12]

It is well known that Freud attempted but failed in his abortive *Project for a Scientific Psychology* (1895) to erect an entire psychology on this mechanistic model of instinctuality and the mind.[13] It is also commonly argued, by a certain group of Freud's followers, that he thereafter repudiated this mechanistic model and developed a true psychology based on introspective analysis of the meanings his patients communicated in their therapeutic conversations. Although there is truth in this view (put forth by many eminent scholars such as Ernest Jones and, later, Erik Erikson and Paul Ricoeur),[14] it disregards both the tenacity with which Freud continued to hold to his mechanistic views and the way newer and more organic biological models began gradually to emerge in his thinking. Even in his later years he revealed his belief that psychological ideas could be reduced to more basic mechanistic levels when he wrote at the end of *Beyond the Pleasure Principle* (1920) a final wistful confession: "The deficiencies of our description would probably vanish if we were already in a position to replace the psychological terms by physiological and chemical ones."[15] But the view of Jones, Erikson, and Ricoeur overlooks the gradual emergence of other kinds of biological models that partially, although never completely, replace the more mechanistic ones.

Niebuhr's View of Freud

Niebuhr had considerable appreciation for what he called the "realism" of Freud's view of human nature. Niebuhr believed Freud's picture of human beings as fraught with self-interested passions to be a definite improvement over the liberal and optimistic anthropologies that dominated the Enlightenment and the early half of the twentieth century.[16] In addition, Niebuhr appreciated, but was impatient with, what he thought (somewhat incorrectly) to be Freud's mechanistic naturalism and biologism. Niebuhr conceded that Freud had a right to be naturalistic and even mechanistic in a heuristic manner. But Freud indeed was not heuristic about his naturalism. Freud was dogmatic about it, and it was this presumption that bothered Niebuhr, especially its implication that there was no other approach to knowledge and no other forms of knowing except these. And furthermore, if Freud was to be deterministic in his thought (for which, Niebuhr thought, in itself Freud was "not to be criticized"), he should not have confined himself to such a narrow determinism. Niebuhr writes, ". . . the primary problem with his determinism is that he finds the causative factors in a too narrow range of subconscious motives."[17]

But the real problem with Freud's naturalism, Niebuhr thought, was the way it led Freud to misunderstand the complexities of the self. The perspective of historical distance and the advances in our understanding of Freud force us now to admit the lack of subtlety in Niebuhr's critique, not unlike the lack of subtlety in Freud's criticism of religion. Nonetheless, it will prove to be a critique from which Freud can never quite escape. But we know now that Niebuhr failed to understand the full nature of the self in Freud and did not understand the richness of his biological models and the ways some of them, at least, surpass the more mechanistic ones I reviewed above.

In his 1955 volume *The Self and the Dramas of History* Niebuhr stated a succinct version of his criticism of the Freudian theory of self. It was also in this work that Niebuhr shifted his basic categories from nature and spirit to nature and the self. The idea of the "self" in this book had the same qualities of self-transcendence and freedom that "spirit" contained in his earlier *The Nature and Destiny of Man* (1941), but it recognized more fully the social and dialogical character of life as well. "The self," Niebuhr wrote, "is a creature which is in constant dialogue with itself, with its neighbors, and with God, according to the Biblical view point."[18]

But it was precisely this insight that Niebuhr believed Freud's mechanism and his later structural theory, which divided the self into ego, id, and superego, failed to comprehend. "For all of the therapeutic skill of Freudian psychology," Niebuhr told us, ". . . it has confused the realities of the internal dialogue in some degree of obscuring the fact that the self is really in both the 'id' and the 'superego.'"[19] Freud, Niebuhr believed, tended to see the id too naturalistically, too much the formless "cauldron of seething excitement" dominated by the "pleasure-principle" and without "organization" and a "unified will" of its own.[20] Niebuhr wanted to see the id as part of the self, with some capacity for dialogue and freedom as is evidenced by its cunning maneuvers to deceive other parts of the self called the ego and the superego. Furthermore, Niebuhr believed the structural model of the self, infused with mechanism and naturalism as it is, obscured the way the superego is also involved in the dialogue of the self. Freud's naturalism prevented him from seeing the superego as anything more than the result of the "pressure of society upon the 'ego.'"[21] This prevented Freud from accounting for the way the superego can participate in conscience understood as a genuine self-transcending "debate between the self as engaged and obligated to its various communities and the self concerned with its own ends."[22] In this, as we will soon see, Niebuhr was anticipating points that are consistent with the theory of effective history found in the hermeneutic philosophy of Gadamer, Ricoeur, Cushman, and the Richardson team. All would agree with Niebuhr that the linguistically mediated effective history of the past sinks into and shapes even the id. Certainly it forms as well that part of the self that Freud called the superego; even here, it is good to remember that our superegos internalize more than our parents' prohibitions; they internalize aspects of the effective history that shaped our mother and father before they shaped us.

In advancing these criticisms, Niebuhr was not fully sensitive to the ways Freud's therapeutic involvements partially pushed him beyond his early mechanism and naturalism to a more genuine psychological discipline. The trouble was that Freud's philosophical commitments never quite caught up with the moves his therapeutic and self-analytic commitments were leading him to take.

Ricoeur on Freud

In Paul Ricoeur's *Freud and Philosophy* (1970), we read what is, in effect, both an affirmation and correction of Niebuhr's reading of Freud. The charge of naturalism and mechanism is clearly appropriate, according to Ricoeur, to the early Freud. In the early Freud, only the "vicissitudes of the instincts" within an isolated psychism are thematized. Stated bluntly, the Freudian systematization is solipsistic, whereas the situations and relations analysis speaks of and which speak in analysis are inter-subjective."[23] Ricoeur means by this that in the early Freud, his models and metaphors of the mind never permit us to get beyond the tension-reduction compensations of the organism. Real interpersonal and dialogical exchanges of the kind that occur, for instance, in psychotherapy are simply not thematized or accounted for by Freud's early concepts.

But in unthematized ways, much of what Niebuhr has called for in Freud was, when we read deeper, actually there. Ricoeur points out that in Freud's therapeutic studies and in his analysis of dreams, both his own and others, Freud was studying a wish *(Wunsch)*, and a wish was not a raw biological urge but rather a mental idea or representation *(Vorstellung)* of an instinct.[24] When this recognition is added to the additional insight that an instinctual representation always entails some image of an object (an other) that is the source of satisfaction, we must then admit that desire or wish in Freud is mostly depicted as an intersubjective or dialogical phenomenon. Although it was not adequately described by Freud's mechanistic models of the mind, Ricoeur believes that

> The intersubjective structure of desire is the profound truth of the Freudian libido theory. . . . Freud never described instincts outside of an intersubjective context; if desire were not located within an interhuman situation, there would be no such thing as repression, censorship, or wish-fulfillment through fantasies; that the other and others are primarily bearers of prohibitions is simply another way of saying that desire encounters another desire—an opposed desire.[25]

Hence, Ricoeur would say that the situation is far more complex than Niebuhr admits. Rather than a purely naturalistic language of mechanism, Ricoeur insists that there exists in Freud two sets of models or two languages of the mind—an energetic or mechanistic one *and* an intersubjective or, as Niebuhr and Gadamer would say, a dialogical and historical one. The intersubjective or dialogical consciousness is the presupposition of the possibility of interpreting the unconscious and its domination by the tension-reduction desires of the pleasure principle.[26] Even if it is the task of psychoanalysis to displace consciousness and uncover the energies that motivate it, it is only on the basis of this self-transcending and dialogical consciousness that the uncovering of the unconscious becomes possible. We cannot interpret unless we are first self-transcending and self-reflective creatures. But Ricoeur would agree with Niebuhr that although this insight is something that Freud assumed and a truth that his therapy and self-analysis presupposes, it is not well thematized by Freud at all.

This is a perspective on Freud that has been brought out by several interpreters, especially the earlier work of Philip Rieff in *Freud: The Mind of the Moralist* (1961)[27] and the more personal statement by Bruno Bettelheim in *Freud and the Soul* (1983). But even though Ricoeur uncovers these mixed models—the model of energetics and the model of intersubjectivity or dialogue—the resultant image of the human is indeed not unlike Niebuhr's perception of Freud. Both nature and spirit may indeed be there in Freud's anthropology, but as Ricoeur acknowledges, nature is thematized and spirit is either not thematized or at best underthematized. Furthermore, nature is still represented—especially in the early Freud but basically throughout Freud—in tension-reduction terms. Hence, not only is spirit poorly thematized, nature itself is built around a tension-reduction model. This model of nature tends to contaminate the image of spirit (intersubjective dialogue), leading us to think, if we are attentive to Freud, that spirit in all respects follows the dynamics of instinctuality in its drive toward discharge.

One can see this when Freud writes, even rather late in his career, that "The nucleus of the Unc. consists of instinctual representatives which seek to discharge their cathexis."[28] Hence, Freud is here plainly saying that these psychological realities, these intersubjective wishes (these "instinctual representatives"), work on the basis of the tension-reduction patterns of the pleasure-pain mechanism. Hence, there is little doubt, as Ricoeur points out, that the Freudian wish stands at the intersection of nature, culture, and society; it is not just a brute biological reality. But nonetheless, the wish is, in Freud's eyes, always a meaning, an interpersonal reality, which drifts toward the laws of mechanism. In Freud's mixed language (or models) of energetics and dialogue, dialogue and intersubjectivity are constantly succumbing to the laws of energetics and mechanism. But the reverse is not true: it is at best only implicit in Freud how mechanism or energetics can be transformed, enlarged, and developed by the power of dialogue. Freud may have been fully aware that his model of "the instincts is," as he put it, "so to say our mythology."[29] In confessing this, Freud reveals that he was aware that he was basically using metaphors derived from electronics and hydraulics to conceptualize the working of our instinctual wishes. But in spite of his self-consciousness on this matter, the evidence points to the truth that, to the very end, Freud thought all psychological life—all of its cultural, symbolic, and religious expressions—functions according to the laws of these energetic models. It is true that the world of language, representation, and symbol is for Niebuhr and Ricoeur the world of some degree of freedom and self-transcendence, but it is not clear that it was so for the mind of Freud.

Life, Death, and the Metaphors of Ultimacy

Freud's psychology is primarily built on theories about the nature and dynamics of our instinctual tendencies and needs. In terms of the first three levels of practical moral thinking that I mentioned in chapter 1, Freud's psychology concentrates on level three. The question, however, is this: Do Freud's various understandings of our basic psychobiological tendencies and needs function in his thought not only as psychological propositions but also as metaphors of ultimacy—that is, as metaphors that tell us about the nature of the ultimate context of experience and something about our origins, destiny, and the basic value of life? Freud's theory of our basic tendencies and needs does double as a system of metaphors of ultimacy and, indeed, as a veritable cosmology. In addition, these metaphors of ultimacy and their associated cosmology also influence Freud's implicit theory of moral obligation, that is, his ethic.

In several of his later writings, Freud traced the shifts in his theory of instincts that occurred throughout his long career.[30] The account goes like this. In his early years, his clinical work led him to posit two sets of instincts that he called the ego instincts (self-preservation instincts) and the sexual instincts (concerned primarily with the preservation of the race). Then his work with narcissism led him to believe that the ego did not have a separate source of instinctual energy but that, instead, it became an object of the libidinal energy of the id. Finally, in his speculative 1920 volume *Beyond the Pleasure Principle* he divided the instinctual energies of the id into two broad classes that he called the sexual or life instincts and the death instincts.[31]

Although he presents these theories as frankly speculative, within three years—when he wrote *The Ego and the Id* (1923)—he was willing to say this his theory of the life and death instincts and their various fusions was "an assumption indispensable to our conception."[32] Furthermore, it is clear, as Frank Sulloway summarizes, that Freud's new dual-instinct theory was presented to solve substantial issues in his clinical theory: namely, the problem of repetition compulsion (why people compulsively repeat destructive symptoms), the problem of regression, and finally the problem of appearing to explain everything with reference to sexuality after his studies in narcissism had led him to dispense with his earlier instinctual dualism of sex and self-preservation.[33] In addition, it is also clear that the introduction of this distinction between the life and death instincts affected nearly every aspect of Freud's psychology—his theory of anxiety, of dreams, of the structure of the mind, and especially of the superego and culture. These last two topics will be of special interest as we review the influence of his instinctual dualism on his implicit ethics.

What is the content of the life instinct and the death instinct, and do they actually become deep metaphors or metaphors of ultimacy? The phenomena of compulsive hallucinatory repetition of war traumas, tenacious resistance in psychoanalysis, and certain repetitive characteristics of children's play led Freud to question whether the psychic apparatus always and everywhere functioned according to the tension-reduction patterns of the pleasure principle. It was clear to him that upon occasion human beings directly sought out pain, courted disaster, resisted health and cure, and stupidly repeated dysfunctional and destructive symptoms. Although for Freud the pleasure principle was conservative and sought tension-reduction, its primary goal was to "reduce, to keep constant or to remove internal tension due to stimuli."[34] Yet the death instinct went even beyond that. Not just constancy but death itself is its goal—the literal return to the state of inanimate existence. Freud wrote,

> Moreover, it is possible to specify this final goal of all organic striving. It would be in contradiction to the conservative nature of the instincts if the goal of life were a state of things that had never yet been attained. On the contrary, it must

be an *old* state of things, an initial state from which the living entity has at one time or another departed and to which it is striving to return by the circuitous paths along which its development leads. If we are to take this as a truth that knows no exception that everything living dies for *internal* reasons—becomes inorganic once again—then we shall be compelled to say that *"the aim of all life is death"* and, looking backwards, that *"inanimate things existed before living ones."*[35]

Freud thought that he had to go that far to explain the self-defeating repetition of neurotic symptoms and his patients' incomprehensible defiance, at times, of his own curative efforts. The life instincts, or eros, although conservative themselves, function to preserve life by combining through the sexual encounter of germ cell with germ cell to produce new life.[36] If it stands by itself, all life falls under the sway of the death instinct and yearns to return to the inanimate state. If it yields to the life instinct, it combines and reproduces and conserves or preserves itself through the production of new life.

It is very clear that in *Beyond the Pleasure Principle* the life and death instincts have the force of metaphors of ultimacy. This means that they apply to all biological life and constitute the relevant effective forces playing on and influencing human action. Not only do these forces constitute Freud's mythology, they constitute a metaphysics, or at least a cosmology. Hence, as Lee Yearley has recently pointed out, Freud the destroyer of all faiths and all religious cosmologies creates a new one to undergird and support his psychoanalysis.[37] After determining that both Judaism and Christianity rested on the foundations of his Oedipus conflict and its associated neurotic repressions, Freud developed an alternative picture of ultimate things. After determining that the God of the Western religious tradition—its monotheism, its ethical claims, and its redemptive acts—constitutes nothing but a projection of the primitive fear and love that young sons have in response to the arbitrary sexual prohibitions of their father, Freud developed another set of metaphors to represent the ultimate context of experience.

These metaphors used to represent our psychobiological tendencies and needs become metaphors of ultimacy because of Freud's explicit naturalism and positivism. As we noticed earlier, it is Freud's view that scientific knowledge is based on the "manipulation of carefully verified observations"[38] and that this knowledge is the only knowledge there is. It is precisely this kind of positivism and naturalism that combines with his late dual-instinct theory to develop an alternative cosmology and a new set of metaphors of ultimacy. Positivistic thinking is basically "nothing but" thinking—the kind of thinking that says that there is nothing but naturalistic determinants or mechanistic determinants, or, for that matter, nothing but divine or supernatural determinants.[39] So it is appropriate to speak of scientific or naturalistic positivisms or even of theological positivisms, as we frequently do when referring to the theology of Karl Barth.[40] When Freud's increasing affirmation of his two instincts of life and death combines with his scientific naturalism and positivism, the net result is to make these instincts more than humble working hypotheses designed to order discrete arenas of observed data, but instead they are elevated into a cosmology and inflated into metaphors that represent the ultimate context of experience. Freud all but admits this in his close identification of the life and death instincts with Empedocles' two cosmological principles of *philia* and *neikos*. In his article "Analysis Terminable and Interminable," Freud makes a disclaimer and asserts that the eros and death instincts are not, as are Empedocles' *philia* and *neikos,* cosmological principles; instead, they apply strictly to the psychobiological realm.[41] Freud does not quite comprehend, however, that by taking the position that the psychobiological realm is the only relevant context for human action he has indeed elevated eros and death to metaphors of ultimacy, that is, to metaphors that represent the only effective and relevant ultimate context of experience.

To the extent that Freud apotheosized the metaphors of life and death, he used them in ways analogous to the way more explicitly religious people metaphorically represent the ultimate context of experience. Hence, Freud was making his own kind of *faith judgment*. None of us, including Freud, really knows in any direct, tangible, and sensory way what the ultimate context of experience is. What intimations that we have of this ultimate context, we represent, and even investigate, through more concrete metaphors taken from ordinary experience. Freud almost seemed dimly to suspect that he was involved in a quasi-religious kind of thinking when he wrote: "Perhaps we have adopted the belief because there is some comfort in it. If we are to die ourselves, and first to lose in death those who are dearest to us, it is easier to submit to a remorseless law of nature, to the sublime Aνάγχη [Necessity], than to a chance which might perhaps have been escaped."[42]

Freud, then, who debunked all religions and all cosmologies as neurotic, inadvertently developed a cosmology of his own. All past cosmologies, he believed, had led to ethics that were basically neurotic. Although Lee Yearley is using in the following passage the word *cosmogony* rather than *cosmology* and although he makes his point too harshly, he is more right than wrong when he writes, "As a critic of cosmogonies, he assumes that cosmogonies must undergird ethics and then attacks the cosmogonies and thus the ethics. As a creator of cosmogony, he builds a cosmogony that makes morality into a form of pathology."[43] Yet Freud ended by creating not only an alternative cosmology but an alternative ethic. Or perhaps it is more accurate to say that he flirted with a couple of alternative ethics. Although he tried to keep his psychoanalysis free from ethical commitments, he did believe that it was clearly incompatible with certain inherited moral positions, and in tipping his hand on this issue, he left strong clues about the kind of ethics that he believed psychoanalysis implied. In uncovering this, we will also learn how Freud's own metaphors of ultimacy condition and influence his implicit principles of obligation.

Niebuhr and Freud on Vitality and Form

But before turning to a more direct consideration of Freud's implicit theory, or theories, of obligation, I want to insert a brief discussion of the question of vitality and form in Niebuhr and Freud. We saw in chapter 2 how Niebuhr, following the basic commitments of both Jewish and early Christian anthropology, believed that both nature and spirit have vitality and form. In addition, he believed that there was an important analogy in Christian theology between anthropology and metaphysics on the issue of vitality and form. In the Christian vision, Niebuhr tells us—and I believe correctly—God is seen as a perfect union of vitality and form, and humans, at the levels of both nature and spirit, are finite unions of vitality and form. The practical upshot of these affirmations is that both Judaism and Christianity have very positive views of nature and instinctuality. Our instinctuality has form, and although reason, conscience, and spirit may further order our instinctuality, this additional refinement is or can be gentle and uncoercive. Being a civilized person is not a matter of spirit, reason, and conscience beating instinctuality to the ground and forcing it into submission. Nature provides a fundamental order to spirit that spirit further refines. And all of this at the anthropological level reflects the fundamental unity of vitality and form in the life of God. In this, Niebuhr and other Christian theologians believe, Christianity avoids the dichotomy or split between vitality and form characteristic of so much of classical Greek thought. The idealism of the classical Greek view "identified spirit too simply with reason and reason too simply with God."[44] Hence, reason, conscience, or culture (something outside of our vitality) becomes the "source of the order and form which transmute the anarchic vitality of nature into genuine creativity."[45]

It is clear that the relation between vitality and form in Freud's psychology is closer to classical Greek thought than it is to the anthropology and metaphysics of the Judeo-Christian tradition. Throughout the development of his instinct theory, but especially during the middle period when he believes that even the ego functions off the diverted and captured energies of the id, Freud believes that form (morality and culture) comes in all respects from the outside of human nature, that is, from parental prohibitions, the superego, or finally, for those fortunate enough to be analyzed, from analytic insight. Although he begins to attribute some element of form to instinctuality in his later dual-instinct theory in that eros is depicted as striving for the renewal of life through the generative combination of germ cells, Freud never grants this process sufficient form-developing power to alter his understanding of the id as a seething, formless "cauldron." In spite of Freud's association with a variety of twentieth-century movements toward sexual and biological liberation, it would be precisely the view of Christian anthropology that his picture of nature and instinctuality is not positive enough and that his devaluation of these areas may come from the silent metaphysical assumptions concealed in the metaphors he uses to represent both human tendencies and the ultimate context of experience.

Vision and Obligation in Freud

Freud's tendency to split up vitality and form in his theory of nature and instinctuality is not primarily questionable because it disagrees with the traditional commitments of the Judeo-Christian tradition, but because it is also problematic on more strictly philosophical grounds. Niebuhr's own position, which assigns vitality and form to both nature and spirit, although stated too abstractly for certain practical purposes, is more philosophically adequate. William James can help us see this. James's anthropology basically agrees with Niebuhr on this question and states even more forcefully the way in which vitality and form can be thought to be a part of both nature and spirit. I will invoke James again when we look at the question of vitality and form as it emerges in both Jung and the humanistic psychologies. Suffice it now to say that instinct for James is not just formless vitality. Instead, it is full of form, in the sense that it is full of evolutionary adaptive wisdom that has been retained and encoded in our bodily systems due to the refining power of natural selection.[46] All of our basic instinctual capacities, for James, are doubtless adaptive capacities that have served human adaptation well sometime or other in the evolutionary history of humans. They may be ambiguous and need further refinement and channeling by socialization, the superego, or reason, but this process will entail form refining form rather than simply form wrestling to the ground, whether by insight or repression, the obdurate demands of vitality.

James's view of instinctuality holds good today and has the further advantage of being stated in a sufficiently sophisticated way as to be adjustable to a sound understanding of consciousness, will, and freedom. He had a theory of the plurality of instincts, a theory of their adaptive potency and relevance, a theory of their transitoriness (what Erikson would call an epigenetic principle), a theory of how habits inhibit and channel instincts, a theory of how these instincts are in humans always inextricably connected with memory and meanings, and finally a theory of how they both feed and are further ordered by higher-level psychological processes that we might call will and reason. So completely did James anticipate the best of contemporary instinct theory that the great Harry Harlow once said at a major American Psychological Association symposium in 1967 that had he read James on instinct "earlier, he might have saved himself several years of tedious research and agonizing theorizing."[47] All of this theorizing (of both James and the more recent models) points to an image of human instinctuality that brings *vitality and form together,* close to the way Niebuhr speaks about it.

Of course, saying that James and others provide reasons to see vitality and form more closely related at the level of instinctuality is not the same as saying this view of the "nature" in human nature can be used as a valid metaphor for the inner core of reality. The step from anthropology to the wider realms of metaphysics is a step that Freud took too quickly and one that I will not attempt to take at all. My point is a more cautious one. I am simply arguing that if one *were* to use the testimony of our instincts and combine it with wide ranges of other experiences to develop a genuine metaphysical argument about the nature of reality as such, their witness would bring vitality and form into closer proximity than occurred in the vision of Freud. But the implications of other ranges of experience would be needed to complete the argument. The point is, not only did Freud move too quickly from a view of the nature of human tendencies and needs to their metaphorical overgeneralization, he understood these natural instincts somewhat inadequately to begin with and hence failed to gain from them the right metaphorical force.

Freud believed that our instinctuality is socialized, redirected, and sublimated by the repressive forces of civilization.[48] This, Freud thought, had been a necessity for the control and ordering of human instinctuality. But it was a control that cost a great deal of neurosis and needless human pain and suffering—a price that Freud contended was too high to pay. Part of the explanation could be found in the exalted ideals of the Western religious tradition, especially the principle, known in other religions as well, that "Thou shalt love thy neighbor as thyself."[49] Freud made a variety of criticisms of this universalistic principle—that it cannot be kept, that it discriminates against members of one's own family in favor of strangers, that it fails to distinguish between those who are worthy of our love and those who are not, that it fails to take account of our innately aggressive natures, and finally, that the renunciations for which it calls will lead to unhappiness. But the claims about its impossibility and its blindness to our aggressiveness are the most relevant criticisms for our purposes.

Rieff's View of Obligation in Freud

The command to "love thy neighbor as thyself" Freud believed was psychologically impossible. "But, above all," Freud asks, "how shall we achieve it? How can it be possible?" No ethic can be justified if it is psychologically impossible, if we do not have the capacity to fulfill the ethic in question. Philip Rieff has presented an influential interpretation of Freud that depicts his implicit ethic as a kind of philosophical ethical egoism. The ethical egoist, according to the moral philosopher William Frankena, answers the question of what he is obligated to do with the principle that he is to produce as much good over evil as possible *for himself.*[50] Furthermore, in view of the centrality of the pleasure-pain principle in the Freudian economics, it might be argued that Freud's basic ethical commitments were in the direction of an ethical egoism of a hedonistic kind and that he felt that this was the only ethic genuinely possible by virtue of the way we human creatures are actually made. This seems to be what Rieff is suggesting with his concept of "psychological man," which he advances as a summary statement of the implicit ethic found in the Freudian view of human fulfillment. But as Ernest Wallwork points out in an important recent essay, Rieff's influential interpretation of Freud was probably built on a superficial interpretation of narcissism—one that interpreted all forms of love in Freud as finally expressions of self-love.[51] Furthermore, Wallwork believes that Freud's criticism of the principle of neighbor-love did not so much leave Freud as a restrained and prudent ethical egoist, as Rieff's concept of psychological man suggests, but is more a critique of exalted Christian images of love of neighbor that overemphasize needless self-sacrifice. In turn, Wallwork believes that Freud was subtly advocating more properly Jewish images of other-regard built around the concept of respect and reciprocity.

What is probably nearer to the truth is that Freud, like most of us, was unstable in the way he thought about ethics. There is clearly a rather well thematized ethical egoism that runs throughout his writings. It hardly can be otherwise in view of the final weight that he assigns to the conservative models of motivation to be found in both the life instinct and the death instinct. Since the life instinct seeks constancy and the death instinct the total repose of inanimate matter, neither exhibits the natural sense of abundance associated with more genuine other-regarding behavior. I believe that this is true in spite of the subtleties of the processes of narcissistic identification, which we will examine below. There is still the image that runs throughout Freud that to invest one's love in another, and especially the larger society, is to take one's libidinal energies away from oneself. This is the entire theme of *Civilization and Its Discontents* (1930): culture develops at the expense of the depletion of the natural aims of our libidinal energies. In this work Freud writes, "We have treated the difficulty of cultural development as a general difficulty of development by tracing it to the inertia of the libido."[52] Note the same conserving and scarcity-oriented mentality when he writes, "My love is something valuable to me which I ought not to throw away without reflection."[53] Hence, it is not surprising that interpreters such as Rieff and Gilbert Harman have believed that some form of ethical egoism, probably of a restrained and cautious hedonistic kind, was the implicit ethic compatible with Freudian psychology.[54]

Nor is it surprising in view of this cautious attitude toward the possibilities of emotional investment that the interpreter of Freudian psychoanalysis might be inclined to call the culture that this ethic undergirds a culture of detachment. The detachment associated with Rieff's view of Freud is one thing, but a more subtle kind of detachment of the kind described below is probably more authentic. Rather than the detachment of the ethical egoist trying to relate in such a way as to satisfy basic wishes without incurring the losses of emotional overinvestment, the detachment more typical of Freud is a cautious but fair reciprocity that comes from a fear of the fundamental hostility of the world, especially the neighbor. This alternative view we will now investigate.

Wallwork's View of Obligation

Ernest Wallwork has put his finger on another more profound strand in Freud's writings on ethics. Wallwork argues that Freud in his actual behaviors and attitudes is not an ethical egoist opposed to all other-regarding behavior. He is simply against those interpretations of neighbor-love that stretch it to mean that we are to love all others universally with deep affection, that is, to love with "deep feeling" all people equally, even the stranger and the enemy.[55] This is what Freud thought the Christian concept of agape requires, and he believed it to be psychologically impossible. But in its place Wallwork insists that Freud believed in the psychological possibility of a milder, less affective, mutual respect and reciprocity that actually resonate "with the ethics of Judaism more than with those of Christianity."[56]

The key to the psychological possibility of genuine other-regarding behavior is the phenomenon of identification. Within the act of identification, the natural tension between egoistic narcissism and other-regarding object-love is mitigated. As Wallwork points out, "Identification makes it possible for an agent's self-esteem to be raised by a vicarious tie to another."[57] And if the object of identification is the person of a religious leader who has attracted a large following, then even more generalized other-regarding behavior is possible. Through the identification with a religious leader such as Jesus, the believer, as Freud points out in *Group Psychology and the Analysis of the Ego* (1921), can learn to love all those who love Jesus and all those whom Jesus loves.[58] The believer can love himself in identifying with Jesus but can also quite literally love others who are also identified with Jesus.[59] Hence, as Wallwork writes, "Within the Freudian scheme, self-sacrificial behavior is still possible, even though complete selflessness as a motive is not."[60] Of course, Freud thought that this kind of identification with the person of a widely loved religious leader, although opening the possibility of a more generalized other-regarding behavior, was finally unhealthy. The believer is subject to the authoritarian whims of the beloved leader and all of the attendant possibilities of exploitation and manipulation that this entails.

Freud might have fewer reservations about the reality of genuine other-regarding behavior had he considered the possibility of people identifying in their ego-ideal with an abstract concept or belief, such as the idea of equal dignity of all humans or the idea that all persons are children of God. In fact, it might be possible for the religious leader him- or herself to hold this belief as the shared ideal around which all followers would work out their narcissistic identification with him or her and each other.[61] But Freud seems not to have considered this possibility.

Not only did Freud feel that neighbor-love or agape was impossible from the standpoint of the structures of the narcissistic ways of our libido and sexual instincts, but he thought it was clearly impossible from the standpoint of the dynamics of the death instinct. In fact, he believed that the other-regarding behavior that the love commandment entails was inconsistent with both of these two major instincts—instincts that, as we have seen, he sometimes made into metaphors of ultimacy. By the time of the writing of *Civilization and Its Discontents* Freud's death instinct had developed into a more generalized instinct toward aggressiveness. Instead of loving the neighbor, Freud believed that sober reflection suggested that the neighbor had far more "claim to my hostility and even my hatred."[62] The neighbor seems not "to have the least trace of love for me" and if it "will do him good he has no hesitation in injuring me. . . ."[63] This is clearly an expression of Freud's death instinct, which seems all too ready to spring out and strike at strangers with whom one has not developed inhibiting affectional relations. As he states, humans are "creatures among whose instinctual endowment is to be reckoned a powerful share of aggressiveness."[64]

But even here, as Wallwork points out, the death instinct does not, for Freud, so much eliminate the possibility of other-regarding behavior as it does remove the possibility of the more expansive loving initiatives toward the stranger that is generally associated with agape. Freud does leave room for respect and reciprocity. Freud writes that if the neighbor "behaves differently, if he shows me consideration and forbearance as a stranger, I am ready to treat him in the same way, in any case and quite apart from any precept. Indeed, if this grandiose commandment had run 'Love thy neighbor as the neighbor loves thee,' I should not take exception to it."[65] One is to presume that such an unemotional capacity for reciprocity Freud believed to be possible within the limits of narcissism.

Hence, we see a rather direct line leading from Freud's cosmology (his metaphors of ultimacy) to his theory of obligation. Eros and thanatos show us the kind of world we are in, set the limits for the kinds of action that are reasonable, and show us the framework of our moral action. Our metaphors of ultimacy do not dictate in all respects our explicit or implicit theories of obligation. Indeed, this does not happen in our official religious thinking, and it does not happen in the unofficial religious thinking that we find in the psychologies reviewed in this book. For instance, Freud's deep metaphors are compatible with either ethical egoism or cautious views of reciprocity and respect, and he probably oscillated between them. But our metaphors of ultimacy, whatever they are, do lead us to discern the world and its possibilities in certain ways, and this clearly affects our understanding of the nature and scope of moral action.

My point is that in an effort to explain certain specific ranges of clinical data, Freud developed his instinct theories. In connection with attempting to account for the clinical phenomena of hysteria, obsessional neuroses, and phobias, Freud elaborated his theory of libidinal instincts that later became his theory of eros. In an effort to explain repetitive behavior and neurotic resistance, he developed his theory of the death instinct. However, in the case of both eros and thanatos, he gradually elevated them to the functional equivalent of cosmological forces. He went from the level of explaining discrete data to the level of interpreting human experience in general. Ian Barbour has suggested that this is the step that separates the limited models of science from the more encompassing metaphors of religion. He writes, "One of the functions of models in science is to suggest theories which correlate patterns in observational data. One of the functions of models in religion, I submit, is to suggest beliefs which correlate patterns of human experience."[66] If this is what distinguishes the models and metaphors of science from the models and metaphors of religion, it is clear that upon occasion, and more and more toward the end of his life, Freud journeyed onto the terrain of religion. In addition, it was an aspect of his thought that decisively shaped his understanding of the possibilities, limits, and purposes of moral action.

But it was not just Freud who shifted categories from the scientific to the normative. It is a step that many psychologists take but generally in ways so subtle that it is difficult to understand and describe clearly. Its nearly ubiquitous presence in psychology, especially in its more clinical expressions, probably says more about the functioning of the human mind than it does the perversity or lack of discipline of psychologists. As Mircea Eliade and others have argued, humans have an irresistible need to turn the raw material of their experience into orienting myths.[67] We have seen how this process occurred in the work of Freud. But insofar as this happened, his metaphors of ultimacy and the ethics that accompany them should be fair subjects for critical theological reflection and analysis.

Obligation in Freud and in Christian Thought

If Freud's psychology points toward an ethic of mutual respect and reciprocity rather than an ethics of agape, what would be a theological response to his position? More specifically, what would be the response of Niebuhr, whom I will take as a beginning guide to this discussion? Our question is relevant both for a proper understanding of the realities of psychoanalytic psychotherapy and a proper understanding of the potential influence of Freud's thought on our cultural images of human fulfillment and the moral life. It is relevant for a proper understanding of psychoanalytic therapy, because if it were indeed the case that a therapist held in the back of his or her mind a normative theory of human relations built around the principle of reciprocity, this would doubtless enter into the therapeutic transference relation in some way. And if the concepts of eros and thanatos seem to be associated with a morality of reciprocity in contrast to some form of ethical egoism (Rieff) or agape (Christianity), then wherever psychoanalysis is accepted our cultural images of human fulfillment would be tilted toward its implicit norms.

Granting Wallwork's interpretation of Freud, Niebuhr would need to acknowledge in Freud a position that holds that rather minimal levels of reciprocity and justice are the only other-regarding ethical possibilities open to humans in view of their constancy-oriented sexual drives and their overtly destructive and aggressive death instincts. This might entail more direct narcissistic involvement with those members of our own family, but with strangers and more remote acquaintances, it could entail no more than a kind of low-key civil justice. Most of this Niebuhr could have affirmed as far as it goes, but he would have wanted to restore agape to its rightful place in relation to this cautious justice.

Realism in Freud and Niebuhr

On the whole, however, Niebuhr affirmed the realism of Freud's understanding of the ethical possibilities of human beings. Niebuhr was himself critical of the superficial optimism about human nature that he found in various forms of humanism, liberalism, and romanticism. He believed that Freud's analysis of the unconscious springs of all action and its deep involvement in both narcissistic and aggressive impulses had tempered profoundly the progressive views of human nature found in the Enlightenment and all rationalistic views of morality—be they Lockean, Kantian, or Hegelian.[68]

But Niebuhr believed that Judeo-Christian pessimism and realism are more profound than the Freudian forms and for discernible and arguable reasons. Freud, according to Niebuhr, too simplistically locates inordinate human self-regard in our instinctuality and fails to understand the subtle ways in which our freedom and its associated anxieties aggravate and distort this natural self-regard at all levels of human life and creativity. He writes, "Our thesis has been that Freudian realism is defective in explaining the facts of the emergence of self-regard on every level of civilization and in doing justice to the fact that these forms did not represent the inertia of a primitive *id* but the corruption of the freedom of a coherent and organized *ego*."[69] In this passage, Niebuhr is doing two things. First, he is taking a stance somewhat similar to Barbour's on the relation between data and experience. Second, he is pointing to the way that Christian realism anchors itself in an understanding of the corrupting power of freedom, anxiety, and original sin in contrast to the Freudian chaos of nature. We should look briefly at these two points.

Niebuhr was close to the position of American pragmatism on the relation of truth and experience. Although Niebuhr acknowledged, as hermeneutic theorists would today, how history and language qualify experience, he held with James that experience had certain pervasive features somewhat independent of language and history against which moral and religious claims can be tested. In this sense, he had a decided leaning toward the values of a rational and experiential philosophy of religion and the need to affirm only those religious assertions that can be seen most adequately to interpret experience in the broad sense of that word. To do this Niebuhr made a distinction between empiricism in the narrow and empiricism in the broad sense of the term. From the narrower perspective, it refers very much to what Barbour means by sense data. On the other hand, by the broader meaning of the empirical, he has something very close to what Barbour has in mind by experience. We can see this when Niebuhr writes,

> If we make the charge that an empirical culture is blind to some very obvious "facts," it is necessary to define what is meant by "facts." Traditional scientific empiricism recognizes only sense data as facts. But who would deny the validity of the concept "fact" to such "realities" as the self-freedom, the self-corruption of that freedom in self-concern, or the self's "historical character"? These are the kinds of facts with which the average man must deal daily.[70]

This more commonsense empiricism is what the phenomenologists would call "lived experience" or William James would call the "full fact." Niebuhr says that his broader empirical mentality must deal all the time with the reality of these fuller facts about the self. Especially is this broader empirical sensibility aware of the facts of humans' inordinate self-regard or what Christians have called the facts of original sin.

It is precisely in the name of this broader empiricism that Niebuhr argues for centering his realistic and even pessimistic understanding of human nature in the facts of human freedom and anxiety rather than in the facts of our animal or instinctual natures. As is well known, Niebuhr follows Paul, Augustine, and Kierkegaard in seeing the human animal as a spirit with sufficient freedom and self-transcendence to become anxious about its freedom, finitude, and ultimate death. Unlike the animals, Niebuhr tells us, man sees this "situation and anticipates its perils. He seeks to protect himself against nature's contingencies but he cannot do so without transgressing the limits which have been set for his life. Therefore all human life is involved in the sin of seeking security at the expense of other life."[71]

Then Niebuhr goes on to say that the human is "both free and bound, both limited and limitless, is anxious."[72] In addition, Niebuhr tells us that "anxiety is the internal precondition of sin. It is the inevitable spiritual state of man, standing in the paradoxical situation of freedom and finiteness. Anxiety is the internal description of the state of temptation. It must not be identified with sin because there is always the ideal possibility that faith would purge anxiety of the tendency toward sinful self-assertion."[73] By locating the seat of human fallibility in human freedom and anxiety rather than in instinctuality, Niebuhr can maintain his strong and distinctively Hebraic and Christian emphasis upon the reality of both vitality and form at the level of nature. Freud and Niebuhr share a realistic image of the human, but they arrive at it by considerably different roads. Freud sees nature as primordially chaotic; Niebuhr sees nature as a union of vitality and form that is disrupted by freedom and anxiety.

Niebuhr's view of the role of anxiety in response to the indeterminacy of freedom does not replace or downplay the importance of the special kind of anxiety that Freud did address. Freud knew about the importance of separation anxiety and understood the crucial role of experiences with parents and loved ones in inducing it. The Kierkegaardian-Niebuhrian view of the anxiety induced by freedom does not mean separation anxiety is unreal or unimportant. Indeed, from the perspective of the development of the child, separation anxiety is probably the greater problem. Even though they are doubtless even in ways related, we intuitively know that the anxiety of freedom and the anxiety of separation are not identical. We know this when we see even the most emotionally and interpersonally secure of us become anxious in response to the indeterminacy of our decisions, choices, and the freedom that they imply. The problem of the anxiety that undergirds original sin is the problem of an anxiety that only creatures with a modicum of imagination, memory, and self-transcendence can have. For only these creatures can experience the anxiety of freedom both in relation to and yet somewhat in distinction from the experience of separation.

Agape and Justice in Niebuhr

As I said earlier, Niebuhr would have seen Freud's emphasis on respect and cautious reciprocity as an affirmation of the possibilities of justice on the plain of human history. Niebuhr closely associates, but does not equate, justice and mutuality. Mutuality is more affective and tries to promote reciprocity within the spheres of more intimate human interaction.[74] Justice too, for Niebuhr, entails reciprocity but in a less affective, more public and distinctively rational manner; both mutuality and justice for Niebuhr entail attitudes of calculation in an effort to balance gifts and receipts in the spirit of a rather strict concept of fairness. For instance, he relates justice rather strongly to the concepts of equality and impartiality. In one place he states that equality is the "pinnacle of the ideal of justice. . . ."[75] It is clear that Niebuhr's concept of justice is close to what Freud had in mind by reciprocity and respect. And rather surprisingly, Freud and Niebuhr were in basic agreement that other-regarding behavior, in the sense of reciprocal justice, is about the only other-regarding behavior that can be consistently sustained at the level of human history, with all of its elements of sin and inordinate self-regard.[76] Although Niebuhr believed in the possibility and necessity of agape, he taught that only various forms of mutual love and justice are realizable at the level of historic activity. Hence, not only was Niebuhr a realist about human nature, he was also a realist about the possibilities of ethical action within the confines of history. Whether either Niebuhr's or Freud's views on these matters are sustainable is an issue to be debated in the chapters to come.

But there is, of course, finally a crucial point that separates Niebuhr and Freud. Although various forms of mutuality and justice are the practically realizable ethical norms on the stage of human history in view of its finitude and sin, Niebuhr still believed that there was a role in human life for agape or sacrificial love. Although agape could never be completely manifested within the boundaries of human history and although it certainly could never be completely justified by the responses and rewards of history, there still was a place for it as goal and ideal. Agape is for Niebuhr the presupposition for the possibility of both justice and mutual love. A direct and uncomplicated drive for either justice or mutuality, Niebuhr thought, will always come to failure unless infused with the positive, uncalculating, risk-taking initiatives of sacrificial love. Sacrificial love, as Niebuhr argues, is the "support of all historical ethics; for the self cannot achieve relations of mutual and reciprocal affection with others if its actions are dominated by the fear that they may not be reciprocated."[77] So Niebuhr is interested in keeping the idea of sacrificial love alive as an ideal that qualifies and occasionally breaks through and transforms all the other more usual, customary, and ordinary forms of other-regarding behavior that do indeed occupy most of our time and that are themselves, in their own right, difficult to emulate.

In following Wallwork's interpretation of Freud, the distance between Freud and Niebuhr on the issue of human fulfillment has been reduced. Both agree that most of our historical existence is lived in the modality of mutuality and reciprocal justice. Clearly Freud's cautious reciprocity has a different quality to it than Niebuhr's understanding of mutuality. In ways that Wallwork does not fully admit, Freud's image of reciprocity clearly expects the others to take the first step; as we saw, Freud said that he would accept the love commandment if it meant "Love thy neighbor as thy neighbor loves thee." Niebuhr's mutuality calls for genuinely equal initiative; Freud's reciprocity is cooler, hesitant, unequal with regard to the first step. If it fits the Kantian or Rawlsian principle of respect, fairness, and equal-regard, as Wallwork suggests, it does so in a far more anemic and reluctant way than does Niebuhr's mutuality. But in spite of this difference, Niebuhr and Freud roughly agree that their respective versions of justice, reciprocity, and mutuality are all that is possible for humans on any consistent and predictable basis at the level of historic existence. Freud's unwillingness to accept the occasional rejuvenation of agape clearly leaves him in a modality of some detachment, especially with the people outside the immediate sphere of narcissistic involvement. But the fact that Niebuhr would want to keep agape alive as an initiating, transforming yet incompletely realizable ideal would be enough to cause Freud quickly to reassert his argument against the Christian ideal of love. Especially would this be true in view of the distance that Niebuhr is alleged to have maintained between our self-love (eros) and our sacrificial love (agape).

Niebuhr is sometimes thought to separate agape and eros rather drastically. By eros, he has in mind that kind of love that seeks to enrich itself and to earn a reciprocal response.[78] On the other hand, agape is frequently spoken of by Niebuhr as a kind of disinterested, self-sacrificial love that meets the needs of the other without thought of a reciprocal benefit.[79] Stated in these stark terms, Niebuhr would seem to be a perfect example of what Freud believed Christians have in mind when they advocate the principle of neighbor-love. But closer consideration shows that Freud's perceptions of the Christian meaning of neighbor-love do not fit Niebuhr, nor indeed, do they fit the view of early Christianity, as Victor Furnish has recently pointed out.

Freud might believe Niebuhr, at first glance, to be an excellent example of how Christians try to disconnect neighbor-love from narcissistic gratifications, thereby calling for absolute selflessness, self-loss, or self-repression. Indeed, Niebuhr does speak of agape as impartiality and self-sacrifice. But he does not mean this in such a way as to disconnect agape from our natural springs of instinctual motivation. In fact, he directly rejects the positions of Nygren and Bultmann in their strong separation of agape and eros, points we will look at more fully later in our discussion of Nygren. In contrast, Niebuhr writes, "Sacrificial love (agape) completes the incompleteness of mutual love (eros)."[80] It does not call for its destruction or devastation. Furthermore, agape builds on the energies of eros; agape redirects the energies of eros toward the end of promoting the good for the other. "It is significant," Niebuhr tells us, "that Jesus does not regard the contrast between natural human love and the divine agape as absolute."[81] Niebuhr was fully aware of how eros as self-regard and self-involvement functions in natural family ties, group and tribal identifications, the exchanges of business, the erotic attractions of lovers, and in a wide range of other natural, although partial and incomplete, unitive and harmony-producing forces in life. It is clear that Niebuhr believed that agape builds on, transforms, and enlarges these natural energies, rather than burying, repressing, or disconnecting itself from them.

Furthermore, there is no evidence that Niebuhr believed agape meant giving deeply felt affection to everyone universally. But regardless of where Niebuhr himself stood on this issue, recent research on the meaning of neighbor-love suggests that Freud overemphasized, as far as the Bible goes, the role within it of both universalized deeply affective attitudes and the place of selflessness or self-abnegation. Victor Furnish, in responding to Wallwork's discussion of Freud, argues that Wallwork's position would have been stronger had it included an attempt to uncover a more accurate understanding of the various biblical understandings of neighbor-love.

Furnish argues that neither in the Old nor the New Testament is there an emphasis on neighbor-love as deep affection. For instance, Lev. 19:18 reads, "You shall not take vengeance . . . you shall love your neighbor as yourself." Here, Furnish points out, self-love is not commanded but assumed. The principle of neighbor-love does not have to do with affection but rather with refraining from exploitation. And finally, in the Leviticus context, it is not even universal but deals, instead, with obligations to members of one's own tribe. In various New Testament passages such as the second Great Commandment (Matt. 22:38-40) and the Sermon on the Mount (Matt. 5:43), neighbor-love is presented as applying to members outside one's own group and as the hermeneutical key to the law as a whole. But even there it does not have to do primarily with universal affection. Rather, it has to do with "nonretaliation, refusing to show partiality, and active goodwill and service to those in need."[82] In addition, it does not entail self-abnegation but, instead, self-affirmation. What is involved is not inordinate self-love or self-enhancement but rather "acceptance of one's life as a gift and the affirmation that it is good."[83] The idea does not entail selflessness but the using of the self, its needs and potentialities, as a guide and resource to the service of the neighbor, even the neighbor who might be a stranger for whom we would not otherwise be full of natural affection.

Hence, Freud's rejection of the possibility of neighbor-love was based both upon a misunderstanding of what it actually calls for and a highly conservative understanding of the limits of human transformation. Freud had a limited vision of how the constancy-oriented life instinct and the inertia-seeking death instinct—in spite of the fact that we know them primarily as psychical representations and in spite of the fact that he saw them as indeed open to a variety of transmutations—could be transformed into positive activity, not necessarily deep affection, on behalf of other people.

Of course, for Niebuhr and the Christian tradition in general, this transformation is a possibility because of the reality of grace. Grace both *forgives and empowers.* As Niebuhr writes, "Grace represents on the one hand the mercy and forgiveness of God by which he completes what man cannot complete." On the other hand, grace represents power and "accession of resources, which man does not have of himself, enabling him to become what he truly ought to be."[84] The expectation that our lives should be centered on neighbor-love must not be seen as an imposition of an abstract standard held before all humans and used only to condemn them when they fail to live up to its requirements. The difficulties of living a life of neighbor-love is fully acknowledged in the great Christian writings from Paul through Augustine, Luther, and the great neo-Reformation authors such as

Niebuhr, Tillich, and others. If neighbor-love is a possibility, it is one primarily because of a transforming power—a power that Christians have called grace, and that Paul Ricoeur has called the transforming power of certain cultural "figures of the spirit."[85]

But to raise the question of grace is to point once again to the issue of the metaphors of ultimacy that inevitably undergird our systems of practical thought and action. It moves to the question about which set of metaphors we will rest our faith on as best representing the nature and possibilities of the ultimate context of experience. My message has been that our decisions about the metaphors we use to represent the ultimate context of experience are first a matter of faith and shaped by history and community. Freud's decision to overgeneralize the metaphors of eros and thanatos was neither a completely rational nor scientific decision. His imagination went beyond the justifiable inferences of the clinical and scientific data to which he referred. To this extent, his mind was functioning not unlike that of a religious devotee who decides to use the metaphor of grace to represent the ultimate context of experience. Both are moving beyond the explanation of discrete orders of data to an interpretation of the most fundamental features of human experience. But, of course, whether eros and thanatos or God's creative power in creation and grace are the better metaphors to represent the ultimate context of experience is not something that should be decided completely on faith. To make this decision—or to keep it from being a purely arbitrary decision—we must introduce reason and experience once again. But it will have to be a higher form of reason than strictly technical or experimental reason. And it will need to be a broader ranger of experience than the scientifically empirical in the narrow sense. But just what kind of reason and experience can help us make this decision must be a topic to be pursued in a later chapter.

Freud's genius will influence psychotherapy, clinical psychiatric practice, and even some of the fundamental symbols in Western societies for years to come. My effort to isolate, relativize, and deflate the metaphysical and moral horizon surrounding his thought is not designed to discredit the importance of his psychological insights. His early insights into the transference neurosis, his later model of the mind, as well as his highly crucial early insights into mourning and melancholy and the related theory of object-relations—all these contributions will be of enduring significance. Although no psychology, and especially no clinical or psychotherapeutic psychology, can ever completely eliminate its implicit metaphors of ultimacy and moral images, it can attempt to be aware of them and name them for what they are without invoking for them the authority of science. It can then submit these moral and metaphysical horizons to philosophical testing insofar as they appear necessary to orient psychology to the world of praxis. It is in this spirit that I have submitted Freud to the preceding analysis and now turn to perform a similar review of the highly culturally influential patriarchs of humanistic psychology—Carl Rogers, Abraham Maslow, and Fritz Perls.

Self-Actualization and Harmony in Humanistic Psychology

If Christianity celebrates the principle of self-giving love and justice and Freudian psychoanalysis oscillates between ethical egoism and cautious reciprocity, the implicit ethic of humanistic psychology is different still. And, indeed, the case is more simple with humanistic psychology and more important. It is more simple because it will be easier to discern the implicit theory of obligation resident in the humanistic psychologies. On the other hand, it is more important due to the widespread evidence that humanistic psychology has had over the last few decades even more cultural influence than psychoanalysis. Some of the leaders of humanistic psychology are now dead, but their influence lingers on not only in psychotherapy but in education and the particular approach to moral formation known as the values clarification approach.[1]

Humanistic psychology is associated with a loose assortment of psychologies that differentiate themselves from both psychoanalysis and behaviorism. They share what is often thought to be a higher image of humans that makes more room for freedom, creativity, dignity, and the potential of social cooperation. The leading names associated with the tradition were Carl Rogers, Abraham Maslow, and Fritz Perls. Other names, of equal prominence but less closely associated with the phrase "humanistic psychology," were Erich Fromm and Gordon Allport. A less academically respected but still widely read humanistic psychologist was William Schutz. And some would go so far as to say that the logic of Carl Jung's image of human fulfillment follows the basic pattern of most of the humanistic psychologists.

The cultural impact of humanistic psychology has been probably more extensive than that of psychoanalysis. Cultural analysts such as Philip Rieff argue for the widespread cultural influence of psychoanalysis as this has worked through the worldwide core of psychoanalytically trained psychotherapists.[2] But he admits that psychoanalysis has touched the lives and culture most directly of the elites who use these therapists and only then in secondary ways has its influence trickled down to the general population. According to Rieff, psychoanalysis helped to create a new type of personality he called "psychological man." But Rieff argues that psychological man's prudent and restrained dedication to his own internal well-being was soon followed by psychologists and therapies promoting a far less prudent and far more regressive type of character.[3] This was a personality type that took the restrained hedonism and introspection of the Freudian psychological man and allowed it to degenerate into instinctual utopianism. Rieff clearly believes that most of the humanistic psychologists were examples of these debasements of the more restrained hedonism of psychoanalysis and were guilty of promulgating psychologies and therapies of regression.[4] The utopianism of Norman O. Brown and Herbert Marcuse could also serve as examples of this strand of modern instinctual romanticism.[5] Paul Vitz in his *Psychology as Religion: The Cult of Self-Worship* (1977) went so far as to say humanistic psychology is a new twentieth-century religion in which the fundamental object of devotion is the self as self.[6]

Whether or not Rieff's negative evaluation of the humanistic psychologies can be justified, that their influence is extensive can hardly be questioned. In the book, *New Rules: Searching for Self-Fulfillment in a World Turned Upside Down* (1981), pollster Daniel Yankelovich claims to have discovered the outline among young people of a widely shared new ethic that celebrates the values of freedom, spontaneity, introspection, and self-actualization.[7] It is an ethic that receives much of its justification from the ethos of humanistic psychology, especially popular appropriations of the psychology of Abraham Maslow. According to Yankelovich, many of the young people adopting the implicit ethics of humanistic psychology believe that it enjoys the legitimation of science. They fail to recognize it for what it is, that is, one option in ethics among many—and, indeed, not a very respected option at that.

The Case of Mark and Abby Williams

Yankelovich tells the story of an all-too-familiar type of couple, Mark and Abby Williams, who, in the late 1970s when he did his research, made a combined salary of $50,000 even though they were still in their thirties.[8] There were even more Mark and Abby Williamses after the boom years of the 1990s and, of course, they made much more money. Abby, who made the larger salary, was the assistant editor of a magazine published for stockholders by a large chemical company. Mark worked in a public interest law firm in an effort to "humanize the system" and received a lower salary than did Abby. Mark and Abby had been married for six years. They were delaying having children because they still felt that their careers were not yet settled enough to tolerate the disruption of the one child that they did indeed hope someday to have. In addition, Abby admitted in her interviews that there were some strains in the marriage that led her to feel that a child at that time would be unwise.

Abby's responses are full of the language of need and self-fulfillment. She likes being married, but says her needs for sexual fulfillment and intimacy "are not being fully met by her husband." Eventually she hopes to have a child "to fulfill my maternal needs." She wants to travel more, read more, relax more, enjoy life more, and taste the fruits of her labor. At times Abby has fantasies of losing everything—her job, her marriage, her place in life. She sometimes worries whether she is a member of the me generation because, as she says, "I crave so much out of life."

Mark, on the other hand, seems less preoccupied with the question of self-fulfillment, but at the same time seems quite concerned about the frustrations of his job. He is not certain that he is helping anyone, and he also fears he is falling behind in his salary. In addition, he believes it is necessary to maintain outside feminine friendships with a dimension of warmth and intimacy. It is not just the sex, but he claims it "just isn't possible to be truly close to someone unless the relationship has a sexual dimension." Yankelovich says that Mark's language is sprinkled with words such as "dimension," "proclivity," and "process."

But clearly Abby more perfectly exemplifies the culture of humanistic psychology. She is constantly referring to her "emotional needs," her "sexual needs," her "maternal needs," her "need to be challenged intellectually," her "need to assert herself," her "unfulfilled potentials," and her "need to keep growing." Yankelovich says Abby seems to take these metaphors literally, "almost as if she believes the process of meeting her utmost needs is like filling a set of wine glasses at a dinner party: the more needs filled, the greater the self-fulfillment."

Abby and Mark are, Yankelovich believes, concrete examples of the cultural influence of the humanistic psychologies. He writes,

> Early in the postwar quarter-century, the psychology of affluence and the primacy of self merged in a school of thought called "humanistic psychology," or "third force" psychology. . . . These psychologists popularized certain seminal ideas proposed earlier in this century and the last. Heavily influenced by existential philosophy, post-Freudian revisionism, a faith in the infinite flexibility of the human person and inspired by the traditional American values of self-improvement and individualism, they, in turn, influenced an entire literature of pop psychology. Their thinking permeated the culture through such self-help and inspirational books and movements as EST, Gail Sheehy's *Passages*, books on self-assertiveness and other works with titles such as *Looking Out for #1, Self Creation, Pulling Your Own Strings*, and *How to Be Your Own Best Friend*.[9]

There is little doubt that the humanistic psychologies are major forces in shaping contemporary culture, especially in the United States.

The cultural power and attractiveness of humanistic psychology are partially explained by its continuity with significant strands of individualism that have characterized American history. It clearly has profound affinities with what Robert Bellah and his colleagues have recently called "expressive individualism" and what Robert Fuller has called "romantic individualism."[10] This is a style of individualism that has roots in the revivalism of the Great Awakening and, in another way, the romanticism of an Emerson and a Whitman. For these movements and individuals, the truth of life in both religion and morality is mediated through the inner subjectivity of the individual. The task of life is to capture and express this subjectivity. In *Habits of the Heart* (1985) Bellah and his co-authors have traced the interplay between expressive individualism and other strands of American life, especially what he calls utilitarian individualism.[11] In many ways, public life in America, according to Bellah, has been dominated by a calculating attitude that believes ends are more or less given and that what is important is the "effectiveness of the means" to arrive at them. On the other hand, private life in America has been dominated by the modalities of expressive individualism. This split between public and private is itself a problem, but in more recent times the sphere of expressive individualism is widening and being promoted by the modern psychologies and psychotherapies. Although Bellah makes no specific link between historic American expressive individualism and the humanistic psychologies, it is most likely that he has them in mind. In commenting upon the expressive and therapeutic aspects of our culture, he tells us that they exist "for the liberation and fulfillment of the individual. Its genius is that it enables the individual to think of commitments—from marriage and work to political and religious involvements—as enhancements of the sense of individual well-being rather than as moral imperatives."[12] As we will see, the emphasis on individual fulfillment is most typical of much of the ethic of the humanistic psychologies. Bellah et al. believe much of modern psychology is characterized by an individualistic ethic. Richardson and his colleagues agree when they write, "The influence of individualism is powerful in both psychotherapy and contemporary social science. Modern social scientists generally tend—even when claiming to be value-free or value-neutral—to aid in the active re-engineering of human society in directions indicated by fundamental Western ideals of freedom, dignity, and inalienable rights for all individuals."[13]

By the turn of the twentieth century, however, the idea of self-actualization or self-realization took on a different meaning. German and British idealism were major sources for much of the American conversation during that period. The talk of self-realization during the first decades of the twentieth century was closely associated with the ideal of the formation or education of character. It did not speak of the harmonious expression of basic biological desires or tendencies in the way fashionable in contemporary humanistic psychologies. For instance, the vocabulary of self-actualization in the thought of Josiah Royce was mixed with the language of self-restraint, discipline, and loyalty.[14] This was true, in a quite different way, even in the ethics of John Dewey. He too could speak of self-actualization but did not mean by this a theory of biological unfolding of latent potentialities typical of our present-day humanistic psychologists. Self-actualization for Dewey had to do with the formation of character; it involved the affirmation and transformation of basic impulses in the process of learning both to cope with and transform the world in which humans live. Self-actualization and creative adjustment to the environment were brought together in the thought of Dewey.[15] But self-actualization, as we will discover, takes on new meanings in the psychologies of Maslow, Rogers, and Perls.

The following analysis of the principles of obligation and the metaphors of ultimacy in humanistic psychology is not an evaluation of the therapeutic effectiveness of these schools of psychology. Indeed, I have little doubt that they are often very helpful, as can be the case with a variety of therapies for even a greater variety of reasons. My concern is rather at the level of their cultural impact and the way they promote images of human fulfillment that help define our understanding of the good life. At this level, I have, in *Pluralism and Personality* (1980), characterized humanistic psychology as a culture of joy.[16] By culture of joy, I meant an image of the good life that sees it consisting primarily of a rather uncomplicated matter of giving expression to and actualizing the innate human potentials that everyone has. These potentials are seen primarily as positive, benign, creative, and socially constructive. Through a simple process of discovering one's own potentials and expressing them, individual fulfillment can be experienced and social harmony achieved. This is why I call it the culture of joy.

In addition to the general cultural influence of humanistic psychology, it has had a distinctive impact upon the life of the church. Brooks Holifield in his *A History of Pastoral Care in America* (1983) credits the influence of Erich Fromm and Karen Horney on Protestant theological thought with setting the stage for much of the recent romance in the church with humanistic psychology.[17] Indeed, my own early writings and the widely read early books of Thomas C. Oden were strongly influenced, especially at the level of their anthropologies, by the work of Carl Rogers.[18] James Walker in his *Body and Soul* introduced Perls into theological and pastoral care circles.[19] Before that, Seward Hiltner's writings, which were immensely influential on Protestant pastoral care throughout the middle decades of the last century, were significantly influenced by Rogers.[20] And indeed, it is commonly acknowledged that Abraham Maslow had a direct, almost unmediated impact upon the churches just as he did on the culture as a whole.

The Common Features of Humanistic Psychology

The common feature of Rogers, Maslow, and Perls is their shared use of the concept of *self-actualization* to account for the fundamental aspects of human motivation. They also share a strong tendency to inflate its original meaning and move subtly from a descriptive to a normative use of the concept. Carl Rogers in his 1951 book *Client-Centered Therapy* provides an excellent example of what I have in mind when he writes, *"The organism has one basic tendency and striving—to actualize, maintain, and enhance the experiencing organism."*[21] Rogers invoked this particular organic model of motivation with considerable self-consciousness. He also believed it was different from the models of motivation found in both psychoanalysis and behaviorism. It is, indeed, a type of organic model built, as we will soon see, on a deeper metaphorical image. It was Rogers's attempt to capture in summary fashion the basic tendencies and needs (my level three) that make up the human organism.

The deeper metaphor informing the organic model of self-actualization is doubtless the metaphor of *growth*. Rogers's work in therapy, his hundreds of hours of direct contact with suffering and anguished individuals and a comparable amount of time listening to and analyzing the recordings of therapeutic sessions, convinced him that people everywhere had a strong inner push propelling them in the direction of growth—growth in "differentiation," in "autonomy," in "self-responsibility," and finally in higher and more inclusive degrees of "socialization."[22] In one place he simply states, in contradiction to Freud, that in the patients with whom he has worked the "forward direction of growth is more powerful than the satisfactions of remaining infantile."[23] Whereas Freud's models of constancy and death were based upon metaphors of inertia and resistance to growth, Rogers's model sees life, even the life of troubled and anxious people, through metaphors of forward movement, growth, and expansion.

But he is not alone in these perceptions. Rogers believed that he was building upon the insights of the great Kurt Goldstein, who was one of the first to employ within clinical psychology the model of self-actualization. His work with both healthy individuals and brain-damaged veterans from World War I convinced him that healthy individuals function on different motivational patterns from those who are sick or severely injured. For instance, the tension-reduction models of motivation seem to apply to those who, because of sickness or injury, could not handle tensions well and who required all of their energy to survive by maintaining life in an unchanged state. In contrast to this, normal and healthy activity appeared to Goldstein as much more holistic and open-ended. To account for this, he put forth his understanding of an "actualization tendency," which asserted that the basic motivation of life "is toward activity and progress."[24] Rather than reduce tension or return to the state of inanimate matter, Goldstein argued that normal life seeks, within a stable range, to maintain tension and to "actualize itself in further activities, according to its nature."[25] But as we will see below, although all of the authors in humanistic psychology that I am reviewing in some way use Goldstein's principle of self-actualization, they all make it into a normative ethical concept in ways in which Goldstein himself never intended.

Maslow and Perls use the organic model of an actualization tendency in ways similar to Rogers. In *Motivation and Personality* (1954), Maslow writes that "various recent developments have shown the theoretical necessity for the postulation of some sort of positive growth or self-actualization tendency within the organism, which is different from its conserving, equilibrating, or homeostatic tendency, as well as from the tendency to respond to impulses from the outside world."[26] In one of the articles included in his *Toward a Psychology of Being* (1962), he states that on the basis of his own research on creative persons and on the basis of the work of many other psychologists and psychiatrists, "we can certainly now assert that at least a reasonable, theoretical, and empirical case has been made for the presence within the human being of a tendency toward, or need for growing in a direction that can be summarized in general as self-actualization, or psychological health."[27]

And what does self-actualization include? What is the self-actualizing person like? Such a person possesses a lot of truly wonderful qualities, specifically a

> growth toward each and all of the sub-aspects of self-actualization, i.e., he has within him a pressure toward unity of personality, toward spontaneous expressiveness, toward full individuality and identity, toward seeing the truth rather than being blind, toward being creative, toward being good, and a lot else. That is, the human being is so constructed that he presses toward fuller

and fuller being and this means pressing toward what most people would call good values, toward serenity, kindness, courage, honesty, love, unselfishness, and goodness.[28]

No reader of these words can do other than to admit the profoundly admirable nature of these qualities. But it is also the case that the more reflective reader will question whether all those qualities are truly directly encoded in some single, master motivation to actualize our potentialities. In another place, Maslow speaks of the self-actualization tendency as a matter of becoming "everything that a person can become,"[29] further suggesting that all of the above qualities are genetic capacities that will gradually unfold if the proper environmental supports are present.

And finally, the writings of the late Frederick Perls follow the same general outline. He too makes great use of Goldstein's model of self-actualization but actually employs the term "self-regulation" in its place. The concept of self-regulation functions in his thought identically to the way the actualization tendency functions in the psychologies of Rogers and Maslow. It refers to a hypothesized internal growth and balancing mechanism that, when relied upon, guides the individual toward more expansive levels of creativity, autonomy, responsibility, and social sensitivity. It functions more or less unconsciously to balance our various needs within the context of changing environments. In *Gestalt Therapy* (1951) he writes, "In the struggle for survival the most relevant need becomes figure and organizes the behavior of an individual until this need is satisfied, whereupon it recedes into the background (temporary balance) and makes room for the next *now* important need."[30] Even though Perls has introduced a wide variety of powerful new therapeutic tools (for instance, the procedure of guided fantasy), the belief in the efficacy of self-regulation constitutes the theoretical center of the theory of how they work. Trouble to the human organism comes about when self-regulation is not permitted to be carried through, when it is frustrated or inhibited, thereby crippling its natural balancing powers. The procedure of guided fantasy is designed to *live our fantasy through,* thereby permitting the self-regulation tendency to complete its normal and natural balancing functions.

Self-Actualization as Moral Imperative

In *Pluralism and Personality* I made the observation that the interesting yet regrettable thing that happens in these humanistic psychologies is that the concept of self-actualization gradually and subtly becomes transformed from a purely descriptive concept, as it basically is in Goldstein, to a moral category. Not only is it argued that we have an actualization tendency that, if experienced and felt, balances certain basic biological and psychological tendencies and needs, it is also claimed that the actualization tendency is sufficient for the solving of higher-level moral problems as well.[31] In addition, I also pointed out that the hidden hypothesis implicit in these psychologies was the principle of the near utopian harmony of all individual interests, wants, and desires. I wrote that "in this literature there is the remarkable implication that, when all people are fully aware of their own organismic needs and completely attuned to their own valuing processes, an almost preestablished harmony of wants and desires will reign over society and conflict will be at a minimum if it does not altogether disappear."[32] Since the appearance of this work, additional support for this interpretation of the culture of humanistic psychology (the culture of joy) has come to my attention. With these new resources, it is possible to state even more emphatically both the nature of the implicit principles of obligation and the hidden metaphors of ultimacy that undergird the more explicit focus of this brand of humanistic psychology.

But what evidence actually exists to support the charge that these psychologists convert the actualization tendency from a descriptive hypothesis (which in itself may be a questionable empirical hypothesis) to a moral category? This can be seen in the general claim, made both implicitly and explicitly by humanistic psychologists, that the self-actualizing tendency is a trustworthy guide to decision making in all aspects of life, including those that are normally called moral. In his *On Becoming a Person* (1961) Rogers writes that the person who relies on his or her own organismic self-actualization tendency discovers "that it is a suitable instrument for discovering the most satisfying behavior in each immediate situation."[33] In a later passage he becomes even more exuberant in his praise of the moral wisdom of the body. He writes that "fully functioning" individuals—individuals who rely totally on their own actualization tendency rather than on the expectations of others—have learned that ". . . doing what 'feels right' proves to be a competent and trustworthy guide to behavior which is truly satisfying."[34] It is clear that Rogers is here presenting the idea that what is "satisfying" to our basic need to actualize our own potentials is a trustworthy general procedure in all decision making, even moral decisions.

We can see this same subtle conversion of self-actualization from a descriptive principle to an ethical norm in the work of Maslow. Health is defined as living in accordance with one's basic nature—that actualization tendency. And then Maslow asks the normative question: "By this conception," he wonders, "what is good?" And he answers, "Anything that conduces to this desirable development in the direction of actualization of the inner nature of man. What is bad or abnormal? Anything that frustrates or blocks or denies the essential nature of man."[35] In his essay "Psychological Data and Human Values" Maslow argues that knowledge about the schedule and hierarchy of human natural growth toward self-actualization can provide a naturalistic grounding to a general theory of value. He writes, "For one thing it looks as if there were a simple ultimate value for mankind, a far goal toward which all men strive. This is called variously by different authors, self-actualization, self-realization, integration, psychological health."[36]

But Fritz Perls is even more forthright in converting his model of self-regulation into a moral norm. In his essay "Morality, Ego Boundary, and Aggression" he places in opposition to one another the external morality of culture and tradition and calls this kind of ethics heteronomous and alienating. Then he contrasts this to the internal morality that automatically flows forth from the biologically based self-regulation tendency. This latter kind of valuing process is the guide to authentic living.[37]

We see in these passages a drift in the argument from the assertion that the tendency toward self-actualization *is* the basic nature of humans to the assertion that it is *good* and that, therefore, all humans *should* pursue the life of self-actualization. In the essay "Self-Realization as Ethical Norm: A Critique" Isaac Franck has cogently argued,

> The principle step in the argument, then, is the inference from the alleged fact that the need to self-actualize is a central propensity in man's behavior, to the conclusion that self-actualization and its products and consequences are morally good and ought to be pursued and encouraged. The ethical norm, the criterion for ethical judgment, is thus allegedly contained in or built into the phenomenon and pursuit of self-actualization, and the logical guarantee of the correctness of the ethical judgment is allegedly contained within this propensity itself. From the descriptive psychological premise "Man has a tendency toward self-actualization," is inferred the normative and prescriptive proposition, "All self-actualization is, *by virtue of its being an instance of self-actualizing*, good, and ought to be encouraged."[38]

This kind of thinking, possibly found as well in Allport, Fromm, and even Jung, probably goes to the heart of why psychology in general, and humanistic psychology in particular, has such widespread cultural impact in our time. People unconsciously recognize that they are receiving more than descriptive science from these psychological schools. They are receiving alternative ethical visions that are indeed clothed in the aura of value-neutral science. In addition, as we have seen, they are receiving a normative ethical vision that resonates with certain strands of American history.

But the truth is that these psychologists never actually derive ethical norms from the principle of self-actualization even though they talk as though they do. It is more the case that they make certain judgments about the goodness of some human propensities independently of the fact that these propensities are alleged to be natural products of one's actualization tendency. Hence, according to Franck, the highest good proposed turns out in fact "to be not self-realization, but something else." What they do is prescribe that "*certain aspects* of the self and not the entire self . . . ought to be actualized, namely, only those aspects of the self . . . that are considered by these psychologists to be 'good.'"[39] That these propensities are good is not deduced from the alleged fact that humans have a tendency to actualize them. Franck concludes:

> The purported "goodness" of some propensities and the "oughtness" that is attached to the idea of their realization, are thus not at all intrinsic to the fact that men have an intrinsic tendency to realize them. The claimed goodness or

oughtness of these propensities is completely extrinsic to the "need" for their realization, and the justification of the claim that they are good rests upon some other foundation.[40]

In transforming self-actualization from a descriptive to a normative principle, these psychologists, and all those who imitate them, are not only making a logical error; they are also, according to Franck, going far beyond anything that Kurt Goldstein intended when he first put it forward as a model to order human motivation. Goldstein noticed that self-actualization was indeed a tendency in the brain-damaged soldiers and heart attack victims that he studied. But it was also the case that self-actualization for these impaired individuals entailed pain and self-restriction. But, Goldstein observed, whether a particular individual chooses self-actualization or self-restriction entails a decision that cannot be deduced from the actualization tendency itself.[41] Furthermore, in his more social writings, he tended to equate complete self-actualization with immaturity and held that some degree of renunciation and self-restriction is an imperative that must counterbalance self-actualization.[42] In view of the positions he took on these matters, it is a clear distortion to ascribe to Goldstein some of the ideas cherished by Rogers, Perls, or Maslow—that is, that self-actualization can serve as an ethical norm, that what promotes it is "good" and what blocks it is "bad," that humans should be exhorted to self-actualization, and that self-actualization provides a single fundamental goal for all human beings.

Self-Actualization as Ethical Egoism

But there is another line of objection that can be brought up against the moral horizon of the self-actualization theorists. The first line of argument against them was primarily a logical one; it said that they do not do what they claim to do, that is, derive an understanding of the morally good from the alleged factual claim that we human beings have a tendency to actualize ourselves. But the second objection is more properly an ethical one. It has to do more directly with an evaluation of the implicit moral claim of those psychologists that self-actualization *should* be the base principle of our lives and is, in addition, a trustworthy guide for all practical decisions. This raises the question, just what kind of moral principle is the principle of self-actualization?

Most moral philosophers would tend to see it as an example of philosophical ethical egoism. By referring to it as "philosophical" ethical egoism, I am signaling that it has the weight of a serious philosophical tradition behind it. The philosophical ethical egoist is not necessarily egotistical, self-centered, or rude. In fact, the ethical egoist might indeed exhibit the height of civility. In this sense, ethical egoism does not refer to behavior as such but to the kinds of reasons a person advances to support his or her ethical choices. Ethical egoism is a particular species of the teleological approach to ethics. Teleological approaches to ethics, as William Frankena points out, "say that the basic or ultimate criterion or standard of what is morally right, wrong, obligatory, etc., is the nonmoral value that is brought into being."[43] By the nonmoral good, the teleologist has in mind some of the different ways we use the word *good* in other than the strictly moral sense of that term. For instance, we may speak of a good steak, by which we could have in mind the taste of the steak or its nutritional qualities. To speak of a good steak would be in no way to ascribe moral qualities to the steak. We would not be saying that it is an honest or just steak or that it keeps its promises—qualities we normally associate with being moral. The same would be true if we spoke of a good automobile; we would not be saying that it was truthful or fair but that it has the nonmoral value of goodness or efficiency, comfort, or style. The teleologist is one who says that the moral thing to do is to promote more nonmoral good—more nonmoral food, clothing, transportation, warmth, health, wealth, or good times. To be a teleologist obviously requires some theory of nonmoral value, that is, some theory of what the nonmoral good for human beings really is. As I will show below, if this is the sense of the word *good* when they speak of the goodness of self-actualization, then indeed the humanistic psychologists may have a point. But that is precisely my argument; they speak of self-actualization not only as a nonmoral good. Recently, the outstanding moral philosophies of both Paul Ricoeur and Martha Nussbaum have argued that all ethics begins in teleology, i.e., begins in our efforts to realize the good in some nonmoral or premoral sense of the word.[44] The difference between their positions and the implicit ethic of humanistic psychology is that these two philosophers take the additional step of subordinating the individual pursuit of various premoral goods, as relevant to morality as they are, to an ethic of justice between humans.[45] This is also the position of this book.

An ethical egoist is a teleologist who says, implicitly or explicitly, that the moral thing to do is to promote more nonmoral good over evil for oneself.[46] The ethical egoist, in order to be consistent, is not just advocating this as a moral position for him- or herself, hoping secretly that everyone else will be altruistic and self-sacrificing. Rather, the ethical egoist is presenting this as a consistent principle for all people to follow. And certainly this is what our three humanistic psychologists are doing. Self-actualization is the nonmoral good that all humans should pursue to the degree that this is possible. Ethical egoists are teleologists who feel morally obligated to actualize the nonmoral good for themselves in contrast to actualizing the nonmoral good for the wider community or the largest possible number of people, as do teleologists of a more utilitarian bent.

But Rogers, Maslow, and Perls are ethical egoists of a particular kind. They are nonhedonistic ethical egoists in contrast to hedonistic ethical egoists. Hedonistic ethical egoists are those ethical egoists whose theory of the nonmoral good is centered primarily in the value of pleasure. If Rieff's or Harman's interpretation of Freud is the correct one, in contrast to that of Wallwork, then it would be appropriate to call Freud's implicit ethic a kind of ethical egoism of a hedonistic kind. This would be true because the reduction of tension (Freud's understanding of pleasure) for oneself, even though it should be done cautiously and prudently, is seen as the primary task of life.

But the humanistic psychologists we are reviewing are not hedonists in this sense of the word. They are more nonhedonistic in their theory of the nonmoral good. Nonhedonistic ethical egoists may identify the nonmoral good "with knowledge, power, self-realization, or with what Plato called the mixed life of pleasure, knowledge and other good things."[47] The nonhedonistic ethical egoist has a broader theory of nonmoral value than does the hedonist. In the case of Rogers, Maslow, and Perls, the nonmoral good or valuable is primarily associated with the actualization of our biologically innate potentials; it is self-realization in this nonmoral sense of the word that is at the center of the theory of value that animates their theories of human fulfillment. There may indeed be mild experiences of pleasure, joy, or aliveness accompanying the actualization of these potentials, but it would not be pleasure in the more sensual sense of the term nor in the technical Freudian sense of tension-reduction.

Philosophical Criticisms of the Culture of Joy

A variety of criticisms, both philosophical and theological, can be advanced against the implicit theory of obligation found in our three humanistic psychologists. And to present this critique is not to suggest that there is no psychological value in this particular culture of psychology. My goal, instead, is to analyze and critique the implicit culture, the ethic within and the surrounding justifying metaphors, of this powerful and popular school of psychology.

The philosophical criticisms are simple and compatible with the theological criticisms I will also present. We already have been exposed to Isaac Franck's contention that the humanistic psychologists do not derive self-actualization as a moral norm from the self-actualization tendency as a description of human motivation. What they do is identify a variety of goods that they recognize to be morally justifiable on grounds independent of the facts of human motivation (our various tendencies and needs) and then attribute them to our biologically grounded actualization tendency.

But in spite of the fact that they do not derive, in any simple sense, *ought* from *is* in the way they suggest, their resultant implicit ethical egoism is itself morally problematic. Most moral philosophers would say it is not even a properly moral point of view. First, it does not really perform the function of moral concepts because it provides no way to solve conflicts between opposing interests, claims, or needs. If my first obligation is to the actualization of my potentials, if my potentials and the potentials of my neighbor conflict with one another, it is clear that on the grounds of self-realization alone there is no way for me to solve this conflict. Hence, self-actualization and the nonhedonistic ethical egoism that it implies cannot be universalized. Since the time of Kant, universalizability has been seen to be a necessary component of a properly ethical idea.[48] This has been the case whether or not the moral stance has been utilitarian or more deontological in the strictly Kantian style.

In recent years the function of universalizability in moral language has been powerfully restated by Kurt Baier, R. M. Hare, William Frankena, and many others.[49] By universalizability I mean, at the simplest and most common level, that anything a person claims to be right or morally justifiable for one person in one set of circumstances ought to be judged as right for another person in similar circumstances. But it is precisely this that the ethical egoist cannot logically and consistently do, without in the end exposing himself or herself to all kinds of potential injustices. As Frankena says, ". . . it cannot be to one individual's advantage that all others should pursue their own advantage so assiduously. As Kant would put it, one cannot will the egoistic maxim to be a universal law."[50]

But, as Frankena so insightfully points out, most ethical egoists, whether hedonist or nonhedonist, save themselves from blatant self-contradiction by consciously or unconsciously supporting their argument with a rather gigantic assumption—an assumption that must at minimum be seen as metaphysical and might in some instances justifiably be seen as theological. In addition, it is an assumption expressed by various metaphors that are themselves sometimes clearly and sometimes diffusely present in the writings of these psychologists. These ethical egoists assume a kind of preestablished harmony in the world that functions in such a way as to assure that "what is to one person's advantage coincides with what is to that of all the others."[51] This view postulates that the actualization of all potentialities is basically complementary, that differing potentialities can never really conflict, and that, for this reason, all people can pursue their own interests without fear that they will conflict with or be extinguished by the interests of other people. It is only if such a set of assumptions can be justified that it would be possible to live a life of uninhibited self-actualization without the threat of perpetual self-contradiction and continuous interpersonal and social conflict.

Metaphors of Harmony in Humanistic Psychology

But this raises the question: Do the humanistic psychologies of Rogers, Maslow, and Perls make certain assumptions about a hidden, preestablished harmony of all basic potentialities that makes the life of self-actualization a possibility without inevitable self-contradiction? I believe that one can indeed find such assumptions, frequently communicated through a variety of subtle metaphors. These metaphors function like metaphors of ultimacy, a concept I described earlier and exemplified by the metaphors of life and death to be found in the later writings of Freud. Metaphors of ultimacy tell us something about the ultimate conditions of the world in which we live and present a picture of what is morally possible within that world. If we can spot the presence of such metaphors in these three humanistic psychologies, we will have before us further evidence as to how they function not just as psychologies but as religio-ethical interpretations of life as well.

A brief acquaintance with David Norton's *Personal Destinies: A Philosophy of Ethical Individualism* (1967) will further sensitize us to the metaphors embedded in much of humanistic psychology. Although Norton does not explicitly attempt to uncover the deep metaphors in humanistic psychology, he does try to set forth a fully developed philosophy of the ethic of self-actualization. Taking his bearings from the classical Greek philosophy of Plato and Aristotle, but not necessarily following either of them in detail, Norton argues that each individual is born with a unique constellation of potentialities that he calls the person's *daimon*.[52] Life is primarily a matter of bringing forth or *leading* out *(eudaimonia)* one's unique set of potentials—one's *daimon*. Eros as the aspiration to achieve is an expression of our own *daimon's* pushing toward self-actualization.

According to Norton's summary of this tradition, the moral task of life is to bring the possibilities of our own potentialities, our own *daimons,* into actuality. Our *daimons* are real, but initially they have the reality of possibility. The moral task of life is to give our *daimons* the reality of actuality, of genuine operative existence in our lives.[53] We have the freedom to be either faithful or unfaithful and to adhere to or defy our own *daimons,* but we do not have the freedom to change them. *Eudaimonism* is completely devoid of asceticism. In Norton's presentation of the philosophy of ethical individualism, there is no need to suppress or repress errant or recalcitrant aspects of human nature. One need only remain loyal to the telos of one's own *daimon*—one's own unique set of innate, biologically grounded potentialities.

Although Norton does not set out to unearth the basic philosophical commitments of humanistic psychology, it is clear that he believes he has in fact provided the philosophy that their commitment to self-actualization entails. His book is dedicated to Abraham Maslow, who is himself referred to several times throughout the book. Carl Jung is perceived by Norton as a psychologist of the "inner voice," by which he means the inner *daimon* as the fundamental source of conscience.[54] He makes no reference to Rogers or Perls, but he openly chooses the term self-actualization to represent his philosophy because of its widespread currency in contemporary culture, a state of affairs for which we can legitimately credit the humanistic psychology movement.[55]

But for the moment it must stand as a hypothesis, not a proven conclusion, that Norton's position serves as a convenient philosophical crystallization of the ethic implicit in this brand of psychology. This is of special interest, however, because of my search for the metaphors of ultimacy undergirding this kind of thinking. It was Frankena's argument that the kind of nonhedonistic ethical egoism that one finds in humanistic psychology—and, we must admit, in Norton's ethic of self-actualization as well—requires certain postulates about the preestablished harmony of all potentialities. And, indeed, we find precisely such a presupposition in Norton.

We see this in Norton when we examine his answer to the question, how in his ethic of self-actualization does one conceive of the possibility of social justice and interpersonal harmony? Norton believes these moral goals are possible because of the reality of a metaphysical principle that he calls complementarity or "congeniality of excellences."[56] By this he means to suggest a general worldview that holds that all potentialities are unique, cannot and do not duplicate one another, cannot conflict, are in fact mutually reinforcing, and have particular and noncompeting requirements for their actualization.[57] All of this fundamental lack of conflict is a genuine possibility if people actually live according to the needs, requirements, and direction of their own *daimons.*

Social justice and harmony, according to this view, are automatic by-products of people living according to their *daimons.* Individuals in contact with their own *daimons* know who they are, have an identity, and know what they need to actualize this identity. Because they know who they are and what they need, they never wish for more than is required to actualize and maintain their *daimons.* Since all *daimons* are of equal value, all *daimons* deserve what they need for their actualization but no more. Hence, Norton's ethical egoism, as Frankena suggested, is saved from the ravages of self-contradiction by the invocation of a metaphysic of preestablished harmony communicated by metaphors of complementarity and congeniality. *Congeniality* and *complementarity* are words used to conceptualize an easy fit or congruence among attitudes and tastes in social interaction. However, in Norton's usage they become metaphors representing the hidden relation among all biological potentialities. They become, in fact, quasi-religious metaphors of ultimacy telling us about the nature of our ultimate environment and the most fundamental context of our experience. But as a metaphysical representation of experience, they must be seen as entailing dimensions of faith of a religious kind. It is the way Norton must believe the world finally is in order to avoid the self-contradiction of this ethical-egoist theory of obligation.

But do we actually find such metaphors of harmony in the writings of the humanistic psychologists? Norton's ethic may seem, upon first sight, to be a suggestive philosophical encapsulation of the accompanying metaphors of ultimacy functioning in humanistic psychology. But can these metaphors of harmony, complementarity, and congeniality applied to the relation of our various potentialities, needs, and tendencies actually be found in humanistic psychology? It is my belief that they can be found in this psychology and that where they cannot be found they are nonetheless logically required, as both Frankena and Norton suggest. They are required to keep the ethic of self-actualization from falling into self-contradiction.

My first evidence comes from a personal experience during my years as a graduate student at the University of Chicago. I can remember with great vividness a theoretical seminar given at the Counseling Center of the University, which was, at that time, strongly oriented toward the client-centered theories of Carl Rogers. I can recall an overly enthusiastic young professor testing out one of her theories—a theory that she believed to be a logical out growth of Rogers's psychology and one she felt her empirical and clinical experience verified. It was an idea that especially applied to families, but one that also could relate to all kinds of human groups. It was the exciting idea that the self-actualization of the potentials of any one member of the family could occur without interfering with or impeding the self-actualization of any other member of the family.

What an attractive idea this was to all of us ambitious, growth-oriented young graduate students! We all hoped that this was indeed the way the world actually was. And it seemed reassuring to discuss this within a counseling center located in the psychology department of a prestigious research-oriented university. In fact, our young professor presented this idea not as a philosophical, metaphysical, or perhaps even a religious idea but rather as a scientific idea or at least an idea that could submit to some kind of empirical investigation. We knew that Rogers's psychology held up self-actualization as a model for mental health, but at the time most client-centered therapy occurred within the confines of one-to-one psychotherapy. But when placed within the context of family or group interaction, its moral qualities began to dawn on us and its potential for tension and social disruption began gently to gnaw at our consciences. The same pangs of conscience appear to have touched the authors of *Re-envisioning Psychology*. The individualism of humanistic psychology, they believe, has afflicted the family therapies. They acknowledge that on first glance, these therapies appear to reject individualism because they seem interested in the family as a whole. But on closer examination, these authors conclude that "family therapists incorporate a cultural ideal of family life that was developed as part of the societal accommodation to and support of modern individualism."[58]

But our professor's idea of the potential harmony or congeniality of all self-actualizations within a family or group seemed to provide an answer, at least for the moment. We students were not at that time very good philosophers either of the social sciences or of morality. Although we worked with scientific psychology all of the time, we were like most graduate students in psychology courses: we really did not think much about questions regarding the logic of scientific explanation, the nature of moral statements, or the logical status of metaphysical claims. We were in a psychology class, and we more or less naively believed that everything discussed within the boundaries of a psychology class must be psychology, just as we also tended to believe that everything printed and published within a psychology book must be psychology. It took me some years to realize that this was not necessarily so.

Uncovering the foundational metaphors of any system of thought, including a psychological system, frequently entails searching for them in the nooks, crannies, and margins of a psychologist's thinking or writing. For here, in these less formal precincts, the psychologist often reveals certain assumptions or postulates that are required to complete and make sense out of the more formal and public aspects of his or her work. Psychologists, like everyone else, need to live in a unified world. They have a need to make sense out of that world just as do their more conventional or less scientific neighbors. Their professional and scientific work often gives them the satisfaction that it does because it fits into or is completed by more informal ideas and commitments that they carry in the back of their minds. These more private worldviews are often expressed by the metaphors that they use, the unsaid implications of their sentences or lines of reasoning, and the general ethos and tone conveyed in their writings.

Rogers gives evidence for his belief in the ultimate harmony of all potentialities both by using the metaphor of harmony to refer to human nature but also by allowing it to imply more than he explicitly argues for or states. An example of this can be found in the essay "To Be That Self One Truly Is," in which he glowingly writes about the trustworthiness of our animal natures. He tells us that the more a person is able to let "flow" and experience his basic biological feelings, tendencies, and needs, the more "they take their appropriate place in a total harmony of his feelings."[59] Such a "constructive harmony" can also be found in the animal kingdom, even in the lion, the arch "symbol of the ravening beast." Rogers writes about the natural harmonies that exist between the lion and his environment; he eats and sometimes kills when he is hungry, yet he does not "go on a wild rampage of killing, nor does he over feed himself." The lion also satisfies his sexual desires, but he does not venture on "wild and lustful orgies."[60] The lion's various "tendencies and urges have a harmony within him." Furthermore, the lion also seems to be in harmony, according to Rogers, with the outside world. The lion is "in some basic sense, a constructive and trustworthy member of the species *felis leo.*" Then Rogers suggests that all of this inner and outer harmony can apply to humans as well if they only learn to rely on their own biologically grounded actualization tendency. If a person can do this, and become

> truly and deeply a unique member of the human species, this is not something which should excite horror. It means instead that one lives fully and openly the complex process of being one of the most widely sensitive, responsive, and creative creatures on this planet. Fully to be one's own uniqueness as a human being is not, in my experience, a process which would be labeled bad. More appropriate words might be that it is a positive, or a constructive, or a realistic, or a trustworthy process.[61]

The implication is clear: the natural harmonies and congenialities that balance inner needs both with one another and with outer realities are available to both animals and human beings if they only rely on these tendencies as their trusting guide to life. Such examples of the subtle functioning of images of harmony as metaphors pointing to the ultimate context of experience are widespread throughout Rogers's writings.

Robert Fuller in his *Americans and the Unconscious* (1986) argues that the basic metaphors functioning in Rogers have to do with "flow" and "process" and point to an emergent evolutionary metaphysics similar to that of Bergson, Smuts, Teilhard de Chardin, and possibly Emerson.[62] Although this may be true, it is also true that in Rogers's vision the flow of experience and the flow of the deeper strata of reality are basically in harmony with one another and that this underlying harmony can assure a complementarity among people who are themselves honestly following their own self-actualizing tendencies. Process, flow, and harmony come together in the deep metaphors of Rogers's psychology.

The metaphors of harmony in Maslow's writings are most obvious in his development of the concept of synergism and in his description of peak-experiences. Self-actualizing people, concerned with the realization of their own potentials, can harmonize with the interests of others because of the tendency toward synergy. Toward the later years of Maslow's life, he became attracted to Ruth Benedict's understanding of synergistic societies—societies that enjoy a high degree of peace and harmony because they seem to be so arranged that "one person's advantage is the other person's advantage rather than one person's advantage being the other's disadvantage."[63] Not unlike the way the humanistic psychologists have turned Goldstein's concept of self-actualization from a descriptive to a normative concept, Maslow gradually turned the concept of synergy from a biological concept to an ethical and then even a metaphysical concept. Maslow's journal *Eupsychian Management* (1965) gives us an insight into the implicit world images out of which Maslow functioned and that helped give him confidence in his more formally worked out psychological ideas. In this frankly personal and speculative volume, he fantasizes about the features of the good society. It would be the synergistic society with institutional arrangements

> which fuse selfishness and unselfishness, by transcending their oppositeness and polarity so that the dichotomy between selfishness and altruism is resolved and transcended and formed into a new higher unity: this to be done by institutional arrangements so that when I pursue my selfish gratifications I automatically help others, and when I try to be altruistic I automatically reward others and gratify myself.[64]

The word "automatic," standing as it does as a kind of ontological link between "selfish gratifications" and "helping others," strongly suggests that Maslow believes in the reality of a deeper harmony of interests and potentials. In another place, he seems to describe reality, not just in some but in all respects, as enjoying this fundamental harmony. He writes, "Under ideal conditions—that is, of healthy selfishness, of deepest, most primitive animal spontaneity and free choice, of listening to one's own impulse voices—one embraces one's fate as eagerly and happily, as one picks one's wife. The yielding (surrender, trusting response, receptivity) is here the same as in the embrace of the two people who belong together."[65] What is clear in this passage is that the moral ideal is also that which is most deeply natural, that which is the closest to "primitive animal spontaneity" and one's "own impulse voices." In addition, it is suggested that the very key to morality is to be found, without qualification, in this automatic reciprocity of selfish and other-regarding acts. Hence, we are left with the idea that if we can become simple and natural, we can also transcend the irritating tension we find in the everyday world between our own self-actualization and the needs of others. All of this conjures up a world of preestablished harmony as the presupposition of the possibility of Maslow's synergistic morality.

The images of harmony fuse at points in Maslow's writings with what must be called virtually monistic metaphysical metaphors. By monistic images I mean symbols and metaphors that are used to paint an image of the world whose apparently independent parts are so interrelated, interdependent, and harmonious that they are all identified with one another and identical with the divine itself. I do not mean to say that Maslow publicly reveals himself as a pantheist or a Hindu monist or anything so clear and obvious as that. I mean instead that in the nooks and crannies of his thought, and especially in his descriptions of peak-experiences, monistic images crop up. Monism is characterized by the idea that the sacred is a unified, motionless, timeless, unconditional, and self-caused perfection and, furthermore, that the human self in its depth is a manifestation of the divine life itself. According to Maslow, the peak-experiences that some individuals undergo have a quality of timelessness and motionlessness not unlike the way God is described in certain monistic philosophical or religious traditions. Maslow's list of adjectives alleged to describe the peak-experience contains such monistically sounding words as "wholeness," "perfection," "completion," and "self-sufficiency."[66]

In these descriptions of peak-experiences, Maslow is distinguishing the kind of cognition connected with peak-experiences from the cognition of ordinary consciousness. A peak-experience is characterized by a kind of Being-cognition and is involved with the perception of ends and intrinsic values. Ordinary cognition is characterized as deficiency cognition and is primarily interested in purposes, interests, and means to ends. What is at stake here is not the validity of Maslow's distinction between the two levels. Nor am I quarreling with his description of them, even though his characterizations are often very abstract and provide little if any raw data to support his claims. My concern has more to do with his generalization of this description of Being-cognition into a vision of God and the world. One can see this when he writes,

> The philosophical implications here are tremendous. If, for the sake of argument, we accept the thesis that in peak-experiences the nature of reality itself may be seen more clearly and its essence penetrated more profoundly, then this is almost the same as saying what so many philosophers and theologians have affirmed, that the whole of Being is only neutral or good, and that evil or pain or threat is only a partial phenomenon, a product of not seeing the world whole and unified.[67]

Maslow is telling us that in peak-experiences, as he describes them, we may be getting our most accurate insights into the nature of being.

In another application of his description of peak-experiences to the nature of God he writes, "The gods who can contemplate and encompass the whole of Being and who therefore understand it must see it as good, just, inevitable, and must see 'evil' as a product of limited or selfish vision."[68] Not only is the peak-experience the key to Being, it also reveals that the shape of the world as it stands is basically inevitable and that evil is finally an illusion. These views, as we will see more clearly later with the help of Niebuhr and James, are basic concepts of a monistic religious view.

Hence, for Maslow, as it was for Rogers, the actualization of our various potentials can be morally justified as our primary obligation simply because the world, at its depth, is basically harmonious, and all undistorted and basic needs, potentials, and self-actualizations complement each other and lead to mutuality and reciprocity.

Harmony and Anxiety in Christian Thought

There would be no fundamental objection by Niebuhr to the strong affirmation by the humanistic psychologists of harmonizing forces at the foundations of our nature. Niebuhr would say that humanistic psychology is simply an extreme state-ment of the intimate relation between vitality and form that always has been fun-damental to the Judeo-Christian tradition. While Freud, as we saw, comes close in his theory of instinctuality to tearing asunder vitality and form by rendering instinct primarily as vitality and assigning form only to tradition, the superego, or insight, the humanistic psychologists present us with almost a perfect identity of vitality and form, even at the level of finite existence. Following one's actualization tendency, they tell us, is a trustworthy guide for the promotion of both individual happiness and social harmony. The presupposition of this advice, as we have seen, is the massive assumption by these psychologists about the fundamental harmony of all potentials, interests, and needs, if they are authentically and directly pursued. Niebuhr, on the other hand, can affirm both the smaller harmonies of nature and, to some extent, the larger metaphysical harmonies of all creation. His objection—and I believe the fundamental Christian objection—to the humanistic psycholo-gists would be to their uncritical overgeneralization of the images of harmony and their naïve tendency to overlook the way both spirit and anxiety inevitably frag-ment and bring strife to all of life's easy mutualities and complementarities.

The final difference between the central witness of the Judeo-Christian tradition and the romanticism of humanistic psychology is the latter's uncomplicated under-standing of the relation of vitality and spirit. As we saw in chapter 2, Niebuhr believes that the central themes of Judeo-Christian anthropology represent nature and instinctuality as infused with spirit (freedom and self-consciousness). Hence, nature is never just nature and instinctuality in humans never manifests itself as simple instinctuality. This was a truth that in chapter 3 Ricoeur in his theory of how instinct interpenetrates with representation and James with his idea of the way instinct is fused with memory and intentionality helped us grasp. The same under-standing of nature and instinctuality would be true of the actualization tendency; it too is infused (from Niebuhr's, Ricoeur's, and James's perspective) through and through with spirit. The difference between this aspect of Christian anthropology and the doctrine of the human in the humanistic psychologists is that the latter does seem at times to envision consciousness becoming totally identified with the organismic actualization tendency in such a way as to bring none of the disrup-tions, ambiguities, and disequilibria to nature and instinct that Niebuhr would see as the consequences of the anxiety that spirit and self-transcendence inevitably, but not necessarily, inject into human affairs.

Niebuhr fully acknowledges the partial harmonies of nature and instinctuality. He speaks freely of both the "vitalities" and the "forms and unities of nature."[69] He fully acknowledges that the "natural cohesions" of nature are indispensable foundations of the forms and unities added by tradition, civilization, culture, and rationality. For instance, he writes that the "natural impulse of sex is . . . an indispensable condition of all higher forms of family organization" and the "natural cohesion of tribe and race is the foundation of higher political creations."[70]

Niebuhr would see the humanistic psychologists as a manifestation, within the precincts of allegedly scientific psychology, of the romanticism of such philosophers as Rousseau and Nietzsche, such Christian pietists as Spener and Zinzendorf, and such economic and political theorists as Adam Smith and the French Physiocrats. It is almost amusing to notice the philosophical analogies between the theory of the humanistic psychologists and the economic thought of the fathers of Western capitalism. Both believe in the inevitable complementarity of all fundamental human interests and needs. "The idea is that if only government will not interfere with the operation of natural laws in the economic sphere, justice will be established through a harmony preestablished in nature."[71] There should be little mystery, then, as to why the heirs of capitalism have found such hope and reassurance in the implicit promises of a preestablished harmony among all those who pursue the actualization of their own potentials as this is celebrated by humanistic psychology. One could argue that humanistic psychology is the psychology most compatible with the values and worldview of capitalism.

The Christian is so struck by the unity of vitality and form throughout the created world that he or she believes that it is also a fundamental characteristic of the nature of God. In contrast to some rationalistic and idealistic cosmologies (and that of Freud's) that separate a formless material stuff from a forming mind, the "Biblical doctrine of creation derives both the formless stuff and the forming principle from a more ultimate divine source, which it defines as both *logos* and as creative will, as both the principle of form and the principle of vitality."[72] As far as it goes, the Judeo-Christian position on the relation of vitality and form is far closer to that of the Romantics and that of the humanistic psychologists than it is to Freud and some of the idealistic and rationalistic positions originating with more platonically oriented Greek philosophy.

But the major difference is in the relation of nature and spirit and the role of anxiety in human life. The humanistic psychologists are aware of the reality of anxiety but see it predominantly as socially induced. Anxiety is provoked by the threats of punishment or separation that powerful parental figures make toward their children early in life. Anxiety is primarily externally, sociologically, interpersonally, and situationally created; it does not come forth from some deeper ontological quality in the very nature of human existence as it does for Christian anthropology, especially that Christian anthropology shaped by the insights of Augustine and Kierkegaard, like Niebuhr's.

Niebuhr writes, "Man is insecure and involved in natural contingency."[73] In an effort to overcome this insecurity human beings "over-reach the limits of human creatureliness" and in so doing "disturb the harmony of creation."[74] This anxiety is intrinsic to the human condition and cannot be overcome no matter how sweetly parents treat their infants. The Kierkegaardian-Niebuhrian perspective of human anxiety does not neglect the importance of situationally and interpersonally induced anxiety; it just does not consider it as being exhaustive of the full range of human anxiety. There is a deeper, more abiding, and inescapable anxiety that comes directly from the fact that humans are creatures of spirit and self-transcendence and have the capacity to sense the inevitable contingencies of life.

Following Kierkegaard, Niebuhr believes in a kind of ontological anxiety due to the human awareness of finitude and its contingencies. But not only is it the insecurity of finitude that makes us anxious, it is also the awareness of possibilities, that is, the awareness of limitless possibilities that in and of themselves invoke within us the anxiety of indefiniteness. Kierkegaard distinguishes dread, by which he means anxiety, from fear: "One almost never sees the concept dread dealt with in psychology, and I therefore call attention to the fact that it is different from fear and similar concepts which refer to something definite, whereas dread is freedom's reality as possibility for possibility. One does not therefore find dread in the beast precisely for the reason that by nature the beast is not qualified by spirit."[75]

Niebuhr sees human beings as responding in one of two general ways in an effort to secure themselves against the insecurities and indefiniteness of freedom. They either take the strategy of pride and the "will-to-power" or they take the strategy of avoiding freedom by identifying with the vitalities and comforts of the finite world.[76] In both cases, whether pride or sensuality, it is anxiety that tempts humans to convert their natural self-regard into the inordinate self-regard that the Judeo-Christian tradition always has called sin. Of course, anxiety itself does not *cause* sin; there is always the possibility that humans will have the perfect trust in God necessary to accept and take into themselves the insecurities of finitude. But anxiety is the occasion for the temptation to which the human spirit inevitably yields, although not because of anything that one might explain as a matter of causal necessity.[77]

Therefore Niebuhr and the humanistic psychologists would both agree on the reality of certain fundamental harmonies in the created order, but Niebuhr would contend that they are never unambiguously available to us because of the inevitable distortions and ambiguities of spirit. Spirit is a source of distortion just as it is a source of order and positive creativity. Hence, humans must use, but not totally rely on, the form-producing powers of nature; this is true simply because nature, even in the form of our own biology, is never unambiguously available to us. There would be no possibility of finding sufficient order in life by relying for all decision making on the actualization tendency of the individual organism in quite the way that the humanistic psychologists seem to believe possible.

In addition, our instinctual nature is probably not nearly so innately unified as the humanistic psychologists seem to believe. There may or may not be a central drive toward self-actualization, but whether this is the case or not, there are doubtless many lesser instinctual tendencies with their singular functions, special timetables, and unique stabilities and instabilities. There doubtless are processes within the human organism that attempt to hold all of these lines of instinctual development together, but due to the general plasticity of human instincts, the richness and variety of environmental pressures, and the factors of existential and interpersonal anxiety, this plurality of bodily tendencies, our sexuality as well as our innate cognitive capacities, our effectance tendencies as well as our tendencies to play and relax—all of these lines of development can be seen from an evolutionary point of view as adaptive, useful, and good in the specifically nonmoral sense of the word.

This was William James's point of view. As we have seen, he spoke of a pluralism of instinctual tendencies and lines of development. He mentioned most of the ones listed above and more. In fact, he may have gone too far in his vision of our various instinctual tendencies. But that is not the point. The point is that he recognized quite early that there are several different lines of development, that many of them have instinctual foundations, that they all have their positive adaptive functions, and that under certain circumstances they can come into tension with one another and maybe even conflict with one another. James sees humans as the richest of all creatures in their instinctual endowments. "Man has far greater variety of impulses than any lower animal," James insists. When humans appear to hesitate and guide their action by deliberation, it is not because they have no instincts or that their instincts are weak and ineffectual. It is because humans have so many instincts "that they block each other's paths."[78] Humans possess all the impulses that animals do and "a great many more."[79]

The idea of multiple lines of development, all of which have their adaptive functions yet nonetheless are potentially conflictual, is now a widespread idea in a variety of modern disciplines. Anna Freud makes reference to it in psychoanalytic circles with her 1963 article "The Concept of Developmental Lines."[80] John Gedo and Arnold Goldberg extended the concept in their *Models of the Mind* (1973).[81] But it is interesting to note that it is also a fundamental idea in the literature of sociobiology. In his *On Human Nature* (1978), Edward Wilson constructs an analogy between human lines of development and rolling balls down a mountain slope. Each line of development "traverses a different part of the landscape, each is guided by a different pattern of ridges and valleys."[82] All of these trends, acknowledging both the adaptive wisdom of our instincts yet admitting their plural and potentially conflicting nature, are poorly recognized by the humanistic psychologists.

When the pluralism of human instinctuality and its lines of development is added to the way human instinctuality gets mixed up with memory (James), linguistically mediated intersubjectivity (Ricoeur), or spirit (Niebuhr), then the simpler, more unified, and unmediated appeals to a regulating biology in humanistic psychology appear all the more insubstantial. The philosophical weight clearly rests on the side of Niebuhr and James on these issues in contrast to the simpler position of the humanistic psychologists. Here even Freud would come closer to Niebuhr and James than to Rogers, Maslow, and Perls. As we saw in chapter 3 with the interpretive help of Paul Ricoeur, Freud's concept of instinctual representation is his special way of saying much the same thing as Niebuhr when he describes humans as a unity of nature and spirit. So even if it is possible that there is an actualizing tendency, which James's theory of instinctuality would lead us at least to question, it is still not possible that it can ever be mediated to us without the distorting anxieties of spirit.

Harmony and Monism

Even though there may not be an actualizing tendency that works with quite the authenticity, wisdom, and benevolence that the humanistic psychologists would have us believe, there is still plenty of evidence that nature and our instinctuality are important, although not sufficient, sources of the harmonizing forces of life. They are a source of partial harmonies that then must be completed by spirit, reason, morality, and, according to Christianity, by a transforming grace that it has said comes from God. The Judeo-Christian doctrine of creation always has affirmed these partial harmonies. And, indeed, we will see further evidence for them from a variety of psychobiological theorists in the course of this book. But there are good philosophical and theological reasons to resist the subtle drift toward the monism and uncomplicated romanticism that can be found in the humanistic psychologists, especially in the writings of Maslow.

Niebuhr addresses the issue of monism primarily within the context of his critique of mysticism. Although overstated and sometimes inaccurate, Niebuhr's critique of mysticism is relevant because it is primarily a critique of monistically oriented forms of mysticism. There are, of course, more theistic forms of mysticism. Niebuhr saw mysticism as always first turning the inner self into a sacred reality and then identifying and merging this self with the divine itself.[83] Of course, this does not always happen in more theistic forms of mysticism, which Niebuhr seems to ignore. Niebuhr may have neglected them because, indeed, these forms get close to Niebuhr's own style of spirituality. But his critique of monistically oriented mysticisms argues that they end in both a destruction of individuality and a tendency to render illusory the realities of evil in the finite world.[84] Niebuhr's critique, then, is primarily a moral critique; monism minimizes the sense of individuality prerequisite to the possibility of moral action. His critique would apply to all forms of evolutionary mysticism, inner-worldly mysticism, or Taoism insofar as they function to deemphasize the responsible individuality of the human self. In addition, monistic mysticisms tend to minimize the reality of evil and thereby lower one's sense that there are any really serious problems in the world that need to be addressed. Anytime the ethos of the preestablished harmonies of life is as developed as it tends to be in the humanistic psychologists, there is a drift toward the minimization of the importance of transforming moral action. The world is so sufficiently whole and harmonious that for them the only moral task to be concerned with is one's own growth.

William James had a more accurate understanding of the difference between monistic and theistic views of mysticism. He recognized, in ways that Niebuhr did not, that the over-beliefs connected with at least some mystical experience leave room for a transcendent God and an individuated person in a finite and differentiated world. The mystical experience in these forms is more an encounter than it is a merger and total union. These more individuated forms of mysticism James called "pluralistic" mystical experiences, and they indeed can constitute significant leverages to bring about transforming moral action.[85] But James anticipated Niebuhr's skepticism about more monistically oriented forms of mysticism. These do indeed, he thought, promulgate metaphors of merger, union, and total identification with the divine. In the process, they create metaphors of ultimacy that depict the universe as a place of such security, such harmony, such total interdependence, that the kind of individuality that we generally assume in life and that is required for moral action seems undercut if not caused to disappear all together. In terms of my language of metaphor and obligation, James would say that the subtle drift toward monism to be found in at least Maslow, and possibly in the others, represents the world as a place with such security that obligation is not required—or at least no other obligation than to actualize one's own potentialities.

In Niebuhr and James we have before us another set of metaphors and a different understanding of the obligations that should guide life. In the case of humanistic psychology we have seen how ethical-egoist theories of obligation seemed to require metaphors of harmony and even metaphors of monistic unity. In the case of Freud, we saw the influence of his metaphors of life and death on his critique of the love commandment and his own move toward an ethic of minimal reciprocal respect. We have seen in these psychologies metaphors that function analogously to the more explicit theistic assumptions of the Judeo-Christian tradition. We have seen, at least preliminarily, that the theistic metaphors function to affirm nature as a source of both form and vitality but, at the same time, bring both judgment and transforming grace when the anxieties of spirit become the occasion for the inordinate pride and sensuality of sin. Whatever the differences between these new psychologies and the Judeo-Christian tradition it cannot be that the psychologies are without metaphors of ultimacy and principles of obligation while the theologians are burdened with such ancient baggage. We see that the differences are really more a matter of alternative decisions and commitments at these metaphorical and obligational levels. We see, in fact, a subtle process of psychology gradually becoming both religion and ethics.

Obligation in Humanistic Psychology and the Christian Tradition

Both the concept of mutual love and the idea of agape are different principles of obligation than is the nonhedonistic ethical egoism that one finds in our three humanistic psychologists. Mutual love does *not* mean that in all instances one should act to realize one's own potentials but that as a secondary consequence, affectional and harmonious relations will more or less automatically follow. In mutual love there is indeed regard for the other, although it is always expected that this regard will be reciprocated. Hence, in mutual love of the kind Niebuhr speaks about, one is not just actualizing one's own potentials; one is loving the other and finding something truly outside one's self that one wants to support, enrich, and help to flourish. It is also true that in mutual love one also always expects a return. In ethical egoism, however, the actualization of the self is the primary goal and the regard for the other a secondary consequence.

The difference is small but important. This is why Freud's standard of reciprocity, especially when seen in the light of the subtle metapsychology of his theory of identification, is a more genuinely moral principle than the ethical egoism of Maslow, Rogers, and Perls. If we follow Wallwork's interpretation, through identification with the other (either directly or through a third figure such as Christ) our love for the other can also be experienced as regard for the self as well. We are actually members of one another and our love of the other does not rob from us the energy required to have regard for the self. But nonetheless, in Freud's understanding of reciprocity and Niebuhr's understanding of mutual love, it is never expected that our love for the other can sustain itself without reinforcement by the regard, appreciation, and kindness of the other.

Hence, mutual love requires more self-transcendence (although possibly not much more) than is envisioned as either possible or necessary in the metaphysics and ethics of the humanistic psychologists. But one further step into transcendence is needed for the accomplishments of agape. If agape is the presupposition for the possibility of sustained mutual love, as Niebuhr argues, then the tension between humanistic psychology's implicit theory of obligation and the ethic of Christianity is aggravated even further. But this story can be more successfully told in chapter 6, in which I will labor hard to develop a pragmatic theory for making judgments about the relative adequacy of differing metaphors of ultimacy and the different principles of obligation with which they become associated.

The Value of Humanistic Psychologies

The critique of the humanistic psychologies that I have advanced deals primarily with these psychologies as culture. It deals with the horizon or fringe of these psychologies that appeals to the cultural imagination and that projects a view of the meaning and purpose of life. This critique deals mainly with the literature of humanistic psychology, that is, with the publicly available documents that are read by the wider literate population as well as various psychological practitioners. At this level, I believe my analysis is correct.

Yet humanistic psychology obviously has some therapeutic value. I would like to list three such values. I will discuss two of them now and then amplify the third in later chapters. Psychotherapy based on the insights of humanistic psychology has the value (1) of providing a transitional space within which the client can recapture certain initiatives, (2) of making available a warm and affirmative environment within which the client can reconcile various value conflicts and sometimes build on the strengths of former socializations, and finally (3) of providing the grounds for the reconstitution of damaged and defective self-esteem and self-regard.

The work of the social anthropologist Victor Turner helps illuminate the first point. From his perspective, all healing and therapeutic systems—whether ancient or modern, religious or ostensibly secular—pass through a threefold movement of separation, liminality, and reaggregation. In applying these categories to healing and therapeutic rituals, Turner was extending the work of Arnold van Gennep, which was originally focused on initiation rites in various primitive cultures.[86] Almost immediately, one can intuit the relevance of these categories for the ordering of the modern psychologies and especially the humanistic psychologies. Modern therapies too are marked by a moment of separation in which a patient's former socializations, introjections, and community loyalties are looked at, reflected upon, examined, and quite likely brought into question, either in part or as a whole. Then there may be a period of liminality, by which Turner means a period of betwixt and between, when the client neither is completely content with his or her old values nor has replaced them with new ones. The final phases of therapy may be a time of reaggregation during which the client reestablishes what Jerome Frank calls a new "assumptive world"—a new belief and value framework that usually creatively combines aspects of old values with new ones that have been more autonomously chosen.[87] Obviously, as Turner would be quick to point out, in more primitive societies the moment of reaggregation involves a deeper and more internalized acceptance of a set of values and beliefs that have been predetermined by the society.

It is now rather widely argued that the modern therapies to some extent follow this pattern.[88] But if that is the case, the therapies based on the humanistic psychologies may make their greatest contribution to the first two stages, especially to the stage of liminality. The encouragement to experience the valuations of the actualization tendency invites the client gradually to substitute self-evaluation for parental, tribal, class, or wider social evaluations. This helps the client to "separate" or differentiate from the other communities of evaluation.

This then leads to the moment of liminality when the client is between older socialized values and not-yet-developed newer, more satisfactory, self-chosen values. It is during this period that the client-centered methods of Rogersian psychotherapy and the guided-fantasy methods of the Gestalt therapies may have particularly noteworthy power in educing from the client deeper levels of self-initiative and personal agency. And for many individuals experiencing mild self-confusion or fragmentation over value conflicts these therapies may be particularly powerful in providing the psychological space necessary for the arousal of deeper capacities for freedom, initiative, and agency. It is not clear, however, that these therapies are very effective in helping people through the stage of reaggregation. Here, as we have seen, the ideology that claims that these therapies are value neutral and help only to educe from the client values consistent with his or her own self-actualization is clearly illusory. For in reality, if the humanistic therapies function in therapy in ways consistent with their own official value commitments (and frequently, of course, they do not), then they would in reality be leading clients to use their newfound freedom and initiative to support an ethical-egoist view of life—something that may indeed be happening throughout those sectors of society influenced by the humanistic psychologies. As a transitional or liminal therapy designed to increase freedom and initiative, the humanistic psychologies have immense power. But as an implicit philosophical and quasi-religious view of life, they may take away from our society more than they give in return.

The second point can only be argued by reinterpreting what happens in the humanistic therapies in a way that diverges significantly from how these psychologies generally conceptualize the process. For these psychologies, the therapeutic relation communicates the warmth, acceptance, and empathy necessary for the client to experience his or her own actualization tendency and to, more and more, derive from this psychobiological tendency the values that will guide life. In reality, however, the process probably works much differently. Arnold Green in "Social Values and Psychotherapy" makes a telling critique of Rogersian therapy that probably applies to all of the humanistic psychotherapies. Rather than desocializing patients from the introjected values of their parents and childhood communities, Green believes that the warmth and permissiveness of the client-centered approach gives the counselee a chance to sort out old values. In the end, the client uses the freedom of the counseling situation to reaffirm many of the values inherited from parents or early communities—values that, at the same time, Rogers himself seems to affirm. This is why Rogers believes, Green argues, that actualization is so trustworthy; those clients who follow it appear always to "grow" and "mature" and "do the right thing." But is it because they are following their actualization tendency, or are they reincorporating old standards and values that they can now accept because they are no longer being pressured to do so? This is close to the idea developed in van der Ven's Formation of the Moral Self.[89] Using the hermeneutic theory and ethics of Paul Ricoeur, he shows how much of the field of moral education, which is itself significantly influenced by humanistic psychology, may sometimes appear to produce more moral people. But it does so, not because it actually helps people learn to trust their own actualization tendencies, but because it creates a safe environment that permits people to once again confront the traditions that shaped them in order to interpret and reincorporate them in new and more productive ways.

Green believed that the latter was the case. This is why client-centered therapy works best with individuals who already have sufficiently internalized systems of values to be able to use these values as a resource for the purpose of reconstruction. However, if clients do not have these values, as indeed the growing number of character disorders in our society seems to suggest, then the therapeutic methods of the Rogersian and other humanistic therapies may not be effective at all. Green writes specifically about the therapy of Rogers,

> The client who has sufficiently incorporated early moral norms of conduct, learning that he does not have to continue fighting against them in his permis-

sive yet limited relationship, after talking out his aggressiveness and hostility, allows socially acceptable roles and goals, incorporated prior to the development of the specific self-aggrandizement trend, to be reincorporated at a deeper level of self.[90]

If this is an accurate characterization of what frequently happens in these therapies, what they say they do and what actually happens is very different. In many cases, these therapies create both heightened degrees of freedom and agency as well as greater social responsibility. But their ideologies are different, and if we were to take them seriously, as many people do, their influence would finally create more social confusion and turmoil than their actual ministrations would create health.

Husbandry and the Common Good
in Skinner

B. F. Skinner, the great behaviorist and father of the behavior modification movement, demonstrates even better than either Freud or the humanistic psychologists the ways in which modern psychologists fill out the explicit focus of their psychological ideas with unconscious or unthematized religious and ethical ideas. The discovery of these metaphors of ultimacy and principles of obligation in Skinner's writings is all the more surprising in view of the vigor with which he reduces both religion and ethics to the laws of operant conditioning. The human mind, it appears, is structured in such a way as to go right on thinking with metaphors of ultimacy and general principles of obligation even when our ideologies and transient philosophies tell us that they are useless or nonexistent.

Both as a scientist and as a novelist Skinner is very direct in revealing his interest in creating a culture of control. In Skinner's utopian novel *Walden Two* (1948) Frazier, the founder of a Skinnerian-styled experimental community, repeatedly denies the relevance to his society of general moral principles, philosophy, religion, and history. At one point Burris, the narrator of the novel, observes with some approval that "Frazier shied away from generalities. Walden Two was not founded on them, but on specific behavioral and cultural laws."[1] But "generalities" is both Skinner's and Frazier's way of speaking about general principles or what I have called principles of obligation. In setting up the community and establishing its code of conduct, Frazier admits that the founders of Walden Two studied the great classics of world literature, but not in the way that hermeneuticians such as David Tracy and Paul Ricoeur would tell us to study them, that is, by discerning their vision or their way of being-in-the-world.[2] Frazier tells his visitors, "Simmons and I began by studying the great works on morals and ethics—Plato, Aristotle, Confucius, the New Testament, the Puritan divines, Machiavelli, Chesterfield, Freud— there were scores of them."[3] Strange indeed, one might think, to learn that Skinner the metaphysical behaviorist presents Frazier as founding his controlled community upon the ethical classics of world history. But it seems not so strange when we hear Frazier tell us that "We were looking for any and every method of shaping human behavior by imparting techniques of self-control."[4] Not fundamental ethical principles, not basic visions or metaphors by which to understand the nature of reality, but rather technologies for "shaping human behavior"—this is what they were looking for as they searched through the classics of world literature.

In one place, Frazier tells his audience that

> We can make no *real* use of history as a current guide. . . . Nothing confuses our
> evaluation of the present more than a sense of history—unless it's a sense of
> destiny. . . . Race, family, ancestor worship—these are the handmaidens of his-
> tory, and we should have learned to beware of them by now. What we give our
> young people in Walden Two is a grasp of the *current* forces that a culture must
> deal with. None of your myths, none of your heroes—no history, no destiny—
> simply the *Now!* The present is the thing. It's the only thing we can deal with,
> anyway, in a scientific way.[5]

Of course, Gadamer, Ricoeur, Cushman, and Richardson and colleagues would
all want to greatly broaden Frazier's definition of "current forces." Current
forces, for them, would not only entail various material reinforcements; they
also would include everything communicated by the idea of effective history.
The effects of history also are operating in our lives whether or not Frazier and
Skinner want to recognize them. But in ways that neither Skinner nor Frazier
understand, a dedication to a specific view of history, particular principles of
obligation, and discernible metaphors of ultimacy surround and animate their
single-minded commitment to the power of science to solve the problems of the
world. But some may argue, "We should only take seriously Skinner's science of
operant conditioning and forget his dreams, his utopias, and his reformist goals."
If we take that attitude, however, we overlook more than a half of Skinner's
mind—a very important half that filled out, completed, and made sense of the
other half that was, indeed, the only half to which he ever gave official public
recognition. The modern psychologies function within larger contexts of meaning about the way the world is. It is within these larger images of life that psychologists think their psychologies fit and make sense. Their psychologies do not
stand alone but fit within a larger image of the world that may or may not make
good philosophical sense.
    Behaviorists such as Skinner are frequently animated by vastly different visions
of the world and different ethical principles than are the humanistic psychologists.
The differences between them are not just explained by their respective scientific
commitments. The humanistic psychologists are interested in individuality, and
they imaginatively project a world in which individuality is morally and metaphys-
ically possible. The behaviorists, or at least Skinner, are much more interested in a
world of cooperation, smooth social coordination, and the spontaneous happiness
that comes from enjoying a secure and rewarding place within that social world.
Skinner is, however, completely preoccupied, both philosophically and vocation-
ally, with the technologies of behavior formation that he believes are necessary to
achieve such a cooperative, happy, and adaptable community, and he is totally
oblivious to the quasi-religious vision and truncated Kantian principles of obligation that implicitly energize his images of such a community.

A Science of the "Current Forces"

Skinner's basic psychological ideas must be understood within the history of behaviorism, a history dominated by the great names of Pavlov, Watson, and Thorndike. Of the three, Skinner is closest to Edward L. Thorndike and his concept of the law of effect. Skinner, like Thorndike, was convinced that the effects or consequences of our behavior finally shape, control, and determine it. Both Skinner and Thorndike broke apart the stimulus-response (S-R) paradigm of Pavlov and gave their exclusive attention to the study of the response (R) and the environmental consequences to which it led. The environmental consequences or "effects" constitute reinforcements that are, according to Skinner, the final determinants of behavior.

But Skinner went beyond the mentalism of Thorndike and arrived at a dogmatic, radical, and metaphysical behaviorism that denies that there are any internal mentalistic phenomena—thoughts, emotions, feelings, motivations, or intentions—that shape behavior independently of the schedule of environmental reinforcements and rewards that ultimately control our behavior. Thorndike's idea of "trial-and-error learning" suggested that our inner mental processes might control or at least play a part in varying our response to the environment. But Skinner will have none of this talk about inner mental control; the environment and the reinforcements that it mediates to our responses constitute the sum of psychological realities.

The issue is really a matter of the nature of science—what must be done in order to ground psychology as a true natural science. Doubtless deep in his heart Skinner does believe in the reality of thoughts, feelings, emotions, and intentions, but he does not believe that psychology can be truly a science if it attempts to study them directly. So he must deny their reality, for if he acknowledged their existence he would have to admit that his science of external behaviors was either wrong or incomplete.[6] Skinner seems unwilling to acknowledge either of these possibilities.

In contrast to a science of our mental life, Skinner advocates a science of what Frazier called the "*current* forces which a culture must deal with."[7] By "*current* forces," as I pointed out earlier, Skinner has a much more narrow idea in mind than is communicated by the concept of effective history. He has in mind only those environmental facts called reinforcements that shape and mold our responses, that is, our behaviors. Psychology as a science should study the various types, organizations, and patterns of reinforcements to determine how they shape human behavior. For instance, there is the all-important distinction between positive and negative reinforcements. Positive reinforcements add a pleasant or rewarding consequence to a response or behavior. A negative reinforcement removes a painful or aversive stimulus from a response.[8] Adding food, sex, and excitement to a response are examples of positive reinforcements, while removing noise, a bright light, and an electric charge from a response are possible negative reinforcements. As Skinner writes, "In both cases the effect of reinforcement is the same—the probability of response is increased."[9] However, in passing, I want to add that hermeneutic philosophy should broaden the concept of effective history to include some of these material reinforcements that Skinner has in mind. The effects of history are not just a matter of meanings; meanings surround material effects and trends that are also mediated by the past.

And then there is the important distinction between punishment and aversive control. Skinner is against punishment as a means of social and cultural control. In this, he is clearly a humanitarian. "Punishment," as he tells us, "is used to induce people *not* to behave in given ways."[10] Punishment adds an unpleasant or painful consequence to a behavior. It does this, at least temporarily, to extinguish the behavior, but it does not put a positive or more desirable behavior in its place. On the other hand, aversive control removes unpleasant consequences as a reward for finding better, more correct, or more positive behaviors. This, according to Skinner, is what parents, teachers, and governments should do to elicit the behaviors that they wish: they should reward people for the correct behaviors instead of punishing them for what is wrong.

But there are other important distinctions, only some of which I need to mention for our purposes. For instance, Skinner distinguishes between continuous and intermittent reinforcements. Of the latter, there are reinforcements that follow a "fixed-ratio" schedule and those that follow a "variable-ratio" schedule.[11] The former is the method of reinforcement used in the payment of piecework. The latter can be illustrated by the capricious schedule of reinforcements associated with gambling; the gambler really never knows when the "big win" will come, but he or she keeps frantically playing, hoping that it will come soon and often. It is out of the womb of variable-ratio reinforcement that the gambling addict is born.

Skinner believes that psychology as a science of behavior should concern itself with just these kinds of descriptions, analyses, and predictions. It is out of such a science that a practical technology can be discovered for shaping and controlling behavior. Skinner is no intellectual elitist; he sees no sharp distinction between a pure science of behavior and a practical technology for the fashioning of culture and society. Science always and everywhere, like everything else, finds its *raison d'être* in its practical consequences.[12] And in view of his notable contributions to education through the teaching machine (the precursor of the contemporary teaching computer), to the cure of phobias, to psychotherapy, and to the correction of criminal behavior, Skinner's accomplishments must be taken with seriousness by both the culture at large and its religious leaders.

Natural Selection as a Metaphor of Ultimacy

There are several places in Skinner's writings where he compares his concepts of operant conditioning and environmental reinforcements with Darwin's idea of natural selection. An environmental reinforcement refines our responses by selecting those that seem to lead to the most favorable consequences. This is what Skinner has in mind in *About Behaviorism* (1974) when he observes that "There are remarkable similarities in natural selection, operant conditioning, and the evolution of social environment."[13] Elsewhere he writes, "The Law of Effect, formulated nearly three quarters of a century ago by Edward L. Thorndike, owed a great deal to Darwinian theory, and it raised very similar issues."[14] In *Beyond Freedom and Dignity* (1972) he hints at the analogy between environmental reinforcements and natural selection even more strongly. "The trouble was that the environment acts in an inconspicuous way: it does not push or pull, it *selects*. For thousands of years in the history of human thought the process of natural selection went unseen in spite of its extraordinary importance. When it was eventually discovered, it became, of course, the key to evolutionary theory."[15] Later in the same book, he talks about the similarities of cultural and biological evolution. "A culture, like a species, is selected," he tells us, "by its adaptation to an environment."[16] However, cultural evolution, Skinner believed, is more Lamarckian than biological evolution. The accomplishments of cultural evolution must be transmitted and learned; they are not passed on through genes and chromosomes as are the novel emergences and mutations of free variation at the more strictly biological level.

Two comments should be made about Skinner's understanding of the relation between environmental reinforcements and natural selection. First, Skinner sees his program as carrying into psychology what he believed to be both the worldview and the more credible scientific dimensions of the Darwinian theory of evolution. Second, the theory of natural selection as a model for both evolutionary change and learning is also, in the hands of Skinner, a metaphor of ultimacy—a metaphor that accounts for the ultimate context of our experience.

The concept of natural selection is a theoretical model. As both Barbour and McFague point out, a theoretical model functions to illuminate one aspect of experience in the light of another.[17] In the case of Darwin the theoretical model of natural selection helped him illuminate the way species evolve and change by applying it to certain aspects of the practices of animal husbandry. It is a model that in Skinner's thought acquires the status of an "ontological" model. An ontological model, according to McFague, is seen as corresponding to reality and, for that reason, is therefore permanent and essential.[18] Such a view contrasts with what are sometimes referred to as "low" views (in contrast to "high" views), which believe that scientific models are useful but dispensable and have primarily an "as if" function in scientific language. But Skinner's use of the model of natural selection goes beyond what is normally meant by ontological models. Not only does the model refer to something real, natural selection together with environmental reinforcement *exhausts* the factors that shape and change life; there is for Skinner *nothing but* natural selection and environmental reinforcement.

The idea of natural selection grew out of Darwin's observation about how farmers promoted certain characteristics in their stock by selectively breeding those animals that possessed the desired quality. As Darwin wrote in *Origin of the Species* (1859):

> We cannot suppose that all the breeds were suddenly produced as perfect and as useful as we now see them; indeed, in many cases, we know that this has not been their history. The key is man's power of accumulation selection: nature

gives successive variations; man adds them up in certain directions useful to him. In this sense he may be said to have made for himself useful breeds.[19]

The habits of husbandry developed by farmers constituted metaphors out of which Darwin gradually elaborated a model for the understanding of evolutionary change. The model is based on an analogy: as the farmer selects for breeding those animals with characteristics that he likes, the environment selects those species with characteristics that survive within the particular ecological niche that the species occupies.

But Skinner takes this model and, as do many evolutionary thinkers, makes it into another metaphor—this time a metaphor to represent the ultimate context of experience. The word *selection* remains, but it has vastly different meanings within the various contexts. When applied to the farmer, it refers to his *intentional* and free manipulation of desired animal characteristics through breeding. As a scientific model explaining evolutionary change in species, the selection of the environment becomes blind; the environment has no intention or purposes. When applied as a metaphor once again to account exhaustively for the ultimate determinants of all experience, selection is still blind; it implies, however, that at the very depths of life there are only random selective determinants, that they are capricious, mechanical, and without humanly intelligible purposes, and that finally they control all aspects of life and the world.

We see in Skinner another example of how a thoroughgoing positivistic mentality in science can inadvertently give rise to statements and attitudes that become quasi-religious and faithlike in nature. A model taken from one area of human experience (in this case animal husbandry) is applied to another discrete area (in this case the area of evolutionary change at the biological level). But gradually the implication arises that this model accounts for everything that is relevant to human affairs. There is *nothing but* natural selection. Here the imagination has leaped ahead of itself. A limited scientific model has now taken on broader, even cosmological, meaning. A new worldview has been constructed. It may be a worldview that understands itself to be rejecting traditional religious views of life and, indeed, that task it does accomplish, at least to some degree. But in its tendency to go beyond specific empirical areas of data and to use a limited scientific model to account for the ultimate (in the sense of most determinative) context of experience, it begins to imitate the nature of religious thinking. We saw it happen in Freud's use of the metaphors of life and death. We saw it happen in humanistic psychology's expansion of the actualization tendency into more exhaustive metaphors of harmony. We see it again in the case of Skinner and the model of natural selection.

That the discovery of the role of natural selection in evolutionary change does not necessarily have to be inflated to the level of an exhaustive model accounting for all the determinants of life can be seen in Darwin himself. Darwin modestly restricted the principle of natural selection to biological change and did not elevate it to take the place of God, God's creation of the world, and God's direction of its overall destiny. Toward the end of *Origin of the Species* he writes,

> I see no good reason why the views given in this volume should shock the religious feelings of any one. . . . A celebrated author and divine has written to me that "he has gradually learnt to see that it is just as noble a conception of the Deity to believe that He created a few original forms capable of self-development into other and needful forms, as to believe that He required a fresh act of creation to supply the voids caused by the act of His laws."[20]

Darwin realizes that rather than invoke the idea of special creation of separate species, "it accords better with what we know of the laws impressed on matter by the creator, that the production and extinction of the past and present inhabitants of the world should have been due to secondary causes, like those determining the birth and death of the individual."[21] But these secondary causes that govern the processes of evolution do not eliminate the possibility of a primary cause that got the entire course of life going in the first place. Darwin concludes his book: "There is grandeur in this view of life, with its several powers having been originally breathed by the Creator into a few forms or into one; and that, whilst this planet has gone cycling on according to the fixed law of gravity, from so simple a beginning endless forms most beautiful and most wonderful have been, and are being evolved."[22]

Although this distinction between primary and secondary causes, probably borrowed from Aquinas, leans more toward deism and its associated images of a remote and detached God than is popular today, it does serve to remind us that the positivistic steps that Skinner feels impelled to take are not the only alternatives open to us. Paul Tillich's more ontological model, in contrast to the Aristotelian-Thomistic cosmological model, is more in favor today.[23] Rather than speaking in terms of causes and making distinctions between distant and past primary causes and the ongoing secondary causes of natural selection, Tillich used the metaphor of "ground" to convey the idea that God is the continuous source of the power of life (the power of being) and that within this a variety of more discrete causal determinants such as natural selection can function. Regardless of the different models one might employ, Skinner never considers any alternatives. He, like Freud, spontaneously gravitates toward his own scientific and positivistic models without entering into a reasoned discussion of the issues, all the more suggesting the faithlike nature of his final stances.

Form and Vitality in Skinner's Anthropology

Niebuhr's anthropology can help us gain a clearer understanding of the issues at stake in Skinner's image of the human. Niebuhr believed that human nature is characterized by a dialectical relation between nature and spirit. In addition, both nature and spirit have form and vitality. The application of the metaphors of form and vitality to nature means that our human instinctuality is not only a source of energy and motivating power, it is in some way a source of self-regulation. The belief that spirit has both form and vitality signifies that spirit not only is a source of regulation and order for the person as a whole but is also a source of self-transcendence and aspiration. If this is a reliable distillation of the philosophical essence of Christian anthropology, Skinner can be located quite easily with respect to it. First, for Skinner, human nature is not a dialectic between nature and spirit because there is for him no such thing as spirit. There is in humans no such thing as self-transcendence, self-objectification, and the corresponding freedom that comes with it. All of these human features Skinner writes off as belonging to what he dubs the literature and tradition of freedom and dignity and its associated images of "autonomous man."[24] This is a view that his own dogmatic behaviorism, he believes, has discredited. But what is even more surprising and interesting is that Skinner in his own way agrees with Freud in seeing nature and instinctuality as primarily a matter of vitality that receives its form, regulation, and patterns from the outside. It comes not so much from spirit as it does from the operant reinforcements in the environment. Once again, as it was for Freud, form and vitality at the level of nature are split apart. Nature and creatureliness are, as they were for Freud, devalued at a fundamental level. Form for Skinner comes completely from the outside, from sources that are external to and transcend our animal nature.

It is the interpretation of creation and the natural order that is at stake. From a Judeo-Christian perspective, Freud and Skinner, in their different ways, undervalue nature and drift in directions that an earlier Christian age would have called Manichaean and dualistic. Humanistic psychology, on the other hand, overvalues the created order and sees it as a flawless source of preestablished harmony that can be easily actualized if the situationally induced threats and anxieties of life can be removed.

But the view resident in our Western religious traditions, both Judaism and Christianity, is more subtle and more philosophically justifiable. Nature is a source of both vitality and self-regulation. But when the anxieties of life are magnified by the imaginings of our spirit (our attempts to secure ourselves through our grandiosity and pride or our sensuality and flight into finitude), then this anxiety fragments the form-creating and harmonizing dimensions of our creaturely beings. Creation is not evil, but it is incomplete, and it can be further unbalanced by the sinful ways that we cope with the inevitable anxieties of life.

On more strictly philosophical and scientific grounds, Skinner's view of nature can be seen to be confused. Even though he celebrates on a variety of occasions his continuity with Darwin, as a matter of fact there are important differences between them. William James's comments on the one-sidedness of Herbert Spencer's theory of evolution also apply to Skinner. Both Herbert Spencer and Skinner emphasize only one-half of the relevant causal forces that Darwin accounted for in his theory of evolution. Spencer, a contemporary of Darwin and the great herald of the relevance of evolutionary theory for biology, sociology, and psychology, was like Skinner in attending to the importance of natural selection but forgetting the significance of free variation. In his early essay "Remarks on Spencer's Definition of Mind as Correspondence," James was critical of Spencer's definition of mind as that aspect of the human organism that guides it toward favorable adjustment to the environment.[25] James believed this view sees mind as far too passive and far too determined by the pressures of the environment. Moreover, the Spencerian view of mind was really not even faithful to the full dimensions of Darwin's theory. It emphasized, as does Skinner's today, only natural selection and it forgot the role of free variation. Consequently, Spencer overlooked the role in the mind of inner, subjective interests, tendencies, and needs and what they bring to the selective realities of the environment.

Free variation was for Darwin a mysterious random process whereby the organism generates accidental variations in its own genetic structure. Darwin was not clear about how these accidental variations come about; today geneticists are inclined to attribute them to the disturbances in the genetic structure caused by radiation or by failures, for some reason, in genetic transmission. However it occurs, to recognize this feature of evolutionary change requires that we acknowledge the existence of the internal tendencies, needs, and interests that we bring to experience. These interests are the product of free variation; they are not implanted or imposed by the contingencies of the outside environment. They are, as James put it, "brain born"; they are a product of free variation.[26] These interests, tendencies, and needs are indeed retained by environmental selection if, for some reason, they give us the strengths and adaptive responses necessary to cope with our environments. But the selective powers of the environment do not create these tendencies and interests. These interests guide us in our selective approach to our environment; they bring partial form and pattern to our lives just as they receive further form and pattern from the selective forces of the environment. Had Spencer and, in turn, Skinner paid more attention to what evolutionary theory has to say about these internal vitalities, tendencies, and interests, there would have been in both of them a more balanced understanding of the relation of form and vitality at the level of what is truly natural and creaturely in our human nature.

Obligation and Value in Skinner

Skinner's explicit approach to matters of ethics and morality (matters of obligation) appears to follow rather closely from his metaphors of ultimacy. Although at the evolutionary level he is aware that Darwin spoke of both free variation and natural selection, it is clear that Skinner was far more interested in natural selection and, at the level of his learning theory, made no effort to find analogues to free variation. Had he looked for such analogues, he might have paid more attention to what some philosophers and psychologists call our cognitive capacities and what today constitutes the prestigious field of cognitive psychology. They are a product of what James called "brain born" free variations that the species *homo sapiens* accidentally acquired and that are foundational to the human capacity for reason, language, imagination, and mature ethical reflection. Had Skinner attended to such things, he would have had to acknowledge that what he called "autonomous man" is not a complete illusion, although doubtless more limited by a variety of constraints than the Enlightenment and the twentieth-century cult of individualism were inclined to admit. Since life for Skinner was at all levels primarily under the control of natural selection and environmental reinforcement, he believed that there was no possibility for the freedom and reflectiveness necessary for anything approaching genuine ethical thinking.

We saw earlier how Skinner in *Walden Two* represents Frazier as shying "away from generalities," by which is meant that Skinner does not believe in the reality or need for general moral principles. The community of Walden Two is built on concrete laws of behavioral engineering. This theme is carried forth in his *Beyond Freedom and Dignity.* In the middle of this book, Skinner spends several pages trying to convince the reader that all moral language—all statements containing the words "should," "ought," "good," "bad," or "normative"—can really be reduced to contingencies of reinforcement. In short, the language of morality tells us what to do to get reinforced. For instance, he tells us that in the sentence "To get to Boston you should (you ought to) follow Route 1" we are really saying that "If you will be reinforced by reaching Boston, you will be reinforced if you follow Route 1."[27] Yet Skinner seems to realize that in this example he has not given us a genuinely moral statement but rather one in which the word "should" is really not used to communicate obligation. The sentence is not saying that we have an obligation to go to Boston.

So shortly he advances another illustration. He admits that the words *should* and *ought* have different meanings within the context of sentences where people are being induced to behave for the good of others such as the sentence "You should (you ought to) tell the truth."[28] But Skinner translates this to mean "If you are reinforced by the approval of your fellow man, you will be reinforced when you tell the truth."[29] And then Skinner concludes, "The behaviors classified as good or bad and right or wrong are not due to goodness or badness, or a good or bad character, or a knowledge of right and wrong; they are due to contingencies involving a great variety of reinforcers, including the generalized verbal reinforcers of 'Good!' 'Bad!' 'Right!' and 'Wrong!'"[30] And then finally with his characteristic confidence and bluntness, Skinner writes, "The 'norm' is simply a statement of the contingencies."[31]

What is unfortunate about Skinner's argument is that it obscures a good point about how societies should be organized by trying to convert it into a normative statement about the nature of ethical principles. What is good about the argument is that it points to an insight that it is well to keep in mind: any moral principle that a society wants to be widely accepted as a constant guideline to everyday behavior had better be supported with well-designed reinforcements and not just left up to the goodwill of the people. There may be goodwill on the part of many people, but there are always the unenthusiastic, the neglectful, the conflicted, the unfree, and the unscrupulous. In order to get widespread compliance, it is good to have a principle or rule supported with positive reinforcements and, in some cases, aversive ones as well.

Although the importance of supportive reinforcements might be an arguable point in moral psychology, it is not a genuine argument addressing the nature of ethical principles.[32] Skinner's argument about the origins of ethical principles is really an old one put forth by the associationist schools of psychology of an earlier day. William James was familiar with their arguments and advanced an early version of present-day structuralism in refutation of it. The older associationists believed that our moral ideas and feelings were built up through the conditioning of various experiences of pain and pleasure.[33] But James did not believe that this accounted for all morality, although he acknowledged, as we must today, that it accounts for some. He thought instead that our moral ideas arise through successive cognitive conversions built around our developing capacity for inference and generalization. As James pointed out, gradually, or in some cases more suddenly, it "dawns in one the judgment that 'nothing can be right for me which would not be right for another similarly placed.'" Or it occurs to one that "the fulfillment of my desires is intrinsically no more imperative than that of anyone else's."[34] When this conversion of thinking occurs, the kind of mental operations involved in the reversible thinking found in the golden rule and the principle of neighbor-love begins to emerge. The discovery of our higher principles of morality is never a product of simple reinforcement although, indeed, once we discover them, we may in fact wish to support them with such reinforcements.

With regard to Skinner's example of truth telling mentioned above, it is more accurate to say that because society has discovered through an act of moral cognition the importance of truth telling as a moral principle necessary for social order then we also try to reinforce it with rewards and punishments. In one place Skinner calls justice "simply a matter of good husbandry."[35] By this he seems to mean that there is no such thing as an ethical principle called justice, but rather it is a matter of using reinforcements economically and sparingly so that there will be plenty left to maintain those actions the planners and controllers believe desirable. What strikes the careful reader of Skinner, however, is the extent to which he unknowingly invokes time and again the idea of justice and uses it as a genuine ethical principle to guide his allocation of social reinforcements rather than being a simple product of them.

One can see this most clearly in *Walden Two*. On one occasion Frazier tells his guests, "You may have noticed the complete equality of men and women among us. There are scarcely any types of work which are not shared equally."[36] Here equality and justice between the sexes is unwittingly presented by Skinner as a presupposition guiding the organization of reinforcements, not the products of such reinforcements. To assure such justice and equality, Frazier arranges a grand variety of reinforcements (most of which would be seen as highly controversial) that he thought would enhance the role of women in society. In the ideal Walden Two society, couples would marry early. Women would bear children between the ages of sixteen and twenty-three. The community would support the young woman in raising her children. The young woman's education and self-development would resume in her early twenties and last the rest of her life. She too, like any man, would be free to assume roles of leadership in business, politics, and the professions. All of these ideas are interesting and might indeed be reinforcing. But these proposals must be seen as the results of prior visions about and commitments to justice and equality and not, as Skinner thought, simple reinforcements from which the idea of justice comes as a mere consequence. We may not achieve justice without the supporting reinforcements of which Skinner speaks. But it is indeed possible to think of justice without these prior reinforcements. And this possibility is exactly what Skinner's behaviorism denies.

But such errors in conceptuality are precisely what Skinner commits time and again in spite of his denials. In another place in *Walden Two*, Skinner has Frazier launch a vigorous attack against democracy. And he does this in the name of justice. Democracy, he tells us, is the "spawn of despotism." Skinner presents Frazier's case with passion and deep sympathy for the oppressed.

> "Democracy is power and rule. It's not the will of the people, remember; it's the will of the majority." He turned and, in a husky voice which broke in flight like a tumbler pigeon on the word "out," he added, "My heart goes out to the everlasting minority." He seemed ready to cry. . . . "In a democracy," he went on, "there is no check against despotism, because the principle of democracy is supposed to be itself a check. But it guaranteed only that the *majority* will not be despotically ruled. . . . The majority are an elite. And they're despots. I want none of them! Let's have government for the benefit of all."[37]

What is interesting about this quotation is that we once again observe in it Skinner's unconscious prior commitment to a higher principle of justice against which he critiques distorted forms of majority rule. Government for the "benefit of all" must be seen as *equal* benefit or *just* benefit. In fact, the principle of justice that Frazier presupposes is more rigorous than that ordinarily presupposed by democracy. Western democracies have tried to guarantee procedural justice and equality of opportunity; Skinner in his idea of equal benefit obviously wants equal consequences and equal results for all. Except in general terms, this is a degree of justice that goes beyond anything that Western democracies have ever striven to realize. It comes closer to the theory of justice behind rigorous Marxism and invariably leads to a controlled and closed society.

In contrast to Skinner's explicit rejection of general principles of morality and the language of *should* and *ought,* we have seen how his practical psychological writings are riddled with highly general moral presuppositions that he in fact invokes to guide his behavioral engineering. Skinner's explicit moral interests emerge once again in his more recent *About Behaviorism.* Here he reveals that it is his dominant life goal to find a way to "produce the largest possible number of highly intellectual, energetic, brave, patriotic, and benevolent men."[38] He wants to help create a nation of individuals with "strong behavior." By this he means a large number of individuals who are more committed to the "future of the culture" than they are to "their own actualization and fulfillment."[39] Here, once again, we see Skinner, the metaphysical behaviorist, using explicitly moral language. First of all, it is quite clear just what kind of ethics Skinner is rejecting. He is vigorously repudiating the kind of ethical egoism connected with the philosophy of self-actualization that we found in the humanistic psychology of Maslow, Rogers, and Perls. He is also reacting against the kind of ethical egoism that we uncovered in Rieff's interpretation of Freud. Skinner is interested in the general welfare of the nation or larger group and not just the actualization of individuals.

But if Skinner is clearly rejecting a morality of ethical egoism, is it possible to discern the kind of ethics toward which he is actually leaning? I believe that it is. I once thought that Skinner was an implicit utilitarian. It seemed to me that Skinner's interest in the welfare of the group over that of the individual plus the implicit theory of value to be found in Skinner all pointed toward a utilitarianism of some variety. Utilitarianism is one of those species of teleological ethics that answer the question of obligation by saying that we are always to act in such a way as to produce more nonmoral good than evil. The ethical egoist is also a teleologist because he or she always tries to produce more nonmoral good than nonmoral evil for himself or herself. But the utilitarian, as Frankena reminds us, is one who tries to produce in all one's moral action "*the greatest possible balance of good over evil* (or the least possible balance of evil over good) in the world as a whole."[40] Of course, in teleological ethics, the word *good* is frequently used in its strictly nonmoral sense, that is, it is used to refer to such things as health, food, clothing, safety, or beauty— objects or experiences that are said to be good but not necessarily said to be morally good. Still in general, the utilitarian believes there is a moral obligation to produce as much nonmoral good as possible for the largest possible community of people. It is an aggregative ethic rather than a distributive ethic; it is the greatest good for the most people even if, for some reason, a substantial group of individuals cannot be included.

There are times when Skinner sounds like a utilitarian with a primary commitment to the nonmoral value of survival. In *Beyond Freedom and Dignity* Skinner writes, "Survival is the only value according to which a culture is eventually to be judged, and any practice that furthers survival has survival value by definition."[41] If utilitarianism in the service of the nonmoral value of survival is the basic moral commitment of Skinner, then the full weight of the contemporary criticism of utilitarianism can be aimed at the implicit ethic guiding his practical psychology. The standard criticism against utilitarianism centers on its contentment with the simple increase of good for the *largest* number of people. The utilitarian, in fact, should be morally content even if the greater balance of good over evil for the community as a whole is purchased at the cost of considerable suffering and injustice for a minority of the people. Utilitarianism is interested in the aggregative total of nonmoral good and not necessarily the just distribution of it. Hence, utilitarianism can easily lead to unfortunate amounts of injustice, that is, the suffering of the few for the greater good of the many.[42]

As we saw earlier, this is precisely the criticism that Skinner in *Walden Two* leveled against democracy. Democracy, Frazier complained, is the despotism over the minority by the majority. He wants government that produces equal justice for all and by that he seems to mean equal results for all. In view of the evidence in *Walden Two* I am now more inclined to believe that a rather anemic form of a neo-Kantian principle of justice such as John Rawls's principle of justice as fairness lurks behind and guides Skinner's practical psychology of behavioral engineering.[43] Standing somewhat blind to individual particularities (or at least blind to one's own individual needs and advantages), Frazier has tried to design a culture that is genuinely just in the rather strict sense of being equal. But it is also a culture that aspires to be just or fair with regard to results and not with regard to procedures and opportunities. Walden Two is run by an elite group of technological planners and managers whose primary qualification is their experience in behavioral engineering. These planners also seem to be committed to justice because, as Frazier insists, they consult the population of Walden Two about their needs in order to design appropriate contingencies of reinforcement. And then Frazier adds, "The only effective technique of control is unselfish"[44]—another typical unconscious resort by Skinner to an ethical principle that his own dogmatic behaviorism allegedly makes impossible.

But the planners of Walden Two are not concerned with justice at the level of procedure, that is, at the level of equal expression of views that can count in such a way as to shape policy other than through the beneficent and paternalistic judgment of its planners. Hence, Skinner does have a truncated concept of justice, but he does not have a concept of what John Rawls would call the primary goods of liberty and opportunity.[45] Most Western views of justice, especially those influenced by Kant, see liberty and opportunity as both the presuppositions of justice as well as the primary values that justice guarantees. Opportunity and liberty guarantee justice in procedure as well as result. In fact, from this view, without procedural justice of freedom and opportunity, a justice of consequences would be illusory. Justice as equality is what Niebuhr means by justice, but it also includes procedural equality for all involved. Niebuhr writes that equality is the "pinnacle of the ideal of justice."[46] But Niebuhr, as we will see below, is even more concerned than is Rawls to guarantee the procedural justice of liberty and opportunity. Niebuhr's realism and his understanding of how original sin (our anxiety and inordinate self-concern) corrupts our use of power lead him to have profound skepticism of any social arrangement that concentrates power in the hands of a few—even if that few would be Skinner's well-trained and conscientious behavioral engineers. But such a fear is not shared by Skinner for there is for him no freedom to be corrupted by anxiety. Concern with the prerequisites for procedural freedom cannot fit into Skinner's theory of justice; this is so because it belongs to the concept of autonomous man that he has already ruled out as inconsistent with his theory of behavior as totally shaped by the contingencies of the environment.

The Deeper Metaphors of Husbandry

At this point the contradictions in Skinner's practical psychology begin to multiply and overwhelm us. He denies general moral principles yet assumes them time and again. He denies freedom yet exhorts us to plan the schedules of reinforcement that will guide our lives—a planning that seems to assume some capacity for freedom and intentionality. Skinner wants a society of rigorous justice with regard to results yet one of paternalistic rule with regard to procedures.

The contradictions in his thought stem from the fact that there are in reality two sets of metaphors of husbandry functioning in Skinner's thought: one sanctioning a deterministic world shaped totally by environmental reinforcements and one providing the framework for the possibility of a world of care, concern, and the detailed arrangement of a nurturing environment. Skinner seems only to be aware of the more mechanistic metaphors of husbandry that he officially depends on and is unconscious of those metaphors of husbandry he uses that include the possibilities of free and intentional caring—the kind of intentional caring that good caretakers enact when providing for and protecting the animals in their charge.

We already have seen how the evolutionary models of natural selection evolved out of Darwin's observations about how farmers selectively breed their stock in order to improve their more desirable qualities. Skinner, in his own concept of reinforcement, builds on this metaphor but ostensibly removes all of the dimensions of human action that make caring and managing domestic animals as something relatively free and intentional. One is struck by the number of times the word *husbandry* is used in *Beyond Freedom and Dignity*. A few examples are in order. It is, for instance, a matter of good husbandry that we give credit to people "in inverse proportion to the conspicuousness of the causes of behavior."[47] Good husbandry explains why we do not commend people who are "obviously working simply for commendation."[48] In addition he writes that "fairness or justice is often simply a matter of good husbandry. The question is whether reinforcers are being used wisely."[49] Time and again, Skinner seems to be invoking the metaphor of good husbandry to describe a situation of wise and economic management of the people for whom we have responsibility so that high levels of constructive activity are unleashed without the useless squandering of precious resources. But doesn't he here as elsewhere get more out of the metaphor of good husbandry than the blind process of positive and negative environmental selections and reinforcements?

An examination of Skinner's three-volume autobiography suggests that a combination of childhood experiences made the husbandry metaphor so vivid and potent for him. Caged, well-cared-for, and sometimes performing animals and birds were an ever-present part of his home life in Susquehanna, Pennsylvania.[50] "I had a cage-like mousetrap," Skinner tells us, "that caught mice alive, and I used it to catch chipmunks." He complains that he could never tame them, although he doubtless tried. And he further laments that not much could be done with frogs, toads, lizards, and turtles but that he did "make ladders and teeter-totters for them to perform on."[51] But even more important, perhaps, was his warm relationship with Mary Graves, his teacher at both school and church, who took him on Sunday walks to introduce him to the delights and beauties of nature.[52] But wherever it came from, one cannot read Skinner's works and autobiography without sensing that we have in him a person who feels deeply about the suffering and waste in this world and is so driven to do something about it that he is willing to sacrifice the value of freedom in order to remove pain and promote a greater sense of well-being—an impulse and strategy that large portions of humanity now seem willing to follow in their flirtation with more totalitarian forms of government.

At a deeper level than he consciously acknowledges, Skinner sees the world as analogous to farmers and their livestock or gardeners and their flowers. Farmers or gardeners have an obligation to manage and care for their animals and plants. Good husbandry leads one first to provide for the good of the flock or garden as a whole and second, the good of the individual animals and plants. In such a world at least the husbanders have sufficient self-transcendence and freedom to weigh different courses of action and plan the best contingencies of reinforcement to govern that for which they care. But it is a partial and even random freedom that Skinner never acknowledges with sufficient consistency to remove the gross contradictions that mar his project.

Skinner's strange world of care without freedom, of happiness without decisions, is not without the deep desire we found in humanistic psychology for a world of perfect harmony. Whereas the harmony sought for by Rogers, Maslow, and Perls was a perfect complementarity among all human interests and potentialities, in Skinner it is a perfect congruence between what we seem to really want and the schedule of reinforcements that make up our environment. The best environment for Skinner is one whose schedule of reinforcement perfectly fits the structure of needs and tendencies of the species *homo sapiens.* Such a harmonious fit between our needs and tendencies, on the one hand, and our contingencies of reinforcement, on the other, is for Skinner analogous to the relation between freedom and predestination in certain forms of Presbyterian theology. This affinity was first discussed by Daniel Shea over ten years ago in his essay "B. F. Skinner: The Puritan Within."[53] In the best of worlds we feel free, not because we actually are, but because there seems to be a perfect fit between our inclinations and the influences that play on us from the external world. Skinner has written that he can now see that "the point [of *Beyond Freedom and Dignity*] could be summarized as a scientific defense of the radical dissenting Protestantism of early nineteenth-century England."[54] In another context Skinner wrote that Jonathan Edwards "formulated responsibility within a determined system of behavior."[55] And he quotes Gilbert Seldes on Edwards approvingly when Seldes writes, "Freedom consists not in making a choice but in pursuing an inclination."[56] All this suggests that Skinner believes that his perfectly planned operant environment is the secular counterpart to Presbyterian obedience to the providence of God; in both worlds he believes there is a perfect harmony between inclination and external reinforcement without the intervening trials and anguish of freedom. Whether or not Skinner is correct about the nature of radical Reformed Christianity, we can see in this his deep desire to find harmony between wants and the world of our environmental reinforcements without the agonies of moral decisions.

A Theological Response to Skinner

From a theological perspective, the most obvious difficulty with Skinner is the rigidity of his metaphysical behaviorism that denies the possibility of freedom. But I want to discuss this difficulty as both a theological and a philosophical problem. From the perspective of the Judeo-Christian tradition, one would have no difficulty with Skinner's emphasis upon the conditionedness of the human creature—no difficulty, that is, if he were not so thoroughly one-sided about it. The emphasis upon the creatureliness and finitude of humans in Judeo-Christian anthropology leaves ample room to acknowledge this conditionedness. As Reinhold Niebuhr suggests, this tradition "insists on man's weakness, dependence, and finiteness, on his involvement in the necessities and contingencies of the natural world...."[57] But this same understanding of the human resists admitting that we are totally and completely subject to the contingencies of our environment and that there is no margin of freedom whatsoever in our response to them. The doctrine of the freedom, transcendence, and responsibility of humans does not mean that we are totally free and completely unconditioned by either internal impulse or external reinforcements. In fact, it means just the opposite. It means that in spite of our massive conditionedness by these forces, there is still a sufficient modicum of transcendence over them to make it possible for us to alter, however slightly, the course of our lives.

The acknowledgment of the reality of freedom and self-transcendence, no matter how small, leads to the acknowledgment of the inevitable appearance of anxiety in the imagination of human beings. The presence of anxiety, no matter how elementary, leads to the prideful or sensuous grasping after an idolatrous security based on the created values and actualities of this world. This idolatrous effort to secure oneself against the contingencies of this world is the essence of original sin as Kierkegaard and Niebuhr so forcefully have argued. And it is this original sin that distorts our natural self-regard into the inordinate self-regard that has motivated much of the injustice, exploitation, and overt violence that has characterized the human scene throughout its long history.

It is because of the inevitability of inordinate self-regard that a theology informed by the Judeo-Christian tradition would have the strongest possible skepticism about the possibility of a planned society engineered and managed by a core of benevolent technical elites schooled in the efficiencies of operant conditioning. Skinner's good-hearted planners and managers, unchecked by the people they shape, reinforce, and reward, would inevitably drift toward the unjust and inordinately self-seeking use of this power. The concept of original sin profoundly illuminates the problem that Skinner overlooks. Technical elites have their anxiety as do all other people. Their anxiety would be the anxiety of the secure and of those who already have power. But this is just the point: it is among those who have power that anxiety and the will-to-power can take its most subtle and destructive forms. Niebuhr reminds us that sin can take the form of "pride of power in which the human ego assumes its self-sufficiency and self-mastery and imagines itself secure against all vicissitudes."[58] Niebuhr continues, "This proud pretension is present in an inchoate form in all human life but it rises to greater heights among those individuals and classes who have a more than ordinary degree of social power."[59] This clearly would include Skinner's behavioral engineering elites. In *An Interpretation of Christian Ethics* (1958) Niebuhr tells us that the injustices of power "will grow not only because it is the tendency of all power and privilege to multiply its demand and pretensions, but also because shifting circumstances will transmute the justice of yesterday into the injustice of tomorrow."[60] Niebuhr would grant that a center of power is a necessity for the cohesion of any society, but injustice "inevitably flows from its unchecked expression."[61] But without an anthropology that conceives of humans as self-transcending creatures who can resist the unjust will of others— even their ordained technical elites—the grounds for checking this inevitable flow toward injustice will not be found. It is only in a free society of self-transcending and mutually critical individuals that the power of operant conditioning can be justly employed.

It is precisely because the anxiety of freedom and the reality of original sin lead to the corruption of all centers of social power that Niebuhr believes so firmly in the necessity of democracy and procedural justice. Democracy is the organization of social life around the principle of relatively free individuals who can mutually check one another's power. Niebuhr writes,

> Modern democracies tend towards a more equal justice partly because they have divorced political power from special social functions. They endowed all men with a measure of it by giving them the right to review the policies of their leaders. This democratic principle does not obviate the formation of oligarchies in society; but it places a check upon their formation, and upon the exercise of their power.[62]

Skinner unwittingly collapses political power and special social function in his theory of behavioral engineering elites, which is precisely the step that the theory of original sin would warn against. It is true that democracy can lead to the unjust rule of the minority by the majority, as Skinner so astutely points out in *Walden Two*. But insofar as the majority fails to rule justly, it will eventually be checked by the opposing wills of the minority and the self-contradictions toward which injustice inevitably leads. It is only with some degree of freedom as a presupposition that nations and communities can be expected justly and uncoercively to employ the tools of operant conditioning for the benefit of all.

Hence, Skinner's insistent call for us to plan better the contingencies of reinforcement of our environment is only a possibility if some modicum of freedom is presupposed by the members of the community planning the new environment. It is only on the basis of some capacity for freedom that humans can band together in a process of deliberation to design the partial determinants and reinforcements of their environment. Judeo-Christian anthropology, which sees human beings as a synthesis of nature and spirit, of conditionedness and self-transcendence, can legitimately absorb the insights of behaviorism as long as behaviorism does not insist on its most radical metaphysical expressions.

William James had his own version of human beings as a synthesis of nature and spirit. He was fully aware of the human self as a socially formed but reflective subject. His view of the self was not in this respect too distant from what Niebuhr had in mind by spirit. James was also aware of humans as participating in nature with a rich instinctual repertoire that had developed out of the interactions of free variation and natural selection down through evolutionary history. In addition, James was especially aware of the role of consequences in shaping and stabilizing our instinctual responses to the world. In other words, James had his own early theory of operant conditioning and reinforcement. He pointed to the consequences of our actions and how these rebounded upon us to form and shape our behaviors. He was aware that new "sets" in the brain are produced by the "motor affects" of our actions.[63] In speaking about how to form new habits or break old ones we no longer desire, James advised individuals to accumulate "all the possible circumstances which shall reinforce the right motives: put yourself assiduously in conditions that encourage the new way."[64] By "encourage the new way," James means the same thing as Skinner would say if he said "reinforce the new way." But it is also the case that James is telling his readers purposefully and intentionally to arrange "all the possible circumstances which shall reinforce the right motives." He is asserting a small degree of self-transcendence over past reinforcing circumstances sufficient to make it possible for us intentionally to design new contingencies of reinforcement. It is, in effect, the will organizing a supportive environment so that it need not resort to fresh new fiats of creative self-assertion at every step in the way. It is precisely the modest but crucial capacity of the spirit for self-transcendence that makes it possible for the members of a community to join together and plan the reinforcements of their common life.

What James and Niebuhr explicitly allow for in the transcendence of the self over nature, Skinner doubtless does in the unthematized and relatively unconscious margins of his thinking. It is strange to see how some of us fail to become conscious of aspects of the assumptive world we make use of anyway. This is what happens with Skinner in his repression and denial of the freedom and intentionality that he in fact assumes. It is through his own capacity for self-transcendence that Skinner time and again invokes his rigorous deontological view of justice—a view of justice closer to the Kantians than to the utilitarians and a view that made him critical of the utilitarian domination of the minority by the majority in American political history. But it is a freedom and self-transcendence that not only Skinner but many other mechanists, positivists, and determinists in our culture seem unable to acknowledge—even though their every action presupposes such freedom and self-transcendence.

The Contribution of Skinner

In spite of Skinner's truncated psychology and philosophy, he brings home a powerful truth to American religious and cultural life. Both American culture and religion, especially cultural Protestantism, have unrealistically high visions of individual autonomy and freedom. That we have some capacity for self-transcendence is something that is patently clear and universally assumed in our practical actions; that this freedom and autonomy are as unfettered and unconditioned as most Americans and western Europeans like to pretend is something that is patently not true. Here Skinner has much to say. There is a general carelessness about the design of our environments that riddles our civilizations and makes us blind to the effects of our social arrangements. Some modern Protestants, with their celebration of justification by faith and their near pathological fear of justification by works, seem oblivious to how the consequences of our actions rebound to shape us. Further, they seem blind to the importance of the reinforcements of our daily institutional arrangements. Since all well-being is supposed to be grounded in faith and trust in God, the more mundane contingencies of our work space, our home life, our modes of transportation, our entertainment, and the shaping power of what we innocently and often unconsciously do in our daily routines seem to so many of us as inconsequential. But Skinner can wisely point out that every little shift makes a difference.

Not in the name of control but in the name of a freedom that needs the reinforcements of a favorable environment, there is clearly a place in the future for the practical psychology of human engineering of the kind that Skinner proclaims. In the life of our churches, the environments of our schools, the arrangements of our work, the patterns of our home life, and finally in the links connecting home and work, a careful attention to the contingencies of reinforcement that promote healthy and just living is of crucial importance.

6

Making Judgments about
Deep Metaphors and Obligations

The psychotherapeutic psychologies reviewed in this book illustrate the mixed language of many contemporary psychologies. Although all of these psychologies contain elements of real psychological truth and many propositions that are logically of a descriptive or empirical kind, they also have concepts that are normative in a more strictly ethical and religious sense. For that reason, the modern psychologies have filled a larger void in contemporary life than we sometimes recognize. Amidst the secularization of modern life, its multiplicity of plausibility structures, the differentiation of the various spheres of our lives from official religion, and the increasing privatization of our religious forms, psychology in its myriad of contemporary forms has dropped into the widening gap between self and society with the promise of ordering our interior lives. But it has come as neither a neutral scientific technology nor a neutral scientific explanation of human action. Psychology is not simply, and has not been simply, an objective scientific set of concepts unencumbered with metaphysical and ethical overtones. It is more accurate to say that the modern psychologies have filled the space left by the alleged decline (or at least transformation) of institutional religion because they have indeed functioned as alternative faiths. They have been animated by, and to some extent have contained, quasi-religious visions and have pointed to, or at least seen themselves as compatible with, some kinds of ethical norms in contrast to others. In the minds of some people, psychology competes with religion not as psychology but more properly as something that itself begins to take on the logical form of religion.

In this chapter I invite the reader to pause for a moment to think about another set of issues. So far we have been uncovering the deep metaphors and implicit ethics that lurk in the horizons of the modern clinically oriented psychologies. As we uncovered these metaphors and principles of obligation, we have been laying them alongside the metaphors of ultimacy and ethics of selected interpretations of Christian thought. So far, we have done little more than that. We have, in effect, been involved in a prolonged project of excavation. We have doubtless not uncovered everything that is to be found. And in some instances, we may have misnamed or misidentified the new object we have uncovered. But if the reader continues to remind himself or herself that the entire study is illustrative, then there is a sense in which the details, although important, are not crucial. Since we are not uncovering the deep metaphors and ethics of all psychoanalysis but just Freud, not all of humanistic psychology but just Rogers, Perls, and Maslow, and not all of behaviorism but just Skinner, out goal is to show how sometimes (at least in these figures) psychology becomes more than psychology. And if I am generally right about how it happens in the figures we are studying, my argument will hold even if I make occasional errors on specific issues.

Before turning to Jung and two recent but powerful psychoanalytic figures (Erik Erikson and Heinz Kohut), I want to illustrate another kind of conversation. This is the conversation built around the question: Is there anything to be said about which deep metaphors and which principles of obligation are better for the quasi-religious and ethical tasks to which they have been put? Simply to uncover the way scientific models become quasi-religious metaphors does not in itself address the question of whether these same metaphors could indeed serve our religious purposes better than the traditional Judeo-Christian ones. The same is true with the implicit ethics surrounding these psychologies. To identify the implicit principles of obligation within a psychology is not necessarily to say that a psychology's ethics is wrong or that a theology's ethics is good, right, or adequate. Here I want to illustrate one approach to a critical conversation between theology and modern psychologies with regard to their respective deep metaphors and principles of obligation. Once again, the conversation will not be definitive; many issues will go untouched. The issues, as one can imagine, are multiple and difficult. But if I am relatively successful in outlining a strategy for assessment and in demonstrating that coherent discourse is possible about such matters, then I feel that my efforts will have met sufficient success to have justified the effort.

We have found both metaphors of ultimacy and principles of obligation in and around the psychologies we have reviewed. In most cases the metaphors of ultimacy have been internal to the psychologies we have reviewed. Unqualified and overgeneralized mechanistic metaphors were prevalent in the early Freud and inflated metaphors of life and death in the later. The inflated metaphor of natural selection is squarely a part of the writings of Skinner. On the other hand, although the metaphors of harmony are not directly announced in the humanistic psychologies, poetic imagery implying them is everywhere and, in addition, the ethic of self-actualization seems to require them. Principles of obligation such as nonhedonistic ethical egoism are directly a part of humanistic psychology's conceptual apparatus and are unambiguously implied by the concepts of self-actualization and self-regulation. On the other hand, Freud's ambivalent shifting between a more hedonistic ethical egoism and a cautious ethic of respect is more a matter of what he believed his psychology allowed or was compatible with than an ethic he explicitly taught. The same is true for Skinner's work, in which it is a matter of discovering a truncated Kantianism that he neither recognized nor could imagine possible within the limits of his dogmatic behaviorism.

In all three cases, psychology becomes more than psychology. It becomes an arena for the exercise of our unsuppressible and unquenchable thirst for religious myth and moral order. Without the utmost stringency in curbing our religious and moral proclivities, we will project them into our supposedly secular mental endeavors, even our scientific enterprises. Without the most modest and self-limiting approaches to our scientific work, our theories and conceptual schemata will spill beyond the limited observational grounds that gave them birth, and they will become metaphorical models organizing wider areas of experience.

The writings of Mircea Eliade, Carl Jung, and William James have, in different ways, pointed to the almost irresistible tendency in humans to find mythical meanings in their experience. So far, it has been my intent to show that Freud, the humanistic psychologists, and Skinner projected such meanings into their scientific work. In the chapters that follow, we will examine in the same way the work of Jung, Erikson, and Heinz Kohut. Eliade speaks of the universal urge in humans to find in their experience a sacred center, a point of origin, and an indication on the basis of this origin of what their destiny will be.[1] Jung speaks of our tendency to project our inherited archetypal patterns into our experience and to find, almost everywhere, numinous experiences of archetypal mothers, fathers, children, heroes, grandfathers, and symbols of wholeness.[2] William James believed that humans have a deep desire to encounter and find a response from a confirming face and to believe that this face rests at the very heart of the universe. James thought that humans are inevitably religious because of this deep need to believe that they live in a world that will respond to their passional needs.[3]

All of these perspectives, with varying degrees of adequacy, might help account for the emergence of metaphors of ultimacy in the thought of these psychologies. But Stephen Toulmin's explanation of the process may be the most pertinent to the figures we have studied here. Toulmin believes that we convert our scientific theories into scientific myths in an effort to answer our insecurities about life. The Atlas myth had its power because of our "fear that the Earth itself may be insecure."[4] This is the motive "behind many of the old stories. Fear . . . not mere ignorance, was responsible for Poseidon, Wotan, Ceres."[5] These motives remain strong today even though our ignorance may be less than our ancestors. And this insecurity makes us look for a ground of meaning and an anchor to our morals even in our scientific theories. In so doing, we convert them into scientific myths.

According to Toulmin, we make a descriptive scientific theory into a scientific myth not only by overgeneralizing it but by taking a certain attitude toward it that the facts themselves do not imply. Our scientific work may lapse into religion when we start taking various attitudes toward these facts and descriptive theories. Toulmin argues that the attitude that we adopt toward nature or a theory that alleges to describe nature "cannot be settled in the way in which one establishes what the facts of nature are."[6] Freud, for instance, may have been involved in an act of religious imagination not only when he invoked eros and the death instinct and generalized them beyond the facts of the repetition compulsion but also when he adopted the attitude toward the death instinct that "there may be some comfort in it," and that perhaps it is better to submit to the "remorseless law of nature . . . than to a chance which might perhaps have been escaped."[7] Our new scientific myths are modern forms of religious thinking insofar as they attempt to answer our insecurities, give us generalized images of the world, and form the attitudes we should take toward the value of life, the nature of death, and the grounds for morality. Freud's attitude toward life, shaped in part by his new cosmology, also set the terms for his final moral vision and his understanding of the limits of moral expectations. It set the terms for his effort to deflate the moral demands of the love commandment that he believed had weighed so heavily on the Western conscience.

If it is the case that both science and theology must communicate through models that are themselves systematically developed metaphors, then we can see how potent our cultural disciplines are or can be in guiding our perceptions of reality. We both make discoveries through the lens of our metaphorical models and learn to see and perceive the world through these models. If this is the case, then the models that a particular discipline chooses to order its observations will limit its vision to what those models are able to account for and comprehend. Hence, one possible definition of reductionism can be stated in terms of a discipline's tendency to reduce the phenomenon it is studying to the metaphorical models that it prefers to use.[8] Human beings are complex phenomena and can be understood adequately only if a variety of metaphorical models are used to account for their action. Human action is thick enough and multifaceted enough that many different kinds of models need to be used to account for its various aspects. If humans are simultaneously physiochemical, biographical, psychological, sociological, and spiritual (self-transcending) creatures, then it is clear that a variety of models and metaphors are needed to comprehend all of these different dimensions. Reductionism can come from the bottom up or top down. It can come from the bottom up when we attempt to use models and metaphors designed to comprehend our physiochemical reality as exhaustive of the full reality of the human. But it can also come from the top down when we use models primarily designed to comprehend our psychological or spiritual dimensions as exhaustive of the full phenomenon of the human. Keeping our models straight, keeping them confined, keeping them accurate, and keeping them humble are the very essence of disciplinary integrity in the study of human action.

Disciplines that are designed to account for highly discrete ranges of observed data, such as chemistry or physics, may be able to make progress with a limited number of fairly specific metaphorical models. But disciplines such as theology that are attempting to account for experience in general must resort to a wide range of metaphors and models. In theology there is widespread use of such metaphorical models of God as creator, governor, or redeemer, as well as models of covenant and models of God's action as liberating or sustaining. Often when a critic of theology develops his or her attack, there is a concentration on one of the models without reference to how it dialectically relates to the others. For instance, David Norton in *Personal Destinies* reasserts the Feuerbachian and Marxist argument that the worship of the father God in Judaism and Christianity alienates humans from their own essence, their own powers.[9] But in developing this point of view, he has in mind only one set of metaphors used to convey the Christian story—those such as father, king, or ruler that cluster around the metaphor of God as governor. Furthermore, he ignores how these metaphors of transcendence or of "God the distant" (as Peter Homans speaks of them)[10] are balanced and qualified by images of immanence and closeness found in the metaphors of God the creator, God the sustainer, and God the suffering servant.

Throughout these pages I have introduced the distinction between observed data (sometimes called sense data) and wider human experience. We saw this distinction advanced in the writings of both Ian Barbour and Reinhold Niebuhr. I made the claim, with the help of this distinction, that the models of science were primarily designed (or at least should be) to order more or less discrete realms of observed data, that is, so that something can be touched, counted, measured, or even introspected in some controlled and publicly verifiable way. From the perspective of hermeneutic philosophy, these two types of experience should be seen as points along a continuum. Experience as sense data is never completely objective; it is a product of distanciation or abstraction from our broader patterns of experience. Neither these sense data nor the broader patterns suggested by the radical empiricism of James and Niebuhr are ever completely disconnected from our linguistic and cultural traditions—our effective histories. Nonetheless, distinguishing these two types of experience, if not made absolute, is useful. If science in its more distanciated forms deals primarily with sense data, theology deals more with broader or wider patterns of human experience. The metaphors of theology, especially after they have become elaborated into more systematic metaphysical models, have as their task to order wider areas of lived human experience, for example, our sense of continuity over time, the full fact of our sense of responsibility, the meaning of loss, or the sense of permanence, lastingness, or even transcendence. Hence, it is wrongheaded to test religious or metaphysical models in terms of their capacity to account for discrete realms of observed data. It is foolish to ask Christianity to explain the workings of an atom smasher, the speed of light, the chemical functions of our blood systems, or the dynamics of repetition compulsion or obsessive neurosis. On the other hand, it would be foolish to ask for a chemical formula or a theorem in physics to account for our experience of the goodness of creation, the joy of living, or our hope for renewal. We should not ask religion to perform the functions of an empirical science, and we should not ask our sciences to account for the qualities of our experience and our belief in its deepest possibilities.

But it has been my claim that what claims to be science is frequently not simply science. In the case of the psychotherapeutic psychologies we have studied, all of them have given birth to scientific myths that in turn have implied cosmologies or metaphysical systems. If this is true, *then these scientific myths (and their metaphysical implications) and the myths, metaphors, and stories of the Judeo-Christian tradition are at this point on equal footing.* In view of this, two fundamental questions need to be addressed: (1) Are these metaphysical models truly required by the particular scientific tradition from which they come? and (2) are these metaphysical models adequate to experience in the broad sense of that term?

The answer to the first question for Freud, the humanistic psychologists, and Skinner must simply be "No!" Neither Freud, the humanistic psychologists, nor Skinner need the metaphysical models that they allow their controlling metaphors to become. All of them permit these models to appear even within the context of their professional roles as scientists. Scientists are individuals who, within the context of their professional activity, remain skeptical about ultimate things. That is, they try not to take a stance; their task, instead, is to come up with adequate descriptive and explanatory models to account for specific ranges of observed data. But in each case we have reviewed, our "scientists" of human behavior have gone beyond this. Although Freud said that psychoanalysis had no *Weltanschauung* other than that of the scientific method, he nonetheless inflated his theory of the life and death instincts, originally designed to explain our tendency to hang on to our neurotic symptoms, into cosmological realities. The motives of the humanistic psychologists are different. Determined to demonstrate that the goal of self-actualization can be socially benign, they paint a vague and poetic background picture of a world where all self-actualizations are finally harmonious. The situation of Skinner is different still. He inflates the idea of natural selection into a metaphor of ultimacy through a process of negation. His positivism does the trick. His metaphysical behaviorism leads him to dogmatize his doctrine of positive and negative reinforcement, to eliminate the realities of freedom and consciousness, and to elevate natural selection to the central reality of the universe, even without the balancing evolutionary reality of free variation. Although all of these psychologists make their central metaphors into metaphysical models in different ways, none of them needed to do this—either in the name of science or in order to explain some aspect of the observed data over which they preside. But they did it all the same. They may have needed to do this, however, in order to satisfy some more or less private opinions about religion or, perhaps, morality.

With regard to the second question, I will not say in this book all that needs to be said. I mainly want to point to the validity of the question. It is now popular to say among some psychologically oriented people that "metaphysics is really a matter of metapsychology." I hope that what has been said so far in this book will make the reader reluctant to agree too readily with that dictum. The argument can just as easily be reversed. It is partially by virtue of some of Freud's prior metaphysical decisions, that is, that there is no other knowledge besides scientific knowledge and that physiochemical realities will someday be demonstrated to be determinative of all aspects of human action, that his psychology both took some of the forms it did and made some of the extensive and incautious claims it made. Similar statements could be advanced about the humanistic psychologists and about Skinner. This is not to say that the psychologist qua psychologist actually requires a specific metaphysic in order to do his or her scientific psychological studies. But to understand the broader meaning of one's psychological concepts and their place in the wider scope of things, some kind of metaphysic is doubtless sooner or later required. But in this book I have not so much been concerned with the metaphysic that is needed by psychologists as the metaphysic that sneaks into their psychological systems because of a reckless and incautious use of their dominant metaphors.

Psychology in its most scientific forms makes neither metaphysics nor ethics the focus of its interests, although it inevitably makes assumptions about both. But psychology as psychotherapeutic discipline needs both a critical metaphysic and a critical ethic. Since the psychologists we have been studying were all practice-oriented and used their psychologies to cure, shape, or educate human beings, it was impossible for them to avoid either metaphysics or ethics. Practical action can avoid neither because practice needs metaphors pointing to the way the world really is and it needs principles of obligation guiding the praxis of therapy or, as in the case of Skinner, the praxis of behavior formation. This points, then, to an idea that I alluded to in the first preface of the book and will return to briefly in the conclusion: we must have in our time two models of psychology just as we must have two models for the social sciences in general. One model of psychology would be to develop a fund of psychological knowledge that would be as value free as possible, although it can never fully achieve this goal. This, of course, is today the reigning model in the academy of psychology as a scientific discipline. The development of such a discipline may be difficult, but it has not been the argument of this book that it is impossible.

The second model of psychology would have analogies to the contemporary discussion in sociology that calls for a social science grounded in a critical theory of the good society. This is a project in sociology associated with the Frankfurt School and Jürgen Habermas, and before him Max Horkheimer, Theodor Adorno, Herbert Marcuse, and others.[11] There are those connected with the Frankfurt School who would argue that all sociology and social science should be guided by and subsumed under a critical social theory. By critical social theory is meant a normative theory of the way society should be, the way it should function, and the way it should be transformed. This view believes a more neutral and scientific social science is impossible and will inevitably be captured by the dominant ideologies of a particular culture. Thus, all social science should be incorporated into a critical and normative theory of social reality. A sign that this discussion is now moving into the wider precincts of the academic social sciences can be found in the publication of a highly provocative collection of essays entitled *Social Science as Moral Inquiry* (1983).[12]

The position of this book is close but not identical to the Frankfurt school and the work of such theorists as Habermas. I propose not just a *critical theory* but a *critical hermeneutic theory* of the social sciences. Yes, this second model that I am describing would be contextualized by a wider critical theory of the good society and the good person. But following Ricoeur more than Habermas and the Frankfurt school, this critical theory would be located in a hermeneutic theory that takes effective history and the classics that shape it more seriously. Habermas and his associates are Kantians; once they have Kant's categorical imperative, i.e., the idea of determining if our moral maxims are consistent with what could be willed as a universal law,[13] they don't really need history and its classical narratives that orient us to the broader meaning of life.[14] This is why Paul Ricoeur develops his critical theory within the context of hermeneutic philosophy. He claims that the human sciences need to be contextualized within the view of the human that the great narratives of the past open to our imaginations. Nonetheless, Ricoeur believes that something like the Kantian critical moment is needed as a submoment within hermeneutic philosophy to critique how these classics manifest themselves in actual concrete circumstances.[15] A critical hermeneutic theory of society takes history, its religious classics, and hence theology as sources for its vision of the good person and the good society. Critical theory alone tends to neglect history and its religious classics.

There are analogies now emerging in the field of psychology to this discussion in sociology and related social science disciplines. Habermas himself has contributed to the call for a psychology grounded in a critical and normative theory of person and society, but others have entered into the discussion as well.[16] Ricoeur envisions his hermeneutic philosophy as providing a context for more intentional scientific psychology. Although I do not agree with those who want to abolish all attempts to develop a relatively scientific psychology, I do agree that much of psychology—especially the psychotherapeutic and developmental psychologies—needs to be part of a wider hermeneutic, critical, and normative theory of person and society. Hence, society needs two models of psychology—one more properly scientific, descriptive, and predictive and one more self-consciously critical and normative.[17]

Acknowledging this leads us back to the psychologies we have studied with new appreciation. The difference between the psychologies we have studied and the new critical psychological theory that is now in order is that the latter discipline would be much more self-conscious about the philosophical grounds for its normative metaphors and principles of obligation. It would assume that the development of these metaphors and principles would entail the use of other disciplines such as philosophy, hermeneutics, ethics, and even theology. In addition, such a discipline would assume that the more scientific psychologies might contribute to, but certainly not dictate, the normative and critical theories that would guide this kind of psychological theory. Hence, in this style of psychological theory, the bridge between normative and descriptive statements will be intentionally pursued, and what Freud, the humanistic psychologies, and Skinner did by accident and under the pretense of science will then be done intentionally and through a combined program of empirical and normative analysis and conceptual work. But such a new type of psychological discipline would need to possess the philosophical grounds upon which to make judgments about the "relative adequacy" of different metaphors of ultimacy and different theories of obligation.

Making Judgments about Deep Metaphors

In order to have a dialogue of the kind needed to make comparative judgments about the adequacy to general experience of metaphors from different disciplines, one has to move into the kind of inquiry represented in the work of such metaphysicians as the later William James, Alfred North Whitehead, Charles Hartshorne, Schubert Ogden, Robert Neville, and classical or modern Thomistic metaphysics.[18] Questions about the ways the world can be seen as one, about the relation of the one and the many, about the nature of consciousness, freedom, and causality are metaphysical questions. All such questions cannot be settled on strictly psychological grounds, even though psychology as well as other empirical disciplines may be able to make, as Stephen Toulmin suggests, a contribution to their clarification.[19] But this conversation, although a possible one, is not central to this book.

It is more relevant for our purposes to argue for the importance of moral experience as at least one aspect of the test of the relative adequacy of a metaphor of ultimacy. Experience is made up of more than its moral dimension; it consists of our relation to physical objects, their relation to each other, our relation to other people, our relation to and experience of time and space, and our relation to actualities that are largely or solely material as well as actualities that may be primarily spiritual. But central to all aspects of our experience is our awareness of our agency and our capacity to entertain alternative courses of action, some of which can be argued to be more morally responsible than others.

In looking at the adequacy of a metaphor of ultimacy from the perspective of how it supports the moral dimension of life, I will follow closely William James's three principles for the verification of religious claims. In *Varieties of Religious Experience* (1902) James mentions three criteria for evaluating religious experience: "immediate luminousness . . . philosophical reasonableness, and moral helpfulness."[20] Since I have demonstrated the various ways in which scientific models can function as metaphors of ultimacy and, to this extent, serve quasi-religious functions within their respective psychological systems, I will use James's system to evaluate the way these metaphorical models support moral experience. James's view is a classical expression of the pragmatic approach to the testing of religious claims; it emphasizes the centrality of moral experience as a test of religious ideas. But, in addition, James's view of the moral test of religion is built on a model of moral experience that sees morality as the fair and just enhancement of a variety of other human interests as well.

James's three criteria are complex, and the role of moral experience in judging religious or quasi-religious models constitutes only one-third of the total procedure. James was willing to let immediate luminosity, the first criterion, count. If someone says that a religious model, metaphor, or experience does something for them—makes them feel better, is renewing or consoling, or conveys insight—James thought that such testimony ought to count for something in its evaluation. So when Freud says that he gets some consolation from his cosmology of the forces of life and death, James would want to take that testimony into account. James thought, however, that a philosophical evaluation of religious symbols, metaphors, and their attendant experiences needed more than personal testimony, although he admitted that it did indeed need that.

James's second criterion, philosophical reasonableness, actually leads him into what are commonly recognized to be idealistic modes of thinking. Philosophical reasonableness was for James a kind of principle of external coherence that demanded that a religious experience and the over-beliefs it implied (what I have called its metaphors of ultimacy) must be consistent with other known states of knowledge. It is through this principle that James in *A Pluralistic Universe* (1910) was led into an essentially metaphysical enterprise.[21] In order to employ this principle, one must be interested in a variety of concerns about the cognitive adequacy of religious models and metaphors.

It is not my intention to illustrate to any significant degree the cognitive and, indeed, metaphysical approach to the verification of theological and religious claims. My concern is to move on to the illustration of James's third criterion, the moral approach. But it is important to point out that to some extent our discussion has been involved already in James's second criterion. We have been doing this in our treatment of the principles of vitality and form in the Christian faith and the modern psychologies. The argument has been that the unity of vitality and form in the divine life is a fundamental intuition of the Christian tradition. And because human beings are seen as created in the image of God, they too, in fragmentary and incomplete ways consistent with the limitations of both finitude and sin, exhibit a unity of vitality and form. In fact, according to the Christian, all of the created world exhibits, in different ways, this unity. We saw this unity collapse in the psychology of Freud, intact but romantically unmindful of the unbalancing forces of sin in the writings of Maslow, Rogers, and Perls, and once again nearly absent in the work of Skinner. Throughout this discussion, not only did I use the testimony of the Christian tradition, as interpreted by Niebuhr, but I tested this tradition's anthropology on the relation of vitality and form with evidence from the modern sciences of the human. At the level of anthropology, the findings and arguments of these disciplines are relevant for the clarification of the vitality-form issue. The work of James, Anna Freud, Gedo and Goldberg, and Wilson were pressed into the discussion. I argued that there is much evidence from the human sciences that suggests the unity of vitality and form at the instinctual level; I also argued that disunities of life come from the way the anxieties of the self turn the pluralistic harmony of our instinctuality into conflict and competition.

But what I did not do, as I explicitly mentioned in the chapter on Freud, was to generalize or synthesize these fragments of data and arguments back into a cosmology or metaphysics. I did not argue that because of the evidence for the unity of vitality and form at the level of human nature, this is also true of the nature of the most fundamental aspects of the universe and can be demonstrated to be so independently of any claims of special intuition or revelation. In addition, I did not, and do not, deny this as a valid and potentially useful enterprise and part of the full task of submitting religious claims to philosophical assessment. That is, it is valid to ask if the same vision of the relation to vitality and form can be established whether one begins with the claims of revelation or whether one begins with a generalization and careful building up into a larger vision of the more discrete knowledge of various specific disciplines. But this has to be done cautiously. As Toulmin reminds us in *The Return to Cosmology* (1982), data and knowledge from several different fields of research have to be brought together. One cannot rely only on one or two disciplines, for instance, psychology or perhaps biology. This was the mistake of Freud. And it must be done intentionally, considering counterarguments, test cases, and the relevant perspectives of several disciplines. This is an entirely respectable enterprise and one that should be pursued consciously and systematically. As we have seen, it has happened unconsciously and unsystematically even within the clinical psychologies we have been studying. They have allowed their preferred metaphors frequently to become overgeneralized into metaphysical postulates and visions. It is not that what they did is totally inappropriate; rather it is that it was not done intentionally, systematically, carefully, and judiciously using the testimony of a wide variety of disciplines. It is only then that the information from a discrete discipline can join with the information from others and give insight into the fundamental features of experience in general. This task, one that I respect and believe to be possible, is something I will leave, however, to the hands of others.

It is James's second principle that is closest to the central ideas about verification in the recent thought of Ian Barbour and Sallie McFague. Neither of them makes much of a place, in the way James does, for the evaluation of religious or quasi-religious models from the perspective of the kind of moral sensibilities that they inspire. Barbour lists five criteria: simplicity, coherence, adequacy to supporting experiential evidence, extensibility (fruitfulness in ordering new experiences), and comprehensiveness (coherent ordering of diverse types of experience with a single metaphysical system).[22] Barbour believes that these same five criteria function in the area of science; he believes they function in religion as well. The difference is that with religious models (or the scientifically oriented metaphors of ultimacy of the kind we have studied), judgments are less precise and the ranges of experiential evidence larger and more difficult to handle. Nonetheless, a reasoned discussion about the adequacy of religious models to experience can, according to Barbour, go forward. McFague advances a similar but shorter list and is more interested in judging the adequacy of models within a single paradigm, be it scientific or religious, than in judging the adequacy of models between paradigms and traditions.[23]

Barbour discusses the possibility of using moral and psychological criteria to judge the adequacy of metaphors and models of ultimacy (James's third criterion), but for the most part rejects them. For him, to judge a religious model in terms of how it meets psychological or psychobiological needs or how it inspires moral attitudes, principles, or actions requires that such judgments be made in the light of a certain cultural or religious paradigm. Such moral or psychological judgments are for him, then, always relative to that paradigm. What is considered morally good or psychobiologically needed is always dependent, he believes, on the larger vision of the world implicit in the particular controlling paradigm.[24]

But I find this point of view on the paradigm-dependent status of moral judgments peculiar, especially since earlier in his book Barbour argued that although scientific judgments are highly paradigm dependent, they are not completely so.[25]

One wonders why he believes that scientific judgments can achieve some independence from paradigms but that moral judgments or judgments about psychological needs cannot achieve such independence.

A paradigm, as the term is used by Thomas Kuhn, who introduced it into the philosophy of science, is a tradition in scientific inquiry that rests upon a community of methodological, epistemological, and metaphysical assumptions incarnated in certain "standard examples" of what good research entails.[26] When we think about a paradigm from the perspective of its communal traditions, it is possible to argue that religious traditions are also paradigms and have certain analogues to scientific paradigms. Both see the world from the perspective of their assumptions, which themselves are not subject to scientific verification, and their methods and tests for truth are largely determined from within these paradigms. Kuhn's theory goes on to say that paradigms are changed, not on the basis of the accumulation of pure experimental evidence, but by virtue of revolutions wherein the fundamental assumptions governing the paradigm are overthrown and a new paradigm emerges. The outstanding example of such a series of revolutions can be found in the field of physics in the shift from Aristotelian to Newtonian physics and then to relativity theory.[27]

Kuhn's theory of paradigm-dependent verification in science was first thought to mean that there could be no communication and testing of findings between paradigms. This is now being challenged, and Kuhn himself seems to have slightly modified his position. Although still holding out for the incommensurability of paradigms, he now believes that some communication between them can occur.[28] But whatever Kuhn's position on this matter finally turns out to be, it is clear that Barbour himself believes that scientific observations and the rational analysis of them do finally count, as difficult as it is, for the modification and renovation of a particular paradigm.[29] Not only does he believe this is possible for scientific paradigms, but he apparently believes it is also possible for discussions between different religious faiths and, by implication, discussions about the relative adequacy to experience of a religious model such as Christian theism or the metaphors of ultimacy such as we found in Freud, humanistic psychology, and Skinner.

One wonders, then, just why Barbour believes that some paradigm-independent judgments are impossible in matters pertaining to morality. The assumption behind that would have to be that there is nothing rational, in any independent sense, about any kind of moral judgment and that moral judgments *in all respects* are both derived from and justified by the more irrational dimensions of our religious and cultural paradigms. These are the reasons Barbour rejects a pragmatist approach to verification of the kind espoused by James.

But such an argument overlooks the inner core of morality that can be relatively more adequately justified independently (at least in the formal sense) of appeals to religious paradigms, that is, independently of our deep metaphors and their accompanying narratives and symbols. I cannot enter fully into this knotty problem here, nor do I need to in order to illustrate my point. I only need to make the point with regard to the theories of obligation that we have confronted so far within this study—the ethical egoism of the humanistic psychologies, the theory of just consequences in Skinner, the cautious reciprocity in Freud, and the more expansive mutuality and agape in Niebuhr. To develop my argument, I will employ Niebuhr temporarily (even though we will soon return to balance some of his own one-sidedness). After arguing the point that one can speak of a rational core to morality that can be envisioned independently of surrounding religious and cultural metaphors, I will conduct a brief test of the already-discussed psychologists' respective theories of obligation. After this I will use the rational core of morality as a partial test of the relative strengths and adequacies of various metaphors of ultimacy. But I must first establish the rational core of morality.

Some form of mutuality gets to the rational inner core of morality. It entails a particular form of rationality, that is, the capacity to think reciprocally and reversibly. Lawrence Kohlberg has pointed out that in order to think mutually, in the sense of justly and fairly, one has to make logical inferences of the kind, "If this is a claim that I think is justifiable in this situation for me to make on my neighbor, it is also a claim that is justifiable for him or her in a similar situation to make on me." When a person goes through such an intellectual procedure, one is thinking reversibly. One can be content with the rationality of one's moral judgment when one can trade "places with others in the situation being judged."[30] As Kohlberg writes, "This, of course, is the formal criterion implied by the Golden Rule: It's right if it's still right when you put yourself in the other's place."[31] Mutuality as a principle of obligation exhibits these rational features. Of course, prior to being considered and justified as a rationally adequate principle of obligation, the principle of mutuality stood in the context of an effective history and its religious symbols. We know it as the principle of neighbor-love (love neighbor as self) or the Golden Rule. Variations on the Golden Rule, as is widely known, can be found within the context of the effective histories and background symbols of a variety of religious and philosophical systems. It stood within these systems long before Kant tried to establish its independent philosophical validity through his transcendental deduction of the so-called categorical imperative. From the standpoint of hermeneutic philosophy, it is not clear Kant would have tried to establish the categorical imperative philosophically and critically if the Golden Rule and its Christian analogue—the principle of neighbor-love—had not been a part of his own effective history and consciousness prior to his philosophical work. From the standpoint of this book, one does not need to choose between the principles of the Golden Rule and neighbor-love as they can be found within the context of religious narratives and as they can be grounded in the rational arguments of Kant. Both can be accepted if, in addition, it is acknowledged that Jesus' teachings about the status of persons as children of God contribute even greater depth and seriousness of justification than does Kant's argument that persons deserve respect and treatment as ends because of their status as rational agents.[32] Critical hermeneutics of the kind that undergirds the argument of this book can acknowledge the importance of tradition— even the greater profundity, in this case, of the Christian tradition—without denying the additional usefulness, clarification, and critical distance that Kant's categorical imperative gives to our understanding of the inner core of morality.

Because of this, mutuality can be seen to accomplish the basic task of morality better than our other alternatives. We have seen already that philosophical ethical egoism cannot solve genuine conflicts of interests, and for this reason we cannot consistently wish that people everywhere and always act in such a way as to actualize themselves first. Skinner's truncated justice of consequence finally cannot be seen as rational morally because it leaves out an important element that needs to be figured in our mutuality and justice from the beginning—our capacity for degrees of freedom that permit us to enter into deliberations about mutuality. Only Freud's cautious mutuality in the sense of reciprocal respect begins to approach the fully reversible thinking that exhibits the rational core of morality. The inner core of morality is a rational process, and because of this, some paradigm-independent judgments about morality can be made.

Certainly there are many instances in the world's religions whereby theories of obligation appear to be derived from the commands of God, but this is not my point. The point is a philosophical one about justification. It goes back to Socrates' famous question to Euthypro: "Is something right because God commands it, or does He command it because it is right?" If one takes the latter alternative—and even most religious people do when they pause and reflect on the question—then one soon thereafter must admit that "what is right is so independently of whether God commands it or not."[33] This is the standard philosophical argument for the independence of morality from religion that one hears put forth in the somber quarters of moral philosophy. And it is my judgment that the argument is basically correct, as far as it goes. But the argument really only says that the *inner rational core* of morality is *logically* independent from religion (or from metaphors of ultimacy). It is not an argument for the independence of morality from religion *in all respects*. Indeed, as we have seen, our deep attitudes about the world as revealed in our religions or our metaphors of ultimacy do affect our moralities in their *full embodiment*. Hence, when we think about the inner rational core of morality, we can say that morality is formally or logically independent of religion and certainly independent of religion for its justification. We do not need religion to envision conceptually mutuality in its formal sense or to recognize its moral qualities. But when we think about morality from the perspective of its full embodiment, religion and our deep metaphors very much come back into the picture to influence morality. We need religion to help us envision the kind of world in which mutuality and justice can take place.

Deep Metaphors, Freedom, and Morality

If the inner core of morality can be seen as independent of justification by religio-cultural paradigms, it is this core that must be used to test the moral adequacy of various deep metaphors that represent the way the world is. A distinction needs to be made between the idea of the "core of morality" and William James's more amorphous concept of "moral fruitfulness" if we are to advance and make workable James's idea of the moral test of religion. The first and most obvious question to raise about any metaphor of ultimacy is this: Does it provide for the possibility of the freedom and self-transcendence that are the presuppositions for the possibility of mutuality? This, in the end, was primarily what James had in mind by his pragmatic test of religious ideas and experiences: Do they support and stimulate the freedom and self-transcendence that morality seems to require? James believed that most forms of pantheism, monism, and mechanism do not.[34] Even certain forms of classical theism do not. This is why on philosophical grounds he gravitated toward what he believed popular Judaism and Christianity always in fact held, that is, a limited theism that both required moral seriousness and, at the same time, left room for human freedom and responsibility.[35]

How, then, do the deep metaphors in these psychologies rate in supporting a degree of freedom and self-transcendence necessary for the purposes of actualizing the core of morality? Of course, this question would not even be justified to put to a psychology if that psychology did not allow its scientific models to become over-expanded and evolve into metaphors of ultimacy. But since in the case of these psychologies this has indeed happened, then the question is clearly in order. The answer is that, in one way or another, freedom is denied or deemphasized by these psychologies. In saying this, I am looking at these psychologies from the perspective of their conceptual systems and the view of life these systems tend to project when simply read as cultural documents. I am not speaking about them as they tend to function in practice. The practitioner may bring back into focus, frequently unconsciously, many of the presuppositions about freedom and self-transcendence that the conceptual system itself cannot readily handle. *But it is these psychologies as conceptual systems and cultural documents influencing and sometimes confusing our images of life and the world that we are centering on in this study.*

For instance, Freud's early mechanistic metaphors and his later determinism of the life and death instincts all seem to eliminate the possibility of freedom. Of course, we know that this does not actually happen in Freud's therapeutic practice. As Paul Ricoeur and others have demonstrated, some modicum of freedom as an unthematized or implicit dimension of genuine intersubjectivity pervades Freud's thinking and practice through and through.[36] The very possibility of psychoanalysis presupposes some freedom on the part of the client to accept responsibility for reflecting on his or her experience, understanding this experience, and developing new interpretations of it. But that is just the point Ricoeur makes: Freud's explicit theories and his preferred models and metaphors do not account for what he must necessarily assume.

Certainly the same would be true for Skinner's dogmatic behaviorism. His basic models and metaphors and the extremities toward which he pushes them fail to account for the freedom that he otherwise assumes when he challenges us heroically to plan our environments. The uncovering of these implicit assumptions about freedom and the metaphors or husbandry upon which they rested was part of our goal in the chapter on Skinner.

The status of freedom in the humanistic psychologies is more subtle. There is a great deal of talk about and affirmation of not only freedom but spontaneity and creativity as well; however, the logic of their psychological positions and their metaphors of ultimacy actually do not require it. In short, in the best of all worlds as envisioned by our humanistic psychologists, freedom would not be required. Alternative values would not be freely entertained and deliberated over because our basic biological actualization tendency would provide us, at a subreflective level, with the right values and the right alternatives; freedom and the deliberation of alternatives would not be required. Freedom, reflection, and deliberation would descend to attentive listening to our biology. In addition, in the world of humanistic psychology, if everyone was truly faithful to his or her own basic potentialities, the basic harmony of all potentialities would eliminate conflict and remove the necessity for strenuous deliberation about alternative courses of action. So, strangely, in spite of the humanistic rhetoric of these psychologies, the deterministic shadow of biologistic metaphors taken to the extreme is cast over their formulations. The moral inadequacy of their fundamental metaphors is once again revealed; they are neither consistent with the demands of freedom nor consistent with their own unthematized assumptions about freedom.

In contrast to these psychologies, the metaphors of ultimacy of the Christian tradition explicitly allow for and promote understandings of human freedom and agency. This does not mean that a recognition of the conditionedness of human experience is lacking. As we saw in Niebuhr's interpretation of this tradition, the creatureliness of humans and how they are profoundly conditioned by both their animal nature and their environmental context are fundamental to what it means to say that humans are a synthesis of nature and spirit. Human conditionedness included for Niebuhr "the necessities of nature, of sexual and racial limitation, of geography and climate, and of the dominant drives of his own creaturely nature."[37] Nevertheless, we saw the ways in which God is defined in this tradition as self-transcending freedom and how the capacity for some self-transcendence and some freedom gets to the very heart of what it means to affirm that humans are made in the image of God.

In addition, within the Christian tradition the major models for the representation of God as the ultimate context of experience tend to portray God as compatible with the possibility of freedom on the part of human beings. In other words, God's power is not so overstated as to become a monolithic omnipotence controlling all events and squeezing out all room for freedom and initiative on the part of humans. This is true for the heart of the tradition, and it is my conviction that both Niebuhr and James are faithful to it. In spite of the significant differences between them on the nature of God, they both stand *against* the classical metaphysical tradition, which was so concerned to protect God's aseity (God's self-caused nature) that it envisioned God as beyond all influence from the finite world, as eternal in all respects, as omnipotent in all respects, and as beyond both enjoyment and suffering. Niebuhr signals his disassociation with such a tradition in his affirmation of the appropriateness of the category of the "person" in speech about God.[38] It is only through the metaphors of personality, he insists, that God's nature as free can be safeguarded. But we also see in Niebuhr his rather muted but still quite visible appreciation for Charles Hartshorne's neoclassical understanding of God as relative, passable, and surpassable.[39] By this Hartshorne meant that God is conditioned by the world through God's capacity to know, feel, and influence the world and all humans. But for that very reason God is also *affected* by the events of the world, open to the subjectivity and initiatives of humans, and therefore can be moved in both enjoyment and suffering. William James, who along with Whitehead was a major inspiration for Hartshorne's understanding of God, developed a model of God in his *A Pluralistic Universe* that he believed consistent with the popular piety of the Judeo-Christian tradition and that depicted God as in some sense finite.[40] God in his view is the dominant, although not the sole, agent in the creation, maintenance, and transformation of the world. But God's agency and God's participation in these events do not, for James, eliminate the need and importance of human freedom, initiative, and participation.[41]

A full debate about the relative adequacy of the models of ultimacy in the Judeo-Christian tradition, as represented by James, Hartshorne, and Niebuhr, is beyond the scope of this book. As I indicated above, to compare and argue for their strengths in relation to the models implicit in the modern psychologies require a full-blown metaphysical discussion beyond what can be pursued on these pages. What is more important is to point out that these modern psychologies have backed themselves into a position that now requires such a discussion. In addition, regardless of how the fuller conversation comes out, at the moral level the models of ultimacy of the Judeo-Christian tradition are more compatible with (and actually encourage) the kinds of assumptions about the reality of human freedom that we inevitably resort to in the normal course of everyday living and that are presupposed by the rational core of morality.

The Function of Multiple Metaphors

Not only are theistic metaphors potent with regard to their capacity to represent God (the ultimate context of experience) as influencing human life yet allowing ranges of human freedom, these metaphors have added range and depth because of their multiple expressions. This is to say that the Christian tradition has never experienced God in only one way; it has experienced God in several ways and from the perspective of several different modalities of God's action. Assuming a plurality of images and metaphors for the representation of the ultimate context of experience has the advantage of actually bringing together the full range of the Christian's many responses to the perceived action of God. This is a factor of adequacy that the deep metaphors of the social sciences and the psychologies do not appear to have even though they do function religiously. Not only have the ones we reviewed failed to comprehend the reality of human freedom and the moral essence of life, they are often, even as quasi-religious metaphors, one-sided in accounting for the richness of life in general as well as of the religious life in particular.

The Christian tradition has tended to use the metaphors of God the creator, God the judge or governor, and God the redeemer to speak of its various experiences and responses to the God it discerns as the ultimate context of experience. One can find these various metaphors in almost any theological summary of that tradition. One can certainly find them in the theology of Reinhold Niebuhr. But one of the best summaries of their various meanings can be found in the theology of his brother, H. Richard Niebuhr. In his introduction to H. Richard Niebuhr's *The Responsible Self* (1963), James Gustafson points out that Niebuhr was not speaking of three different Gods or one God who functions in three unrelated modes. God is equally redeemer and governor when God is creator. And God is equally creator and governor when redeemer. Gustafson summarizes it as follows:

> For purposes of theological-ethical analysis, however, we can make distinctions between our responses to God the Creator, God the Governor, and God the Redeemer. We can analyse characteristics of response without judging the response itself to be segmented and clearly differentiated, in the same manner that we can affirm God to be Triune without denying that he is One.[42]

We experience God as creator when we experience the goodness of various aspects of life and acknowledge that it is a goodness that we ourselves have not created. We experience God as creator when we experience the various aspects of life—nature, our neighbor, culture—as good gifts that are there prior to our own efforts and that beckon to be acknowledged in gratitude and thanksgiving. We experience God as judge and governor when we experience various aspects of an ordered life that also have about them a sacrality and weight that transcends individual and social interests as such. In fact, moral action for H. Richard Niebuhr is "human action in response to the governing action of God upon us."[43] God as governor is especially confronted in experiences of limitation and finitude.

And finally, Christians experience God as redeemer and as a source of renewal and revitalization within the midst of human brokenness. God the redeemer is still the governor and creator, and Christians experience this creativity and governance within the midst of God's activity as redeemer. The Jew experienced God's redemptive action in the exodus, and the Christian finds it both there and in the life and death of Jesus Christ. In fact, the religious person is inclined to see God as the final author of all experiences of renewal and redemption.

The metaphors of God the judge and governor depict God as morally serious and the agent and final promoter of all genuinely moral action among human beings. Not only is the God of the Judeo-Christian tradition compatible with and, indeed, desirous of human freedom and moral responsibility, this God is experienced as a positive source of moral inspiration and actual moral truth. It is human anxiety and the sin that flows from it that tempt humans not to pursue the morally serious life. Yet this same God who measures all of our shortcomings also is the source of all the grace, empowerment, and forgiveness that renew our quest for the morally serious life.

What strikes us as we review these basic metaphors of the Christian faith and compare them with the metaphors of ultimacy of the modern psychologies is the richness and multidimensionality of the metaphors of the Christian faith. The deep metaphors of the modern psychologies—life or death, harmony, natural selection, etc.—tend to be singular and one dimensional. Because these psychological metaphors are indeed used within a culture that carries with it the larger metaphors of ultimacy of its animating religious traditions, then in reality we never experience what it would mean to live only with the metaphors of science. But it is an interesting mental exercise to think of what it would be like if all the world experienced amnesia and forgot all religious traditions. What then would happen if no one could remember the images or conjure up the feelings connected with the old metaphors of ultimacy of these founding religious traditions? What if all cultures everywhere had only the deep metaphors of the sciences? I say "sciences" because there are certainly other sciences that have their metaphors of ultimacy besides these clinical psychologies. Could we live within the horizon of these sciences alone? Could we live with their scientific mythologies and these alone? I would wager that we would find them too uncomplex, too one dimensional, and insufficiently rich to take account of the fullness of the actual range of practical living. Therefore, the very diversity of the metaphors of the Western religious tradition is a factor that argues for their relative adequacy. And indeed it is the very essence of reductionism to attempt to squeeze the richness of experience into the boundary of a limited metaphor—one indeed first designed to comprehend a limited sphere of life. If the reader does this exercise, he or she will gain insight into the central argument of this book, i.e., that the modern psychologies cannot stand alone and on their own foundations. They need to be nurtured by the narratives, deep metaphors, and associated principles of obligation found in our religious classics, specifically those animated by the creation stories of Judaism, Christianity, and Islam—narratives that find uniquely powerful completion in the ethics and eschatology of early Christianity. The drive to found psychology on completely objective grounds, it must be recalled, serves just this alienating cultural dysfunction.

How Metaphors of Ultimacy Shape Morality

Some form of mutuality is the core of morality. I say this on philosophical grounds, and when I do I realize that the statement stands in some tension with Christian perspectives, such as Reinhold Niebuhr's, which elevate agape as self-sacrificial love over mutuality. But setting that issue aside for a while, let us go beyond the issue of freedom as a condition for moral action and look again at the way the deep metaphors of these psychologies influence their implicit ethics and at the difficulties that they have in supporting mutuality as the core of morality.

Mutuality is the core of morality, and this is true without total dependence for its justification on religio-cultural paradigms or deep metaphors. On the other hand, certain deep metaphors can so depict the world as to make mutuality either impossible or unnecessary. This happens in different ways in different systems of thought, and it happens differently for each of the psychologies that we are studying. Freud's early metaphors of mechanism and tension-release engender the idea that both the world and other people are basically an *intrusion* to which we momentarily accommodate in order to meet some of our basic needs. In the long run, our deepest wish is to retreat from the world and its various involvements and demands. It is this world image that gives rise to the "culture of detachment" that can sometimes surround psychoanalysis in its more strictly orthodox forms. A somewhat different image of the world emerges from Freud's later dominant metaphors of life and death. In this vision, the world at its depth emerges as overtly hostile. In spite of our impulses toward life, people want finally to die in their own way. And, because of the close relation between the death instinct and aggression, all people want to express their destructive tendencies in their own way. This explains why Freud was prone to assume a fundamental antagonism between all humans, especially between strangers. Hence, the image and evaluation of the world to be found in Freud led him to believe that it would not support loving initiatives toward the other—be it neighbor, stranger, or overt enemy. A cautious reciprocity was all that humans were capable of and to demand more would lead to neurosis. Although reciprocity and mutuality have much in common (both to some extent exhibiting the formal rational features that make up what I have called the core of morality), as a matter of fact the complete lack of initiative, of taking the first step, in Freud's view of reciprocity makes his ethic function in a considerably different way than what is implied by the idea of mutuality as the core of morality. Although Freud gets close to an ethic of mutuality, as we have seen earlier, its cautious character strips it of the kind of fully reversible thinking that would lead one to take initiatives. For indeed, if in some instances Freud would want the stranger to take the first step and show him "consideration and forbearance," then according to the principle of fully reversible thinking Freud would have to admit that he should take the first step and show such consideration and forbearance to the stranger.[44] Freud's metaphors of ultimacy function in such a way as to obscure in Freud's mind the requirements of the rational core of morality.

On the other hand, humanistic psychology paints a picture of the world as so harmonious, so trusting, and so balanced that all persons can pursue without qualification an ethical egoism centered on the actualization of their own potentialities and do so without fear of conflict and destruction to their neighbor. The image of a world where all authentic potentialities complement one another obscures the necessity of mutuality as the rational core of morality. Reversible thinking on moral issues is not necessary. Because there can be no conflict between my potentialities and the potentialities of others, it is not necessary for me to reach out and imagine how the other person feels about something and to moderate my claims or restrict the actualization of my potentialities in such a way as to make it possible for others to meet their needs as well.

And finally, Skinner so relates his metaphors of ultimacy to the relentless power of natural selection that selection itself becomes something of an arbitrary god whose pressures on our lives must be adjusted to at all cost. In ways that Skinner does not understand, this scientific myth takes on the proportions of a Calvinistic theory of predestination. Further, to rise above these forces requires a heroic act of self-transcendence on the part of his elite core of behavioral engineers who attempt to suppress the freedom of individuals in the name of a kingdom of equal yet forced consequences for all. Hence, Skinner's metaphors of ultimacy tend to distort the rational core of morality toward an ethic of justice without mutuality. It is a justice without mutual participation of free and self-reflective humans working together to shape the lives that they must finally live together.

The metaphors of ultimacy of the Christian tradition support the rational core of morality in a way that the deep metaphors of these psychologies do not. This is true first of all, as we have seen, because a limited theism of the kind found in popular Christianity, Niebuhr, and James provides for the capacity of the freedom and self-transcendence in humans that mutuality presupposes. God influences, challenges, and stimulates the human will, but God does not control it in all respects. Hence, the God of the greater part of the Jewish and Christian traditions is depicted as leaving enough freedom to humans for them to have the agency and self-transcendence necessary to enact the mutuality implicit in the principles of neighbor-love and the golden rule. But in addition to this, God is often depicted as a God who can enjoy human beings, receive contributions from human beings, have fellowship with humans, and yet at the same time take initiatives through self-sacrificial love to restore mutuality when it is threatened. But fully to understand the way the metaphors of ultimacy of the Christian religion support the rational core of morality, we must pause for a fuller discussion of the relation of agape and eros and the pressures that contemporary discussions surrounding humanistic psychology put on this discussion. And then we will return once again to consider the way the limited theism of the Christian tradition supports the rational core of morality.

Health, Obligation, and Neighbor-Love

I want to conclude this chapter by illustrating the full meaning of the revised correlational approach to the theology of culture. This approach, although beginning in faith, tries to present public reasons for faith's intuitions. Furthermore, it takes seriously the answers explicit or implicit in various non-Christian interpretations of life found in the culture. These interpretations often have great wisdom and may constitute correctives to the perspectives of faith. For although the deep metaphors and ethics of the Christian faith are in tension with these cultures of psychology, at the same time these psychologies have played an important and occasionally creative function in contemporary religious life. A brief review helps illustrate what I mean by a revised critical correlational discussion between Christian thought and the modern psychologies.

For instance, these psychologies have had an interesting impact on contemporary religious ethics and its attempt to understand the meaning of neighbor-love. In one way or another, all of these psychologies have placed on the cultural agenda the role of self-regard in health and ethics. And although they have each had vastly different ways of handling this issue, they have had the collective effect of insisting that there must be a more positive relation among self-actualization, self-regard, self-esteem, *and* love of neighbor than at least some historic religious interpretations have been inclined to admit. But the modern psychologies are not the only source of this more balanced perspective on the nature of neighbor-love. The modern psychologies are, in effect, simply pulling to the front some older classic themes on the subject. In brief, *these psychologies are having the effect of balancing certain interpretations of neighbor-love historically associated with Protestantism with views that have been historically associated with Judaism and Catholicism.* Hence, it is not the psychologies all by themselves that are doing this balancing but the psychologies functioning to remind us of older alternative traditions. These psychologies have helped us understand the power and relevance of these traditions.

The humanistic psychologies raise the issue the most directly. It is simply the question of the relation of self-love or self-esteem to the love of the other. This is the third value of humanistic psychology that I listed in chapter 4. On the whole, early psychoanalysis addressed this question indirectly through the issue of narcissism. And we saw with Freud that he believed that humans could only love those people with whom they are in some way narcissistically involved. This is the psychoanalytic way of saying that we can only love others if we are getting something out of it for ourselves. But strictly speaking, Freud reduced the question of narcissism to the question of libidinal satisfactions and attachments. Self-esteem or self-love was not for Freud an independent line of development, that is, independent of libidinal satisfactions and involvements. But it is interesting to note that the more recent psychology of the self put forth by Heinz Kohut and extensions of this perspective by John Gedo and Arnold Goldberg have begun, like the humanistic psychologists before them, to conceptualize self-esteem as an independent line of development.[45] I will discuss and evaluate these developments in psychoanalysis, and some parallels in the work of Erik Erikson, in a later chapter. In a far less direct manner, the same issue comes up in Skinnerian behaviorism. Even here, the entire concept of reinforcement functions to show that our behavior is shaped by rewards; this suggests that all altruism and love for the other are undergirded by processes of reinforcement.

But for purposes of simplification, I will state the issue about the relation of self-love to other-regard from the perspective of the humanistic psychologists. Carl Rogers's 1958 review of Reinhold Niebuhr's *The Self and the Dramas of History* focuses the issues well. It is safe to say that Rogers was rather deeply offended by Niebuhr's book. He saw it as dogmatic, exhibiting a certitude that Rogers found foreign to his own self-image as a scientist. But Rogers was especially upset with Niebuhr's understanding of human brokenness or sin as self-love and pride. He tells us that only when we view individuals "in the most superficial or external basis are they seen as being primarily the victims of self-love."[46] To the contrary, on the basis of the great masses of people that Rogers has treated, he believes "the central core of difficulty . . . is that . . . they despise themselves, regard themselves as worthless and unlovable."[47] From here, Rogers goes on to make the basic humanistic psychology case for the relation of self-love to love for the other.

> Actually, it is only in the experience of a relationship in which he is loved (something very close, I believe, to the theologian's agape) that the individual can begin to feel a dawning respect for, acceptance of, and finally, even a fondness for himself. It is as he can thus begin to sense himself as lovable and worthwhile, in spite of his mistakes, that he can begin to feel love and tenderness to others. It is thus that he can begin to realize himself and to reorganize himself and his behavior to move in the direction of becoming the more socialized self he would like to become.[48]

Similar statements can be found in the other humanistic psychologists. The logic of the position is clear: the problem of human existence is not self-love but self-hate, and once a person feels self-love (feels the self is loved and lovable), then automatically love for the other will follow.

Several things need to be said about Rogers's remarks before moving on to the main point, the relation of self-love to the love of the other. First, Rogers failed to understand that in Niebuhr self-love and pride are the symptoms and not the cause of human sin. Anxiety over the possibilities and insecurities of life, although not the cause, is at least the occasion for the inordinate self-concern that Niebuhr calls self-love and pride. Rogers misses the subtlety of Niebuhr's Augustinian-Kierkegaardian analysis of human self-transcendence and anxiety and how they lead to inordinate self-concern.

Furthermore, Niebuhr, as does the theological tradition from which he works, is not saying that humans have no right to basic natural self-regard. Niebuhr is fully aware of, and acknowledges repeatedly, the self's natural self-regard and the rightful place it has in human life. He and the theological tradition he represents are fully aware that humans must have sufficient self-affirmation to be cohesive selves with enough capacity for initiative to take basic responsibility for their lives, to deliberate, and to make fundamental decisions, moral and otherwise. The modern psychologies have been extremely helpful—in fact are making their primary contributions—in charting the various ways this natural self-affirmation develops, the conditions that foster it, and the developmental deficits that impede it. Niebuhr, whose objectives are somewhat different, simply assumes this self-love—as does the love commandment when it says, "You shall love your neighbor as yourself" (Matt. 22:39; Mark 12:31; Luke 10:27). As we will see more fully later, natural self-love was taken for granted in primitive Christianity and most of the Hebrew tradition that fed it.

It is not this natural self-love but the "inordinate self-love" occasioned by our inability to handle our existential anxiety that the Christian tradition primarily addressed in its doctrine of sin. It is our tendency to be concerned for ourselves "beyond natural requirements."[49] It is not ordinate but inordinate self-love that is at issue. As Niebuhr writes, "Man loves himself inordinately."[50] It is this inordinate, exaggerated self-love that fuels both our pride and our sensuality, both our self-glorification and our slinking freedom-denying retreat into the sensual. And it is this inordinate self-love that Niebuhr believes functions in all of us no matter how good a father or mother we have had, no matter how warm and supportive our environments have been, and no matter how successful our psychotherapy has been. It is this kind of problem that Niebuhr has in mind with his analysis of original sin and that Paul Ricoeur has in mind with the concept of the "servile will" he believes summarizes so well the idea of sin in the apostle Paul. It is a captivity of the will into which we ourselves have put ourselves because of our anxious grasping after security in the face of anxiety.[51]

It is, I cannot point out too strongly, the problem *par excellence* of adulthood. It is the problem we all have left over when we have all the health, all the interpersonal love, all the self-actualization and self-cohesion that any human can reasonably expect in this world. Even those with this kind of health will still try to secure themselves at the expense of others, reach beyond what they truly need, vault themselves with pride, or overprotect themselves in sensuality—do all of these things even though it is really not necessary for the basic requirements of living. It is very difficult for modern people, so aware as we are of the lessons of the modern psychologies about all the developmental hazards that lurk to rob us of the growth of natural self-love, to acknowledge the problems that are left over when we have achieved a high degree of appropriate self-regard, self-esteem, and the health that goes along with these qualities.

In addition, it is difficult for us to keep this aspect of human brokenness in mind when we are as aware as we moderns are that at all times throughout the human life cycle, our anxiety over our freedom gets mixed up with the genuine developmental anxieties, deficiencies, assaults, challenges, twists, and traumas that do invariably afflict us all and some more than others. Children do have mothers who sometimes ignore them, fathers who punish irrationally, siblings who compete, friends who torment, uncles who seduce, etc. All of these experiences create their own kinds of anxiety, cripple self-esteem, and diminish a sense of self-actualization and agency. The disciplines of psychology have made an indispensable contribution to modern life by throwing light on how early oedipal and preoedipal defects affect both later development and the capacity to love and show regard for the other. But the modern psychologies can and do work to obscure that element of freedom that functions in many of these traumas, especially as the child grows older. We can say it this way: the traumas of life condition and exacerbate the existential anxiety that will always be a part of life even if there are no developmental deficiencies. It is not that our interpersonal, familial, or developmental anxieties are one thing and our existential anxieties about life's general contingencies and limitless possibilities are another. There is a continuum between them. Our existential anxieties are always there, and we become progressively aware of them as consciousness matures. Our familial, developmental, and interpersonal anxieties amplify and particularize our existential anxiety. But if the tendency to grasp in overdetermined and desperate ways for security in the face of developing freedom is a universal and ontological feature of human life, then it must be acknowledged that the temptations of sin qualify and are a factor in all our other developmental processes. They are there even if we have the healthiest of environments. They are also there aggravating and compounding those experiences of life that push us toward unhealth. These subtleties Rogers and the other humanistic psychologists seem unable to grasp.

It is entirely possible to argue that Niebuhr and other Protestant theologians do not make enough out of the problem of self-hate and the loss of self-esteem in their analysis of the human condition. This is indeed arguable. It is, in fact, probably the case, although it must be admitted that the entire analysis of the role of divine love and grace in human affairs is partially designed to show how God empowers our agency and restores our fundamental self-respect in order to be attentive, once again, to the demands and opportunities of life in the Kingdom of God. But the full range of problems that humans face when afflicted with depleted self-regard is something modern psychology has told us more about than have the theologians. But to acknowledge this should not obscure the truth that original sin is the profounder problem. For it is the problem left over when relative health has been achieved. And original sin itself illuminates why our own inordinate self-concern can do so much to undercut the ordinate, natural, justified, and necessary self-esteem and self-regard of others. Our own sin is a causative factor in the wounds that are ubiquitously afflicted on the self-esteem of others.

Self-Actualization and Agape

There still remains an issue that humanistic psychology in particular and the modern psychologies in general have rightly been pressing on modern theology, especially modern Protestant theology. This concerns a widespread tendency to make self-sacrificial love the central goal of human fulfillment. This concerns the nature of agape and how it is to be interpreted. Certainly in some form or other, agape must be presented as a crucial ideal of human fulfillment for those claiming loyalty to the Christian tradition. But the question is: How must agape as love of the other be interpreted? Niebuhr interprets it to mean self-sacrificial love for the other and, in principle, for all others. And as we have seen, although he does find a place for mutuality as the controlling norm of the Christian life within the context of a fallen and sinful human existence, he certainly makes self-sacrificial love the ideal of human life. In addition, it is not clear what role in human life he would grant to the need for self-actualization, self-love, or self-realization. As a result, Niebuhr is an example (although by no means the most pure example) of the Protestant tendency to formulate the norm of human ethical activity around self-sacrifice to such an extent that one cannot rightfully formulate the proper role of one's obligation to oneself and the actualization of one's potentials. In short, the humanistic psychologies have functioned to push the interpretation of neighbor-love in the direction of equal-regard for self and other—a formulation, however, that humanistic psychology by itself has been unable to achieve. But at the same time, neither has it been a formulation that Protestant theology, and particularly Niebuhr, has been able to affirm.

Although Niebuhr believes that a faithful rendering of Christian thought means that mutuality and the self-regard that it assumes do have a place within the realistic possibilities of history with all of its sin and finitude, the norm of the Christian life is indeed agape defined as impartial and self-sacrificial love. Jesus Christ is the perfect exemplification of this sacrificial love and the cross is its perfect symbol. Niebuhr writes, "Christ as the norm of human nature defines the final perfection of man in history. . . . it is the perfection of sacrificial love."[52] It is a love on behalf of the other that takes no thought for the self. It depicts a love that "seeketh not its own." Such a love is a possibility by virtue of the nature of God. The essence of God is sacrificial love, and this love is disclosed through the person of Jesus Christ. Although this love is an "act in history . . . it cannot justify itself in history."[53] By this, Niebuhr means that sacrificial love will doubtless meet tragedies and losses at the level of history and that at the plain of human affairs it will go unrewarded. Although the promises of the Christian message do guarantee that sacrificial love will find its ultimate reward and victory beyond history in the fulfillment of the Kingdom of God, at the level of history agape or sacrificial love must act on behalf of the other without expectation of any personal completion of satisfaction. Hence, Niebuhr is almost Kantian in the way he separates virtue and happiness.[54] The good person with virtue who does his or her duty and loves the other impartially and without thought of reciprocity should expect no reward in his life but can indeed look forward to the happiness that virtue deserves in the life to come. Therefore, Jesus warns his disciples to be sanguine about historical hope: "In this rejoice not, that the spirits are subject unto you; but rather rejoice because your names are written in heaven" (Luke 10:20).[55] Effective historical action entails a certain degree of indifference to one's own historical fate. This, in turn, requires faith "in a dimension of existence which is deeper and higher than physical life and which makes it possible for" the faithful person to confess: "Whether we live, we live unto the Lord; and whether we die, we die unto the Lord: whether we live therefore, or die, we are the Lord's" (Rom. 14:8).[56]

There are both attractive and problematic features in Niebuhr's understanding of agape, especially around its ideality and its superiority to mutuality and equal-regard. But let us look further at his understanding of the relation of agape to mutuality. Niebuhr says it bluntly: although agape is the ideal, "it is not . . . right to insist that every action of the Christian must conform to agape, rather than to the norms of relative justice and mutual love by which life is maintained and conflicting interests are arbitrated in history."[57] Here Niebuhr appears to be in a conceptual bind and maybe even a contradiction. On the one hand, agape is the ideal, but on the other, mutuality and relative justice seem to be the norms that actually function to mediate conflicting claims at the level of history. Can he solve this tension?

Furthermore, agape itself seems to be for Niebuhr the presupposition for the fulfillment of mutuality and relative justice. And, of course, it is within the context of mutuality that eros finds whatever realization in history that it can find. The appropriate relation among eros, agape, and mutuality is the issue we must now consider if we are to determine what is really at stake between the concern with self-love and self-regard in the modern psychologies and the role of sacrificial love in the kind of Christian tradition that Niebuhr represents. Mutuality and relative justice permit, as Niebuhr sees it, some degree of self-actualization and self-regard. He speaks of this under the rubric of his discussion of eros. *Eros* is a Greek word for the natural tendency in humans to seek their own good, seek the higher good, and actualize their own potentialities. Mutuality does find room for the self-actualizations and self-affirmations of eros; it accomplishes this because of its concerns with reciprocity and some degree of balance between giving to others and receiving in return. Even here, the mutuality that Niebuhr speaks about goes beyond the philosophical ethical egoism of our humanistic psychologists. We saw with them that self-actualization and self-affirmation were the first obligation, and then it was assumed that mutuality would more or less automatically follow. The mutuality that Niebuhr speaks about and the eros he tries to satisfy go far beyond this: they entail relative dimensions of justice and equal-regard that necessitate restraining and pruning some actualizations and balancing them with the needs of the other and the constraints of the environment.

Self-actualization, and the self-affirmation and self-love that it requires, clearly do have a place for Niebuhr at the level of the mutuality that is our major possibility within the limitations of sinful and finite history. But Niebuhr's main point—and the point that so drastically separates him from Freud—is that mutuality all by itself cannot fulfill itself. It gets too concerned with the calculations of reciprocity and will not reach out and risk a love for which it will get little or nothing in return. Hence, it cannot, in itself, restore and balance situations where reciprocity is not forthcoming. Mutual love needs to be extended by infusions of agape and self-sacrificial love in order to give it the strength to risk love when the prospects for reciprocity seem remote. Niebuhr states his view with characteristic force when he writes,

> Sacrificial love (agape) completes the incompleteness of mutual love (eros), for the latter is always arrested by reason of the fact that it seeks to relate life to life from the standpoint of the self and for the sake of the self's own happiness. But a self which seeks to measure the possible reciprocity which its love towards another may elicit is obviously not sufficiently free of preoccupation with self to lose itself in the life of the other. Considerations of prudence thus inevitably arrest the impulse towards, and concern for, the life of the other.[58]

This gallant and insightful passage does, however, leave Niebuhr with the problem that agape, as the goal of human fulfillment, is the presupposition of mutuality; on the other hand, mutuality itself is not the goal of history but a compromise ethic designed to address the realities of a sinful world. Such a view leaves Niebuhr in the uncomfortable position of suggesting that in the ideal world—possibly in the Kingdom of Heaven—there would be no mutuality but only continuous and repetitive self-sacrificial activity on the part of neighbors who perpetually give but never, in return, receive. Niebuhr's position conjures up the rather bizarre picture of everyone running around sacrificing themselves for the other and having none of their own needs met or actualized in return. Such an image, of course, finally reduces itself to absurdity. If my neighbor is always giving and never receiving, then my neighbor can no longer constitute an object for my own sacrificial giving. And if I am perpetually giving and never receiving, then I can never be an object for my neighbor's sacrificial giving. This, one must admit, does not constitute a very attractive picture of what the ideal community or Kingdom of God, either on earth or in heaven, might be. Few of us would want to live in such a world. And it is precisely this emphasis upon self-sacrifice as the goal of life that has been the object of such energetic attack by contemporary feminist theologians. The appeal to the normative goal of self-sacrifice can so easily be used to force subordinate groups such as women or blacks into submissive and exploited social roles. In the name of self-sacrifice, women and certain minorities have opened themselves to being manipulated and dominated by oppressive elites through the course of Western history.

There is some evidence that Niebuhr would not want to end up being responsible for depicting such a vision of the ideal community. But as a matter of fact, he has done little to protect himself. There are grounds, though, for believing that he does want to find a greater place for eros and mutuality than this final vision suggests. For instance, Niebuhr clearly wants to distinguish himself from the more extreme Protestant understanding of the relationship between agape and eros. In the second volume of *The Nature and Destiny of Man* he is critical of the way Anders Nygren in *Agape and Eros* (1939) makes such a radical separation between agape and eros. Niebuhr writes that Nygren's analysis has the "virtue of revealing the contrast between the pure and the disinterested love which the New Testament regards as normative and the egotistical element which is connoted in all love doctrines (eros) of classical thought."[59] But, Niebuhr continues, "he makes the contrast too absolute. . . . It is significant that Jesus does not regard the contrast between natural human love and the divine agape as absolute. He declares, 'If ye then, being evil, know how to give good gifts unto your children, how much more shall your Father which is in heaven give good things to them that ask him?'" (Matt. 7:11).[60] Furthermore, as we saw in chapter 3, Niebuhr believes that agape is fed by the energies of eros; sexuality, tribal fidelities, class identifications are all examples of eros and feed agape even as they are transformed by it into more genuine and disinterested concern with the other.

Hence, Niebuhr worked hard to move to the left of Nygren on the relation between agape and eros, self-sacrificial love and self-actualization. Still, although he saw a much closer relation between agape and eros than did Nygren, he ends by making self-sacrifice the ideal of human fulfillment and thereby relegates mutuality (and the role that eros plays within it) to a secondary status. Nygren, on the other hand, saw agape as completely disconnected from all aspects of natural human striving for the good. He saw Christian ethics as radically discontinuous with all eudaemonistic expressions of ethics, which Norton helped us understand in chapter 4 and which are generally associated with Greek philosophy. Nygren saw Christian ethics as totally different from the central thrust of all ancient Greek systems of ethics. Greek ethics were, according to him, individualistic and preoccupied with the "Highest Good" understood as that which can satisfy the individual. This preoccupation with the Good meant that

> the dominant question was that of eudaemonia, happiness; and although different answers might be given—the answer of Hedonism, that happiness is the pleasure of the moment; or Aristotle, that it consists in activity and the attainment of perfection; or of Stoicism, that it is ataraxia, independence and indifference towards the external vicissitudes of life—yet the statement of the question remains always the same.[61]

Nygren argued that Christianity created a revolution in ethical thinking that disconnected ethics completely from eudaemonistic strivings for the good, for self-actualization, and for the increase of value. It would follow, then, that Nygren would also insist that Christianity can have nothing to do with many of the modern psychologies because of their decided eudaemonistic commitments.

Nygren saw agape as directly the result of God's love flowing through the faithful into the life of the human object of this love. It is spontaneous, free, disinterested, and totally unpredicated upon the value of the object of love. Following Luther, Nygren contends that Christian love does not come from our own natural energies but "has come to us from heaven."[62] The Christian is "merely the tube, the channel through which God's love flows."[63] And in flowing through the Christian to the other, God's love completely bypasses natural human strivings for self-actualization and mutuality. Nygren finds the eros image of love not only in Greek ethics but in gnosticism and Plotinus. Paul and Luther are the chief examples of the stringent view of agape as self-sacrificial love that Nygren believes is fundamental to Christianity. Augustine, on the other hand, developed a creative synthesis between eros and agape in the doctrine of *caritas*. This synthesis, in turn, became fundamental for much of later medieval Catholic thought. But Nygren also rejects this synthesis as still building sacrificial love too squarely on the upward striving natural energies of humans rather than the downward flowing and transformative grace and love of God. But it is precisely this view of love—the *caritas* model—that I will now turn to as a model for synthesizing the values of self-affirmation and self-actualization with the values of other-regard and sacrifice so fundamental to the Christian tradition and so intuitively convincing as basic to any workable ethic. It is the *caritas* model of love that will enable us to bring together the idea of health with a viable model of responsibility.

Self-Actualization and Equal-Regard

There is a significant alternative to agape as sacrificial love. It is the concept of love as equal-regard. This point of view has continuities with the older Catholic view of Christian love as *caritas* articulated by Augustine. In recent decades Martin D'Arcy and Robert Johann are associated with *caritas* views of Christian love.[64] In Protestant circles Daniel Day Williams gives expression to a position that has many of the features of the idea of love as *caritas*.[65] Yet the single most powerful Protestant statement of the concept of equal-regard can be found in Gene Outka's groundbreaking study entitled *Agape: An Ethical Analysis* (1972). One of the fullest contemporary Catholic interpretations of *caritas* that directly uses the idea of love as equal-regard can be found in Louis Janssens's 1977 article "Norms and Priorities in a Love Ethics."[66]

The importance of the principle of neighbor-love can be seen in the fact that the New Testament repeats the commandment "you shall love your neighbor as yourself" no less than eight times (Matt. 19:19, 22:39; Mark 12:31, 33; Luke 10:27; Rom. 13:2; Gal. 5:14; Jas. 2:8). And it states the highly analogous golden rule twice (Matt. 7:12; Luke 6:31). Janssens believes that the fundamental meaning running throughout all of these uses of the principle of neighbor-love is: "Love of neighbor is impartial. It is fundamentally an equal regard for every person, because it applies to each neighbor qua human existent."[67] Janssens resorts to the basic metaphors of the Christian faith—every person is a child of God and redeemed by Christ—to ground the basic valuation of the other, and indeed all others, as of "irreducible worth and dignity."[68] Being impartial, agape is independent of the personal qualities of the other, the other's attitudes toward us, and our own liking or aversion toward the other.

So far, Janssens sounds remarkably like Nygren and Niebuhr. In fact, at this point, the position is quite Kantian in the sense that impartial, fair, and reversible thinking and behavior of the kind associated with Kant's categorical imperative or the neo-Kantian principle of justice as fairness to be found in the thought of John Rawls form the leading thrust of the direction he would take us. In fact, equal-regard as Janssens defines it is virtually identical to my earlier characterization of mutuality as the rational core of morality. But then, suddenly, this Kantian sounding principle of impartiality and fairness takes on a tone quite foreign to Nygren and Niebuhr. The impartiality that agape requires applies to both self and the other. He writes, "In accord with the impartiality of agape, we maintain that one is to have equal regard for self and for others, since the reasons for valuing the self are identical with those for valuing others, namely that everyone is a human being."[69] And then Janssens invokes Gene Outka, who writes:

> Valuing the self as well as others remains a manifest obligation. One might adopt as a formal contention the utilitarian formulate that each person ought to count himself as one but no more than one and ought never to accord himself a privileged position. . . . Just as the neighbor ought to be regarded as a

human being prior to a particular human being, so the agent ought to value himself in the same way. The agent's basic self-regard, then, ought not to be simply dependent on the number of achievements or the extent to which he is found likeable, but on his being as well a man of flesh and blood and a creature of God, a person who is more than a means to some other end.[70]

In taking this position, Janssens and Outka are occupying a very identifiable terrain on the question of the relation of self-regard to neighbor-love. Outka provides a helpful typology of positions on this issue. He claims that there are four recognizable value judgments in theology on self-love: "as wholly nefarious; as normal, reasonable and prudent; as justified derivatively from other-regard; and as a definite obligation, independent of other-regard, though for some coincident with it."[71] In terms of these types, it is clear that Nygren would see it as wholly nefarious and that Niebuhr would see it as normal and reasonable but inevitably distorted and excessive when compounded by human sin. Neither, however, sees it as obligatory and coequal in obligation with that of loving and helping the neighbor. Such a position is very close to yet very far from what the humanistic psychologists are saying. They certainly lend their support to the position that self-regard (self-actualization and self-love) is obligatory, but they do not state that other-regard is of equal importance. They also state too facilely how automatically other-regard will follow when self-regard is adequate. And this happens because propositions and descriptions that should apply to highly circumscribed concepts of health are allowed to spill over and become more generalized images of human fulfillment and even of human obligation. Or to put it in the language of an earlier chapter, the transitional moments of liminality are frozen and allowed to become the end of life.

How, then, does Janssens's position handle the highly crucial question of the nature of self-sacrifice and the symbolism of the cross? For without stating the role of self-sacrifice in a Christian theory of obligation, one of the major clusters of symbols pertaining to the Christian life is ignored. But this in itself is not a philosophical objection. To leave out the symbol of the cross and what it has suggested about the role of sacrifice in the moral life may be inconsistent with the Christian theological tradition, but it still may make perfectly good philosophical sense. It is my view that the theologian of culture should be interested in both levels of truth and consistency.

But Janssens has, I believe, a particularly interesting and powerful way of stating the role of self-sacrifice within the idea of neighbor-love as equal-regard. Clearly, without finding a place for the role of self-sacrifice within this ethic, equal-regard can easily degenerate into simple preoccupation with reciprocity. It can quickly become a matter of calculation about whether or not the other treats me equally; if not, I might have no obligation to treat the other equally. And then the situation that Niebuhr envisions where mutuality cannot sustain itself and sinks to calculated reciprocity and back scratching would soon obtain.

Janssens's ethic of equal-regard and mutuality guards against this by finding within it a definite place for sacrifice. *But, in contrast to Niebuhr, self-sacrifice is not the ideal of the Christian life. Instead mutuality and equal-regard are the ideal, and sacrificial love is derived from them.* Janssens states it plainly: "In short, self-sacrifice is not the quintessence of love. . . . Self-sacrifice is justified derivatively from other regard."[72] And by other-regard, Janssens means the regard for the other that is a part of the equal-regard of mutuality. We must regard and love the neighbor equally to ourselves, and we must do this even if the neighbor does not respond and does not regard us equally and, in fact, actively works against us. Hence, we must sacrifice some of our own interests and even expend energy to regard the other even if the other fails to reciprocate. We are to do this not as an end in itself but as part of the more fundamental obligation of mutuality and equal-regard for self and neighbor. As long as humans live in a world of finitude and sin, perfect mutuality will not prevail within the context of human affairs. There always will be unbalance, inequality, and injustice. The Christian concept of agape, according to Janssens, does entail an active, self-giving, self-sacrificial effort to restore mutuality when it has broken down. As Janssens writes, "After the model of God's love in Christ who loved us and gave himself up for us, our love is to include self-giving and self-sacrifice as long as we live in a world of conflict and sin. We should love our enemies and persecutors, take the initiative in forgiving, overcome evil with good, and even lay down our life for our friends."[73] But Christians should do this not as an end in itself but as a transition to the restoration and maintenance of true equal-regard and mutuality.

Such a position as Janssens puts forth preserves the importance and necessity of sacrificial giving in the Christian theory of obligation. But it does this in a different way than did Niebuhr; it does not make sacrifice the end, goal, or ideal of history. Janssens's position is a subtle but vital reversal of Niebuhr; whereas for Niebuhr mutuality is the compromise and transitional norm to accommodate sinful and fallen historical existence, for Janssens self-sacrifice is the compromise and transitional norm to accommodate the realities of fallen existence. As a consequence, Janssens's redefinition of agape along the lines of what he calls the *ordo caritatis* can find a place for all three elements that we have been dealing with: self-actualization and self-sacrifice, equal-regard for the other, and appropriate self-sacrifice as a transitional ethic on the way to restoring mutuality. The cultural agenda of the humanistic psychologies has put pressure on the reformulation of certain Protestant excesses in the definition of agape (found to a considerable extent in Nygren and to a lesser extent in Niebuhr). But this pressure has been just that, a pressure for reformulation, for the full resources of reformulation are resident within variations inside the Christian tradition itself, as Janssens's thoughtful retrieval of the idea of the *ordo caritatis* so amply demonstrates.

But to get the full flavor of what this reversal of priorities means, we should add several qualifications to the position that Janssens holds. Impartiality of self-love and other-regard means that we must distinguish between meeting the other's needs and submitting to exploitation by the other. We should resist the latter because it makes us into an object and robs us of our dignity. Not only have we no obligation to make ourselves someone's doormat, we have "something of an oblig-ation not to do so."[74] Second, we should resist exploitation by the other not only for our own sake (our own dignity), but we should so resist it for the good of the other. Furthermore, we should not needlessly sacrifice ourselves if in the process of doing so we will be endangering the health and safety of those individuals who are depen-dent upon us. And finally, it is entirely consistent with Janssens's position to admit the appropriate claims of particular relations, attachments, and commitments such as those between parents and children, between spouses, and between friends and neighbors. Equal-regard does not mean that we should sacrifice the needs of our own children or spouse in an effort ourselves to meet immediately and directly the needs of all other children and all other spouses. What it means is that as we claim the necessity of meeting the needs of those with whom we are directly related and directly responsible, we also have the responsibility to work actively so that other parents and other wives and husbands will have the resources and strength to meet the needs of those with whom they are especially related. Particular commitments are to be respected as a part of the necessities of life, but it is also the case that I must realize that my particular commitments are no more important than those of oth-ers and that finally, the doctrine of equal-regard means that our various special familial, friendship, and neighborhood attachments must be regarded equally. All of this is another way of saying that the concept of neighbor-love does not mean equal deep affection for all people as Freud thought that it did. It means instead a kind of equal, active, and friendly respect for the personhood, self-actualization, and particular attachments of the other. My claims and interests are no more important than those of the other and, indeed, the basic self-hood and fundamen-tal needs of the other are entitled to equal-regard both by me and by the commu-nity as a whole.

Agape, Equal-Regard, and the Bible

I turn to a major source of the classical teachings on love shaping Western cul-tures—the Old and New Testaments or, as is often said today, the Hebrew and Christian scriptures—religious classics that are, for the most part, neglected in the hermeneutic philosophies of Cushman and Richardson, Fowers, and Guignon. The direction of much contemporary scholarship on the meaning of neighbor-love or the love commandment in the Old and New Testaments seems to support Janssens's and Outka's interpretation. Victor Furnish points out that the early Holi-ness Code expressions of the love commandment in Leviticus 19:18 and 19:34 serve primarily as an injunction restraining revenge and the holding of grudges. They apply primarily to members of one's own group, that is, to "the people of Israel."[75] In both cases, self-love is simply assumed and taken as a guide to love of the other. In the New Testament the love commandment is frequently combined with Deuteronomy 6:5 on the love of God and is then formulated as the double com-mandment to love both God and neighbor (Matt. 22:37-39; Mark 12:30-31; Luke

10:27). Paul uses the love commandment twice (Gal. 5:14 and Rom. 13:9) as an adequate summary of the whole of the law. James 2:8-9, a favorite passage of Janssens, depicts neighbor-love as the antithesis of partiality and, in effect, tends to identify neighbor-love with impartiality much in the way that Janssens argues.

Although versions of the love commandment can be found in both Hellenistic-Jewish and Palestinian-Jewish sources, Reginald Fuller believes that Jesus learned it primarily from the Jewish wisdom literature.[76] In addition, it is commonly acknowledged that there are versions of the injunction to love one's neighbor outside specifically Christian or Jewish sources. This gives rise to the suspicion that we are dealing here with a natural product of the human mind of some universal significance and not just a particularistic moral formulation typical of a certain religio-ethical tradition. Neighbor-love interpreted as equal-regard may indeed embody what I have called the rational core of morality.

In the Synoptics, neighbor-love became absolutely central to the message of Jesus. Certainly, as we have seen, the love commandment is not unique to Jesus, but the centrality that Jesus gave to it in his total message may have been unique among his contemporaries. As Furnish points out, it was, along with the command to love God, presented by Jesus as the summary of the law.[77] In addition, it was seen as the hermeneutic key to the interpretation of all the law. Finally, the flourishing of neighbor-love was seen by Jesus as a fundamental characteristic of the coming of the Kingdom of God.[78]

Furnish agrees with Janssens and Outka that agape as neighbor-love does not entail self-sacrifice and self-giving as an end in itself.

> It is misleading to describe what is required by the biblical commandment as "selfless love" and as involving "self-abnegation." The *giving* oneself to the neighbor in love is something different from that. It is the investment of one's self in another, and that must and does presuppose a fundamental acceptance and affirmation of oneself ("You shall love your neighbor *as yourself*"). What is involved here is not "self-love," but the acceptance of one's life as a gift and the affirmation that it is good.[79]

Although Furnish does not go as far as Janssens in using the language of equal-regard, it is clear that neighbor-love for him presupposes and requires a basic fund of self-regard.

But a step even closer to the position of Janssens can be found in an essay by Luise Schottroff. Schottroff is especially interested in what love of neighbor means when it is extended to include even the enemy as it is in Matthew 5:38-48 and Luke 6:27-36. But Professor Schottroff cautions us against seeing it as a simple ethic of passive nonresistance that applies equally to our personal enemies as well as hostile magistrates, governments, and foreign nations. Schottroff believes that such injunctions as "Love your enemies and pray for those who persecute you . . ." are appeals to early Christians to strive actively to confront and transform their enemy so that the enemy will respect them as human beings of dignity and worth. Jesus is, in effect, rejecting the way of violence advocated by the Zealots, although Rome was not the enemy of the early Christians in the same way as it was for the Zealots. Nonetheless, the point is to love the enemy nonviolently yet actively in an effort to transform the enemy to regard Christians with adequate respect.

> The enemies are to abandon their enmity; in other words, they must undergo a change of attitude. The command to love the enemy is an appeal to take up a missionary attitude toward one's persecutors. This brings out the universal all-embracing claim of the salvation offered by Christianity. Even the enemies of the community are to be given a place in its common life and in the kingly rule of God.[80]

The Christian is not to accept passively the evil of the enemy but to try actively to transform the enemy, offering the enemy salvation and a new capacity to treat the exploited party with a new respect. Schottroff believes that the nonviolent transformative programs of Gandhi and Martin Luther King are good modern illustrations of the proper meaning of neighbor-love as applied to those who are our enemies.

Self-Regard and Agape: A Summary

My argument on the relation of self-regard to neighbor-love has been complex. I hope that it has demonstrated the importance of both the classics of history and the possible role of the modern psychologies for enhancing our normative understanding of the moral structure of love. Put simply, the modern psychologies, especially the humanistic psychologies, have put pressure on the culture as a whole and theology in particular to build a greater place for self-regard into their models of human fulfillment. Although this has been a message heard to some extent by the culture as a whole, it has seemed to have special relevance to certain Protestant expressions of the moral life. As we have seen, Anders Nygren in his summary of what he considers to be the normative themes of Christianity, especially Protestant Christianity, fits the implicit criticism of humanistic psychologies. Niebuhr, on the other hand, finds a more central place for self-regard and self-actualization in his concept of eros, but he still subordinates both self-regard and mutuality to the higher ideal of self-sacrificial love. Finally, in the reformulations of the *caritas* model in the work of Louis Janssens, we found the model of agape as equal-regard. This same model still finds a strong place for self-sacrificial love as an active stance that we should take in continuing to offer the possibility of mutuality to the neighbor even when the neighbor fails to reciprocate. This model has the virtue of incorporating the insights from the modern psychologies on the importance of self-regard to health. At the same time, this model balances self-regard with the moral requirements of equal-regard for the other. This is an important corrective to the humanistic psychologies because of their inability to restrict their concepts to the arena of health and because of their tendency to expand the concept of self-actualization (and the self-regard it requires) to a broader moral norm that then becomes indistinguishable from a form of philosophical ethical egoism. And finally, the concept of agape as equal-regard (Janssens's *ordo caritatis*) appears to be consistent with some recent biblical scholarship on the meaning of the love commandment.

Health and the *Ordo Bonorum*

One other set of ideas of Louis Janssens and the tradition of ethics that he represents is important for our purposes. We should pause to examine his theory of the premoral good (the *ordo bonorum*). This concept, similar to what contemporary ethics (especially William Frankena) calls the nonmoral good,[81] throws a great deal of light on a proper understanding of health and is relevant to points that we will pursue in our discussion of the psychology of Carl Jung. It helps us understand the great role the modern psychologies played in providing theories of the premoral good that our principles of obligation, mainly mutuality, help us to order and distribute justly. The principle of the *ordo bonorum* helps us understand what the psychologies have to contribute to our moral fulfillment. We intuitively know that our modern psychologies are morally relevant, but it is difficult for us to say just how they are. The answer is that the modern psychologies are one important source, along with tradition and our intuitive awareness, of our understanding of certain premoral goods that our moral principles in turn justly organize.

The premoral good refers to the various ways that we use the word *good* in the nonmoral, in contrast to the moral, sense of the word. Premoral goods are not directly moral goods because we do not attribute moral qualities to them as such, but we do indeed see them as objects or experiences good to pursue and, in this sense, relevant to any theory of ethics. As Janssens says, there are "realities in us and outside of us which, because of their properties, provoke in our experience a positive reaction in the sense that we enjoy them and welcome them as 'valuable' and hence 'worthy' of promotion (*prosequenda*)."[82] These are such realities as life, physical and mental health, pleasure, joy, friendship, and such cultural values as technology, education, science, and art. It might be better to call these goods or values premoral rather than nonmoral, as does Frankena. They are premoral goods because in themselves they are neither moral nor immoral, although they can become involved in structures of organization and mediation that are themselves either moral or immoral. Moreover, the word *premoral* helps communicate the important truth that it is precisely the task of ethics impartially to organize, coordinate, and mediate conflicts among premoral goods and whatever natural hierarchies we might discover within them.

Janssens points out that there are at least two intrinsic ambiguities resident in the realm of premoral values, or what he sometimes calls the *ordo bonorum*. For instance, anytime that we actualize one set of premoral goods we almost always usher into existence a set of premoral disvalues. Automobiles are a premoral good, but they have brought with them traffic, pollution, and tragic accidents. Modern medicine provides us with many magnificent treatments, but many of these treatments bring with them regrettable side effects. Second, there is the ambiguity implicit in the fact that humans can actualize only one set of premoral goods at a time. "When here and now we choose a certain action, we must, at the same time, and at least for the time being, omit and postpone all other possible actions."[83] Janssens quotes Henri Bergson's "Every choice is a sacrifice" to capsulize this state of affairs. This ambiguity has the most telling relevance to much of humanistic psychology, which often speaks as if there were no choices one has to make in one's actualization and as if all actualizations are simultaneously possible. Although these ambiguities are not morally evil in themselves, we humans may indeed handle them all the worse when they become involved in our own anxiety and our sinful and untrusting attempt to secure ourselves against anxiety. But nonetheless, these ambiguities in our pursuit of premoral goods call for the moral life—the *ordo caritatis*—as a means toward the just and mutual organization of these premoral goods.

This distinction between the moral and premoral good helps us understand a variety of things about the modern psychologies. The modern psychologies make a contribution to the full task of ethics by helping to clarify some of the relevant premoral goods that are so fundamental to life. They help particularize the meaning of the premoral idea of health. Health, as distinguished from the *ordo caritatis*, might from this perspective refer to the capacity to accept, experience, and affirm the natural tendencies that humans have and that constitute their most basic sense of the premoral good. Healthy persons are ones who can experience and accept their basic tendencies: for instance, their need for attachments early in life and analogous forms of relatedness later in life, their need for appropriate degrees of both dependence and independence, their developing sexual tendencies, the need and capacity for relaxation and joy, their bodily processes in general, their needs for self-definition, and their maturing tendencies toward intimacy and generative care. Of course, in composing this list, I have not proved that these tendencies and needs are actually fundamental to human existence and truly are examples of basic premoral goods. This list is an amalgam of premoral values celebrated in such various psychologies as humanistic psychology, Erikson (whom we will review later), Freud, Maslow, and perhaps Jung (whom we will also review). My point here is more formal and illustrative. If this list, or some similar list, could be demonstrated to include truly fundamental premoral goods for humans, then it would be relevant to our definitions of health but in no way exhaustive of our definitions of morality. Health would entail the free acceptance and self-affirmation of these realities as premoral goods in our lives, but the moral task would be precisely the task of ordering them within ourselves so that they can enter into our relations with others when these relations are guided and directed by the *ordo caritatis*—the principle of equal- or reversible-regard as the rational core of morality.

Conclusion and Summary

In this chapter, we have tried to illustrate the full scope of a revised correlational approach to a hermeneutic understanding of the dialogue between Christian thought and the modern psychologies. We have both followed and somewhat revised William James's approach to the pragmatic evaluation of religion. I did not deny the value or possibility of the metaphysical approach to the test of religious claims, nor do I believe that James completely rejected this approach. But I put the accent on the moral evaluation of religion, leaving it to others with metaphysical skills to pursue the other approach.

To further the moral evaluation of the deep metaphors of the psychologies we have studied here, I attempted to state the rational core of morality. I argued that the rational core is mutuality understood as equal-regard and that mutuality can be seen as the rational core of morality independently of any particular religion or the deep metaphors and view of the world typical of any religion. Using the rational core of morality, I tried to state the inadequacies of the deep metaphors of psychoanalysis, humanistic psychology, and Skinner to support the possibility of genuine mutuality and equal-regard.

On the other hand, although mutuality and equal-regard can be both intuitively grasped and philosophically argued as the rational core of morality independently of appeals to religion, nonetheless I argued that the metaphors of ultimacy of any religious view do influence the full embodiment of our principles of obligation, including mutuality as the rational core of morality. Furthermore, it is clear that some religious views support mutuality better than others. On that basis, I gave reasons why the deep metaphors (that is, the limited theism) of the Christian religion provide genuine and positive support to mutuality as the rational core of morality.

I concluded the chapter by illustrating the contribution of contemporary psychology, particularly the humanistic psychologies, to a more adequate understanding of mutuality as the rational core of morality and to a better understanding of its relation to eros and agape. This entailed a retrieval of the Catholic doctrine of the *ordo caritatis* and the characterization of agape and self-sacrificial love as a transitional ethic designed to restore life to mutuality rather than making it the goal and end of the moral and Christian life. This entailed some criticisms of powerful Protestant understandings of the relation of agape and mutuality. Although better on this issue than frequently acknowledged, Reinhold Niebuhr himself received some of this criticism. But the emphasis on healthy self-esteem, stated so powerfully by the humanistic psychologies, was placed within the larger ethic of mutuality and equal-regard. It is the hope that this ethic will, on the one hand, save us from the rampant ethical egoism of contemporary society and, on the other, save such groups as women and minorities from suffering oppression and exploitation in the name of appeals that they should sacrifice themselves for the sake of others—appeals that sometimes lead to self-abnegation rather than to truly appropriate forms of self-sacrifice.[84]

With this chapter on how to make judgments about the adequacy of different metaphors of ultimacy and principles of obligation behind us, we can resume our critical conversation between Christian thought and the modern psychologies by plunging into the mysteries of C. G. Jung and the subtleties of the psychologies of Erik Erikson and Heinz Kohut.

Creation and Self-Realization in Jung

In the remaining chapters, I want to resume our search for the metaphors of ultimacy and principles of obligation in some of the modern psychologies. But in looking at Jung in this chapter and Erik Erikson and Heinz Kohut in the next, I will not only try to carry our conversation forward, but I will look more carefully at level three of our levels of practical moral thinking—the tendency-need level. I have called this the psychological level par excellence. The indices of the basic psychological needs and tendencies that we bring to experience are the heart and soul of what modern psychology has to offer the modern mind. Modern psychology's great contribution to modern culture may be its insights into what Paul Ricoeur called the "archaeology" of the subject, of the basic psychobiological infrastructure behind our subjectivity. These psychobiological tendencies and needs, as hermeneutic philosophy teaches, never function directly and simply on human life. They always are known in part through the mediation and language of custom; that is, they are always developed and amplified dialectically in relation to what we unfelicitously call the "feedback of experience." In addition, within the idea of experience, we must also include the influence of the great figures or monuments of culture such as classic religious documents, art, literature, and architecture. These monuments project ways of being-in-the-world that have been understood from generation to generation to have profound and enduring significance. These monuments of culture, to varying degrees, play back upon our experience and dialectically qualify and shape our archaeologies of our basic psychobiological needs and their developmental history.

The modern psychologies, as sciences, should specialize in discovering these basic psychobiological needs and their possible developmental embellishments. But these psychologies cannot themselves dictate which objective poles of experience (which classical religious and cultural monuments) should qualify our archaeologies. Psychologists may be able to make a contribution to this discussion, but they cannot provide all the answers themselves. But the question of which culture psychology should serve is a vital question that psychologists can never avoid even though they can never fully answer it themselves. Even though the modern psychologies are not moral sciences in their essence, they are indeed moral sciences at their edges and horizons. Moral questions precede, shape, and follow the more properly scientific work of both clinical and experimental psychology. The partitions that separate the psychologies from moral philosophy must be translucent and not opaque. The line that separates them from the moral sciences must be dotted and not a firm and bold black slash.

In spite of the fact that the modern psychologies alone cannot provide their own moral context, they can make a contribution to the question of moral norms. Morality orders fundamental human needs and tendencies. Although our human needs and tendencies alone cannot dictate the moral principles we use to order them, it is still the case that our practical moralities must know what these needs are, which are more central, which are foundational to others, and what their timetable of ascendancy and decline is throughout the human life cycle. The modern psychologies, along with other disciplines, hold the promise of contributing to our knowledge about these tendencies and needs.

This knowledge offers modern civilizations two benefits. First, it offers certain frameworks for the partial explanation of some of the motivating factors of human life. Notice that I did not say these psychologies will teach us the *causes* of our behavior. *Human action is not caused; it is intended.* But this statement is not to deny that human action has its psychobiological needs and tendencies, some of which incline action in typical directions. But insofar as humans act, in contrast to react, their own intentions further shape and form the inclinations of their tendencies and needs. Nonetheless, psychological knowledge may help us explain or account for the psychobiological substrata that feed our intentions. The dynamic clinical psychologies, for instance, will never be able to explain human action totally; they will help us be sensitive to the psychobiological needs that constitute a precondition of our intentions. In addition, they will help us understand the various patterns, constellations, or gestalts that develop in human life in our effort to satisfy our needs within the constraints and pressures of particular environments.

But there is a second function for the psychologies in modern culture. This has to do with the indirect way that they can enter into the task of ethics. We intuit this use of the modern psychologies, but seldom formulate it with care. But insofar as our general principles of obligation—be they the principle of neighbor-love, equal-regard, mutuality, justice, or whatever—organize genuine human need, sooner or later the kind of knowledge in which the modern psychologies specialize must enter into our ethical deliberations. Jung and Erikson are examples of modern psychologies who offer richer theories of psychobiological needs and tendencies than can be found in Freud, the humanistic psychologies, or in Skinner. In recent decades sociobiology and evolutionary psychology have advanced strong claims that they can provide the most adequate archaeology for the modern social sciences.[1] It is not my objective to argue that either Erikson or Kohut are correct in detail. But I do believe that the kind of thinking they represent will be increasingly important for the future. They indeed may make an important contribution both to the psychodynamic interpretation of human action and to a theory of human needs and tendencies. The latter contribution constitutes an important, although incomplete, aspect of the human attempt to think about the norms of action. But in spite of their richer and more accurate psychobiological models, these psychologies also contain their deep metaphors and implicit principles of obligation that need to be understood and that invite theological reflection. We turn, now, to the psychology of Carl Gustav Jung.

The New Interest in Jung

The psychology of Carl Gustav Jung is in the process of being taken seriously, not just by the core of urban and cultured elites who have constituted its therapeutic clientele and not just by the cultured *literati* who have used it as a guide to the meaning of myth and symbol, but by an interesting new generation of biologists, neurologists, ethologists, and anthropologists. Jung's biologism has gained new respectability, or at least it has gained a new hearing as a source of fruitful hypotheses. It is now widely thought that although Jung may not have been right about many of the details of what he taught, he may have been generally onto something that needs to be looked at once again. Jung is currently being reread in the light of sociobiology, evolutionary psychology, neurobiology, and ethology, and his psychology is gaining a grip on the imaginations of certain members of a new generation of social scientists who are turning to biology for orientation and grounding within their various disciplines.

Jung is emerging from several decades of being viewed as a befuddled genius who spent his life rummaging through ancient mythology and his own dreams in an effort to reconstruct an alternative to the Christianity that he saw collapsing all around him. As Philip Rieff has written,

> Accepting as the leading premise of his psychology the failure of established religions in the West, Jung looked back on his entire life as the fortunate unfolding of a counter-myth, one that saved him from the fate of his father. In his development, from the dreams and visions of childhood on to the hypotheses of old age, Jung traced the convergence of divinely inspired messages and scientific intellection into a religious psychology—that form of faith he considered best adapted for use in the twentieth century.[2]

According to Rieff, Jung used the language of scientific psychology to elaborate a new faith and, indeed, a rather remissive faith at that. Rieff believed Jung was fascinated with myth and fantasy as ends in themselves, not for what they do to ennoble life but because they are avenues of access to the unconscious. Whereas myth had been used pejoratively in the nineteenth century and equated with that which was considered ignorant, childish, and primitive, Jung was one of the first of a long line of twentieth-century intellectuals who championed a "meliorative sense of myth"—myth as a source of wisdom, vitality, and renewal.[3]

Hence, my task of exposing the religio-ethical horizon of select modern psychologies is both easier and more difficult in the case of Jung. In spite of his own self-understanding as a scientist taking a purely phenomenological approach to the study of psychology, Jung lapsed into both religious and ethical judgments at every turn. His psychological models quickly became metaphors orienting his readers to the meaning of life, and his descriptions of health and wholeness rapidly became moral prescriptions. Since both religion and ethics abound everywhere in Jung's writings, the difficult task soon emerges of determining just what religious vision is present in his thought and just which theory or theories of obligation are dominant.

But in spite of the rambling and lumbering character of his thought and in spite of his sense of being a prophet to an age that had allowed the acids of scientific rationalism to erode its faith, some rather hard-headed minions of the academy find new inspiration in his writings. The British-American social anthropologist Victor Turner, who once saw religious symbols as basically the playing out of various antistructural releases to institutional and social-structural conflicts, makes an interesting turn toward Jung at the end of his life in one of his last major lectures. In commenting upon the milk tree ritual of Ndembu women that he had written about many years before, he adds a Jungian note that was entirely absent from his earlier commentary: "One might speculate that the Jungian archetype of the Great Mother and the difficulty, resolved among the Ndembu by prolonged and sometimes painful initiation ritual, of separation from the archetypal power of the Great Mother is in some way connected with the milk tree symbolism and with the ritual behavior associated with it."[4] In making such a statement, he is aware that he is bringing into question assumptions about the pervasive social conditioning of human action that constituted the assumptive bedrock of his generation of British anthropologists.

In taking this step toward Jung and neurobiology, Turner relies heavily on the English psychiatrist Anthony Stevens's book *Archetypes: A Natural History of the Self* (1982). Stevens gives new credibility to Jung's theory of archetypes by linking it with developments in contemporary neurobiology and ethology. Stevens argues that there is indeed evidence in these emerging disciplines that something like Jung's archetypes actually exist. The archetypes have, Stevens tells us, "evolved through natural selection."[5] In addition, they are "directly comparable to the 'innate releasing mechanisms' responsible for Lorenz's 'species-specific patterns of behavior' and Bowlby's 'goal-corrected behavioral systems.'"[6] Jung was a Darwin of the mind, a point that Stevens makes about Jung in ways highly analogous to Frank Sulloway's characterization of Freud in his *Freud: Biologist of the Mind.*[7] As Darwin sifted through the animal species of the world looking for anatomical homologues and as ethologists look for behavioral homologues, "so Jung traced homologues in symbols."[8] "It was this insight," Stevens believes, "which caused him to formulate the theory of archetypes, which attributed the universal occurrence of homologous symbols and mythologems to the existence of universal structures within the human mind."[9] Jung and Stevens share this interest in the universal structures of the mind with a variety of contemporary scholars: Noah Chomsky in linguistics, Konrad Lorenz and Niko Tinbergen in ethology, and Robin Fox in anthropology.[10] Earlier analogues to Jung's theory of the archetypes can be found in Plato, Kant, and Kepler, although these older philosophical predecessors failed to understand the biological grounding of these universal structures that they believed to be present in the human mind.

Furthermore, new interest is being focused on Jung as a possible bridge between the more biologically oriented American school of psychoanalysis often referred to as ego psychology (associated with Heinz Hartmann, David Rapaport, and Erik Erikson)[11] and the powerful new British school of object-relations (associated with the names of W. R. D. Fairbairn, Harry Guntrip, and Donald Winnicott).[12] Jung's concept of the complex may constitute a bridge that provides a model for showing how our various biological needs become integrated with the internalizations of our various object-relations and imagos built up from our early childhood social experiences.[13] Jung's theory of the complex suggests, in effect, that our object-relations (our relations with meaningful people in our early environment) actualize our various psychological needs or archetypes. Hence, according to this theory, our psychological representations (the inner psychic images of our social experiences) are actually a combination of the archetypal needs that we bring to experience and an internalization of images of the objects (or people) that relate to these needs. The promise of the concept of the psychological complex is that it can supply British object-relations theory with a model of psychobiological need (including relational needs) that it lacks. At the same time, it can suggest to the American school of ego psychology ways to make more thorough use of object relations thinking without giving up its appreciation for the biological infrastructures of human behavior.

But whatever scientific status Jung's psychology may ultimately enjoy, it is abundantly clear that his psychological writings are not only or simply science. And it will be these writings as intriguing blends of orienting metaphors, moral discernments, and theories of psychological needs and tendencies that will occupy our attention.

Psychology as Science and Moral Praxis

At the beginning of his autobiographical *Memories, Dreams, Reflections* (1961) Jung made a revealing statement about the relation of his psychology to his own personal struggle to become a self.

> My life is a story of the self-realization of the unconscious. Everything in the unconscious seeks outward manifestation, and the personality too desires to evolve out of its unconscious conditions and to experience itself as a whole. I cannot employ the language of science to trace this process of growth in myself, for I cannot experience myself as a scientific problem.
>
> What we are to our inward vision, and what man appears to be *sub specia aeternitatis,* can only be expressed by way of myth. Myth is more individual and expresses life more precisely than does science. Science works with concepts of averages that are far too general to do justice to the subjective variety of an individual life.

> Thus it is that I have now undertaken, in my eighty-third year, to tell my personal myth. I can only make direct statements, only "tell stories." Whether or not the stories are "true" is not the problem. The only question is whether what I tell is *my* fable, *my* truth.[14]

Jung is saying that in both his life and his psychology, the language of myth has been central for deepening his understanding. He is also suggesting that his own experience was a key source of his psychology. In addition, his psychology was the central instrument through which he struggled to overcome the conflicts of his life and achieve a sense of an integrated and actualized self. Much later in his autobiography he makes just this point.

> My life is what I have done, my scientific work; the one is inseparable from the other. The work is the expression of my inner development; for commitment to the contents of the unconscious forms the man and produces his transformations. My works can be regarded as stations along my life's way. . . . All my writings may be considered tasks imposed from within; their source was a fateful compulsion.[15]

As James Olney points out, in Jung the science of psychology inevitably "merges with the psychic process itself."[16]

In effect, then, the science of psychology for Jung becomes a moral science that undergirds a moral practice. Furthermore, the process of psychological growth becomes a moral process—even, as he says in *Psychology and Religion* (1938) about the Carpocratians whom he admired, a matter of "practical intelligence."[17] The process of self-realization and the honest and ruthless self-awareness that it requires are really a matter of acting *prudenter,* that is, acting "wisely," and "prudently, sensibly, intelligently." There is no denying, Jung insists, "that practical intelligence functions here as a court of ethical decisions."[18] Sacrificing one's ego (and the superficial twentieth-century technical rationality to which it is beholden) so that the deeper rationality of one's unconscious archetypes can speak forth is, to Jung, a simple matter of practical moral intelligence. It just makes good practical moral sense. Hence, psychology as science and the processes of life converge for the purposes of practical moral living. But the question is: What kind of moral life did Jung envision? What kind of moral vision did he wittingly or unwittingly make his psychology serve? What were his psychology's basic metaphors and implicit principles of moral obligation, and how did metaphors and morality interact with his theory of psychological need in the final mix that constituted his religio-ethical vision? In the writings of Freud, Skinner, and the humanistic psychologists, psychology as religio-ethical vision remains closeted, suppressed, and denied. In Jung, such an understanding of psychology is fully admitted, especially in his final *Memories, Dreams, Reflections.* But the question remains, what kind of religio-ethical vision in Jung does one actually find?

It is refreshing to learn that Jung, in spite of his imprecise understanding of the boundaries of psychology, did have some very timely insights into psychology's philosophical foundations. He was fully aware that psychology as a science never escapes its grounding in metaphorical thinking. Jung was convinced of the truth of what I have been arguing throughout the pages of this book, that is, that at the edges of the clinical psychologies there is a variety of deep metaphors that are themselves not scientifically established. The clinical psychologies (which still claim to be scientific in some sense) do not put pure objective concepts in the place of the metaphors and symbols of more religious and mythical accounts of human experience. A more accurate picture is that the modern psychologies substitute one set of metaphors for a more ancient set of metaphors. These psychologies enjoy the status of being called scientific only insofar as the new metaphors can, at least in part, be tested by appeals to aspects of observed experience. Ralph Manheim's translation of a section of *Psychological Types* (1921) states it even better than the similar section in the *Collected Works*. He translates Jung as saying,

> Every attempt at psychological explanation is, at bottom, the creation of a new myth. We merely translate one symbol into another symbol which is better suited to the existing constellation of our individual fate and that of humanity as a whole. Our science, too, is another of these figurative languages. Thus we simply create a new symbol for that same enigma which confronted all ages before us.[19]

In another work, we see how Jung had a basic sensitivity to the role of models in psychological theory. Although he says nothing about the relation of metaphors and models, he does seem to understand the tentative and exploratory role of our scientific models when he writes that science is not a question of "asserting anything, but of constructing a *model* that opens up a promising and useful field of inquiry. A model does not assert that something *is* so, it simply illustrates a particular model of observation."[20] But as knowledgeable as Jung was about the role of metaphor and model in the construction of a psychology, he was unable to keep his own metaphors and models tentative enough to guard against constructing a view of life complete with both a metaphysics and an ethics.

When one is doing, as was Jung, what logically must be called a kind of moral philosophy (if not moral theology) while calling it scientific psychology, such an endeavor is bound to be flawed. In this chapter I will show how Jung's image of human fulfillment was built on an image of wholeness that is finally and needlessly confused. Both his metaphors of the self and his metaphors for God tried to come to terms with the reality of evil in ways that were unstable and self-contradictory, both logically and morally. *In addition to developing an implicit ethic that is indistinguishable from ethical egoism, he developed an ambivalent theory of evil.* In order to facilitate self-acceptance in both himself and his patients, Jung tried to incorporate evil into his understanding of both human wholeness and divine perfection. In doing this, he often lapsed into a kind of double talk that revealed he was not so much making a serious intellectual point as he was tweaking the nose of an overly rationalistic and moralistic culture. Insofar as he was playing the role of cultural trickster, we can forgive him his inconsistencies. But to the degree he presented his view on wholeness, both human and divine, with the seriousness of a scientific writer, we have no alternative but to tweak his nose in return as well as the noses of all his followers who take his vision of life so seriously. *On the one hand, he often materializes evil and makes it a subvoluntary ontological substance located at the very heart of reality, both human and divine. At other times, he presents evil as no more than the culturally despised and suppressed side of unused human potentiality.* Here evil is simply that part of human potentiality that the prejudices of particular historical epochs teach us to disparage. Insofar as Jung held the first view, he exceeded both Freud and the Manichaeans not only in dividing the universe into dual and antagonistic realities, but in bringing this dualism right into the center of both the divine essence and the human self. *But insofar as he took the second view, he reveals that he was faithful to the official Judeo-Christian view about the fundamental goodness of God, the created order, and all authentic human aspirations.* He also reveals that what he calls evil is more a matter of a distorted will, as both Paul and Augustine argued, than a consequence of an ontological split in either God or the created order of the world. It is my view that this latter interpretation is more accurate to Jung. For this and other reasons, Jung should be seen as a particularly complex example of what we have called the psychological culture of joy.

Archetypes and Wholeness

Jung reports that as a young boy he had a sense of having two personalities. In his autobiography he refers to them as personality No. 1 and personality No. 2. These two personalities, he tells us, were not a "'split' or dissociation in the ordinary medical sense."[21] Personality No. 1 was his everyday personality as a boy coping with school, his friends, and the expectations of his parents. Personality No. 2, Jung tells us, was far more important to him. In this mode of existence he felt older, wiser, more in contact with nature, his dreams, and the night. It was his feeling for the reality and importance of this second personality, he believed, that gave him his very first sense that there existed at a deeper level of the personality something like the unconscious archetypes that he developed into a psychological theory later in life.

Jung makes some revealing remarks about his parents in terms of his boyhood distinction between these two personalities. His mother was closer to personality No. 2 than was his father, especially at night. He experienced her as better grounded than his father, more empathic and admiring, yet at times more frightening. He was also more comfortable with his mother and experienced a greater sense of loss and abandonment when she was unavailable. His father, on the other hand, was more identified with personality No. 1—his official, public, and Christian self. There was a level at which Jung seemed to love and trust his father, but there was another level, a deeper level, where Jung seemed to pity his father for his lack of relatedness to the deeper vitalities of life and for his failure ever to have had a truly enlivening and renewing religious experience in spite of his public role as a minister. But it would be years later, primarily through his efforts to understand both his own dreams and those of his patients, that he gradually began to elaborate his theory of the archetypes.

My question at this point is simple: What did Jung's theory of archetypes contribute to his final theory of human fulfillment? In his discussion of human health and wholeness, did Jung elaborate a theory about the ends and goals of life? And if so, what was it and how can it be evaluated? To discuss Jung's theory of the archetypes is to discuss, in terms of my three levels of practical thinking, his theory of tendencies and needs. The archetypal level is the instinctual level of human existence. Our archetypes are the fundamental psychobiological tendencies and needs by which humans organize their experience. Jung is in some respects close to Freud and the humanistic psychologists; the instinctual dimension of life is both the source of our primary motivations and a ground or base that gives us orientation in our understanding of health. But Jung's theory of archetypes represents human instinctuality as far more complex and multifaceted than was the case either with Freud's theory of the life and death instincts or the humanistic psychologists' theory of the one great master drive called the actualizing tendency. Whereas in the late Freud there were two great master tendencies and in the humanistic psychologists basically one, there is in Jung a veritable choir of instinctual voices all trying to sing their special songs, although not always at the same time. Jung is more like William James when the latter said that human beings are the richest of all creatures in terms of the wide range of instincts that they bring to experience. In *Principles of Psychology* James writes that "Man has a far greater variety of impulses than any lower animal."[22] Later he says that a human is forced to live a life of deliberation and choice not because "he has no instincts" but "rather because he has so many that they block each other's path."[23] Humans have as many instinctual tendencies as do animals and "a great many more."[24] Jung's understanding of humans' tendencies and needs is a great deal closer to the instinctual pluralism of James than it is to the simpler theories of Freud and the humanistic psychologists.

But Jung's instinctual pluralism is more robust, muscular, and dramatic than anything ever envisioned by James. James's theory was wrought out of a combination of introspection, ethological observation, and the state of experimental studies available during his lifetime. But he never used his or other people's dreams. Jung's theory of archetypal instinctual pluralism comes primarily from the interpretation of the vivid and dramatic symbolism of dreams. Jung grasped, as did Freud, the psychical representations of our instincts in our dreams and our symbolic life in general. In doing this, he renounced the scientific principle of being as economical in one's explanation as possible. In the spirit of early American psychologists such as James and McDougall, Jung tended to posit a fresh and distinct instinctual tendency behind almost every slightly different psychical representation or behavioral tendency.

The Complexes

Before Jung began to develop, in any systematic way, his theory of the archetype, he achieved worldwide fame for his work on a psychological phenomenon that he called the complex. In his early clinical psychiatric work at Burgholzi Mental Hospital in Zurich, Jung developed the concept of the complex to explain the conflictual mental activity—the delays, the silences, and the ambivalences—that he saw in his patients. There were certain kinds of symbolic and behavioral activity in his patients that seemed to be autonomous and outside of their conscious control. Jung talked about these complexes as feeling-toned groups of associated ideas and spoke about them as being "split off" from consciousness in ways not unlike the manner in which the British school of object-relations speaks about split-off object representations. Jung researched this psychological phenomenon through the experimental use of his word association test—a diagnostic procedure that led to his receipt of the honorary Doctor of Laws, along with Freud, at Clark University in 1909.

In his clinical and experimental work on the complex, Jung began to notice what he called a nuclear element, a central core of the complex that was marked by a peculiar intensity of feeling.[25] At the same time, this core or nuclear element seemed to be constellated by images of people and events that came out of the actual life of the patients he was working with. This led Jung to hypothesize that the complex was made up of two elements: an archaic, instinctually grounded tendency or form (some kind of basic human biological need) and images of people and events that fit or become "associated" with this need.[26] The nuclear element of the complex was the ground for Jung's theory of the archetypes that he gradually amplified over the years and that constituted the foundational component of his psychology.

The Archetypes

Jung's mature theory of the archetypes contains the following components. Archetypes are basic forms or patterns of the mind that humans bring to their experience and around which they organize their experience. They are inherited forms and emerge through natural selection within the evolutionary history of the human race. Although they are inner psychobiological forms, they represent our experience of the outer world and, to that extent, do have some adaptiveness to the structures of the outer world. Jung appropriated the word *archetype* from Augustine; it has some similarity with Plato's forms and Kant's a priori structures of the mind.[27] But they differ from both of these philosophical concepts in their explicit biological origins. In this Jung follows much of the modern philosophical temperament that sees mind as an instrument of the body; insight into the forms of the mind is primarily a psychobiological matter. There are many archetypes: for example, there is a father and a mother archetype; a masculine (animus) and a feminine (anima) archetype; archetypes of the hero, the wise man, paradise, and the guide; and archetypes for all of the structural components of the personality such as ego, persona, shadow, and the self. They all, in their appropriate season, actively struggle for expression; the archetypes seek to manifest themselves on the basis of a kind of epigenetic ground plan with some archetypes seeking expression early in the life cycle and others later.

There are models of dualism and complementarity that run throughout Jung's theory of the psychic structure.[28] For instance, there are dualistic dynamics within each of the archetypes. More specifically, there is what Jung calls a positive and a negative pole within each of them; for instance, the mother archetype, independent of our experience with our empirical mothers, has within it the experience of the good archetypal mother and the experience of the bad, terrible, angry, and vengeful archetypal mother. Something similar is true of all the other archetypes. The positive and negative components of every archetype complement and balance each other.[29] If consciousness begins to orient itself too much around one or the other pole of a particular archetype, the contrasting pole begins to emerge in an effort to rebalance the psychic whole. But differing archetypes have a complementary relation to each other. Especially is this true of both the father and mother as well as the animus and anima archetypes. If consciousness becomes oriented too exclusively around one or the other of these sets of archetypes, the contrasting archetype at biologically appropriate times in the life cycle begins to manifest itself in order to balance the total psychic equilibrium.[30]

The archetypes express themselves through symbols. Psychological symbols are the psychic and ideational manifestations of the complexes that we discussed above. Because the archetypes are pure form and have no content (no ideational material) of their own, they get their content from our actual experience of people and events in the outside world (from effective history, as hermeneutic philosophy would say) and therefore express themselves through the symbolic and ideational dimensions of complexes.[31]

But are these concepts actually thinkable? Do they make sense? Although, as we have seen, science and Jung's own individuation process become identical in his psychology, the questions of intelligibility and evidence are still appropriate. In probing his own dreams and those of his patients and in drawing analogies between them and the symbolic heritage of the world religions was Jung just spinning a great hoax? Or are there such things as archetypes and do they express themselves in dreams, our typical behaviors, and our fundamental wants and needs? Or, as Ricoeur might ask, are archetypes "diagnostic" of the depth—the archaeology—of the surface narratives and symbols we live by?[32] There is a new group of psychiatrists, psychotherapists, and neurobiologists who believe that such psychological realities as archetypes actually exist.

Archetypes and the New Biology

Anthony Stevens's *Archetypes* constitutes a major publishing event destined to breathe new life into the analytical psychology movement; it may also save this movement from spiritualization in the writings of Morton Kelsey or mystification in the writings of James Hillman.[33] Stevens attempts to show how Jung's archetypes can command support from a variety of movements in ethology and neurobiology. On the other hand, his book has the special virtue of never reducing either the Jungian image of human fulfillment or the Jungian concept of individuation to strictly simple deterministic processes of biological unfolding and maturation. Stevens helps deepen appreciation for the biological foundations of the archetypes without obliterating the ethical, reflective, and decisional dimensions of the Jungian view of human growth. In this he is doubtless more faithful to Jung himself than is the reductionism and determinism implicit in the archetypal psychology of James Hillman, especially in his *Re-Visioning Psychology.*[34] It is my conviction, however, that neither Stevens nor Jung ever quite understood the role of ethics—even though they both say much about it—in the individuation process.

In addition to his own efforts, Stevens presses a wide range of both ethologists and neurobiologists into the cause of rendering Jung's theory of the archetypes biologically and scientifically respectable. John Bowlby's two-volume *Attachment and Loss* (1969, 1973) is the most central text.[35] Relating both clinical and ethological observations, Bowlby developed the idea that all infants have a fundamental attachment need—a phylogenetically inherited need to be physically related to, held, caressed, and admiringly responded to by their mother. He also argued that the mother has a similar instinctive emotional bond with her infant.[36] Stevens seizes on Bowlby's attachment theory and argues for analogies between it and Jung's theory of archetypes. Both entail the belief in an unlearned instinctive set of biological tendencies that humans bring to and use to organize experience. The entire field of ethology epitomized by the works of Lorenz, Tinbergen, Eibl-Eibesfeldt, Robert Ardrey, and Desmond Morris as well as the newer findings of sociobiology and evolutionary psychology assume the existence of species-specific biological characteristics that led the various animals to adapt to their environments in species-typical ways.[37] Stevens writes, "Once one conceives of archetypes as the neuro-psychic centers responsible for coordinating the behavioral and psychic repertoire of our species in response to whatever environmental circumstances we may encounter, they become directly comparable to the 'innate releasing mechanisms' responsible for Lorenz's 'species-specific patterns of behavior' and Bowlby's 'goal-corrected behavioral systems.'"[38] Not only ethology, but both molecular and neurobiology are also seen as confirming aspects of archetypal theory. Stevens turns to the theory of biological replication as this is illuminated by the concept of the DNA molecule discovered by Francis Crick and James Watson. The DNA molecule is the key to a gene's replication of itself. In the gene's replication of itself, a "characteristic" pattern is passed from generation to generation and "it is the pattern which forms the replicable archetype of the species."[39] The DNA molecule passes on to a gene's successors the "genetic instructions for all the programmes it is potentially capable of executing."[40]

But there is more. Recent developments in neurobiology are seen by Stevens to have Jungian overtones. But here Stevens seems to have a larger company of support, especially in the research and writings of R. W. Sperry, J. P. Henry, E. Rossi, and

G. E. Schwartz. The work of Roger Sperry in the 1950s and 1960s at the University of Chicago and later at the California Institute of Technology demonstrates that humans have "two minds," one localized in the left hemisphere and the other in the right hemisphere, and that they each have their own special functions—the right involved primarily in synthesizing data into wholistic precepts (art, religion) and the left involved in language and abstract, analytical thought (science, logic, technology).[41] In 1977 Ernest Rossi published an article in the *Journal of Analytical Psychology* attempting to translate a variety of standard Jungian concepts into the new experimental data on right and left hemisphere functions. Rossi associated Jung's two basic attitudes of introversion and extroversion with the right and left hemisphere respectively.[42] In addition, he parceled out Jung's famous clarification of mental functions (upon which the widely used Myers-Briggs personality inventory is based) to the two hemispheres. Thinking and feeling were thought by Rossi to be closest to the dominant left hemisphere and intuition and sensation were assigned to the minor right hemisphere.[43] Rossi also associated the archetypes with the right hemisphere and the ego and persona with the verbal and abstracting functions of the left hemisphere.[44] Finally, Rossi argued that the "individuation" process and what Jung called the "transcendent function" (both terms to be described more fully below) could actually be seen as "the integration of the rational and abstract processes of the left hemisphere with the synthetic holistic patterns of the right."[45]

Stevens expresses appreciation for Rossi's suggestive first attempt at interpreting Jungian psychology with the recent breakthroughs in the experimental analysis of hemispheric functions, but he is inclined to agree with James Henry that Rossi was too quick to restrict the archetypes to the right hemisphere and that he failed to take account of those more primitive parts of the brain as possible locations for archetypal activity. Henry places the archetypal systems in the phylogenetically older limbic system and brain stem.[46] In making this move, Henry may be closer to the more sophisticated model of the brain developed by the neurologist Paul MacLean. MacLean advances the position that the human brain actually has three levels. The cerebral hemispheres are primarily a part of the newest stage of brain evolution—the neomammalian brain or neocortex. Below this and phylogenetically much older are the paleomammalian brain (the limbic system that controls basic human emotions such as sex, fear, and apprehension) and the still older reptilian brain (which controls basic sources of vitality as well as cardiovascular and respiratory systems).[47] Both Stevens and Henry believe that the right hemisphere may have especially intimate relations with these older sections of the brain, but that archetypal potentials as such are probably more fundamentally related to these subcortical paleomammalian and reptilian functions. Yet all three agree that the left hemisphere can influence and even repress or inhibit "via the corpus collosum" the entire "right hemisphere limbic affectional system."[48]

This capacity of the left hemisphere to repress or inhibit the right hemisphere and other more primitive parts of the brain earns it the privilege of being called the dominant hemisphere. In addition, since Western society seems biased toward left hemispheric activity, there are doubtless additional cultural reasons why the synthesizing activity of the right hemisphere has been suppressed and maybe even split off in the psyches of many individuals. Following the work of Jouvet, Stevens suggests that dreams may perform the important function of integrating our conscious experience with the older "archetypal biogrammer" characteristic of the species.[49] In addition, it is the aim of Jungian psychotherapy, Stevens believes, "to reduce the left hemisphere's inhibition of the right hemisphere and to promote increased communication in both directions across the corpus collosum."[50] This corresponds to what Jung called the transcendent function. "The transcendent function," Stevens insists, "resides in the mutual influence of conscious and unconscious, ego and Self."[51]

This is a taste of the direction Jungian psychology is going, at least in some sectors of the movement. Whether or not it is influencing actual Jungian psychotherapeutic practice, it has certainly served to suggest that the Jungian model of the human mind and its understanding of the psychotherapeutic process may have some scientific corroboration from quarters outside itself. Some analytical psychologists are fascinated and delighted by this movement within Jungian psychology; others are doubtless fearful that analytic psychology will import foreign elements into its domain and disclose it from its rightful concern with the description and interpretation of the symbolic life of humans as it is revealed in dreams, art, and the world's religions.

Vitality and Form in Jung

Jung's theory of archetypes leaves us with an image of an instinctively rich organism naturally guided by epigenetic timetables to express its various potentials over time in a spontaneously self-balancing way. There can be conflicts between the different archetypal potentials, and these conflicts can be aggravated by the vicissitudes of culture and history. But Jung believes there is an inner telos within the organism toward "balance" and "wholeness," whatever these words are finally thought to mean. To the extent that this is true, Jung's psychology can be understood to have strong affinities with the eudaemonistic tendencies of humanistic psychology, as David Norton in his *Personal Destinies* has suggested.[52] Jungian psychology is, as I have indicated, a variation of the culture of joy. Yet it is a more complicated eudaemonism than one finds in Rogers, Maslow, or Perls. The epigenetic unfolding of the organism is more complex, more multidimensional, and more open to risk and conflict. As I already have pointed out, there is a great commitment to instinctual pluralism in Jung as there was in James. In the latter the pluralism is even looser. For James the various instinctual tendencies finally must be unified more with culture and will, although even he holds that there are strong basic biological unifying propensities. But for Jung these unifying tendencies are more powerful even though they do indeed work to balance a far greater range of quasi-independent archetypal voices, promptings, and urges. In Jung's psychology the process of growth (what Jung called the individuation process) entails more conflict, more innate polar ambivalence, than is the case with the humanistic psychologies.

But the forces pushing the human organism toward self-actualization, balance, and wholeness are just as strong and, in the end, *almost* as trustworthy as they are for humanistic psychology. Vitality and form, to use once again the Niebuhrian categories, find an intimate although complicated union in Jung as they do in humanistic psychology and in the Christian doctrine of creation. But note that I insert the qualifier "almost" in describing the trustworthiness of the archetypes. There are some important nuances that make a difference and must be mentioned.

Ethics and Individuation

For both Jung and his interpreter Anthony Stevens, there is a close relation between the natural processes of archetypal unfolding and the process of individuation, but the two are not identical. In the humanistic psychologies, as we saw, the direction the actualization tendency *naturally* goes and the direction it *should* go are the same; the natural direction of growth and its normative view of human nature are identical. This is not quite so for Jung, but the difference is difficult to discern. And there is characteristic ambiguity that plagues the writings of Jungians on this issue. This is certainly the case with both Jung and Stevens.

We see it in Stevens and the contradictory things he says about the role of the self in the individuation process. He tells us that from "the moment of conception the possibility of individual development is inherent in the genetic structure of the new individual. . . ."[53] This basic archetypal structure Jung called the self, the "matrix . . . out of which the conscious individual personality emerges. It is the Self which determines the stages of ontological development, functioning as individual guide and mentor, leading the growing child on towards consciousness, personality, and effectual existence."[54] Stevens reminds us that Jung called this overall archetypal actualization and personality development the process of *individuation*. Stevens follows the words of Jung in defining individuation in a way that must be recognized as consistent with a theory of self-actualization that Rogers, Maslow, and Perls could themselves affirm: "Individuation is an expression of that biological process—simple or complicated as the case may be—by which every living thing becomes what it was destined to become from the beginning."[55] But then Stevens seems to retract this romantic image of individuation as a simple process of unfolding and adds a series of problematic qualifications with which Jung, as we will see, would doubtless agree. Let me quote Stevens at length.

> No ego can ever incorporate the wholeness of the Self. Incarnation entails sacrifice: it means fragmentation ("disintegration") and distortion of the original undifferentiated archetypal state: many aspects of the Self will prove unacceptable to the family milieu and consequently are relegated to the shadow (Freud's personal unconscious), while others will remain unactualized and will persist as unconscious and latent archetypal potential, which may or may not be activated at a later date. Thus, in every individual life-span some distortion of primary archetypal intent is unavoidable: we are all of us, to a greater or lesser

degree, only a good enough version of the Self. This fact is of the utmost psychiatric significance, because the extent of the distortion is the factor that makes all the difference between neurosis and mental health. Moreover, the life-long struggle of each individual to achieve some resolution of the dissonance between the needs of the conscious personality and the dictates of the Self is at the very heart of the individuation.[56]

This passage conveys the full flavor of the problematic relation between the natural unfolding of the archetype and the individuation process. I also want to quote at length his attempt at a solution to the problem, a solution (as incomplete as it is) that is also doubtless faithful to Jung.

Here lies the essence of the critical distinction which must be made between *individuation* and the biological unfolding of the *life-cycle*. The two processes are, of course, interdependent in the sense that one cannot possibly occur without the other, yet they are fundamentally different. The life-cycle is the indispensable *condition* of individuation; but individuation is not blindly living out the life-cycle: it is living it consciously and responsibly, and is ultimately a matter of ethics. Individuation is a conscious attempt to bring the universal programme of human existence to its fullest possible expression in the life of the individual.[57]

This highly illuminating passage tells us much about the meaning of individuation, but it raises many unanswered questions as well. What is really meant by the claim that individuation is "ultimately a matter of ethics"? What is meant by the insistence that the "life-cycle is the indispensable *condition* of individuation"? And furthermore, if it is the ethical task of individuation consciously to "bring the universal programme of human existence to its fullest possible expression," how much "expression" is possible and how much is enough? This last question is especially important in light of Stevens's earlier claims that "no ego can ever incorporate the wholeness of the Self" and that in every individual life span "some distortion of primary archetypal intent is unavoidable." This is the fundamental ambiguity in both Stevens and Jung himself; on the one hand the goal of life is to become that person one is "destined to become from the beginning," and on the other this goal entails an ethical task that involves some principle of selectivity about which archetypal possibilities should or should not be actualized at various moments in the life cycle and throughout the cycle as a whole. Stevens acknowledges the need for such an ethical principle of selectivity, but does not further identify its content. Is his interpretation of Jung accurate? Does Jung also see the individuation process as distinguishable from the simple biological unfolding of the life cycle? Is the natural unfolding of the archetypes in the life process for Jung the "condition," as Stevens would say, of the more focused and necessarily ethical process of individuation (hermeneutic philosophy would call it an ethical-interpretive process)? Let us turn back to Jung himself for the answers to these crucial questions that Stevens has helped us pose.

The same ambivalence and unclarity found in Stevens can indeed be found in Jung. There are times when Jung speaks of the individuation process as a simple matter of the unconscious archetypes following their own natural inclination toward actualization and consciousness, the final state being a condition of wholeness whereby the archetypes, in all their antinomous richness, have found a final balance in the conscious personality. At other times, however, Jung speaks of how consciousness must guide the process and why consciousness must refuse to become overidentified with any one archetype. But even though Jung, like Stevens, is vague about that principle of selectivity that consciousness should use in order to guide the actualization of the archetypes, in the end it may be clear enough for us to identify it. The end of the story—to anticipate it slightly—is this: Jung's attempt to define the nature of optimal human fulfillment—individuation, wholeness, and actuality—constituted a confused but needed effort to uncover a theory of what William Frankena calls the nonmoral good (and what Janssens calls the premoral good or what certain classical philosophers called the *ordo bonorum*). The balanced archetypes typical of mature individuation constitute a theory of psychobiological nonmoral goods; it is a theory of what humans want, quest after, and need in order to be human. To the extent that Jung's theory of archetypes is a definite theory of the nonmoral good, far richer and more complex than that of either humanistic psychology or psychoanalysis, it is a definite contribution to our theory of health and human fulfillment.

But for Jung, as was the case with the humanistic psychologists, each person in the individuation process is to order his or her archetypal unfolding by a principle of selectivity that moral philosophers would call nothing other than ethical egoism of a nonhedonistic type. Stevens is right; the individuation process is, even for Jung, an ethical process. It is not a simple automatic unfolding of the archetypal potentials. However, we will see that, for Jung, the individuation process is a matter of guiding the natural unfolding of the archetypal potential by that part of it that is each individual's "unique" core of archetypal possibilities. It is a process of guiding the actualization of the general or universal in each person by the actualization of the unique and individual within the person. Nonetheless, it does indeed boil down to an ethics of self-actualization and an ethics of ethical egoism. Let us turn to a documentation of this interpretation.

Individuation as Natural Tendency of the Life Cycle

One can begin to see how this is so in Jung's *Two Essays on Analytical Psychology* (1956). He develops a theory of the archetypes that sounds remarkably similar to Norton's rendition of the *daemon*. He states that individuation means becoming an "individual," and then goes on to say that "in so far as 'individuality' embraces our innermost, last, and incomparable uniqueness, it also implies becoming one's own self. We could therefore translate individuation as 'coming to selfhood' or 'self-realization.'"[58] Although all humans universally have the same archetypes, they have them in a "unique combination."[59] Hence, more specifically, the goal of individuation appears to be the self-realization of one's own unique combination of the universal archetypes. Jung quickly adds that when a person individuates, he or she does not "become 'selfish' in the ordinary sense of the word, but is merely fulfilling the peculiarity of his nature, and this, as we have said, is vastly different from egoism or individualism."[60] The end of individuation may not be selfishness or egotism in the regular sense of these terms, but it may mean a kind of ethical egoism of the kind we saw in the humanistic psychologies and that is, as we have noticed, problematic on philosophical and moral grounds.

There are times when Jung speaks of individuation as "a purely natural process which may in some cases pursue its course without the knowledge or assistance of the individual."[61] When Jung speaks this way, individuation seems almost coterminous with what Stevens called the natural life cycle; the classical acorn and the oak tree comes to mind. Here is an excellent example: The meaning and purpose of the process is the realization, in all its aspects, of the personality originally hidden away in the embryonic germ-plasm; the production and unfolding of the original potential wholeness."[62] There are times when Jung equates this original potential archetypal wholeness with what he calls the "self." The self must be distinguished from the ego in the Jungian metapsychology. The ego is the agency for relating the human organism to the outside world. In the *Archetypes and the Collective Unconscious* (1956) Jung tells us that the ego "extends only as far as the conscious mind . . . is thus related to the self as part to whole."[63] The self as a whole, of course, is the totality of the archetypes. The transcendent function is the culmination of the individuation process. It is the "blending and fusion" of the unconscious archetypes with consciousness itself. It entails a balancing of the antinomies of the personality: first of all the conscious and the unconscious, then perhaps the shadow and our public ideals, the anima and animus, introversion and extroversion, etc.

This balancing process is accomplished when the transcendent function establishes a "mid-point of the personality." This midpoint is the second sense in which the concept of the self is used in Jung. After the transcendent function, the ego is no longer the center of the personality; the center is "midway between conscious and unconscious."[64] This new point of balance or wholeness in the self is presented in the world's religions by a variety of symbols (Christ, quaternity, mandala, cross, fish). Jung discussed these symbols first in his 1912 masterpiece *Symbols of Transformation,* but returned to them several times in his later works.[65] It is precisely this process of individuation that Stevens, Rossi, Henry, and others are translating into the terminology of the dual hemispheres of the brain.

Individuation and Its Conscious Principle of Selectivity

My concern is more with the ethical meaning of individuation and the wholeness it promises. There are times when Jung, as Stevens suggests, seems to distinguish the individuation process from the natural unfolding of the life cycle; the archetypes and their natural epigenetic timetable, although fundamental for the health of the personality, cannot be blindly trusted and must be guided by consciousness. In one place Jung warns, "Possession by an archetype turns a man into a flat collective figure, a mask begins which he can no longer develop as a human being."[66] Some consciousness of the archetypal process is necessary to keep from overidentifying with these voices and pressures from the unconscious. Jung's disciple, Jolan Jacobi, tells us outright that in the individuation process "one has to expose one's self to the onerial impulses of the unconscious without identifying one's self with them."[67] And in his 1946 article "Psychology of the Transference," Jung makes what appears to be a Stevens-like statement when he says that whichever way we take in the individuation process "nature will be mortified and must suffer, even to the death, for the merely natural man must die in part during his own lifetime."[68] This statement seems to further differentiate the individuation process from the natural unfolding of the life cycle. But if these statements are true to Jung, can we document more thoroughly that the principle of selectivity that distinguishes the natural unfolding of the archetypes from the individuation process is indeed a genuine ethical egoism?

Obligation and Individuation in Jung

If for healthy individuation to occur consciousness must not overidentify with the archetypes, if there is some distinction between the natural archetypally determined life cycle and the individuation process, if consciousness is on the one hand to assimilate the archetypes and stay on friendly terms with them yet on the other hand somehow to guide their actualization, it seems that Jung must indeed then have some principle of selectivity that Stevens says is "ultimately a matter of ethics." In stating that consciousness must somehow both assimilate and differentiate itself from the archetypes, Jung has unwittingly moved into the province of moral philosophy. Jung here seems to be taking a position on the relation of the moral to the nonmoral good. For individuation to be healthy, consciousness must be *acquainted with and experience* as much as possible the nonmoral and natural goods of one's archetypal possibilities. But at the same time, Jung acknowledges the necessity of a subtle process of selectivity whereby some nonmoral archetypal goods are given more attention and others less.

Although Jung uses the rhetoric of morality and employs the language of decision, selectivity, ethics, and even sacrifice, in reality his message is primarily romantic and ethical egoist in ways that parallel the humanistic psychologists. In spite of his rhetoric of selectivity, ethics, and even sacrifice, according to Jung the goal of life remains the actualization of one's unique archetypal ground plan and its epigenetic timetable. The end of life is to actualize and assimilate *all one's unique set of archetypal potentialities*, that is, to be true to oneself in this sense first. In addition, it is Jung's belief, in spite of his moments of rhetoric that might suggest the contrary, that on the whole the natural unfolding of the individual life cycle *is* trustworthy and will mediate to the individual what is best for him or her. This is true because the natural unfolding of the archetypes has an inner telos to express one's archetypal *uniqueness*. The natural unfolding of the archetypes and the ethic of ethical egoism are finally the same. Consciousness is necessary not to order or form the archetypes in ways they would not naturally go; consciousness and its functions of reflection, choice, and sacrifice are necessary to remove the obstacles and avoid the pitfalls that might block or divert the natural inclination of the archetypes to express their uniqueness. This is the dominant ethic and theory of human fulfillment functioning in the Jungian vision of life. We can see this clearly if we review Jung's various reflections on the nature of love and its exemplifications in the symbols of Christ, cross, sacrifice, and the ideas of wholeness.

Jung gives no overall analysis of the principle of neighbor-love anywhere in his writings in the way that Freud did in *Civilization and Its Discontents*. But he does mention it in passing from time to time. For instance, he says in *The Undiscovered Self* (1967) that mass society "needs a bond of an affective nature, a principle of a kind like *caritas,* the Christian love of our neighbor" to overcome the isolation of individuals.[69] But love of neighbor cannot function properly unless humans' ancient proclivity to project their own shadow (repressed sense of evil) on their neighbor is brought under control. Clearly Jung puts his energy into the retrospective task of defusing the shadow rather than the prospective chore of actually defining the nature of neighbor-love in the way that preoccupies Nygren, Outka, Furnish, Janssens, and Niebuhr. Although controlling the shadow's projections by making them conscious is his primary concern, Jung does indeed say interesting and revealing things about what love of neighbor, enemy, and the self actually means.

For instance, Jung seems more interested in applying the injunction to "love one's enemies" to the alienated and despised aspects of one's own self than to the alienated person or group in the external world. He is doubtless correct that some self-forgiveness may be an important condition for the love and forgiveness of the enemy, but it is neither psychologically nor logically true that they are the same thing or that the latter will automatically follow from the former. Hence in his pivotal "Psychotherapists or the Clergy," Jung tells us approvingly that modern man needs to hear no more about sin and guilt but rather wants to "know how to reconcile himself with his own nature—how he is to love the neighbor in his own heart and call the wolf his brother."[70] Hence, love of enemy becomes converted into the love and acceptance of the self. The command to love thy neighbor and enemy gets subtly converted in Jung's psychology to an admonition to realize the self.

In addition, Jung has different and novel ways of interpreting the meaning of sacrifice and the call to the "imitation of Christ," especially his "stigmata." Jung tells us we are not to imitate Christ by following his sacrifice; instead, we should imitate him in the deeper sense of living "our own proper lives as truly as he lived his in its individual uniqueness."[71] There is indeed sacrifice and hardship involved in being true to one's own inner uniqueness. "It is no easy matter to live a life that is modeled on

Christ's, but it is unspeakably harder to live one's own life as truly as Christ lived his."[72] There is little doubt that Jung here is emphasizing a deeper ethical egoism—the actualization of the deeper archetypal self in contrast to the paltry and surface egoism of promoting and defending the specific agent of psychic life called the "ego" or its more socially conditioned component known as the "persona." Even though it is the deeper archetypal self rather than the ego or the persona that we are to be true to, live by, and realize, the position he advocates is nonetheless recognizable philosophically as a form of ethical egoism. Every form of imitation, every form of conforming to external traditions, models, or principles in contrast to the dictates of one's own inner uniqueness is experienced by moderns, Jung says, as "deadening or sterile." Jung tells us with an obvious tone of approval that modern man

> behaves as if his own individual life were God's special will which must be fulfilled at all costs. . . . If I wish to effect a cure for my patients, I am forced to acknowledge the deep significance of their egoism. I should be blind, indeed, if I did not recognize it as a true will of God. I must even help the patient to prevail in his egoism; if he succeeds in his, he estranges himself from other people, for they were seeking to rob him of his "sacred" egoism. This must be left to him, for it is his strongest and healthiest power; it is, as I have said, a true will of God which sometimes drives him into complete isolation.[73]

Hence, using the rhetoric of sacrifice, the will of God, and sacrality, Jung dresses up in religious clothes a form of ethical egoism. It is a nonhedonistic ethical egoism rather than a hedonistic ethical egoism that, as we saw, Philip Rieff and Gilbert Harman believed existed in Freud. Jung's ethical egoism does not make pleasure the primary nonmoral good as Freud is sometimes thought to do. Rather, the primary nonmoral good is the actualization of one's unique archetypal possibilities in all their conflicting yet time-specific grandeur. Under the rubric of a model of health, Jung projected a much fuller theory of human fulfillment that was, as well, a theory of ethical obligation. Consciousness in its differentiation from, assimilation of, and guidance of the archetypes in the process of individuation finally only attempts that selectivity, struggle, sacrifice, and hardship required to be faithful to the realization of one's own unique archetypal potential. This for Jung is not simply a transitional egoism that, as I noted above, is a necessary moment in all therapy. There is too much evidence that for Jung it was unapologetically the clear and final goal of human fulfillment.

Critique of Jung's Theory of Obligation

Much of my critique of nonhedonistic ethical egoism developed in my discussion of the humanistic psychologies applies to the implicit ethics of Jung. Ethical egoism as a systematic ethical position has had its eminent defenders, but everywhere it has the problem of addressing the reality of genuine conflict among the competing claims of diverse nonmoral goods. How does one reconcile those competing claims, especially when the nonmoral good at stake can be judged as truly good and justifiable in that nonmoral sense of the word? For example, I may need some medicine and the other person may need food. Both medicine and good can easily be judged as highly valued nonmoral goods. We do not say that the medicine is in itself moral, nor do we say that the food is in itself moral. We do not assign moral qualities to products such as food or medicine. But they are food things in a nonmoral sense and things we understandably want and need; they both are instrumental to bodily health and well-being, and food is, in addition, intrinsically good as enjoyable to consume. But what happens if there are limited resources and the money needed to buy my medicine deprives the other person of the cash needed to buy his or her own food? How does the ethical egoist solve that problem? If they both act equally tenaciously from the ethical-egoist perspective, they will end in relentless conflict. Hence the ethical egoist cannot generalize his or her moral principle. Or, as Kant would put it, "one cannot will the egoist maxim to be a universal law."[74]

The same problem applies when the nonmoral goods at stake are the human archetypes and their actualization. What happens when a young boy's need to actualize his animus conflicts with a father's need to actualize his anima? Can these two different sets of needs conflict? How much weight should the father put on the son's needs? Should the father permit his son's needs to overrule his own, as some would say the ethic of agape demands? Certainly this is not what Jung seems to recommend. Should the father take his archetypal needs and his son's with equal importance, as Outka and Janssens's interpretation of neighbor-love seems to suggest? Or should the father take care of his own archetypal needs with the hope that in meeting his own first he will also as a byproduct automatically meet the needs of his son? This is doubtless closer to what Jung would want to do. But would he, as did the humanistic psychologists, also assume that this would be possible because of a deeper harmony and complementarity among all archetypal potentialities? Does he believe that he can meet the archetypal needs of others through actualizing his own because finally there is an ultimate hidden harmony of all archetypal possibilities? It is my belief that Jung does envision such a world, and he does so in spite of his apparently rebellious insistence that the shadow and the reality of evil must not only be integrated into the self but be acknowledged to exist in the godhead itself.

The archetypal psychology of Carl Jung may constitute an outstanding contribution to a theory of the nonmoral good. As the actualization tendency in humanistic psychology is, as I argued, something of a theory, limited at that, of the nonmoral good, so too is Jung's elaborate theory of archetypal needs and tendencies. In fact, Jung's theory is a much more developed, complex, and sophisticated theory than anything to be found in the humanistic psychologies. And insofar as a theory or model of the nonmoral good is an essential, although partial, component of any full theory either of ethics or of human fulfillment, the psychologies in general, and particularly Jungian psychology, may have enormous contributions to make to such matters.

But because the modern psychologies, especially the clinical psychologies, have not had a firm sense of the boundary between psychological and moral language, their important contributions to our understanding of health have spilled over into larger religio-ethical models of human fulfillment and ethical obligation. The essential message of Freud, the humanistic psychologies, and Jung is that humans to be healthy must have *some awareness and acceptance of* their own natural inclinations. The humanistic psychologists and Jung went further and endowed these human needs and tendencies with the valences of nonmoral goods and proclaimed that both awareness of them and some degree of actualization or realization are also essential for health. But both of these psychologies, in rightly emphasizing these truths, took another step and converted their models of health into full theories of ethical obligation and normative theories of human fulfillment. In doing this, the truth that to be healthy we need awareness of our psychobiological tendencies, their timetables, and their implicit hierarchies became hardened into what must be acknowledged as nothing other than a full philosophical theory of moral obligation that can rightfully be called nothing other than ethical egoism.

It is one thing to argue that whatever one's theory of obligation it must recognize, acknowledge, and make room for awareness of the self's natural tendencies, needs, and timetables. It is another thing entirely to say or imply, as Jung surely does in his doctrine of "sacred egoism," that the goal of life is to *realize* these archetypal needs without quickly adding qualifications about the moral strategy one must use to balance, adjust, or relate one's own archetypal potentials with those of others. The use of such words as "balance," "*coincidentia oppositorum*," "harmony," and "integration" to speak of the largely internal and unconscious compensatory processes that work to bring into equilibrium our contending nonmoral archetypal tendencies makes the matter of inner self-unification sound far more subpersonal, subethical, and subdecisional than it really is. One can make this point without denying that real, unconscious compensatory processes do exist. Even then they function best, as Jung sometimes acknowledges, when consciousness takes a welcoming "attitude" toward these unconscious compensatory movements.[75]

But as incompletely as the rather automatic and mechanistic language of balance, compensation, and equilibrium accounts for the processes of the self-integration of our nonmoral archetypal needs, this language all the more incompletely accounts for the more specifically moral task of coordinating my archetypal needs with those of my neighbor—be the neighbor my spouse, my colleague, my employer, my friend, or my enemy. Here the tendency in Jung to collapse both neighbor-love and love of enemy into the need to love oneself and be friendly with one's shadow can hardly be considered morally complete even though it can be acknowledged as premorally and preparatorily relevant to freer and more authentic positive moral activity.

Although as a hardened philosophical position Jung's ubiquitous self-realization ethic has little to be said for it, as a transitional attitude toward the self and its possibilities, it has much to be said for it indeed. As I argued before, the ethic of some of the clinical psychologies, especially the humanistic psychologies and Jung, is far more understandable and perhaps forgivable if it is seen as a transitional ethic to cover the liminal transformations that occur during the processes of therapy. Seen from this perspective, the ethical egoism of self-actualization and self-realization becomes a transitional ethic designed to heal and mobilize a fragmented and distorted self so that it will be freer, more spontaneous, and have more ready access to its energies and potentialities for the task, finally, of serving a more worthy ethical goal. The goal of individuation can be placed within alternative moral theories and need not be put to the service only of a nonhedonistic ethical egoism of the kind Jung himself apparently thought was the necessary end of psychological growth.

It is doubtless good for the self to have actualized and balanced its mother and father archetypes, and then later the anima and animus, conscious and unconsciousness, its attitudes of introversion and extroversion, its shadow and persona, and its mental functions of thinking, feeling, sensation, and intuition. It is doubtless a great nonmoral good to have these natural potentialities and capacities available to consciousness, functioning, and in relative balance with one another. When this is the case, one will have access to a greater range of psychological possibilities, actions, and adaptive capacities.

It is possible to bring either a full or a narrow self to, for example, the ethic of neighbor-love defined along the lines of mutuality or equal-regard as I suggested earlier. It is possible to bring an awareness of one's sexuality à la Freud to the task of neighbor-love, or it is possible to exclude it. If one is aware and accepting of one's own sexuality, then one is much more likely to accept and respect the sexual reality and sexual needs of another. Of course, this attitude of acceptance and respect would not in itself dictate the more directly moral task of determining just how one should relate sexually to the other person. Does this attitude of respect and acceptance of this natural psychobiological need mean that I should sleep with the other, caress the other, talk over our sexual needs frankly, attend an x-rated movie, masturbate, jog, release tension through telling dirty jokes, watch women at a sidewalk café, or silently smile at this aspect of myself in view of the frustration of not having a suitable partner with whom to express my sexual needs and tendencies? Knowing and accepting my own sexual needs and those of the other do not in and of themselves tell me which of the many possible ways of arranging my sexuality will be the morally right one in any particular situation. Accepting and respecting my sexuality will increase my own empathy with myself and my empathy with the sexual needs of the other. I can even admit that my sexuality is an important nonmoral good for both me and my neighbor and an inescapable part of life that needs to be appropriately (morally) organized. But this attitude of affirmation and acceptance does not in itself tell us how in more concrete ways our sexuality should be organized—between ourselves and our neighbor, between husband and wife, between parent and child, or between brother and sister. But to say that sexuality is a nonmoral or premoral good (as both Freud and the Judeo-Christian creation myths assert—the latter more forcefully than the former) and necessarily a part of life does not in itself tell us how morally to organize our sexuality. Yet much of the mental health profession (as well as both Freud and some of his interpreters) act as if it did. Of course, they were totally correct in their implicit and explicit claims that libidinal energy is an inextricable aspect of life and that recognition and acceptance of it is a morally relevant attitude. Hence, acceptance of our sexuality is part of the moral task, but not the whole of it. In fact, as part of the moral task, its relation to the whole is precisely the relation of the nonmoral (or premoral) to one's principle of obligation.

The same can be said of self-actualization and the archetypes. They can be seen as other types of nonmoral or premoral good relevant to but not exhaustive of the full task of moral discernment. If there is such a thing as an actualization tendency (as the humanistic psychologists insist), it can be understood as a premoral human good that humans have a tendency to pursue. But awareness of this need and respect for its claims would not in itself dictate how this need could be morally organized with other needs that I may have or with similar needs for self-actualization that others may have. Such also is the case with our tendencies and needs to actualize our archetypal inheritance. Jung believed awareness and consciousness of these archetypal needs were essential for mental health. Health itself is a good, but doubtless a nonmoral good since there are both moral and immoral ways to be healthy. Our need to actualize our archetypes into a balanced and integrated self does not in itself tell us how to relate morally our archetypal ground plans (our total selves) to the need for archetypal self-actualization on the part of the neighbor. One might resort to a variety of mental strategies to accomplish this, many of which I have reviewed in earlier chapters. I have advocated the principle of neighbor-love interpreted along the lines suggested by Janssens, Outka, Furnish, and Frankena. One could even rephrase the image of human fulfillment in Jungian psychology in ways consistent with its dictates. The goal of the individuation process would not be to realize the archetypal ground plan into a consciously balanced self. *Rather, the goal of individuation would be to actualize into a consciously balanced self the uniqueness of our archetypal needs but to do so in such a way as justly and mutually to coordinate this actualization with the archetypal needs of the neighbor.* Sacrifice, according to this view, would take on a rather different meaning than that assigned by Jung. Rather than being the sacrifice of the interests and needs of the conscious ego in the name of the deeper self-realization of the uniqueness of our unconscious archetypes, sacrifice would be the just and equal balancing of the archetypal needs of the self with the archetypal needs of the other. Furthermore, some situations of extreme conflict, if we are to follow Janssens's interpretation of agape, would entail the further management of my archetypal needs in such a way as to offer continued openness to the possibility of and actual work toward restoring a situation of mutuality between the self and the neighbor, which finally would include, of course, all potential neighbors as well.

Evil and Jung's Metaphors of Ultimacy

On the surface of Jung's psychology, one might easily come to believe there is a horrible contradiction that runs straight down the middle of it. This manifests itself in the implicit conflict between Jung's theory of obligation and his metaphors of ultimacy; on the one hand Jung proffers a rather simple nonhedonistic ethical egoism as an image of human fulfillment, and on the other he assumes a kind of ontological dualism that subscribes both good and evil, in the moral sense of these words, to the essential character of God and human beings. The apparent contradiction in this is clear if one compares it to the philosophical monism and implicit sense of harmony that we found in Maslow, Rogers, and Perls. These psychologists, I argued, could will that individuals act in such a way as to actualize themselves first because they held a secret metaphysical belief that all potentialities cohere and are finally sublimely harmonious with one another. Hence, for the humanistic psychologists, all potentialities are good and, it seems, morally good at that since their authentic expression cannot lead to conflict.

But Jung, on the surface of things, holds a different vision. In his concept of the shadow and his understanding of evil, Jung sometimes seems to hold a psychological dualism (which must finally be called an ontological dualism) that sees both human nature and God as split between good and evil possibilities. And indeed the words *good* and *evil,* in these contexts, seem to be used here in a specifically moral sense. Hence, at first glance, Jung appears not to enjoy the escape valve unwittingly yet quite obviously used by Maslow, Rogers, and Perls. He seems to be telling us that our first moral obligation is to realize, albeit in a balanced way, our archetypal potentials while at the same time telling us that our archetypal potentials (as well as the potentials of God) are split down the center between good and evil possibilities. Hence, Jung appears to be bringing together a nonhedonistic ethical egoism as a theory of obligation with metaphors of ultimacy that are dualistic. The result is confusion. If our potentialities are really mixed between the morally good and evil, then self-realization is bound to mean the actualization of evil potentialities that will be directly harmful to the neighbor and possibly to myself as well. Jung's rhetoric about the individuation process necessitating moral responsibility, sacrifice, and heroic ethical struggle does not help because, as we have seen, this language simply means that we are to relinquish the less significant egoist needs of our conscious egos and personas in the name of a deeper and more fundamental "sacred egoism" entailed in the realization of our archetypal needs. Nor does it help to say that our archetypal needs are collective and identical to the needs of all human beings. This only tells us that all human beings have the same fundamental human needs, but it does not preclude the possibility that humans can conflict with one another in an effort to realize these identical needs. Therefore, the appearance of holding together under a single edifice a dualism between moral good and evil and what must be acknowledged to be a clear-cut philosophical ethical egoism is strange indeed.

But all of this apparent contradiction may be on the surface of Jung's psychology. At a deeper level, Jung's work may entail a vision of reality undergirded by some of the same metaphors of harmony and complementarity invoked by the humanistic psychologists. It may be that Jung can counsel both his patients and the wider public to strive for a balance of archetypal needs because he believes that in the end all such needs are complementary both within and outside of the individual self. If this is the case, then his rhetoric about the dualism of good and evil in the human self may be analogous to the rhetoric of his moral language; that is, he uses traditional words in such novel contexts that we lose track of what he is actually saying. What appears to be a psychological and ontological dualism between good and evil becomes, then, a far more contextual and relative matter. Evil becomes nothing more than a fundamental human potentiality—in fact, a nonmoral or premoral good—that is deemed evil because for some reason it is in contradiction to the dominant cultural values that make up the individual and collective superegos of a particular society.

In *The Archetypes of the Collective Unconscious* Jung defines the shadow as a personification of "everything that the subject refuses to acknowledge about himself and yet is always thrusting itself upon him directly or indirectly."[76] Elsewhere he writes that the shadow is the "'negative' side of the personality, the sum of all those unpleasant qualities we like to hide, together with the insufficiently developed functions and the contents of the personal unconscious."[77] But by "unpleasant qualities," Jung appears not to be speaking about our personal unconscious alone; he is also referring to certain natural phylogenetically inherited archetypal tendencies that he wants to call evil. In addition, he seems to be saying that these negative qualities come out of our archetypal heritage. In *Aion* (1951) he writes that the shadow is that "hidden, repressed, for the most part inferior and guilt-laden personality whose ultimate ramifications reach back into the realm of our animal ancestors and so compromise the whole historical aspect of the unconscious."[78] The shadow has a personal dimension to it; it is a collection of personal experiences that have been repressed and relegated to the unconscious. But it also has an archetypal foundation to it as well, and this more archetypal source is what leads Jung to say that evil is a constituent or substantive part of the psyche as well as a constituent part of our psychological representation of the divine.

It is difficult to tell, however, whether Jung is speaking here about evil and good in an absolute or a relative sense. Are these particular phylogenetically grounded capacities for anger, aggression, or competition evil in themselves in Jung's view, or are they evil in some more relative sense? By this I mean are these potentialities evil because their destructive aim is totally gratuitous (hence nonrelative and substantive)? Or are these tendencies relatively evil in the sense of being overdetermined, or in the sense of being contrary to some dominant personal or cultural value, or in the sense of being inappropriately related to other important values? If these potentialities are relative, then Jung does not have a dualism in the moral sense at all. There may indeed be dichotomies in the personality such as the celebrated archetypes of the mother and the father or the anima and the animus. But these would in no way be moral dualisms or dichotomies for which the designations of good and evil would be appropriate. There may be polarities, dualisms, and dichotomies in the human psyche, but they may not be moral dualisms and polarities. But again, Jung may have been trying to convince us that there are. It is difficult to tell what he was trying to say. And it is difficult to evaluate the correctness of his arguments, as is always the case when it is hard to determine what is being said.

Time and again it sounds as if Jung is talking about evil in the more absolute sense of the term. This appears mostly clearly in his well-known attack on the doctrine of *privatio boni* (privation of the good) that early medieval Christian philosophy, especially Augustine, used to account for the nature of evil. Jung understood this doctrine to mean that evil did not really exist and that everything a person does, feels, or thinks is really fundamentally good. Jung, interestingly enough, first got this interpretation of the doctrine of *privatio boni* from one of his patients who tried to excuse his erratic and immoral behavior by invoking this doctrine. Jung was aghast at this, but unfortunately from then on he seemed to make his patient's rather questionable interpretation of the doctrine his own.[79] In the essay "A Psychological Approach to the Dogma of the Trinity" (1948) he says that the theory *privatio boni* "robs evil of absolute existence and makes it a shadow that has only relative existence dependent upon light."[80] And then Jung continued,

> But, as psychological experience shows, "good" and "evil" are opposite poles of a moral judgment which, as such, originates in man. A judgment can be made about a thing only if its opposite is equally real and possible. The opposite of a seeming evil can only be a seeming good, and an evil that lacks substance can only be contrasted with a good that is equally non-substantive. . . . There is no getting round the fact that if you allow substantiality to good, you must also allow it to evil.[81]

Of course, in ways that Jung does not understand, the distinctions he is discussing are not based on empirical psychological observations, but are basically logical and methodological distinctions fundamental to the discipline of moral philosophy, a point I will clarify below.

It is precisely this kind of experience that gave rise to the conviction in Jung that the Christian doctrine of the trinity needs to be revised and enlarged. Jung wanted to change the trinity to a quaternity. In addition to the Father, Son, and Holy Spirit, Jung wanted to include the devil or Satan in our psychological representation of the godhead. After insisting that evil has a substantive reality, Jung retreats and tells us that whatever the metaphysical position of evil and the devil, "in psychological reality evil is an effective, not to say menacing, limitation of goodness, so that it is no exaggeration to assume that in this world good and evil more or less balance each other, like day and night."[82] In his *Answer to Job* (1952) Jung can write that Yahweh (God) "is total justice, and also its total opposite,"[83] is "suspicious" and "jealous of man,"[84] is "dangerous" and needs propitiation,[85] and is a divine being who "fills us with evil as well as with good."[86] All of these statements seem to argue for the fact that Jung, both early and late in his writings, thought that on strictly psychological grounds he could argue for the substantive reality of evil both in the experience of humans and in the appropriate representation of the divine. This is what I am calling Jung's absolute view of evil. It suggests a Zoroastrian, Manichaean, or gnostic view of life. But Jung's dualism appears to exceed the dualism often associated with these movements, for Jung speaks not of two separate principles, or of good gods and evil gods, or of good gods and evil demiurges, but rather of both good and evil right at the heart of a single god.

Therefore, one might think that in Jung one can find an entirely new and different deep metaphor from what can be found in Freud, the humanistic psychologists, or Skinner. Whereas metaphors of mechanism, or, later, life and death abound in Freud, or harmony and complementarity in the humanistic psychologists, or natural selection in Skinner, in Jung it might seem that we have a completely different model. It might indeed appear to be a dualism, a psycho-metaphysics of opposites within a single god. But what is difficult to discern is precisely what Jung's attitude is toward this dualism. Is this coincidence of opposites complementary and supportive? Are the two sides mutually reinforcing, balancing, and corrective to one another? Or are they in genuine opposition to each other as are Freud's eros and thanatos? The answer to this last question is certainly that Jung's dualism is not like Freud's. For Freud eros and thanatos truly oppose one another so that when eros is strong the death instinct is, for a while, submerged or inactive. And it is certainly not the case that life and death somehow balance or complement each other in the way that Jung seems to suggest for his archetypes.

There is much in Jung's writings to suggest that his doctrine of evil is more relative and his dualism more complementary than some of his extreme statements about human and divine perversity might indicate. In several places Jung represents the shadow and evil as quite a relative affair, and this in spite of the fact that the shadow itself has archetypal foundations. In his essay "Psychology and Religion" (1940) Jung says:

> If the repressed tendencies, the shadow as I call them, were obviously evil, there would be no problem whatever. But the shadow is merely somewhat inferior, primitive, unadapted, and awkward; not wholly bad. It even contains childish or primitive qualities which would in a way vitalize our existence, but—convention forbids! The educated public, flower of our present civilization, has detached itself from its roots, and is about to lose its connection with the earth as well.[87]

If we are to take Jung seriously here, then evil becomes an entirely different matter than it seems from those passages where he appears to be representing it in substantive terms. Here Jung is saying that not just part but all of the shadow, both its personal and collective archetypal dimensions, is not evil or wholly bad, but is deemed to be such because it is inferior, primitive, or unadaptive with reference to the dominant styles and values of a particular cultural situation. If this is what Jung means, then that which he might call evil is really not *substantially* evil—evil in and of itself—but evil from the perspective of some particular cultural or moral position. In fact, what from one interpretive perspective may be called evil might, from another, have qualities that could "vitalize our human existence." This is another way of saying that some adaptive or archetypal capacity that from one point of view may appear evil might, in another context and from another point of view, appear vitalizing and renewing. This is precisely, I might add, what his concept of individuation seems to suggest. But if this is true, then much of Jung's rhetoric about evil seems excessive, and in the end he holds a position on the nature of evil not that much different from what actually was meant to be the case in the doctrine of *privatio boni*.

Jung as much as admits the relativity and unsubstantiality of evil in his *Memories, Dreams, Reflections*. Here he tells us that we must beware of thinking of good and evil "as absolute opposites." Recognizing the reality of evil seems to "relativize the good, and the evil likewise, converting both into halves of a paradoxical whole."[88] Further, Jung takes the position of the relativity of evil when he speaks about the amorality of God. Above, we saw instances when Jung seemed to say that God, or our psychic representation of God, contains both good and evil. But in *Answer to Job* he says that God's condition "can only be described as amoral."[89] Later in the same text, he assigns these words to the very mouth of God. "This is I, the creator of all the ungovernable, ruthless forces of Nature, which are not subject to any ethical laws. I, too, am an amoral force of Nature, a purely phenomenal personality that cannot see its own back."[90] But of course, if God is amoral then it is not quite accurate to call God either good or evil. To call God amoral is to say that there is a kind of brutishness to God and that as such God has no intentions of a kind that one could rightly call either moral or immoral, good or evil in the moral sense of these terms. And finally, when Jung is saying that Christianity's tendency to deny evil simply leads to evil's breaking out time and again in unconscious ways, he simultaneously denies that either humans or God have a natural tendency for evil. "A sheer will for destruction," he tells us, "is not to be expected. . . . In all my experience I have never observed anything like it, except in cases of severe psychoses and criminal insanity."[91] This is to say, in effect, that it is only when natural inclinations, in either God or man, are distorted do we find anything like a drive for sheer destructiveness and evil. This final cleansing by Jung of both God and the human psyche of any ontological tendencies toward evil may be evidence that, in the end, Jung actually followed the classical Judeo-Christian view of both the divine and the human more than he realized. If this is the case, Jung may have interpreted his psychological data more in light of his unconscious hermeneutics of the Jewish and Christian classics than he interpreted these classics in light of his psychology.

In his interpretation of Jung, Stevens takes much the same stance on the nature of evil. Evil for him seems to be more relative than substantive. Stevens, when he discusses evil and the shadow, says much that Christians call evil is really "morally neutral."[92] But furthermore, much that particular cultures call evil is really in some way good. For instance, from the perspective of ethology, human aggression plays a positive function in human adaptation.[93] What makes aggression good or bad is not the aggression itself but the "attitude to these fundamental a priori aspects of our nature—how we live them and how we mediate them to the group."[94] So once again, there does not so much seem to be absolute evil in human beings (and in God) as there does positive adaptive potentials that are either somehow misused and distorted or inappropriately repressed and then, inevitably, projected outward onto people and events in the external social world.

This point—that unless people are aware of their shadow they will project the evil they fear in themselves to events in the social world beyond—is an important truth to acknowledge. And there is little doubt that this is the central contribution Jung is trying to make to the reduction of strife in human affairs. Jung is trying to get us to look inward, become introspective, and acknowledge that genuine evil lurks within. The use of introspection to discern one's own evil—a central part of the Christian and Jewish concern with confession (in ways that Jung sometimes seems to forget), is absolutely central and one of the great themes of both psychoanalysis and analytic psychology. But we can argue that humans have a capacity for genuine evil and that this capacity, often buried in our shadow, needs to be confronted and acknowledged without, at the same time, going so far, as Jung sometimes did, as to make evil in humans an absolute, substantial, and autonomous reality. We can present good arguments to support the contention that humans have the capacity for genuine evil without becoming excessive and saying that they are psychologically and ontologically within the grips of a moral dualism of a substantive and even ontological kind.

Jung and Nonmoral Goods

Jung's confused argument is due to a lack of philosophical clarity about the different types of good and evil that exist in this world. He fails to make the simple yet crucial distinction between moral and nonmoral (or premoral) goods and evil. We have discussed this distinction above, but let me say more by way of illustration. We certainly use the words *good* and *bad* in nonmoral or premoral senses. If I say that the weather last Sunday was good, I am not saying that it was morally good. I am not saying that nature willed good intentions toward me and my family. I am saying that the sun shined for most of the day, that it rained gently and warmly for thirty minutes in the late afternoon, and that the temperature was in the seventies. I am simply saying that on that day I experienced nature as providing a great deal of the nonmoral good things in life that are important for human existence. The same would be true if I said that on Sunday the weather was bad. I would simply be saying that it rained all day, that it was cold and chilling, and that I could not play tennis that day. But I would not be saying that the weather was evil or bad in the moral sense of these words. I would not be saying that it willed bad intentions toward me.

Jung might be able to argue his position in a philosophically more acceptable way if he kept the distinction between the moral and the nonmoral good firmly in mind. He could then argue that we have many archetypal and adaptive possibilities in human life. Following his more relative, and less substantive, view of evil, then

Jung would simply be saying that human beings possess a wide range of nonmoral archetypal and adaptive capacities. Some of these capacities express themselves dichotomously. On the whole, these archetypal adaptive capacities are nonmoral or premoral goods in that they broaden our range of adaptive responses to the challenges of life and, furthermore, are so arranged that they balance and compensate one another. Hence, our father and mother, child and adult, anima and animus archetypes are all nonmoral goods that present potentials for living that are important at different times and points in the human life cycle. But as such, they are neither moral nor immoral. Whether any of the archetypes are moral depends upon the attitudes and organizations (the rules) by which we pattern their expression. The same can be said about our anger, aggression, and libidinal sexuality. None of these is evil in itself. In fact, as Stevens pointed out, all of these capacities are adaptively relevant and therefore good in this nonmoral sense. But it does not mean that they are always expressed in such a way as to be morally good. For questions of moral good have to do with the way nonmoral goods, many of which can be conflicting or at least in tension, are patterned in the interaction of persons and groups.

With this fundamental distinction in mind, which is indeed quite consistent with his more relative view of evil, Jung is seen to be far closer than he realized to what is actually meant by the idea of *privatio boni* and what it intended to communicate about the classic dimensions of the Jewish and Christian doctrines of creation. H. L. Philp in *Jung and the Problem of Evil* (1958) chides Jung for accepting his wayward patient's definition of the doctrine. In a style of direct address to Jung, Philp wonders "if your interpretation of his doctrine is not in fact similar to that of your patient . . . , because . . . whatever the doctrine may mean it neither destroys or minimizes the reality of evil."[95] He then continues,

> The *privatio boni* stresses that evil is not a thing in itself but a condition of the thing, and it consists in the privation of the good which by nature that thing should have. Thus deafness implies that a man has been deprived of the particular gift of hearing. It is possible of course for most theological and philosophical terms to be misinterpreted, but that is no argument for not attempting a careful definition.[96]

The doctrine of *privatio boni* does not argue that there is no such thing as evil; it just argues that it is not a thing-in-itself—a substantive and absolute reality independent of human will and attitudes.

Later in his argument, Philp makes virtually the same point that I have made using the distinction between moral and nonmoral good. Philp rightly points out that Jung believes that he is using the word *good* in the same sense as it is used in the doctrine of *privatio boni,* but as a matter of fact he is not. Philp correctly accuses Jung of using *good* "in a moralistic sense—a Protestant approach perhaps as opposed to the Catholic and Eastern Orthodox one."[97] But the concept of good in the idea of *privatio boni* means "fulfilling its purpose or function perfectly."[98] Or, to put it in the terms I have been using, the good of the concept of *privatio boni* has to do with the nonmoral or premoral good rather than the more specifically moral good.

Had Jung rightly understood the idea of *privatio boni*, he might not have objected so strenuously to it. Furthermore, he would have realized that his own view of evil, when stated in its more relative form, was actually quite close to the proper meaning of this classical philosophical attempt to capture the rational meaning of the Jewish and Christian doctrines of creation. Our archetypal potentialities, when viewed from this angle, would be seen as good in this specifically nonmoral sense of the term. They constitute adaptive potentials that have their proper function somewhere and at some time in the total life process. But whether these archetypal potentials are morally good or evil is strictly a matter that pertains to how they are expressed and how they relate to other nonmoral goods (some of an archetypal nature) both within and outside the human psyche.

Creation and Evil

In those moments when he feels impelled to speak of evil in absolute and substantive terms, Jung ends up moralizing nature, especially the natural inclinations of humans. Basic instinctual and archetypal inclinations become endowed with moral intentions. When this moralizing of human nature is projected into our psychic representations of the divine, then God's life is similarly divided into good and evil intentions. The result is that with regard to the divine, Jung, at least part of the time, resurrects a variation of the tragic vision of the wicked and indifferent god. This view is one of several classic ways of handling the problem of evil. Paul Ricoeur in *The Symbolism of Evil* (1967) distinguishes the tragic myth of evil from other options such as the myth of chaos, the myth of the exiled soul, and the Adamic myth. In the tragic myth of evil (what Ricoeur calls the myth of the wicked god) the initiative producing fault and evil in humans "is traced back into the divine and . . . works through the weakness of man and appears as divine possession."[99] In its more primitive versions, "the principle of evil is as primordial as the principle of good."[100] Hence, in the tragic view, evil enters the world through an evil and indifferent god. Humans in their own free decisions and actions are not responsible for sin. Rather they are blind and ignorant and do not understand how their actions lead to the inevitable evil and destruction that follows from these acts. They are simply pawns of superior yet insensitive powers that function beyond their consciousness.

The view of evil found in the myth of tragedy can be distinguished from the myth of chaos. In the myth of chaos, perhaps best represented by the Sumero-Akkadian myth, the Enuma Elish, the creation of the world is coincidental with the defeat of an evil god and the ascendancy of a god of goodness and order. Tiamat, the ruthless and devouring mother, is defeated by the good and ordering Marduk. Evil is the more primordial and good a later development.[101]

The tragic view of evil is also different from the view found in the myth of the exiled soul. In this myth, of which historians have found only fragments but which was immensely influential on the history of Western philosophy, the souls of humans are exiled for some unknown offense from paradise and confined in the body as if flesh itself were a prison and an expiation.[102] This led to the gradual distinction between body and soul and the association of body and the passions with evil itself. This is the crux of the Orphic myth. In a later, more philosophically elaborate version of the myth probably associated with the neo-Platonists, the infant Dionysos was assassinated, boiled, and devoured by the cruel and heartless Titans. Zeus, as punishment, obliterated them with lightning and their ashes became the present race of humans. This is the reason why humans today participate in both the evil of the Titans and the divine nature of Dionysos.[103] This, furthermore, is the reason why the Dionysian soul hungers for release from the evil Titanic body.

It is clear that the more absolute form of Jung's understanding of evil is far closer to the myth of tragedy than either the myth of chaos or the myth of the exiled soul. Jung tells us that God is a dualism of evil and good and assigns no primordiality to one or the other. In the myth of chaos, evil precedes good and good establishes itself by vanquishing evil. And Jung's myth is certainly different from the Orphic myth of the exiled soul. Clearly there is no separation of body and soul in Jung and, even more clearly, no devaluation of consciousness and rationality as good and the body as evil.

But at the same time, his more absolute view of evil is different from the Adamic myth that finally became dominant in normative Hebrew and Christian literature. The Adamic myth sees both God and creation as good. God, this tradition affirms, is good in both the moral and nonmoral senses of the word. God is the source of all beauty as well as of all the world's nonmoral richness that meets life's needs and gives it joy, pleasure, warmth, and happiness. This is represented in the metaphor of God as creator and the evaluation that God's creative activity is good. But God is also called good in the more strictly moral sense of the word. God is just and righteous, does not have favorites, and keeps the covenants and agreements into which God enters. Creation is good, at least in this nonmoral sense, and humans as a part of creation have a capacity to be good in the more specifically moral sense. Moral evil (injustice, war, deception, exploitation) comes into the world through the misuse of human freedom. The fall, as Ricoeur points out, is a "deviation," a missing of the moral mark through a misuse of the will and freedom. The development of the Adamic myth comes out of the Jewish attitude of confession and penitence, a point that Jung often overlooks. The point of the Adamic myth is to confess "a 'beginning' of evil distinct from the 'beginning' of creation, to posit an event by which sin entered into the world and, by sin, death. The myth of the fall is thus the myth of the first appearance of evil in a creation already completed and good."[104] This is clearly not the direction that Jung wishes to go in his more absolute version of evil, although it may be closer to his implicit view. It seems to me that most of the mental health movement in the modern world implicitly functions out of a secularized form of the Adamic myth with its confession of the goodness of the created world as well as our fundamental natural impulses. This, I believe, includes Jung in his more clinical and less speculative moments. Self-acceptance as a presupposition to self-cohesion and self-esteem almost everywhere in the contemporary literature of mental health means acceptance of our primordial impulses as having their natural and beneficent place in human life. Hence, they are good in that nonmoral or pre-moral sense and form a ground upon which to build and shape as we try to fashion their appropriate moral expression.

But the Adamic myth can become too narrowly moral, and Jung, in his rather indirect and diffuse way, may have been sensitive to this possibility. The ethicization of the Adamic myth is addressed in the classic book of Job, an ancient Hebrew text that Jung addressed in the *Answer to Job* written in the later years of his life. Jung thought, as we have seen, that the biblical book demonstrated the twofold nature of God as both morally good and morally evil. He believed that it showed Job, a morally perfect and faithful devotee of Yahweh, as morally superior to Yahweh. It reveals God or Yahweh as entering into a devious pact with his evil son Satan to test Job's faithfulness amidst untold catastrophes that Yahweh permits Satan to visit upon Job's family, wealth, and health.[105] Jung's message, throughout his strange book, is that humans must become conscious of their own shadows, their own capacity for evil, and their own capacity for destructiveness. In giving this interpre-tation to the book of Job, Jung is placing upon it a reading shaped by that part of his thinking dominated by the myth of tragedy that sees God as wicked and humans as fatefully programmed and basically ignorant of what they are doing.

But Jung largely misses the mark about the true meaning of the book of Job. As Ricoeur points out, it is indeed a text that protests against the excessive moraliza-tion of faith in the Adamic myth. In locating evil in the misuse of freedom by humans and in confessing belief in the essential goodness of both creation and God, aspects of prophetic and post-prophetic Hebrew thought began to make an exact equation between the suffering and evil that persons experience and the depth of their sin. This rendered God as a God of retribution who preserved an unbending and exact relation between sin and punishment. The ethical and anthropological view of evil had won out but at great cost to the self-esteem of all innocent sufferers.

Job, who is depicted as morally perfect and pious in all things, becomes the test in an effort to alter or at least mitigate the more oppressive consequences of the vic-tory of the ethical view of evil in the Adamic myth. Job insists upon his innocence. His friends Zophar, Bildad, and Eliphaz, who keep accusing him of hidden sins and self-deluding pretentiousness, are in effect anxiously defending the orthodox view of an exact relation between sin and evil. Rather than showing that God has a twofold nature of goodness and evil, as Jung so insistently argues, the book tries to break the tenacity of the ethicization of the Adamic myth. It tries to soften the mechanical relation between sin and evil. The sinful do not, indeed, always suffer evil. And the morally good are not always exempt—sometimes they suffer as well.

But indirectly, Jung is correct in sensing that the book of Job introduces an ele-ment of the tragic myth into the Adamic myth. But this is done not by showing

Yahweh as evil; both the pact with Satan and Job's own moral perfection are rhetorical devices designed to stage the issue to be debated by Job, his friends, and finally God. Rather, the tragic myth, or parts of it, is introduced through the idea of the mystery of God, the incomprehensibility of God's intention, and the unmerited gift of God's creation. After repudiating the orthodoxy of Job's comforters, Yahweh turns to chide Job himself. In his own way Job, in continuing to insist upon his innocence, is trapped within the hyperethical and retributive view of the Adamic myth. In asking Job, "Where were you when I laid the foundation of the earth?" (Job 38:4) and in pointing to the grandeurs of his creation (the Behemoth, the Leviathan, the hippopotamus), the author of Job is pointing to the mystery of God's creation as gift that means certain aspects of evil must be accepted as part of larger schemes that humans cannot comprehend fully and must accept in faith. As Ricoeur tells us, through these symbols of the magnificence of creation, Yahweh gives Job to "understand that all is order, measure, and beauty—inscrutable order, measure beyond measure, terrible beauty. A way is marked out between agnosticism and the penal view of history and life—the way of unverifiable faith."[106] Reinhold Niebuhr says much the same thing when he writes, "All Biblical theism contains the suggestion that God's will and wisdom must be able to transcend any human interpretation of its justice and meaning, or it would be less than the center of that inclusive meaning which alone can comprehend the seeming chaos of existence into a total harmony."[107] Ricoeur and Niebuhr agree in seeing the book of Job as qualifying the extensive ethical and retributive view of evil to be found in the Adamic myth. It introduces a tragic element that acknowledges the evil that is sometimes already there and to which our own freedom sometimes yields. It evokes sympathy for those who innocently suffer. And it invokes in the faithful a new respect for the unfathomable richness, mystery, and incomprehensibility of God's intentions in creation. It does all of this without giving up the Jewish confession in the goodness of God and creation and the need for confession and repentance (that is, confession of one's shadow and moral wrestling with it) on the part of humans.

Hence, both the book of Job and the psychology of Carl Gustav Jung have as their goal the overcoming of an excessively ethical view of religion by incorporating dimensions of the myth of tragedy. But Jung's resurrection of this myth is unstable and self-contradictory. His misunderstanding of the doctrine of *privatio boni* and his widespread tendency to speak of the adaptive relevance, some time or other, of all the archetypal potentials of humans strongly suggest that a vision of the goodness and harmony of creation is the deeper impulse in his thought. So he too, like the humanistic psychologists, can counsel a form of ethical egoism because of an implicit faith that all individuals' unique archetypal programs are basically compatible. Hence, the principle of selectivity for the actualization of archetypal potentials is fundamentally ethical egoist. This is true with the additional proviso that the task of life for Jung is not to actualize all our archetypal potentials but as much as is compatible with our own *unique* archetypal constellation—our own unique archetypal daemon.

But Jung failed to understand the deeper levels of anxiety and inordinate self-concern and how these facts of human nature invalidate all uncomplicated harmonistic metaphysics and the philosophical ethical egoisms that follow from them. Life and the world have their natural harmonies, but our own anxieties and self-concern inject tension and conflict into life in ways that Jung did not admit fully. The dichotomies and tensions of our archetypal heritage are nonmoral or premoral goods that are relevant for adaptive purposes and easily submit to a valuation about the goodness of the created order consistent with the sensibilities of the Western religious experience. But when the reality of inordinate human self-concern is finally recognized and confessed, from then on the need for other deep metaphors—metaphors pointing to moral governance and possibilities of redemption—tend to emerge. But in the thought of Jung, both the moral selectivity of the individuation process and the redemption of the transcendent function give rise to an image of self-fulfillment that does not go beyond the ethical-egoist actualization of one's own unique potentials.

Generativity and Care
in Erikson and Kohut

In this chapter, I will continue my commentary on the religious and moral horizon of the modern psychologies by discussing some issues common to Erik Erikson and Heinz Kohut. Both analysts have been very influential upon contemporary religious thought and for very similar reasons. I want to bring them into a conversation about the deep metaphors and principles of obligation that may be implicit in their psychologies. Then I will engage them in a fundamental conversation with the deep metaphors and principles of obligation of the Christian tradition.

Today I would suggest that Erikson's dialectical understanding of the relation of the high and low in human maturity is very parallel to Ricoeur's understanding of the dialectical relation between the high in human culture—our religious and cultural classics—and what he called the archaeology of our human motivations. In my book *Generative Man* (1973) I argued that Erikson had a "dialectically progressive" view of human nature. By this rather clumsy phrase,

> we only intend to suggest the rather simple idea that for Erikson the high in man must not exclude the low, just as the civilized must not exclude the primitive, the mature become dissociated from the infantile, or man's progressive advance become estranged from his more regressive renewals. The high and the low remain together for Erikson in a way that is not the case with our other psychoanalytic ethicists. This is the fruit of his *epigenetic principle.* According to this principle, all advances to the higher and later stages of development—toward independence, responsibility, maturity—must include and carry forward, while restating, a lower level of development. Without the early and the low, in both ontogenetic and phylogenetic development, the late and the high in human development is not truly better. Nor is it truly stronger. Unless the high in man somehow includes and restates the lower, the high is weak, anemic, and unstable.[1]

Generative Man was a comparative analysis of the ethical visions of four psychoanalytic writers—Philip Rieff, Norman O. Brown, Erich Fromm, and Erik Erikson. It was an essay in cultural analysis and did not become involved directly in theological issues. In fact, it bracketed all theological issues. Even though it is clear that I believed that Erikson, of the four writers I reviewed, had the psychologically and morally superior view of human nature, I did not argue that case on specifically theological grounds. Although even then I had some identity as a theologian, I only hinted that some day Erikson's concept of "generative man" (which I would now call the "generative human") should be brought into contact with other great historical prototypes of the good person. At the conclusion of the book I wrote,

> Generative man, as portrayed in these pages, has yet to confront in mature dialogue the great historical prototypes, in both the East and the West. Most specifically, I have not answered the question, posed at the beginning of this study, as to the final relationship between generative man and the great Christian image of man which has fed, in one way or another, most of the historical prototypes of the Western world. I have only answered what I believe to be the central testimony of the growing, most clinically responsible part of the psychoanalytic tradition.[2]

In this chapter, I intend to take a step toward this confrontation between the generative human and the Christian image of human fulfillment. I also intend to do this in ways that will include in the discussion some of the themes pertaining to generativity in the remarkably powerful psychology of the self of Heinz Kohut.

Erikson and Kohut are like the other clinically oriented psychologists studied in this book; they have their deep metaphors and their implicit general principles of obligation as well as their more properly psychological theories about central human tendencies and needs. And it may well be that it is precisely the horizon of their psychologies—the periphery that does indeed lapse over into visions about the way things are or into vague concepts of moral obligation—that has made these psychologies so attractive, particularly to people fed by the Judeo-Christian tradition. So my task in this chapter will be the same as it has been before, that is, to distinguish the more genuinely psychological dimensions of their thought from their fringe of metaphors of ultimacy and principles of obligation and, finally, to advance some critical evaluation of these normative dimensions of their systems. I will concentrate primarily on Erikson, but, because of his growing prominence and importance, I will discuss Kohut as well.

For different reasons, neither Freud, Skinner, Jung, nor the humanistic psychologists believed in an ethic of genuine mutuality. On the other hand, Erikson and Kohut do write psychologies imbued with an ethic of mutuality. None of these psychologists, including Erikson and Kohut, arrives at his ethical views on strictly psychological grounds. But it is true that their various psychological commitments do suggest limitations or inclinations to human nature that seem to make certain ethics either unworkable or unnecessary. Hence, Freud thought that an ethic of sacrificial love was impossible and stated his doctrine of mutuality so cautiously that it amounted to little more than an ethic of reciprocal advantage. Jung and the humanistic psychologists thought that neither an ethic of mutuality nor one of self-sacrifice is necessary; the fundamental harmonies of life are thought to be such that an ethic of self-actualization is itself sufficient to guarantee the good life.

That Kohut and Erikson have a better implicit ethic than Freud, Skinner, Jung, or the humanistic psychologies—and I will argue that they do—is only partially due to the kind of psychologies that they respectively developed. Although there is an indeterminate relation between types of psychologies and theories of obligation, Kohut and Erikson have the virtue of having intuited a creative relation between them—one that goes far in suggesting the outlines of a more intentional critical psychology of the kind necessary to guide therapy and establish the links between the arts of healing and the everyday world that the ill hope someday to inhabit again.

Both Erikson and Kohut, to varying degrees, gravitate toward an ethic of equal-regard or mutuality. But Erikson goes even farther and incorporates within his ethic of mutuality an appreciation for the role of nonviolent love or self-sacrifice as a transitional moment on the way to the restoration of mutuality. Insofar as he does this, he comes close to an ethics of *caritas* typical of that developed by Janssens and Outka. Both Erikson and Kohut associated health with an ethic of generative mutuality and care between the various actors—young and old, husband and wife, parent and child—in the human life cycle. Although depending to a considerable degree on metaphors of harmony not unlike those that animate the psychological culture of joy found in Jung and humanistic psychologies, both Erikson and Kohut understand the disintegrating and unharmonizing effects of anxiety in ways that the culture of joy does not. Furthermore, Erikson especially understands how anxiety is a part of the human experience of the contingencies of life and an inevitable counterpart to our human freedom. But because the harmonies of life can be flawed by anxiety and freedom, for Erikson the mutualities that guide life must partially be built on the cogwheeling of their natural affections among people but finally completed by willed fidelities (covenants) and intended acts of care.

Ego Psychology and the Psychology of the Self

We must establish the commonalities and differences that exist between Erikson and Kohut before we can assess how they can both be seen as expressions of what I have called the culture of care. Erikson has been seen as a part of the largely American tradition of psychoanalytic ego psychology. Kohut is the founder of and primary developer of a recent strand within psychoanalysis called the psychology of the self. There are great similarities and much overlap between these two traditions, but there are also important differences.

The American tradition of ego psychology is associated with such names as Heinz Hartmann, David Rapaport, Robert White, and Erikson himself. It is frequently referred to as an American stream of psychoanalytic thinking primarily because it was developed in the United States and became popular on these shores. Actually, many of its developers—Hartmann, Rapaport, Erikson, and Anna Freud before them—were first Europeans. Their central shared interest was the study of the defensive, motivational, and adaptive functions of the central organizing capacities of the personality called the ego. Psychoanalysis under the guidance of Freud had largely been seen as the clinical study of the unconscious and the vicissitudes of the id. While retaining this concern, ego psychology has both studied and found an increasingly prominent role for the agency of the ego.

Hartmann was the central figure in psychoanalytic ego psychology. His *Ego Psychology and the Problem of Adaptation* (1939) is considered the classic text. Here he pictures the ego as relatively more independent from the id and more crucial to the processes of adaptation than did Freud. But in the essays collected for a later volume, *Essays on Ego Psychology* (1964), he made some highly important although not well-developed remarks about a fourth agency of the personality—in addition to the ego, superego, and id—which he variously called the self, self-image, or self-representation. It is this concept that constitutes the bridge between Erikson's brand of ego psychology and Kohut's psychology of the self. In an effort to clarify the meaning of narcissism, Hartmann suggests that we think of it as a matter of the libido cathecting the self or self-representation rather than cathecting the ego, as Freud suggested in his early metapsychological papers.[3] This small but vital observation effectively introduced for the first time the concept of the self into psychoanalytic theory.

Erikson's key concept of identity has much in common with Hartmann's theory of self-representation. In fact, Erikson admits that identity has much in common with "what has been called the self by a variety of workers, be it in the form of a self-concept (Mead), a self-system (Sullivan), or in that of fluctuating self-experience . . . (Schilder, Federn)."[4] But within psychoanalytic ego psychology he credits Heinz Hartmann "above all" with introducing the idea of "self-representation" to account for the very problem in the theory of narcissism that I alluded to above.[5] In this discussion, and in several others, Erikson draws a straight line of influence between his theory of identity and Hartmann's concept of self-representation.

Kohut is similarly indebted to Hartmann. In the preface to his major work *Analysis of the Self* (1971) Kohut lists Hartmann's "deceptively simple but pioneering" conceptual "separation of the self from the ego" as a major stimulus to his own theory of the self.[6] Hence, both Erikson and Kohut correctly can be seen as elaborating in their own ways Hartmann's beginning insights into a fourth agency of the mind, that is, the self.

Of course, there are differences. When speaking about the self, Erikson is much more likely to use the terms "ego-identity" or "self-identity."[7] Kohut, on the other hand, consistently uses the term "self." All three concepts point to the way our psychological identities are shaped by the cultures and histories into which we are socialized; all three beg for development by the fundamental ideas of hermeneutic philosophy—effective history, pre-understanding, and the classical. There are differences, however, at least in terminology, in the major psychological syndrome or pathology they are respectively studying. Erikson is justly famous for coining the term "identity confusion" and describing it both for clinical purposes and for purposes of broader cultural self-understanding. Kohut is equally renowned for refining and giving common cultural currency to Freud's concept of narcissism. Identity confusion and narcissism, although certainly not identical concepts, are highly convergent. Although the concepts are not identical, there is clearly a great deal of overlap in the clinical and cultural phenomena that they are trying to describe.

Both concepts point to a shift in the kind of clinical populations seen by psychiatrists, psychologists, and social workers across our land—a shift that must mean something about what is happening to people in general, not just the people who seek psychological help. There seems to have been a massive move away from the classical neurotic personality who has had an unsuccessfully resolved Oedipal problem that expresses itself in obsessive-compulsive, hysterical, or phobic difficulties of various kinds. Both Erikson and Kohut recognize this trend and with their respective concepts of identity confusion and narcissism are trying to name the new sociocultural trends in human personality difficulties.

Although a full comparison between identity confusion and narcissism is too complicated to attempt here, it will be useful to point to a few preliminary similarities and differences. First, a sense of the "fragmentation" of the self is the key experience for both identity confusion and narcissistic personality disorders. In both cases, there is a noncohesive self and a lack of firmness of self-experience and self-definition.[8] *Depression, emptiness, hypochondria* are words liberally used by both Erikson and Kohut to describe these respective clinical phenomena. In some of the more extreme cases, various kinds of regressions occur—infantile clinging or withdrawal, sexual promiscuity, a reactivation of Oedipal dramas and incestual wishes, a radical testing of friends, parents, and therapist to find a durable affirming and confirming face—all of which seem to be secondary strategies to reinstate the primary goal of establishing and maintaining a unified identity.

But there are certainly divergences in tone, context, and understanding of causality in the way Erikson and Kohut think about these two social and clinical problems. Erikson has done most of his work on the nature of identity confusion amidst his study of adolescent psychological problems. Identity confusion is both a normative crisis of adolescence (all modern adolescents undergo it to some extent) and, in some instances, a pathological phenomenon requiring clinical intervention and treatment. Its precipitants are multiple. Certainly developmental difficulties centering in the preoedipal stages of life are a fundamental source of the weaknesses in the self that make up identity confusion. Erikson's theory of the preoedipal nuclear conflicts between basic trust versus mistrust and autonomy versus shame and doubt share the limelight with some of the early British object-relations theories of Melanie Klein, W. R. D. Fairbairn, and D. W. Winnicott in showing the importance of preoedipal experiences for the development of a healthy, firm, and cohesive identity or self. But Erikson is aware of other factors that work in conjunction with these preoedipal deficits. Social factors such as rapid social change, the dislocation and confusion inflicted on families living in a highly differentiated and mobile society, and the pressures on adolescents and young adults for complex syntheses of sexual, vocational, political, and ideological commitments all work with, intensify, and even freshly aggravate old serious and not so serious preoedipal deficits.

Reading Erikson on identity confusion leads one to see the wisdom of a multi-dimensional approach to the task of alleviating the problem. Therapy addressing preoedipal deficits would be only one among many approaches to the problem, crucial for some of its expressions but relatively irrelevant for others. Certainly, when reading Erikson, one begins to think of the kind of social philosophy needed to bring an overheated, highly differentiated, and rapidly changing society into some kind of order. This, of course, is a task in social ethics that Erikson does not directly attempt, but it is indeed a subject about which he constantly makes hints. In addition, reading Erikson leads one to think about the kinds of ideologies and worldviews necessary to guide young people in making the complex syntheses that identity formation requires. Erikson makes it clear that in a complex society relatively healthy young people can confront trauma and even appear sick if they are prematurely forced to make these syntheses, choices, and commitments without workable ideological frameworks to guide them. As a psychiatrist, Erikson implicitly or explicitly calls for strategies from all of these directions in addressing the phenomenon of identity confusion.

Kohut is much more restricted in his discussion of solutions. Only occasionally in his writings does he even allude to the possible sociological and cultural forces that may stand behind and precipitate the largely parental failures in empathy that lead to the blows in self-esteem, the sense of emptiness, the lack of cohesiveness, and the general self-enfeeblement that make up narcissistic personality and behavioral problems.[9] Kohut keeps his eyes directly on the therapeutic interview and what it reveals about both the deficits in the early formation of the client's self and the deficits in the selves of the surrounding parental figures.

Hence, one always has the impression when reading Kohut that narcissistic problems are somehow deeper than problems of identity confusion. Of course, this is not necessarily true. Erikson was fully aware of the role preoedipal injuries to the self can play in the creation of identity confusion, but he was also aware of how stresses later in the life cycle also contribute. One also suspects that Kohut would look for preoedipal deficits and imagine that he found them when in reality the stresses were later, more situational, and more relative to the incomprehensibly complex, pressured, and unsupported tasks of coping and synthesis that we place on people in modern societies throughout the life cycle, but especially on adolescents and young adults. Erikson awakens, more quickly than does Kohut, the social reformer in us all. But for those who have the task of doing their work within the confines of the clinic, Kohut is clearly the more useful of the two. But one of the ironies of the relation of psychoanalysis to society is the possibility that the same analytic tools that help us to see things so clearly in the consultation room may lead us to see things rather poorly in the society as a whole.

There is one other important difference between Kohut and Erikson that should be noted. This is the difference in epistemological point of departure. Erikson's observational standpoints are multiple, and he believes that this is justifiable even from a psychoanalytic point of view. Erikson certainly believes that analysts must give priority in the study of human nature to the standpoint of the free associations, introspections, and empathic communications special to the analytic interview. But Erikson is clearly a part of that movement beginning with Hartmann that believed that psychoanalysis should have strong continuities with general psychology and therefore use the multiple epistemological vantage points of general psychology.[10] Hence, in addition to the insights gained directly from the analytic interview, Erikson makes more objective observations of children playing, borrows concepts from biology (the epigenetic principle), and does participant-observation anthropological studies. And he sees all of these as sources for the enrichment of psychoanalytic theory.

Kohut is much purer in his epistemological starting point. In a landmark article written in 1959, "Introspection, Empathy, and Psychoanalysis," he takes the position that the only legitimate modes of observation for psychoanalysis as a genuine psychological discipline are introspection and empathy.[11] Psychoanalytic epistemology begins with the observation of external behaviors such as words, symbolizations, acts, etc. Then the therapist introspects his or her own experience to surmise what such words or acts might mean had he or she said or done these things. Then, lastly, the therapist empathically places this introspection back into the life of the client and infers that maybe this is what it means to the client. Psychological knowledge within the context of analysis is built on the careful development, testing, and revision of introspectively derived and empathically amplified knowledge of the other person. At the same time, Kohut rejects the use of all other disciplines external to the introspective and empathic situation provided by the psychoanalytic interview—for instance, biology, anthropology, sociology—unless they can somehow be used as guides to the understanding of introspectively derived materials.

But these differences in epistemological starting point also show up in their terminological preferences: *identity* by Erikson and *self* by Kohut. Kohut and his followers believe that the concept of identity is basically a sociological concept, belongs to the discipline of sociology, and should not be used in psychoanalysis at all. In fact, two followers of Kohut, John Gedo and Arnold Goldberg, argue in *Models of the Mind* (1972) that the concept of identity in the therapeutic context may result in "externalizing problems which pertain to the formation of the archaic nuclear self into the social context of the patient in adult life."[12] It is my opinion, however, that Erikson's concept is large enough to encompass both the self in its archaic formations and the self in its sociological definitions and that therein rests its power. Furthermore, the two perspectives are not really separate fields; the parental figures that help form the nuclear self and the self of the child being formed both stand in these sociocultural fields. These fields influence from the very beginning both the parental shapers and the infantile self being shaped. One would want to break up these fields only if one had made a prior decision to erect a science of the human totally from the perspective of the preferred interventional strategy of psychoanalysis (that is, individual treatment built around free association and transference), a decision that the Kohutian school has clearly made. For them the truth is what one can see from the perspective of what one does within a particular specialized mode of treatment. But from the perspective of other disciplines that must necessarily preside over multiple forms of intervention—social work, the ministry, government—it is precisely such bridging concepts as those found in Erikson that are so valuable.

Empathy and Regard in the Formation of Self and Identity

At the most general level, both identity (Erikson) and the self (Kohut) are built out of the internalizations of responses of significant others, both early parental figures who form the archaic nuclear self and later personal and cultural figures who build on and elaborate these earlier formations. Seen from this perspective, both Erikson and Kohut's theories are similar to the American tradition of social psychology (William James, George Herbert Mead, and Harry Stack Sullivan), which saw the self as a social self, in other words, as an internalization of attitudes and gestures of significant others. In spite of the fact that the Kohutians would not like being associated with this tradition, logically they must be seen as consistent with it. In addition, we must be reminded that James and Mead (Mead depended greatly on James) elaborated their theories basically phenomenologically, that is, from the perspective of introspectively grasped experience of the self.[13] What James and Mead did not have, but what Erikson and Kohut contribute, is insightful age-specific developmental understandings of how the self or identity evolves. Of course, to be fair, it must be admitted that the neglected Harry Stack Sullivan provided profound theories about the early development of the self, as Jay R. Greenberg and Stephen Mitchell so appropriately remind us in their *Object Relations in Psychoanalytic Theory* (1983).[14]

Erikson says that the sense of ego identity "is the accrued confidence that the inner sameness and continuity prepared in the past are matched by the sameness and continuity of one's meaning for others."[15] When Erikson uses the term "ego identity," he is signaling his retention of the Freudian structural view of the agencies of the mind: the ego, superego, and id. Ego identity suggests that there is an inner agency (referred to as the ego) that synthesizes experience, even our various and sometimes contradictory experiences of how other people regard us. Seen from the perspective of the ego's synthesizing its various mediated self experiences, Erikson speaks of "ego identity." Viewed from the perspective of the actual images or representations of ourselves that the attitudes of other people place upon us, Erikson speaks of "self-identity."[16] For Erikson parental recognition, confirmation, and regard are the factors that activate and elaborate the developing self,[17] while failures in recognition, confirmation, and regard are the experiences that stunt the development of the self or self-identity. In *Generative Man* I called Erikson's psychology a psychology of the face. The presence of an affirming and confirming face, almost an I-Thou presence in the Buberian sense, is what Erikson is speaking about.[18] But for Erikson, the need to experience a confirming face, not only at the beginning of life but to some extent throughout, is a phylogenetic and ontogenetic requirement. It is a psychobiological need just as basic as food and water; it is certainly more basic than sex. The infant feels recognized when it senses that its very presence has awakened in the parent an inner joy—a joy that is, in turn, radiated back to the infant in the parent's countenance, voice, and touch. The baby feels confirmed when it senses that it is enlivening to the parent. As Erikson writes, "While the baby initially smiles at a mere configuration resembling the human face, the adult cannot help smiling back, filled with expectations of a 'recognition' which he needs to secure from the new being as surely as it needs him."[19]

Erikson agrees with hermeneutic philosophy that self-identity at its more mature level must entail an encounter with the classic cultural figures and ideologies of a person's inherited tradition or effective history. These cultural personages (the great heroes, saints, mythical prototypes) and ideologies are both energized by earlier infantile self-images and function subtly to restructure and expand these earlier images. In healthy human beings there is both continuity and discontinuity between earlier parentally shaped self-representations and identities and later adult identities significantly shaped by dominant religious and political ideologies as well as cultural figures of a society and its traditions.[20] Erikson summarizes most of the elements that go into identity formation in a recapitulation of his thinking, the ironically titled *The Life Cycle Completed* (1982).

> In summary, the process of identity formation emerges as an evolving configuration—a configuration that gradually integrates constitutional givens, idiosyncratic libidinal needs, favored capacities, significant identifications, effective defenses, successful sublimations, and consistent roles. All these, however, can only emerge from a mutual adaptation of individual potentials, technological worldview, and religious or political ideologies.[21]

There is much that sounds similar in Kohut's understanding of the self. Early in *The Analysis of the Self* (1971), he says that the self is not an agency of the personality like the ego, superego, or id. But it is a structure that has "continuity in time, i.e., it is enduring."[22] This seems to echo Erikson's understanding of identity as the center of one's experience of "continuity and sameness." Elsewhere in *The Analysis of the Self* Kohut seems further to parallel Erikson by saying that the mother's exultant response and enjoyment of the total child's "presence and activity" support the growth of the "self experience as a physical and mental unit which has cohesiveness in space and continuity in time."[23] In *The Restoration of the Self* (1977) Kohut argues that the point of origin of the self occurs when "the baby's innate potentialities and self-object's expectations with regard to the baby converge."[24]

All of this makes Erikson on identity and Kohut on the self sound very similar indeed. But Kohut has several unique dimensions to his theory. First, he does not carry the concept of the self, in any major way, into an encounter with cultural objects, ideologies, faiths, and figures. Kohut acknowledges that we encounter these cultural products amidst our development, but the kinds of self-experience that they will invoke seem for Kohut to be determined largely by the contours of archaic imagos. On the whole, little new meaning is opened up by these cultural ideologies and figures in the way Erikson believes happened in the case of Luther's encounter with the Christian message of justification by faith.[25] The later stages of self-formation—what Erikson writes about under the rubrics of identity and ideology—are of little interest to Kohut's more classically psychoanalytic perspective.

Although the main purpose of this chapter is to gain an understanding of the deep metaphors and principles of obligation that stand on the horizon of these two psychologies and not to do a systematic review of their systems, there is one more aspect of Kohut's theory of the self that I must not neglect. This is what he calls in *The Restoration of the Self* the bipolar nature of the self. But the basic ideas that make up this view find their first and most powerful statement in *The Analysis of the Self*. Kohut argued in this book that there are two basic aspects of the nuclear or archaic self: the grandiose self and the idealized parental imago. Both poles of the self are compensatory structures that come about in response to the inevitable failures in the mothering figure's care and empathy. In reaction to these failures, the infant attempts to reinstate the perfection and stability of his original narcissistic relation to the mother by turning his libidinal energies upon himself or upon an idealized parental figure. In his early theory Kohut frankly insists that what makes both the grandiose self and the idealized parental imago narcissistic is the "quality of the instinctual charge" invested in these aspects of the self.[26] These aspects of the self are narcissistic because they are invested with narcissistic libidinal energy. This energy in its state of relative equilibrium endows the grandiose self and the idealized parental imago with qualities of perfection, omnipotence, and durability. However, in *The Restoration of the Self* and *How Does Analysis Cure?* (1984) Kohut repudiates such energistic language and the metapsychology that it implies and speaks instead of the self's independent line of development.[27]

The central characteristic of the grandiose self is the experience "I am perfect," whereas the central experience of the idealized parental imago is "You are perfect, but I am a part of you."[28] To maintain these inner subjective states, both poles of the self require "selfobjects." Kohut makes a succinct definition of selfobjects in his 1978 article "The Disorders of the Self and Their Treatment: An Outline": "Selfobjects are objects which we experience as part of our self."[29] We experience them as something we have control over not unlike the way we control our own bodies. Our early selfobjects are our parents and their deep attitudes toward us. There are two kinds of selfobject: "those who respond to and confirm the child's innate sense of vigour, greatness, and perfection; and those to whom he can look up and with whom he can merge as an image of calmness, infallibility and omnipotence."[30] Clearly the selfobjects of the first kind support or fail to support our grandiose selves. The selfobjects of the second support or fail to support our idealized parental imagos. Empathy, or the lack of it, is the primary attitude on the part of parents that counts for the support, confirmation, and invigoration of these two poles of the self.

Spirit and Nature in Erikson and Kohut

In our earlier discussions of Niebuhr's view of the relation of nature and spirit in the Jewish and Christian traditions, I touched only lightly on a very important shift that Niebuhr makes in his theory of the self from *The Nature and Destiny of Man* to his later statement on theological anthropology in *The Self and the Dramas of History*. In the earlier volume Niebuhr did not give a particularly social definition to spirit. His main concern was to demonstrate the reality of human self-transcendence—the fact that in spite of all biological and social necessities, man has some capacity to stand outside of nature, life, himself, his reason, and the world.[31] More specifically, self-transcendence entails the capacity to make the self one's "own object," in other words, the capacity in one's imagination to get beyond oneself and then to look back on one's self as an object of reflection and evaluation. This is what is meant by *spirit* in this earlier work. But in this early book the social dimensions of spirit are unclear.

In *The Self and the Dramas of History* the capacity for self-transcendence is absorbed into the metaphor of dialogue. The self is a dialogical self that is in perpetual conversation with the self, with the community of other selves, and with the divine. Whereas in *The Nature and Destiny of Man* the human capacity for self-transcendence is identified as the "image of God,"[32] in *The Self and the Dramas of History* the image of God in humans is identified with the human capacity for dialogue. The difference between the two books, however, is not absolute. The dialogical view of humans and the dramatic view of history that accompanies it were always present as subthemes in the earlier work, and the capacity for self-transcendence is a constituent part of what it means to have dialogue in the later book. But regardless of the continuities, the new centrality of the metaphor of dialogue does indeed give Niebuhr's later thought a new emphasis on the social and communal nature of the self and a surprising continuity with the historical and dialogical view of the self found in the hermeneutic philosophies of Gadamer, Ricoeur, and more recently Cushman and Richardson, et al.

The influence of Martin Buber's *I and Thou* (1958) is openly acknowledged by Niebuhr.[33] One also suspects the influence of George Herbert Mead (and possibly even that of his own brother, H. Richard Niebuhr, who was also experimenting at the time with a social view of the self).[34] Although Niebuhr seems to acknowledge how the self is formed by its various communities, he differs from the social determinism sometimes associated with Mead's view of the self. Niebuhr gives great emphasis to the self's dialogue with the self—this inner spiritual awareness of and capacity for relative freedom over all the self's functions and over biological and social influences.[35] But this is why humans' interaction with their communities is always a matter of dialogue rather than simply a matter of socialization and conditioning; the self's own internal dialogue with itself gives it the potentiality for some modicum of critical transcendence over its communities of socialization. As Niebuhr writes, "The self is engaged in a perpetual dialogue with other selves in which its dependence upon others becomes apparent but which also proves its independence over all relationships."[36] This capacity gives the self the ability to criticize the very community or communities that form the self: "The individual looks down upon the community because he is, as it were, higher than it."[37]

By introducing the concept of the self, by making the self a social self, and by stating the place of spirit or self-transcendence within the larger view of the dialogical self, the possible lines of correspondence among Erikson, Kohut, and Niebuhr become clearer. Niebuhr can even agree with Kohut that the narrowly conceived empirical scientific disciplines with their externalistic modes of experimentation and observation cannot comprehend adequately such a self. Niebuhr joins the phenomenologists in saying that naturalistic modes of observation characteristic of the physical sciences cannot comprehend the interior complexities of the self. And Kohut could fully affirm and doubtless Erikson second when Niebuhr writes, "Sometimes the methods of empirical science, drawn from the natural sciences, serve to obscure the facts about the self which can be known only through introspection, and in dramatic encounter."[38] Introspection practiced in the intersubjective situation, as Kohut would suggest, is Niebuhr's fundamental source for genuine knowledge into the self.

In view of the emphasis in Niebuhr on the ambiguity between nature and spirit within the dialogical model of the self, it is not surprising to read in the preface of the second edition of *The Nature and Destiny of Man*: "Since the delivery of these lectures modern 'ego psychology,' particularly as elaborated by my friend Erik Erikson, has developed this paradoxical position of the self scientifically. I agree with this position, but it would have prompted some changes in my statement of the reality."[39] This opens an affirmation that I want to carry further. It is safe to say that all three—Niebuhr, Erikson, and Kohut—hold a dialogical view of the self and that, furthermore, all three, to varying degrees and in different ways, hold a place for the dialectical relation between nature and spirit within this wider dialogical model.

Certainly Erikson firmly anchors his view of self-identity in an understanding of nature, that is, in an understanding of the biological foundations of the human personality. His concept of the "epigenetic principle" and his use, albeit ambiguous, of Freud's theory of psychosexuality find a place in Erikson's image of the human for the vitalities and forms of nature. In the Kohut of *The Analysis of the Self* nature is visible in his theory of the self through his use of libido theory to formulate a theory of narcissism. In both *The Restoration of the Self* and *How Does Analysis Cure?* the nature in human nature subsumes libido theory and becomes something that looks vaguely like the motivation theory of humanistic psychology. He suddenly starts speaking of "innate talents,"[40] a "blue print" of our potentialities,[41] and an "innermost design" that throws us "into a middle-age crisis" if we discover we have not been true to it.[42] But regardless of the competing models of the "natural" in humans, Kohut both early and late finds a role for it within his understanding of the self.

But it is much more complex to state how the self in Erikson and Kohut transcends nature and its necessities in ways similar to Niebuhr. In Erikson this is accomplished by the distinction between the ego and the self or self-identity. The ego is the inner core of a person's capacity for agency and synthesis.[43] The ego matures, partially on the basis of innate maturational timetables and partially under the differentiating impact of experience. Either way, the ego does not just conform in all respects to the self-defining attitudes and gestures of parents and surrounding environments. The maturing ego gradually learns to organize, affirm, reject, elevate, and subordinate its various socially imposed definitions. In short, as Erikson says in "The Problem of Ego Identity" and elsewhere, the ego does a work of *synthesis and resynthesis*.[44] Needless to say, Erikson's view of the capacity for self-transcendence must be understood developmentally; it is greatly influenced by earlier experience. Indeed, for some selves with major early deficits self-transcendence may be small if not almost nonexistent. Nonetheless, some self-transcendence seems possible for everyone who has sufficient symbolic capacities to have a representation of the self.

This developmental perspective on self-transcendence is equally important for Kohut. This is the crucial difference between Kohut and Erikson on the one hand and Niebuhr on the other. Kohut as a clinician is primarily interested in the pre-oedipal foundations of self-development. He is interested in the way the empathic attitudes of a child's selfobjects support the development of its ambitions and strivings and how through a gradual process of moderate empathic failures the attitudes of these selfobjects become internalized into permanent structures within the self of the child. Kohut calls this a process of "transmuting internalizations."[45] In short, it is a process whereby the attitudes that the parental figures have toward the child now become more or less permanent attitudes that the growing child has toward himself or herself.

Because the attitudes of the others are crucial to the development of the child, Kohut does not concentrate, even as much as Erikson, on the ways that the child and, later, the adult may transcend these attitudes, pick and choose among them, and affirm some or subordinate others. And yet Kohut clearly believes that this does gradually become an emerging capacity of the growing person. In "Introspection and Empathy in Psychoanalysis" he openly affirms the reality of freedom. The capacity to discern freedom is, for him, a matter of observational perspective.[46] If we take an introspective or empathic approach in contrast to an external and naturalistic one, Kohut believes we can discern the freedom of the self. But it is safe to say that Kohut never investigates to any noticeable extent this growing adult capacity for synthesizing the various self-attitudes and definitions placed upon one from the outside world. Nor does he investigate the various ways in which the self says yes or no or maybe to its own natural inclinations. All of this is true because Kohut is not very interested in the problems of the relatively healthy adult self. He is not interested in the problems left over after a generally high degree of self-cohesion has been accomplished. Kohut loses interest at precisely the place where Niebuhr begins. Because Kohut's interest is in early development, the emphasis upon self-transcendence, although present, is small.

Although Kohut and Niebuhr have similar models of the self, Kohut is interested in the social resources (the selfobject resources) necessary to bring the self to a high degree of firmness and cohesion. On the other hand, Niebuhr is interested in the problems that the self faces—anxiety, sin, and guilt—even when the self *is* cohesive. Erikson, to some extent, is a bridge figure because he is interested in the preoedipal foundations of the self, but he also emphasizes the continuing challenges to egosynthesis during adolescence, young adulthood, and even into later life. Niebuhr, and the theologians in general, can be justly criticized for seeing the problems of the self too monolithically from the perspective of adulthood and for failing to comprehend, as Peter Homans has pointed out, the development precursors to the adult self.[47] But at the same time Kohut, and to a lesser degree Erikson, equally can be criticized for overextending the problems of the early development of the self and leaving us with the idea that if the self is healthy, there will be no temptations to anxiety and inordinate self-interest of the kind that Niebuhr and his retrieval of the concept of original sin portray as the universal condition of humans. By virtue of the discovery of the importance of preoedipal experiences for the formation of the adult personality, we have tended too much to reduce all adolescent, young adult, and adult problems to early childhood problems. In addition, we have failed to understand that it has been precisely the task of theology to conceptualize those problems of identity and self that remain when relatively high degrees of health and self-cohesion have been obtained. Theology, and the Jewish and Christian traditions in general, have worked to symbolize the problems of life that remain if one has had the best mother, the best father, and the best environment that are possible for this finite world to provide.

It is the task of theology, I would argue, to look forward, think *prospectively,* and project the goals of life. It is the task of the clinical psychologies, of which Kohut and Erikson are examples, primarily to think *retrospectively* and help us analyze the interaction between biology and early parental and social influences in the formation of the self. Theology has few concepts to assist in this retrospective analysis. With the advent of the clinical psychologies with their special languages to accomplish this task, we have a remarkable opportunity to forge new disciplinary alliances that will help provide both powerful procedures for retrospective analysis and powerful normative and prospective images of human fulfillment. It is one of the functions of this book to suggest that a dialogue between theology and the modern psychologies might give hints as to how these retrospectively oriented psychologies and prospectively oriented theologies can reinforce one another. But, as we have seen, the dialogue is complex; the psychologies too have their prospective images of human fulfillment in adulthood, some of which complement and some of which contradict the normative images of theology. Such tension, as I have insisted repeatedly, requires adjudication.

Although Niebuhr, Erikson, and Kohut share to varying degrees an image of the human that emphasizes the ambiguity of nature and spirit within a larger dialogical model, the proportions of these elements vary. The ambiguities of life and the anxieties that they invoke, even for those with the most healthy of preoedipal environments, weigh most heavily on Niebuhr. Niebuhr is fully aware of the situational anxieties included by parents, specific losses, accidents, class, and financial demotions. But Niebuhr is aware of that form of anxiety that is a result of our general capacity for freedom, our transcendence over the brute necessities of nature, and our awareness of what Kierkegaard described as infinite possibility. Kohut's study of anxiety is limited to the anxiety invoked when a child's selfobjects fail to communicate empathy or somehow are forced by the contingencies of life to withdraw too traumatically.[48] Both are important forms of anxiety, although Niebuhr would say that the dim awareness of the anxiety of freedom is more pervasive, fundamental, and in some ways inclusive of Kohut's intersubjective anxiety. Both are a result of the human lack of total embeddedness in a rigid and neatly controlled order of nature.

On the subject of anxiety, Erikson is once again somewhat of a bridge figure between a psychologist such as Kohut and a theologian such as Niebuhr. Although fully aware of the intersubjective anxieties invoked by the child's preoedipal social environment, Erikson also seems to be aware of those inevitable anxieties and crises that come any time the growing person leaves one stage of nuclear conflict and, through inner propulsion and outer circumstances, moves on to another stage. Whether it is the transition from trust versus mistrust to autonomy versus shame and doubt or the later adult transitions from generativity versus stagnation to integrity versus despair, the anxieties accompanying the subtle decisions to cope with the new circumstances of life are increasingly evident throughout the life cycle due to the pangs of freedom. Erikson could write passionately and sensitively about existential anxiety, metaphysical anxiety, and "ego chill" as he did in *Young Man Luther* (1958).[49] He knew he was describing something that was both continuous with but certainly not exhausted by a child's fear of losing a parent or the experience of fragmentation to the self due to a parent's unempathic responses.

Generativity and Obligation

Erikson and Kohut have remarkably similar views of human fulfillment. Although they speak about their visions under the rubric of health or the self's cohesion, both psychologists clearly lapse into normative and ethical meanings. It has been known for some time that the idea of generativity is the normative core of Erikson's developmental psychology; indeed, generativity was the primary subject matter of my 1973 work *Generative Man*. It is not only a concept pointing to the meaning of health, but it is an obvious ethical concept as well, implying both a theory of virtue and a general principle of obligation. It is less well understood—in fact surprising to learn—that Kohut's image of health involves very much the same ideas expressed in slightly different words.

Both Erikson and Kohut see a relatively nonconflictual capacity to care for succeeding generations as both a primary psychobiological goal of life and a basic criterion of health. Erikson goes farther than Kohut in generalizing this need into an ethic. However, on this matter, Kohut is only slightly more cautious than Erikson. Both, however, have little difficulty making the subtle shift between the *isness* of health and the *oughtness* of obligation. At the same time, both of them are strikingly different from the other psychologists we considered with regard to their images of human fulfillment. Their view is different from the Freudian image of the human drive for tension-reduction through undifferentiated union. It is different, although far less drastically, from the nonhedonistic ethical egoism of the humanistic psychologists and its more complicated version in Jung. In both Erikson and Kohut, there is a genuine conflation of concepts of health and concepts of moral obligation. In both cases their thinking is confused, but it is also nonetheless creative.

Generativity and Erikson

In *Childhood and Society* (1950) Erikson defines generativity as "primarily the concern in establishing and guiding the next generation."[50] Generativity is not confined to procreation, although it can include it. In *The Life Cycle Completed* he says it can include the generation of "new products and new ideas" as well as the generation of "new beings."[51] Generativity is part of the adult nuclear conflict of generativity versus stagnation. If past developmental deficits, family, contemporary world images, and contemporary adult anxieties conspire to repress one's generative potentials, individuals can fall back into the business of making themselves "their own . . . one and only child."[52] But the crucial feature in generativity is not simply the capacity to create but, in addition, the capacity to *care* for that which one creates. "Care," Erikson tells us, "is the widening concern for what has been generated by love, necessity, or accident; it overcomes the ambivalence adhering to irreversible obligation."[53] Erikson refuses to equate generativity with creativity for the simple reason that creativity can be unconcerned with caring for that which it creates; generativity not only creates but it maintains and cares as well.

Although generativity must be seen as something of an artistic synthesis, it does have its instinctual foundations. This is certainly what Erikson means when he writes that evolution "has made man a teaching as well as a learning animal, for dependence and maturity are reciprocal: mature man *needs to be needed,* and maturity is guided by the nature of that which must be cared for."[54] Both animals and humans "instinctively encourage in their young what is ready for release."[55] We need to take Erikson seriously when he speaks of "generativity, as the instinctual power behind various forms of selfless 'caring,'"[56] when he speaks of the "parental drive" applied to one's own offspring or to larger causes,[57] and when he writes that he has "postulated an instinctual and psychosocial stage of 'generativity' beyond that of 'genitality.'"[58] Although Erikson indulges in what we would today recognize as sociobiological thinking in postulating these foundations to our generativity, he also sees generativity and care as a product of an artistic synthesis of will and emotion. Really mature forms of generativity entail a subtle synthesis of instinctual needs of various kinds, early ego strengths and virtues, and an artful coordination of these accrued powers with the developmental needs of those for whom we have been assigned to care.

Generativity and Kohut

Although he does not use the term, Kohut develops what must be recognized as a concept of generativity in his critique of Freud's theory of Oedipal conflict as universal and the fundamental ground of the neuroses. In *The Restoration of the Self* and other later writings Kohut begins to repudiate the drive theory that he leaned on so heavily to formulate his earlier view of narcissism. Concepts such as drive, libido, and thanatos are now viewed as biological concepts that should not be used within the basically introspectively grounded epistemology of psychoanalysis. In addition, he gradually took the stand that what appear as unruly and uncontrollable sexual or destructive impulses are not the natural condition of humans, but are instead "disintegration" products; that is, they are the manifestations of the disorganization of normal affection and assertiveness due to the fragmentation of the self.[59]

Hence, the Oedipal conflict, according to Kohut, is not the inevitable and universal phenomenon Freud thought it was. We do not have irresistible sexual attractions toward the parent of the opposite sex and aggressive feelings toward the parent of the same sex as Freud thought. Nor are fathers unconsciously competitive with their sons and mothers with their daughters. The sexual and aggressive overtones of generational relations are due to a lack of parental empathy and the noncohesive self that this produces in their child. The fragmentation of the self turns natural and positive affection and assertiveness into competitive and destructive sex and aggression.

What Kohut does not seem to understand is that he has substituted one model of biology for another. In place of seeing through the actions and feelings of the self impulsive sex and aggression as did Freud, he now sees through the analysis of the self a model of our psychobiological nature that is clearly much closer to the theory of self-actualization found in the humanistic psychologists. We have seen already the proliferation of concepts such as "innate talents," "blue print," and "innermost design" in Kohut. In addition, phrases such as "self-realization"[60] and "man's essential nature"[61] also begin to be used more and more. In fact, by the end of his career in *How Does Analysis Cure?* Kohut seems to have settled on the two broad psychobiological concepts of "affection and assertiveness" to characterize the fundamental motivational directions of human beings.[62] All this movement in motivational theory ends up in quite a startling shift in the psychoanalytic image of human fulfillment—one that is very much built around a theory of the optimal parent. In *The Restoration of the Self* Kohut gives us a clue to an emphasis that becomes increasingly prominent toward the end of his life.

> Optimal parents—again I should rather say: optimally failing parents—are people who, despite their stimulation by and competition with the rising generation, are also sufficiently in touch with the pulse of life, accept themselves as transient participants in the ongoing stream of life, to be able to experience the growth of the next generation with unforced nondefensive joy.[63]

What, in effect, we have in this paragraph is a synthesis of a theory of self-actualization with a theory of motivation that finds a place for a limited altruism; Kohut suggests the existence of a fundamental motivational need to care for the next generation, especially one's own children. Self-actualization and care for the other come together; the most actualizing thing we can do is care for and actualize the strengths of the succeeding generations.

That Kohut has indeed moved to a genuine self-actualization theory can be seen in his theory of Tragic Man, an image of man that he contrasts with what he refers to as Freud's theory of Guilty Man. Since the word "man" is the convention that Kohut felt comfortable using when he was writing these words, I trust the reader will excuse me if I follow him in summarizing his views. The most forceful statement of his theory can be found in his article "Introspection, Empathy, and the Semi-Circle of Mental Health" (1982).

Here Kohut makes one of his strongest cases for distinguishing himself from the commanding authority that Freud always had exercised over the psychoanalytic movement. Kohut directly confesses that he wants to liberate his psychoanalytic colleagues from their typical view of the normal or essential nature of man, "namely, man as an insufficiently and incompletely trained animal, reluctant to give up his wish to live by the pleasure principle, unable to relinquish his innate destructiveness."[64] Such a view of the essence of human nature gives rise to what Kohut calls an image of man as Guilty Man—man as constantly infringing upon the rights of others in an effort to satisfy his own insatiable appetites.

Kohut's revolt is so vigorous that it almost confirms what Freud said about the usurping aspirations of sons toward their fathers. Kohut believes that self-psychology has liberated itself from the pseudo-biological point of view of orthodox psychoanalysis. In addition, Kohut believes that what is useful and good about Guilty Man should be "supplemented by, and subordinated to, the self-psychological view point."[65] In contrast to Guilty Man, Kohut calls his view of the human Tragic Man and tries to counter the evocative power of Freud's employment of the Oedipal myth with a myth of his own choosing—the myth of Odysseus and Telemachus. Kohut is using the word *tragedy* in the sense of Euripides: "striving, resourceful man, attempting to unfold his innermost self, battling against external and internal obstacles to its unfolding; and warmly committed to the next generation, to the son in whose unfolding and growth he joyfully participates—thus experiencing man's deepest and most central joy, that of being a link in the chain of generations."[66]

In the phrase "unfold his innermost self," we find a shift from the conflictual model of the human in psychoanalysis to a genuinely eudaemonistic view of the human continuous with what one would find in Plato, Aristotle, the Stoics, and the Epicureans, a view that David Norton helped us understand in its broad contours in our discussion of the humanistic psychologists. It is not a move from a biological view to a purely psychological view; it is rather a different theory of what the regular and constant biological motivations of humans are as this is captured from the introspective view of the analysis of the self. Odysseus exemplifies a confluence of self-actualization *and* the joyful care of the next generation. Feigning madness when being pressured by Agamemnon, Menelaus, and Palamedes to join them in their Trojan expedition, Odysseus reveals his sanity, as well as his own deepest desires, when his son Telemachus is thrown before the plow that Odysseus is using to work his fields. Rather than plow over his son, Odysseus made a semicircle around Telemachus, thereby revealing both his "mental health" and his strategy to escape the war over Troy. Although the story does not prove anything and is only presented by Kohut as a counter to Freud's myth of father murder in the story of King Oedipus, it is a fitting "symbol of that joyful awareness of the human self of being temporal, of having an unrolling destiny, . . . of the fact that healthy man experiences, and with deepest joy, the next generation as an extension of his own self."[67] Here Kohut unknowingly joins Erikson in conflating self-actualization and the generative care of succeeding generations as the deepest and most constant of human wishes.

The Move from Psychology to Ethics

In both Erikson and Kohut these ideas of generativity are presented first of all as concepts of mental health. But in both cases, they clearly go beyond that and become implicit principles of obligation. In Kohut the step is taken more subtly and less intentionally but just as definitively. It comes from the simple fact that being invested in the next generation is clearly something Kohut values. He sees it as a self-evident good; being invested in one's own children is obviously a good that humans would have to promote even if it were not a deep-seated inclination. But Kohut would argue that fortunately for humans it is a natural inclination. And those who live by it are healthy. Kohut's tack here is clear and analogous to that of the humanistic psychologists: something considered morally good is also a matter of natural motivation. The argument is not different than it is for Maslow, Rogers, and Perls; for them, self-actualization is a good, and it also just happens that it is the basic natural interest of human beings. The result of this, however, is that one has a moral obligation to do that which deep down one wants to do. Or to say it differently, it is morally justifiable to do what one is inclined to do because what one is inclined to do is also moral, in this case taking care of succeeding generations. If what we deeply desired to do was to sleep with our mothers and fathers and aggressively attack both enemy and friend alike, we might call this healthy, but we would not recommend it; that is, we would not hold it up as a moral norm.

But Erikson is much more direct in shifting his theory of health into a theory of obligation. One can quickly admit that Erikson is interested in promoting a healthy ethic. By healthy ethic I mean an ethic not built on repression and one that finds a place for human self-affirmation. But it is also clear that a healthy ethic is not the same thing as a theory of health. Since Heinz Hartmann's *Psychoanalysis and Moral Values* (1960) psychoanalytic practice has officially aspired to be as value neutral as possible. But Erikson is far less cautious and is actually willing to explore the moral implications of psychoanalytic theory as he sees it.

There are three ways that Erikson's concept of generativity goes beyond a simple theory of health. First, Erikson is constantly blurring the borderline between the generative care of our own children as issues of our own genitality and genes and a more widespread care for succeeding generations. Kohut does the same thing. It is one thing to say that we have an instinctual need to care for our own flesh and blood. The sociobiologists E. O. Wilson, R. Dawkins, and G. C. Williams can all advance very convincing arguments that we all do have natural altruistic inclinations toward those individuals, and certainly our own children, who carry our own genes.[68] But this is not to say that we have a more generalized instinct to take care of everyone's children and certainly not everyone's children equally to our own. Humans may need to provide for the care of all children and the cycle of the generations, but acknowledging this moral requirement is not the same thing as saying that we actually have a natural instinct to do all of these things. But Erikson does not protect himself, and he mixes the language of instinct and the language of morality, sometimes in a single sentence. He certainly does this when he writes, "Generativity, as the instinctual power behind various forms of selfless 'caring,' potentially extends to whatever man generates and leaves behind, creates and produces (or helps to produce)."[69] Here we have rendered in a descriptive modality both the language of instinct ("instinctual power") and—by the implication that humans should exercise selfless "caring" for "whatever man generates and leaves behind, creates and produces (or helps to produce)"—the language of obligation. And since we know already that generativity is supposed to have behind it instinctual power, we see this same mixing of language when we read "Generativity, then, is primarily the concern for establishing and guiding the next generation." Here, we have a slight yet significant process of moving from one's own children to a more generalized image of "the next generation." This may indeed be an ethically justifiable thing to do, but that is not my point. My point is that generativity gradually moves from being a scientific concept descriptive of health to a moral concept indicative of obligation.

Moreover, Erikson's ethic of generativity is compatible with, but also in some tension with, his ethic of mutuality developed in the article "The Golden Rule in Light of New Insight."[70] In this article Erikson advances a restatement of the golden rule around his understanding of the kind of mutuality that occurs in all good instances of generativity. In suggesting that generativity has its own instinctual foundations, Erikson is elaborating the naturalistic foundations of an ethic of mutuality. Erikson rephrases the famous "Do unto others as you would have them do unto you" with the words "truly worthwhile acts enhance a mutuality between the doer and the other—a mutuality which strengthens the doer even as it strengthens the other."[71] We see Erikson developing a theory of mutuality and equal-regard not unlike what we found in Janssens and Outka. But there is, at the same time, a huge difference. Whereas Erikson's theory of mutuality is built on a generationally based theory of the nonmoral good. Janssens himself is open to such a theory but does not develop it.[72] But Erikson makes such a theory explicit. Erikson believes that there is an entire range of developmental needs emerging at different times throughout the life cycle. These needs function in complementary ways within the cycle of the generations so that in meeting the needs of our children we are also meeting certain phase-specific needs in ourselves. For example, adults need to see a smiling face from infants just as profoundly as infants need to encounter the warm and confirming face of an adult.[73] Mothers receive pleasure from their suckling infant at the same time that the infant meets its needs for nourishment. Both mothers and fathers have their own "teaching instinct" met in the very act of caring for the young.

But Erikson takes these few observations about the complementarity of the cycle of the generations and generalizes them into a much wider theory of mutuality. He expands this position by saying,

> Seen in the light of human development, this means that the doer is activated in whatever strength is *appropriate to his age, stage, and condition,* even as he activates in the other the strength appropriate to *his* age, stage, and condition. Understood this way, the Rule would say that it is best to do to another what will strengthen you even as it will strengthen him—that is, what will develop his best potentials even as it develops your own.[74]

Here Erikson says that not only is mutuality morally good, but it can build on a wide range of developmentally relevant needs that function as nonmoral or pre-moral motivating goods.

Third, in the golden rule article and in *Gandhi's Truth* (1966) Erikson provides a fresh interpretation of Gandhi's theory of nonviolent or truth action that extends his theory of generativity and his reinterpretation of the golden rule to include self-sacrifice. "That line of action is alone just," Gandhi once said, "which does not harm either party of a dispute."[75] Erikson says in *Gandhi's Truth* that for Gandhi, "Truthful action . . . was governed by the readiness to get hurt but not to hurt—action governed by the principle of ahimsa."[76] Erikson sees this as similar to his reinterpretation of the golden rule even though the form of these statements revolves far more around not doing harm than it does around the more expansive mutual activation seen in his version of the golden rule. Nonetheless, these statements do build into his ethics of generative mutuality a place for self-sacrifice, that is, for the "readiness to get hurt."[77] And it does suggest that he goes beyond mutuality as a totally adequate ethic for all occasions.

"Getting hurt" is clearly an experience that goes beyond mutuality. The person involved in nonviolent action, in order to change the other to more just and mutual action, is suffering or is willing to suffer and get hurt even as he or she does not hurt the other. Such a person is willing to go beyond an ethic of mutuality, at least for a while. As a transitional strategy designed to restore relations to genuine mutuality and justice, such a person is willing to take nonviolent actions that indeed do cost him or her dearly but yet are designed to change the other without doing the other harm. Such an ethic is close to the one I described at the conclusion of chapter 6 as the *caritas* ethic of neighbor-love. Erikson's ethic is quite clearly one that goes far beyond the concept of mental health and far beyond what is a matter of natural generative instinctuality, even as it includes and extends that generative instinctuality.

Both Erikson and Kohut end up stating within the language of mental health a certain version of an ethic of mutuality. There can be little doubt that neither of them would have been motivated to give us their formulations had they not been themselves shaped by an effective history that pointed to the importance of this ethical principle. In both cases, however, it is an ethic of generative mutuality, stated with special reference to the interlocking needs of the cycle of the generations. Kohut tiptoes on the edge of such an ethic, while Erikson plunges directly into the center of it. In the language of Niebuhr, mutuality is for Erikson and Kohut the "norm of history," not because history is fallen and sinful (neither Erikson nor Kohut speak of such things), but because it is seen as the moral ideal—indeed, the healthy moral ideal. Both psychologists go beyond a simple theory of health and move into the realm of morality. Neither psychologist signals to us that in advancing such concepts he is moving out of the realm of psychology and into moral philosophy. In spite of their inability to keep their categories straight, it must be admitted that they accidentally generate a theory of *healthy morality*. Kohut ends up suggesting that it is morally good for us to work on behalf of the younger generation, but he also adds that it is good to do this in such a way as to be fed by our own innermost tendency to do so. We become thereby an enlivening and empathic selfobject to those for whom we have been given the charge to care. Erikson has given us an image of healthy morality—healthy generative mutuality—as well. Our mutuality is healthy when it activates those needs in the other that are ready to be activated while, at the same time, activating some complementary need in ourselves.

What is strikingly different from Niebuhr, however, is the tendency, especially evident in Erikson, to make mutuality the norm of history and to make self-sacrifice, either in the form of a generalized care for all children or in the form of genuine nonviolent acts of *satyagraha* (truth force), a transitional ethic designed to restore the situation of mutuality. Hence Erikson clearly offers a secular version of the Catholic theory of the *ordo caritatis* that we saw so powerfully stated in the thought of Louis Janssens. For in Janssens we saw mutuality as the norm of life and self-sacrifice and the cross as transitional norms that all serious Christians must bear in an effort to restore life to the mutuality and equal-regard for which it was made.

Although Erikson ends (and Kohut nearly ends) with a normative ethic not far from the ideal of the *ordo caritatis* and equal-regard, it is actually a much thicker concept in Erikson than it normally is when expressed in the typical theological treatise. This is true because Erikson's theory of the nuclear conflicts of the life cycle and his theory of virtue or ego strengths constitute a very complex theory of the *ordo bonorum*. His theory of the epigenesis of the various needs and potentials of human life such as trust, autonomy, initiative, etc., constitutes a series of indices of what Janssens calls the premoral good or what William Frankena calls the non-moral good. And it is precisely the premoral good that the more properly moral goods of equal-regard and mutuality must fairly and lovingly actualize among all human beings. I need not get into the details of Erikson's developmental theory or even debate whether it is correct in order to make the more general point that it, as well as any good developmental psychology, can play an important role in ethics by providing at least part of the theory of the *ordo bonorum* that is necessary for ethical thinking.

Janssens says as much when he writes of the developmental psychology of Abraham Maslow that "Recent studies furnish very valuable information with respect to priorities in the domain of premoral values."[78] He then makes some points that were made with Maslow in mind but could easily be adapted to Erikson. Janssens says that developmental psychology has learned that "different premoral values do not hold the same rank and position in the hierarchy of values."[79] This seems to suggest that there may be a distinction between foundational values and teleological values. Trust is a highly important foundational value because so many other premoral values, such as autonomy, initiative, industry, identity, and intimacy, are dependent upon the foundational capacity for trust and the virtue that Erikson associates with it—hope. But in another sense the later premoral values of autonomy, initiative, industry, identity, and intimacy are higher because they involve more complex syntheses. Hence, Janssens can write, "With respect to the distinction between lower and higher values 'humanistic psychology' seems to be very helpful for moralists."[80] Of course by "humanistic psychology" he is referring specifically to the developmental psychology of Maslow. But the point, as I have said, can apply to any good developmental psychology, including Erikson's.

It is not my point, however, to argue that either Erikson or Maslow is correct scientifically in his description of human development. I am making the more abstract point that good developmental psychology can be enormously helpful, as I believe it implicitly has been already, in our ethical deliberations by giving us theories of the range, sequence, and timetable of our basic needs and potentials. In turn, these theories can constitute highly strategic theories of the premoral good that our more directly ethical principles of equal-regard and mutuality should order in the very process of living. When generative mutuality is actualizing and ordering the rich potentials and needs of various stages of the life cycle, then generative mutuality becomes a very thick, rich, complex, enlivening phenomenon indeed, far more potent, suggestive, and usable than the more abstract and philosophical idea of equal-regard.

Deep Metaphors in Erikson and Kohut

Erikson and Kohut are no exceptions to the argument I have been advancing: the modern clinical psychologies contain metaphors that function in close analogy to the metaphors of ultimacy in the great religions of the world. These deep metaphors give these psychologies their images of the fundamental possibilities of life. They convey a set of basic beliefs about what can be expected from life and hoped for in life. They do not necessarily dictate the content of their implicit ethics, but they set a context that supports or constrains what seems ethically possible or required.

Erikson and Kohut have their metaphors of ultimacy just as do Freud, Skinner, Jung, and the humanistic psychologists. Even though they have come out of the psychoanalytic movement and therefore stand in the lineage of Freud, their deep metaphors are actually closer to those of the humanistic psychologists. This is especially true of Kohut, who can, I believe, justifiably be called a humanistic psychologist dressed in psychoanalytic clothing.

But this is almost true of Erikson as well. Harmonistic metaphors are pervasive throughout his psychological writings. These metaphors are only slightly more complicated than those of the humanistic psychologists. Their more complicated features stem from the fact that Erikson is more of an instinctual pluralist than Rogers, Perls, and Maslow. There is no single actualization tendency for Erikson as there was for our humanistic trio. There is, instead, a patterned sequence of various instinctual tendencies or "developmentals" (to use a phrase of Barrett and Yankelovich) that call for actualization at various times throughout the human life cycle.[81] This model of our instinctuality comes from the application within the domain of psychoanalysis of what the distinguished biologist C. H. Stockard called "epigenesis." Erikson's rich (yet patterned and sequenced) biological pluralism (reminiscent of that of William James) gets mixed with his theory of how anxiety further destabilizes our impulses at each developmental crisis. This crisis-oriented and conflictual nature of our developmental journeys works to qualify, mitigate, and finally save Erikson's psychology from the general vision of an easy harmony that so permeates the psychologies of Rogers, Maslow, and Perls.

But in spite of the fact that Erikson's harmonistic metaphors are more complex and less automatic than our humanistic triumvirate, they still clearly tend in that direction. One can see this in two areas of his psychology. One is his persistent assertion that infants and children need a unifying and trusting image of the world. The other is his belief that the human life cycle is welded together by a preestablished cogwheeling of mutually reinforcing needs between the old and the young throughout the human life cycle.

For the most part, Erikson's writings are characterized by a surprisingly consistent psychological point of view. Even though he ranges widely and discusses politics, religion, and a variety of other topics, he for the large part confines himself to comments on the psychological significance of these realms of experience. This is basically true of his comments about the importance of a sense of basic trust for the development of the healthy personality. He says that trust is important for health and that infants, children, and, in fact, all of us need a worldview that suggests that other people and the world beyond basically can be trusted to support what we need for human life. As a psychologist Erikson usually says only that humans *need to believe* that this is the case; he does not generally make ontological statements that the world has ultimately something about it that makes it genuinely trustworthy. Yet his personal conviction that this *is* the case shines through his writings about the role of trust, worldviews, and religion in the formation of the mature person.

A few examples from an abundance of passages will suffice. In *Childhood and Society* Erikson tells us that it is the task of parents to help move the child toward "a final integration of the individual life cycle with some meaningful wider belongingness."[82] In addition, they must be able to "represent to the child a deep, an almost somatic conviction that there is a meaning to what they are doing."[83] This requires a "parental faith" that finds its "institutional safeguard in organized religion."[84] Erikson seems aware that this need for a trust guaranteed by religion does not prove the truth of religion. But his personal orientation may break through when he writes, "The clinician can only observe that many are proud to be without religion whose children cannot afford their being without it."[85]

In *Insight and Responsibility* Erikson says that to communicate self-cohesion and affirmation to the developing infant the quality of the parental relationship should convey an "all-enveloping world-image tying past, present, and future into a convincing pattern of providence."[86] This requires "an adult faith," and one that, as he says in *Youth, Identity, and Crisis,* entails attitudes "toward [both] oneself and the world."[87] But then suddenly the drift of Erikson's statements toward more objective and ontological affirmations about the way the world really is becomes evident when he writes, "only a reasonably coherent world provides the faith which is transmitted by the mothers to the infants in a way conducive to the vital strength of hope."[88] In short, humans need to believe that the grounds for their trust are objective and stamped into the very fabric of the universe. Although for the most part Erikson speaks of this need in psychological and functional terms, there are times when his own faith in this ground of trust shines forth.

But Erikson's faith in a trustworthy and basically harmonious world is most clear in his use of the metaphor of "cogwheeling" that he uses to explain the fundamental biological harmony between the young and the old in the cycle of generations. This metaphor is taken from mechanics to communicate the way gears mesh and wheels fit to propel one another. Here is another excellent example of the way philosophers of science such as Barbour, Black, and Hess say metaphors from one area of experience are used to order another. Here a metaphor from mechanics is used in biology to suggest how diverse human needs between the young and the old actually mesh, correspond, and are finally mutual. In this case the metaphor of cogwheeling is used to suggest the harmonious compatibility of psychobiological needs throughout the life cycle. Biology, read and interpreted through this metaphor, becomes trustworthy and a ground for security. And this happens in ways almost diametrically opposed to the way biology functions in the psychology of Freud. The psychobiological use of the metaphor of cogwheeling takes on the function of God language; it helps biology to function as a signal and an index of the basic trustworthiness of the ultimate context of experience. A mechanical metaphor employed within the precincts of biology hints at a bedrock for the security of life and the compatibility and harmony of its various forms. In his summary of the history of ego psychology, David Rapaport detects the importance of the metaphor of cogwheeling in Erikson when he writes,

> Erikson's theory, like Hartmann's adaptation theory rests on the assumption of an inborn coordination to an average expectable environment. His concept of *mutuality* (1950) specifies that the crucial coordination is between the developing individual and his human (social) environment, and that this coordination is mutual. The theory postulates a *cogwheeling of the life cycles:* the representatives of society, the caretaking persons, are coordinated to the developing individual by their specific inborn responsiveness to his needs and by phase-specific needs of their own (e.g., generativity).[89]

This quotation astutely points to the centrality of the cogwheeling metaphor for Erikson. It provides him with the loose conceptual tool to convey his image of how infant and parent needs correspond and mesh to move each other along throughout the cycle of generations. "Babies control and bring up their families as much as they are controlled by them; in fact, we may say that the family brings up a baby by being brought up by him."[90] And then he adds that whatever "reaction patterns are given biologically and whatever schedule is predetermined developmentally must be considered to be a series of *potentialities for channeling patterns of mutual regulation.*"[91] This fund of cogwheeling needs is the foundation of interpersonal mutuality and harmony; the basic harmonies of life are founded upon the secure ground of reciprocal and mutually reinforcing biological needs.

Furthermore, these mutually reinforcing needs constitute the grounds from which the human life cycle is renewed. In *Insight and Responsibility* Erikson tells us, "The cogwheeling stages of childhood and adulthood are, as we can see in conclusion, truly a system of *generation and regeneration.*"[92] By this Erikson means that the mutually activating needs of the young and the old renew each other, help keep each other on track, and renew each other in life's central task of maintaining and revitalizing the cycle of generations. For as Erikson says elsewhere, "The history of humanity is a gigantic metabolism of individual life cycles."[93] Hence, the suckling needs of the infant awaken both pleasure and maternal instincts in the mother, the dependence of the child both awakens and fulfills the generative teaching needs of the adult, the infant's need for a confirming face both activates and meets the adult's need to see and enjoy the smiling face of the young, as finally the adult couple's need for genital exchange and mutual confirmation gets met in the mutualities of the marital state. Erikson's writings are replete with such illustrations supported by varying degrees of evidence.

There is an interesting interaction between Erikson's functional language about the role of trust and parental faith in human development and his more directly cognitive assertions about the harmonious cogwheeling of needs and tendencies within the cycle of the generations. His cognitive assertions about the latter give a hint of objectivity and ontological weight to his more functional language about trust. The implication is that faith in the trustworthiness of life is justified (not just functionally useful) because the human life cycle is biologically structured to be complementary and mutually supportive. It seems only a short step for the imagination to conclude, as it may do for both Erikson and his readers, that since belief in trustworthy and benevolent providers is functionally good and since the human life cycle is objectively cogwheeled and meshed maybe there are indeed behind it all beneficent forces that create all this complementarity and harmony and make it a fundamental feature of human existence.

That Erikson's images of harmony are never as extreme and secure as those in Rogers, Maslow, and Perls is due, as I suggested above, to his more complicated theories of instinctual pluralism and more fundamental vision of the pervasiveness of anxiety. Anxiety is more than simply socially induced in Erikson; it is a consequence of confronting the contingencies and forced decisions implicit in every developmental crisis. Although it can and does have a social dimension, anxiety is much more a pervasive aspect of human existence for Erikson than it is for the humanistic psychologists. Erikson is far closer to Augustine, Kierkegaard, and Reinhold Niebuhr on the role of anxiety in human life than are Rogers, Perls, and Maslow. Although he never approaches affirming anything like the Augustinian-Niebuhrian concept of original sin, his theory of anxiety qualifies his metaphors of harmony and makes them function much closer to the Judeo-Christian doctrine of creation than do the metaphors of harmony in humanistic psychology. Hence, Erikson is close, although not quite identical, to the religio-cultural vision of humanistic psychology.

But in spite of this closeness, Erikson, as we have seen, never uses this vision to support an ethical-egoist theory of obligation. For Erikson, the harmonies of life are sufficiently qualified and disrupted by anxiety and instinctual pluralism as to require an ethic of genuine mutuality and, indeed at times, an ethic of generative self-sacrifice. The harmonies that support the human life cycle only work to support, not absolutely guarantee, an ethic of mutuality and equal-regard. The cogwheeling of intergenerational needs and tendencies gives our lives a gentle drift toward mutuality; it means that an ethic of mutuality has energies to draw on for support and activation. But it would be an illusion if Erikson were to be used, as sometimes he can nearly permit himself to be used, to support the fiction that these mutualities are so built into the fabric of life that we can appropriate them without ambivalence through a simple process of mindlessly and romantically sinking back into the rhythms of nature.

We have already seen how the later Kohut adopts much of the self-actualization language of humanistic psychology—language about inner potentials, innate talents, blue prints of the self, and innermost designs. But in addition to these affinities with the metaphors of harmony in humanistic psychology, we also have seen that Kohut holds a theory of generative complementarity within the cycle of the generations quite similar to Erikson's. Moreover, Kohut also seems to advocate certain generalized attitudes of trust toward the world as an integral part of his psychology. For instance, toward the conclusion of *The Analysis of the Self* Kohut claims that the successful completion of his kind of psychotherapy with narcissistically disturbed individuals "leads to the acquisition of a number of highly valued sociocultural attributes (such as empathy, creativity, humor, and wisdom)."[94] In discussing empathy Kohut tells us, with obvious approval, that psychoanalyzed individuals will not only have an increased capacity to empathize with others but that they, in addition, will have "a gradually increasing acceptance of the expectation that others will also be able to grasp the patient's feelings, wishes, and needs."[95] Here Kohut is subtly advocating a certain attitude toward the deep possibilities of life. The healthy person—the one who sees the world rightly—can expect that people within that world on the whole will empathize with his or her feelings. This rather nonspecific set of expectations about the responsiveness of the people we meet in the world is almost diametrically opposed to Freud's expectation that most of the people in the world will meet us with hostility and general insensitivity to our needs, wishes, and feelings.

In *The Restoration of the Self* Kohut reveals that he sees the attitudes of parents as metaphors to the genuine possibilities of life. By implication Kohut conveys the idea that the therapist's attitudes in therapy can also function as metaphors filtering and restructuring the analysand's expectations about life and the possibilities of the world. Kohut discusses the case of a young woman who had a dream that she was standing over a toilet urinating with the vague sense that there was something watching her from behind. Rather than interpreting this as a dream about penis envy (as did her previous therapist), Kohut sees it as an attempt on the part of the woman to identify with her more empathic father rather than with her bizarre and emotionally shallow mother. Her mother had warned her never to sit down on toilets outside of the house because of the fear of disease and dirt. The toilet seat was a metaphor of the "mother's hidden paranoid outlook on the whole world." As Kohut so astutely observes, "The toilet seat was the world—an inimical, dangerous, infected world. And the child's healthy move toward the world—in sexual and nonsexual directions—was made impossible by the infiltration of the mother's paranoid beliefs into the child's psychic organization."[96] What Kohut does not seem to understand here is that the language of these comments reveals that both parents and therapists are in the business of conveying certain attitudes and expectations about the way the world is and what to expect from it. One can argue that Kohut as therapist in the transference relation was helping this woman learn how to use the therapist and his attitudes as a more reliable set of metaphors for the way the world really is—a world in which there are fewer dangers, fewer genuine fears, and more supports than this woman's poor mother believed was the case.

Erikson and Kohut both have within their psychologies metaphors of harmony typical of those found in the humanistic psychology. As we have seen, metaphors of harmony are also found, along with other metaphors of ultimacy, in the Hebraic and Christian traditions. From another perspective, these same metaphors of harmony and the goodness and trustworthiness of the created order constitute metaphors of redemption in some modern psychologies. They point to a resource at the depth of life from which energies flow that will revitalize, recreate, and restore broken lives to former states of wholeness. It is clear that in both of these psychologies there are positive sources available in the organism to guide life in the beginning, and these same forces through therapy and other interventions can be unleashed to restore life when it is broken. This logic can be found in humanistic psychologies as well.

What one has in Erikson and Kohut, and even more so in the humanistic psychologies and Jung, are implicit metaphors of harmony and redemption—two of the great foundational metaphors of the Western religious tradition. What is missing in both are metaphors analogous to those of God as governor, that is, metaphors that point to those deep resources and demands stemming from the depth of life that make moral claims and provide moral supports to the life of moral seriousness. Skinner, on the other hand, has metaphors analogous to God the governor. Natural selection, that is, the negative and positive reinforcements of the environment, functions in his psychology, as we saw, as supraindividual powers of predestination. They function almost like the sovereign will of God selecting and pruning out those among us who have not the moral fitness to handle the demands of our environments. Erikson, on the other hand, with his morality of generative mutuality and his superadded ethics of nonviolent sacrificial love, has no deep metaphors calling for and supporting the mutuality and transitional self-sacrifice that he sees so fundamental to life.

It is not that the modern psychologists are any less religious or any less reliant on deep metaphors that require a leap of faith to accept. It is rather, with the exception of Freud, that there is everywhere the romanticism of Christianity's doctrine of creation without the moral realism of this tradition's understanding of a transcendent and morally serious God. Even when the transitional ethic of self-sacrifice is called for conceptually, as it is in Erikson, there are few if any metaphors of ultimacy suggesting that the deeper recesses of life either call for this sacrifice or can provide supporting resources to make it possible. The modern psychologies have their quasi-religious metaphors, but they are noticeably devoid of both metaphors of moral seriousness and metaphors of grace. Hence, the moral expectations of these psychologies, although not absent, are modest. And the resources in life that they envision to empower moral pursuits are weaker still.

Psychology and Society:
Toward a Critical Psychological Theory

In this book, I have treated the modern psychologies more as systems of practical moral philosophy than as simply scientific or clinical psychologies. I have not denied that there are genuinely valid scientific statements and clinical values in these psychologies; I have simply argued, instead, that they are not only or strictly scientific in either the clinical or experimental senses of the term. In effect, however, I have implied that it is very difficult, if not impossible, to develop a clinical psychology that is without the moral and metaphorical overtones that characterize these psychologies. This is because they were born in the context of practical interests concerned with the question of cure and healing. For that reason, they take part in the structure of practical thinking. It is a view of the structure of practical thinking that has guided my analysis of the full reality of these psychologies.

However, I have not done much with what I have called the fourth level of practical moral thinking, that is, the contextual level. In chapter 1 I mentioned very briefly that we would return to a consideration of the social context of the modern psychologies but that for most of the book I would concentrate on them as systems of *practical ideas* designed to guide practical work in the area of psychotherapy or psychological intervention or management. I justified this by taking a distinctively Weberian perspective in this analysis. I respected the ideas in these therapies and the ideas and thought of certain examples of Christian thought. Like any Weberian approach I did not deny the importance of social systemic patterns for the formation of thought, but I took a stand that social systemic forces never completely and exhaustively form the ideas and ideals that guide our lives.

But there are new and powerful approaches to the study of modern psychology that say that it is deeply embedded in the social forces of modern life—particularly the forces of advanced rationalistic capitalism—and that for all practical purposes psychology is an ideological expression of and tool for these social contextual patterns. The argument is that the form of life found in rational capitalism shapes social life in ways that reward individualism, assertiveness, independence, and flexibility. On the other hand, this form of life undermines communities of loyalty, localism, interdependence, and covenanted relations of all kinds. This is a theme, as we have seen, that runs through Cushman and Richardson's team. I agree that modern capitalism has shaped much of contemporary psychology, but it is not the only source and it need not be the only source for the future.

Nonetheless, the argument about capitalism's relation to psychology is worth hearing at length. In *Justice and the Critique of Pure Psychology* (1983) Edward E. Sampson states this position well.[1] He admits that the critique starts with the Marxist assumption that the practical shape of economic life forms human consciousness in a variety of ways. In the case of the West this form of economic life is advanced capitalism, and it shapes the patterns of everyday consciousness and ways of life as well as the concepts and implicit values of academic disciplines such as psychology. He writes, "In other words, the prevailing reality, the world of our everyday existence, is generated by the underlying forms of advanced capitalism: for example, the qualities of our daily work, our career choices and chances, the kinds of conflict we encounter, the ideas, beliefs, and self-understandings we have about our world and our life, and so forth."[2] In addition, the underlying forms of advanced capitalist society, according to this view, shape the disciplines of psychology as well. Let us listen to Sampson again. Although he speaks about the human sciences in general, he intends to cover the disciplines of psychology as well when he says,

> The human sciences enter this model in one important manner: they are the contemporary vehicle that organizes and develops societal self-understandings. Needless to say, they are not alone in this endeavor, as the media and religion also have their hand in developing, organizing, and propagating societal self-understandings. However, the human sciences play an especially central role in that they provide the scientific seal of approval, with all that it connotes in our world today, to the kinds of self-understandings they develop: an added sense of truth, fact, objectivity, and hence legitimacy.[3]

This passage is striking not only for what it suggests about the ideological nature of the modern psychologies but also about how the modern psychologies play integrating functions for contemporary society in ways analogous to religion—another way of making a point similar to the main argument of this book.

If this position were to be taken seriously, then additional, though not necessarily contradictory, light is thrown on my argument. If the modern psychologies serve the ideological functions of reflecting, perpetuating, and legitimating advanced capitalism as the dominant social force in Western societies, and particularly in the United States, then we would expect these psychologies to project a vision of human fulfillment that celebrates the values of individualism, assertiveness, independence, and flexibility. You would expect the psychologies to build an implicit normative view of the person that celebrates the virtues of one who would function well in the competitive individualistic or corporate environments of rational capitalistic societies. At first glance, this might indeed appear to have happened. The drift toward the conflation of images of health with implicit normative concepts of philosophical ethical egoism that we saw in the writings of the humanistic psychologists and Jung might fit this argument almost perfectly. The individualism, assertiveness, independence, and flexibility spawned by advanced capitalism might be perfectly served by, in fact might be seen as actually equal to, the ethical egoism we uncovered in these psychologies. Freud might fit as well, depending on whether we follow Rieff or Wallwork in our understanding of Freud's ethics. And even if we follow Wallwork, his view of Freud's ethic of respect (which can hardly be distinguished from cautious reciprocity) might be seen to fit into an ethic of exchange so typical of the market economy of the capitalist society. Kohut might be seen to fit as well since he never carries his ethic of mutuality far beyond the confines of the intergenerational relations between parent and child. And there is indeed in Kohut much talk about health as fulfilling in mature ways the ambitions of one's grandiose self. Skinner's truncated justice and Erikson's ethic of mutuality and nonviolence strain the argument somewhat. But even here, Skinner's implicit concern with justice could be seen as superficial and primarily subservient to the technical rationality of his operantly conditioned and fully engineered society. And even Erikson's ethic of generative mutuality with its strong reinforcement, against the forces of capitalist disintegration, of the integrity of the cycle of generations can be construed to fit the argument. One might say that without setting this view of human fulfillment within a thoroughgoing critique of the individualizing and community-undermining forces of advanced capitalism, Erikson's generative person will be quickly corrupted and put to the dutiful service of maintaining, not the cycle of generations, but the cycles and engines of the capitalist machine.

Hence, this argument, which gains much of its fuel from the major figures associated with the Frankfurt Institute of Social Research, could appear to explain many of the values of these psychologies. It could make them all seem to express and serve the deep structures of capitalist societies. Further, it could make it appear that my Weberian effort to take the ideas of these psychologies seriously and to compare them critically with the religious thought of representative Christian interpreters was misguided and fruitless. What are at stake here, it could be argued, are not ideas, concepts, deep metaphors, or even principles of obligation. What are at issue are the needs for self-reproduction of a particular form of society into which these disciplines have been unwittingly pressed, and their concepts, whether psychological, ethical, or metaphorical, are simply tools to that end.

This sociological view of the modern psychologies is only partially correct, however. There is little doubt that these psychologies, as practical disciplines, tend to participate in the larger practical activities and interests of the societies that surround them. This is part of the purpose of calling these psychologies, as I have done, practical moral philosophies as well as strict psychologies. But rather than saying that they totally reflect the processes and ideologies of Western capitalist societies, it might be more accurate to say that these psychologies are *responses* to the forces and trends of capitalist societies. The dim outlines of the various demands and interests of capitalist societies are in the background of these psychologies. Capitalistic societies form an agenda with which the psychologies are implicitly or explicitly dealing. Capitalist societies do not necessarily dictate the responses of these psychologies, but they do present a pressure with which, in their varying images of human fulfillment, these psychologies attempt to cope.

Putting the case this way allows for several advantages. It permits me to keep the basically Weberian beginning point of the inquiry I have been pursuing. Moreover, it permits me to take their various responses to the forces of rational capitalism seriously as quasi-independent solutions, projects, and perspectives. As we have seen, their solutions do vary. The optimal images of human fulfillment for these various psychologies, their implicit ethics, and the deep metaphors that undergird them do differ from one another, sometimes only slightly but sometimes strikingly. If these psychologies were all simply unreflective pawns of rational capitalism, they would not possess the distinctions that they do.

This then makes it possible to do a genuine theology of culture. By taking their images of human fulfillment seriously as practical constructive responses to the forces of rational capitalism, I can then justifiably evaluate these responses. And if these responses contain quasi-religious metaphors and implicit ethical commitments, then these practical psychological responses are legitimate candidates for what we called earlier a revised critical correlational conversation with representative interpretations of the Christian tradition. It is my conviction that these psychologies have made responses to the forces of modern capitalist societies of a religio-ethical kind, that their religio-ethical responses are in many ways on the same logical level as the inherited Judeo-Christian responses, and for that reason they are entirely respectable candidates for the exercise in a critical theology of culture of the kind we pursued in these pages.

Critical Theory and the Modern Psychologies

The view presented by Sampson is actually part of a wider movement, inspired by the Frankfurt Institute of Social Research, to place the modern social sciences on a surer foundation. This is a movement first inspired by the writings of Max Horkheimer, Theodor Adorno, Herbert Marcuse, Erich Fromm, and more recently the powerful work of Jürgen Habermas.[4] This was a loose, powerful, and often confused school that was trying to rescue the modern social sciences from the illusion that they were value-free, totally objective, noncontextual, and nonhistorical quests for objective knowledge. This school has insisted that insofar as the modern social sciences (sociology, political science, economics, as well as psychology) continue with their philosophy of positivistic empiricism and the self-deception of objectivity that flows from it, these disciplines will by default unwittingly fall into the service of advanced capitalism. This is to say that they will not be neutral; they will be uncritically value laden—and in ways they will not understand. It is within this context that the work of Erich Fromm can be better understood and appreciated than it was when it first came to the attention of the American reading public.[5] It is also within this context that the work of Herbert Marcuse should be understood. His attempt to synthesize psychoanalysis with Marxism was designed to place psychoanalysis in a historical and normative framework.[6]

The work of Jürgen Habermas has been an extremely powerful addition to this line of scholarship. And recently in the United States some established social psychologists have now begun to take this point of view. In addition to the work of Sampson referred to above, Kenneth Gergen and John Broughton have brought this line of argument into a critique of various aspects of American psychology.

The result of much of this ferment seems to point to a truth that Brewster Smith articulated well several years ago—that much of psychology (especially the clinical, developmental, and social psychologies) cannot stand on its own feet. Psychologists must do their research in close association with the normative disciplines of ethics, political science, and, I would add, hermeneutic philosophy and theology.[7] For instance, psychologists cannot define mental health without having some normative understanding of the kind of society in which one would want to be healthy. One cannot study the psychological formation of conscience without some normative understanding of what constitutes morality—a truth Lawrence Kohlberg in his research on moral thinking has wisely acknowledged.[8] One cannot study the nature of sexuality, the idea of identity, the psychology of work, or the psychology of aging without some prior critical and normative understandings of the dialectical relation between the good person and the good society and what this would mean for these various provinces of life. Hence, our psychologies (as well as our other social sciences) must be critical psychologies. This means that they should be disciplines that self-consciously mix descriptive and experimental work with normative work about the nature of the good person and the good society and their dialectical relation.

Just what to call this new mixed discipline is still a matter of debate. Russell Keat recommends calling it "critical social theory," but has in mind primarily the sciences of sociology and economics.[9] If we were to follow his lead in the area of the clinical psychological disciplines, we might call it "critical psychological theory." Such a discipline would be self-conscious in bringing together under a single discipline normative and descriptive/empirical work in the various areas of psychology. As I have indicated above, an even better tag is to call it a critical hermeneutic theory of psychology. This would signal taking effective history and the religio-cultural classics that have shaped it with more seriousness than does the Frankfurt school, Habermas, Sampson, or Keating. Work toward the creation of such a discipline is now in progress and can be seen even among hardheaded academicians who once would have been horrified by such an idea. Evidence for this, as I have already suggested, can be found in the collection of essays from nearly every quarter of the social sciences, edited by Norma Haan, Robert Bellah, et al., *Social Science as Moral Inquiry*.[10] It can be found as well in Robert Bellah and his associates' *Habits of the Heart* and the partners with whom we have been in conversation throughout this book—the writings of Cushman and Richardson, Fowers, and Guignon.[11]

I am not prepared to say that this new discipline of critical psychological theory should be the only form of psychology. Here I find myself agreeing more with Russell Keat's position as developed in *The Politics of Social Theory: Habermas, Freud, and the Critique of Positivism* (1981). In this book he argues that we need two kinds of social science. I would extend this by saying that we need two kinds of psychology. One psychology would be a cautious, rigorous, and humble psychology that would aspire to be as value free as possible, although it would recognize that it can never achieve this goal. There is a logical distinction between rigorous descriptive statements and statements about norms, and it is useful and important to maintain that distinction as well as we can.[12] For instance, Keat believes that we should never try to argue for the scientific validity of a descriptive statement on normative grounds, that is, on the grounds that it conforms to some normative ethical or religious view of things. Therefore, there is a real usefulness and importance in maintaining a discipline that tries to do primarily descriptive work of a limited kind. But it is his belief, and I concur, that such a psychology would be relatively impotent to address very many problems of actual living. One could never develop a therapy from such a psychology alone and certainly not a personality theory nor a developmental psychology. These psychologies inevitably contain, as I think we have shown, practical normative interests. This is inevitable and acceptable and should be legitimated by self-consciously creating a variety of critical psychological theories pertaining to the various provinces of human life. Psychology of the more value-free variety will be used by psychology of this second type—psychology understood as critical psychological theory. But the strictly descriptive statements of psychology in the relatively value-free form would not claim validity from psychology in the second form; conversely, the normative dimensions of the second type of psychology would never seek justification alone from the scientific descriptions of the first type of psychology. Both forms of psychology could rightly claim to be scientific since both would attempt to be public and follow arguments that could be publicly examined, reviewed, and tested. But they would indeed be sciences in different senses of the word.

Seen from the perspective of this second kind of psychology, the mixed discourse of Freud, Skinner, Jung, Erikson, Kohut, and our humanistic psychologies seems not so much wrong in principle as unreflective, naïve, and philosophically and ethically immature if not downright dangerous. For all practical purposes, to do psychology in the first sense may be impossible, especially for the more clinically oriented psychologies and probably as well for personality theory, developmental theory, and all aspects of social psychology. All these psychologies are too close to the context of practical action to avoid the contours of practical thinking. There is no way to avoid it. So the task is not to avoid it but to base the genuinely practical aspects of these psychologies on critical practical thought. Hence, rather than asking these psychologies to get rid of all their deep metaphors and implicit principles of obligation, the task would be to base their psychologies on better and more critically grounded hermeneutic philosophy of practical moral thinking. Rather than asking Freud to suppress his latent ethical views, one might ask him to review his commitments to cautious reciprocity and his interpretations of the Western tradition of agape and determine whether these are as critically defensible as he thought. Rather than asking the psychologists I have associated with the culture of joy to suppress their moral commitments or their deep metaphors, one would ask instead that they be brought to the surface, critically tested, and replaced if they appear inadequate.

But the question remains: What will be the role of religion and theology in providing the critical and normative background to these new mixed disciplines of critical hermeneutical psychology? On the whole, people such as Habermas and many influenced by him (such as Sampson and Broughton) seem to find no place for the role of religion. Sadly, neither have the more directly hermeneutic perspectives promoted by Cushman and Richardson, et al. Hence, it would seem that the deep metaphors, narratives, and symbols of the Judeo-Christian tradition will be barred from officially influencing these disciplines. Habermas clearly takes this view when he rejects the projects advocated by Paul Ricoeur, Hans-Georg Gadamer, and David Tracy for a hermeneutical retrieval of the classical visions of life in Hebrew, Christian, and Greek culture.[13] But if our view of the inevitable role of deep metaphors in practical thinking is correct, then barring the role of religion may be more difficult than one would think. And if my view that some rational method can be brought to the question of evaluating deep metaphors from the perspective of their metaphysical as well as their moral adequacy, then it may be that even theology—the despised discipline of our times—will have a role to play in this newly evolving discipline of critical hermeneutic psychology. This book has been dedicated to the investigation of this possibility.

Reason and Reactivity
in Ellis, Beck, and Bowen

In this chapter, we will focus on three psychotherapeutic theorists—Albert Ellis, Aaron Beck, and Murray Bowen—who were not covered in the first edition. One might wonder why a family systems theorist such as Bowen is grouped with the typically individual, cognitive approaches of Ellis and Beck. The primary reason for this is that all three theorists identify emotional reactivity as the primary culprit of mental health. All three recognize exaggerated anxiety as a major problem sabotaging a healthy cognitive process. All three understand the solution to the human dilemma as a return to unruffled reason. All three believe our psychological salvation is through clear, creative thinking in the face of stress. All three view the central problems of human life as related to the inability to rationally "respond" to circumstances because of knee-jerk, emotional reactions and "survival thinking." All three see mental health centered in the activities of the neocortex: analyzing, evaluating, and exploring creative alternatives. Put differently, all three could not possibly disagree more with Fritz Perls's frequently quoted suggestion that we must "lose our minds and come to our senses." It is precisely the absence of reason's higher level functioning that creates troubled persons in the first place. The vision of human fulfillment, then, is intricately tied to a Stoic, nonreactionary, almost imperturbable self. Thus, in their own ways, they each advocate a culture of calm reason—a culture that is close to, although not identical to, Freud's culture of detachment.

To help us focus on these theorists, we will make use of a work that the first edition of *Religious Thought and the Modern Psychologies* influenced to a considerable extent; this is the work of Stanton Jones and Richard Butman in their *Modern Psychotherapies*.[1] We give special attention to the manner in which they analyze implicit philosophical assumptions in clinical psychology. In other words, how do they expand our discussion of the religio-ethical horizons out of which psychological cultures operate?

Modern Psychotherapies, a very comprehensive book, is similar to our own effort in two ways: (a) it seeks to explicate the philosophical matrix out of which psychotherapies function, and (b) it focuses primarily on analysis and theological and ethical evaluation, rather than the theory-building part of integration. Like us, the authors believe that a critical analysis of various cultures of psychology is essential before the next steps are taken. Unlike us, they argue primarily on the principle of biblical authority rather than on critical correlational grounds. In that sense, their effort is less public than ours. Put simply, they do not follow our revised correlational method. They make it clear that while they are attempting a dialogue between psychotherapy and Christianity, it is a "dialogue where one side of the conversation, that of the Christian faith, is presumed to have the ultimate standing as truth."[2] God's special revelation in the Bible must take priority over any natural revelation in psychology or any other discipline. Hence scriptural teachings about persons, though they do not qualify as a full-blown personality theory, are taken as the "control beliefs" that guide the discussion.[3]

The Primacy of Reason in RET[4]

Albert Ellis introduced the basic principles of rational-emotive therapy in 1955.[5] While he further developed and refined his position, the basic premises remain the same. In a nutshell, RET argues that emotional disturbance results from distorted thinking. Psychological problems stem from cognitive processes. Human beings act neurotically because they think crookedly. While biological, social, and developmental factors all play a role in the formation of psychological disturbance, their role is clearly secondary to the most important factor of emotional distress, the process of interpreting things. Ellis puts it this way:

> The central theme of RET is that man is a uniquely rational, as well as a uniquely irrational, animal; that his emotional or psychological disturbances are largely a result of his thinking illogically or irrationally; and that he can rid himself of most of his emotional or mental unhappiness, ineffectuality, and disturbance if he learns to maximize his rational and minimize his irrational thinking.[6]

Our critique of Ellis does not question his emphasis on rationality as such but rather his narrow, instrumental view of rationality in contrast to the hermeneutic rationality advanced in this book. For Ellis, emotion should not be considered apart from its attachment to cognition. In fact, thoughts precede and determine emotions. Human beings are constantly assessing, evaluating, and interpreting their life circumstances. These mental processes shape the emotional response. Therefore, emotion is never a "thing-in-itself." According to Ellis,

> a large part of what we call emotion is little more or less than a certain kind— a biased, prejudiced, or strongly elusive kind—of thinking. Although, then, the patient is more than just his ideas, for all practical purposes the fact remains that, especially as regards his emotional disturbance, he is *mainly* his ideas; and that therefore the most important method of helping him overcome his disturbance is through helping him change his conscious or unconscious ideas.[7]

Ellis even argues that distorted thinking not only brings about misery, but is also unethical. As he puts it, "When you make yourself severely anxious or depressed, you clearly are acting against *you* and are being unfair and unjust to *yourself*."[8]

While Ellis is quick to point toward reason as the crucial ingredient in treating emotional problems, he distinguishes himself from the philosophical tradition of rationalism: "In philosophy, rationalism is basically an idealistic and anti-empirical mode of viewing the world: since it holds that reason, or the intellect, rather than the senses is the true source of knowledge. The classical rationalist is therefore a believer in absolutism, since for him reason is the prime and absolute authority in determining what is true and what cause of action one should take in life."[9] For Ellis, reason and logic are tools of scientific investigation. He does not believe that reason and logic contain universal truths in their own right. Rationalism is tenable insofar as the term means opposition to "all forms of supernaturalism, spiritualism, mysticism, revelation, dogmatism, authoritarianism, and antiscientism."[10] But the philosophical tradition of rationalism and its Cartesian preoccupation with indubitable, absolutely certain innate ideas is clearly wrongheaded.

Ellis also does not share the frequent assertion in humanistic psychology that "all feelings are neutral" and that we should not label them positive or negative. Humanistic psychologists have often proclaimed that "feelings are just feelings" and that only behaviors can be evaluated. In contrast, Ellis believes there are "appropriate" and "inappropriate" feelings. Both categories arise from human thinking. But what is their difference?

This crucial difference between appropriate and inappropriate feelings usually has to do with the turning of a desire (which is healthy) into a demand (which is unhealthy). When we *desire* that life or people be a certain way, we are appropriately saddened, disappointed, or frustrated when it is not. But when we *demand* that life conform to our God-ordained expectations, then we feel inappropriately outraged, depressed, horrified, or suicidal. Again, "appropriate" feelings emerge from desires; "inappropriate" feelings emerge from demands. As Ellis puts it, "your dogmatic command that you always *must* get what you desire is illegitimate and self-defeating—because the universe clearly does not *owe* you your heart's desire. And you will interfere with getting your preferences by fanatically demanding that they *have to be* fulfilled."[11] We cannot help wondering on what grounds Ellis knows, in view of his alleged positivistic empiricism, what the universe does or does not owe the people in it. Although his remark about what the universe owes is doubtless a kind of unguarded lapse on Ellis's part, it shows just how difficult it is for even the most skeptical of souls to keep from making some kind of judgment about the nature of the ultimate context of experience.

Stoicism, Ethics, and Ellis

As Jones and Butman investigate RET, they point toward both the obvious and the subtle dimensions of Ellis's ethical and value orientation. On the one hand, Ellis is very explicit in describing himself as a "long-term hedonist." He is most straightforward: "Seek pleasures and happiness today—and also tomorrow! Do cost-benefit calculation to determine if your gains, now and in the future, are too costly."[12] Ellis further believes this ethical egoism is universal. Even ascetics in a monastery are long-term hedonists in that they are anticipating heaven's reward.[13] Recognizing the problems inherent in short-term hedonism, Ellis accents the importance of restraint for the purposes of greater overall happiness. He states the goals of RET as helping people "to think more rationally; . . . to feel more appropriately; and to act more functionally . . . in order to achieve their goals of living longer and more happily."[14] While Ellis claims that he does not *prescribe* values to his clients, Butman and Jones believe he sneaks those values in through the back door under the banner of "rational attitudes." These rational attitudes Ellis deems important include "self-interest, social interest, self-direction, high frustration tolerance, flexibility, acceptance of uncertainty, commitment to creative pursuits, scientific thinking, self-acceptance, risk taking, long range hedonism, non-utopianism and responsibility for our emotional disturbance."[15] These attitudes, argue Jones and Butman, clearly contain embedded values designed to help clients move toward the goals of survival and emotional peace.

Ellis's value-laden rational attitudes are directly tied to his philosophical Stoicism. Jones and Butman indicate that Stoicism emerged during a historical period of socio-political chaos and offered a retreat into one's internal world. Skeptical about exercising any control over the outside world, Stoics believed that they could at least control their inner mental states. Experiencing a cultural decline and military defeats, Greek Stoics wanted an internal mental world free of the unpredictability surrounding them. Again, the goal was inner peace and tranquility. If they remained aloof and detached enough, nothing occurring in the external world would be able to disorient or control the inner life of the mind.

From its beginnings, Stoicism has been criticized for its derogatory view of the emotions and its tendency to resign itself to a kind of fatalism concerning life. A temptation with all forms of Stoicism, including Ellis's, is passivity and disregard for social change. While it *is* important to acknowledge those things we cannot change, the other half of the serenity prayer is to change those things we can. The temptation of Stoicism is to assume that since all problems emerge because of the way we are "interpreting life," then by viewing the world differently, we can make these problems go away. Stoicism easily slides into a conviction that all problems are ultimately intrapsychic in nature. Neurosis is bad hermeneutics.

Edwin Schur offers one example of a provocative critique of this way of thinking.[16] He believes this perspective leads many individuals to think that the origins of all their problems reside within their own psyches. The potential for social change is therefore "cooled out" as these persons are "therapized," and hence the status quo remains the same.[17] Therapy provides a solipsistic inattention to those very structures that oppress. Individuals thus interiorize socio-economic problems. The "aloof self" is viewed as an endless source of problem-solving ability. Psychotherapy thus serves a very important function: It reduces rage over socio-economic injustice. Clients are ongoingly told that they can control any problem by "choosing to not be bothered" by it. Again, this can become a hideout from social involvement. By turning attention away from social and economic injustice, and focusing instead on "why they let these things bother them," clients may be encouraged to do nothing about their world.

More recently, postmodernists such as Sandra Rigazio-Digilio, Allen Ivey, and Don Locke, have also chastised psychotherapy for not considering the importance of socio-economic factors. "Theories of counseling and practice that perpetuate the notion of individual and family dysfunction without giving equal attention to societal dysfunction and to the dysfunctional interactions that can occur between individuals, families, and societies (e.g., intentional and unintentional power differentials) may unwittingly reinforce the oppressive paradigm."[18] While this critique of psychotherapy's neglect of socio-economic contextual issues is often associated with postmodernism, it is important to note that it is essentially an older Marxist critique. While Marx criticized religion for obsessing on an "afterlife," and hence making social change problematic, social critics have attacked psychology for obsessing on an "inner life," which also makes social change problematic.[19]

Although Ellis believes this is an important criticism of much of individual psychotherapy, he does not think it applies to him: "In my early articles and books on REBT [Rational-Emotive Behavioral Therapy], I emphasized that people had better change their inner musts and demands, with which they upset themselves, about the social system. But at the same time, they had better fight against that unfair and irrational system."[20] Ellis points toward his firm stand against the Puritanical social-sexual system of the 1950s. He says, "I think I can say that I was one of the main instigators of the social-sex revolution of the 1960s."[21]

The question must be raised, however, whether Ellis has retained remnants of a Stoic cynicism about changing the outside world and has instead focused on why individuals "allow" external circumstances to "upset" them. The thrust of his therapy has been toward turning individuals away from outside factors and helping them concentrate on their "catastrophizing" and "awfulizing" of injustice. Even if this is not Ellis's intention, clients are encouraged to focus on how they are victimizing themselves through their own exaggerated thinking.

> When you are neurotic, you almost always make yourself that way with illogical and unrealistic thinking. First, you were born with a talent for accepting and creating self-damaging ideas. Then you are considerably aided by your environment—which gives you real troubles (such as poverty, disease, and injustice) and which often encourages your rigid thinking (such as "Since you have musical ability, you absolutely *ought* to be an outstanding musician") . . . but neurosis still comes mainly from *you*. You consciously or unconsciously choose to victimize yourself by it. And you *can* choose to stop your nonsense and to stubbornly refuse to make yourself neurotic about virtually anything.[22]

From a theological perspective, one cannot help wondering why Ellis does not realize that his analysis begs for some deeper explanation—one that might make use of the Kierkegaardian-Niebuhrian understanding of finitude, anxiety, and sin—a sin that not only hurts others but is destructive of the individual's own appropriate search for the goods of life.

At another level, Ellis's position may work to obscure some natural inclinations that Christianity might wish to protect. It should be noted that Stoicism is based on an acquiescence to fate, an intention to align oneself with the "way things are." By telling people, as he frequently has done, that all anger is neurotic, Ellis may be undercutting some of the very natural energy necessary for social change. The point is that the idea of "disturbing oneself" can be pushed too far. Life is then accepted as destiny and injustices continue. While we respect Ellis's ability to help deflate unrealistic entitlement claims on life, he comes dangerously close to blaming the victim in his insistence that we always disturb ourselves. When this happens, not only are people the victims of oppression, but they also blame themselves for "allowing" this oppression to disturb their Stoic tranquility. In the face of unfairness, they then turn their attention toward their own unrealistic "demand" that life be fair. By insisting to themselves that their plight is not horrible, awful, or unbearable, they may tame the very emotions that could propel social changes.

For Ellis's Stoicism, *all* strong emotions are treated with suspicion. Passion is dangerous. Feelings are second-class citizens completely dependent on the thought processes that precede them. The price paid for never allowing ourselves to experience despair is that joy is also off-limits. Living within narrow emotional parameters leads to a calm, but sometimes bland, life.

Jones and Butman point toward the work of Robert Roberts in exposing how Ellis can view the world as noncatastrophic, no matter what. Roberts refers to Ellis's vision of imperturbability as a tendency to be "emotionally flexible and adaptable, relatively content regardless of what happens."[23] Roberts further correlates this to the Judeo-Christian virtues of gratitude in all circumstances, contentment, perseverance, and courage.[24] Yet he makes a most interesting comparison. Ellis encourages his clients to believe that nothing is catastrophic because nothing is of ultimate value. Nothing is momentous, and hence, pain and tragedy are trivialized. The Judeo-Christian tradition, on the other hand, stresses that nothing is ultimately devastating because the future is in the hands of God. What may seem horrible does not have the final word. This is obviously an eschatological view of suffering. Our task becomes rising above that which *seems* unbearable and moving closer to an eternal perspective. Lacking an eschatological view, the price that Ellis pays for viewing nothing as catastrophic is the belief that nothing is of ultimate significance. In positing the belief that nothing is of ultimate value, Ellis demonstrates the validity of our argument, i.e., that all practical judgments make faith assumptions of some kind about the ultimate context of experience. Christianity has its view, and Ellis has his. At the level of their respective faiths, Christian theology and Ellis's amoral vision of cosmic indifference are on the same logical footing. The question becomes, as we discussed in chapter 6, which of these visions and deep metaphors best helps us account for what we intuit about the rest of life—our freedom, moral responsibility, and concern for both self and other?

Perhaps this is one reason Rational Emotive Therapy seems much more prepared to handle the everyday world of exaggerated thinking over minor losses than the larger existential struggles of guilt, suffering, death, loss, meaninglessness, anxiety, and hopelessness. What does Ellis say to clients, for instance, who are in such despair that they don't care if they are being rational or not? His approach presupposes both motivation by and a deep faith in reason. Shipwrecked clients may have neither. The great existential questions of life challenge Ellis's only therapeutic tool—the validity and finality of his particular view of human reason. In fact, some existential thinkers might argue that Ellis lives in fundamental inconsistency with his own standard of rationality. Throughout his career, Ellis has appealed to rationality as if there is a normative standard available. Yet as an atheist, Ellis is hard pressed to find any orderly, reasonable purpose or direction in the ultimate scheme of things. He offers a very small and temporary island of rationality in an ocean of irrationality. This is an unusual brand of Stoicism. As Richardson, Fowers, and Guignon point out, traditional Stoicism "made sense in the context of belief in a living, rational cosmic order that afforded a consoling sense of community with the universe and acceptance of one's place in it."[25] One could detach from everyday emotional ills by committing oneself to the wisdom built into the universe, the Logos. Ellis's Stoicism does not offer a detachment based on this commitment to a larger framework of cosmic or ontological reason.

Two Views of Rationality?

Stephen Evans believes that Ellis works with two different, and potentially conflicting, criteria for rationality.[26] On the one hand, he holds an evolutionary conception of rationality that appeals to something like Darwinian survival value. Rationality refers to that which promotes survival and happiness. Irrationality, conversely, refers to anything that interferes with survival and happiness. Ellis is quite straightforward: "By irrationality I mean any thought, emotion, or behavior that significantly interferes with the survival and happiness of the organism."[27] Or we might say that irrationality is anything that violates ethical egoism.

Yet this standard of survival and happiness is problematic. The simple reality is that Ellis is going to have a hard time identifying a normative standard for happiness. As Evans puts it, "if we take a cross-cultural and historical perspective, there are *vast* differences in what people have taken their happiness to be. We would be foolish—and irrational—to blindly assume that the view of happiness which is taken for granted by the average middle-class person in a consumer-oriented hedonistic society is necessarily correct."[28] Throughout Ellis's writings, he seems to frequently equate happiness with enjoyment, which is consistent with his long-term hedonism. He does not carefully delineate what he means by "happiness" and appears to believe its meaning is self-evident to the reader. Since he is using the standard of happiness and survival as criteria for rationality, it would be helpful if he provided a more specific definition.

Yet this vague understanding of happiness is not Ellis's major problem, according to Evans. Ellis uses a second criteria of rationality—empirical or scientific verifiability. He frequently refers to irrational ideas as nonempirical or unscientific: "REBT holds that most neurotic problems have magical, empirically unvalidatable thinking and that if disturbance-creating ideas are vigorously disputed by logico-empirical thinking they can be recognized as false and minimized."[29] As Evans puts it, "The implicit assumption seems to be that beliefs which are warranted by the 'scientific method' are rational, while those which are not are irrational."[30]

The problem is that these two standards of rationality may very well conflict. While the evolutionary view argues that the criteria of reasonableness is happiness and survival, the empirical standard insists on limiting ourselves to those beliefs that are scientifically warranted. But what if the beliefs derived from the scientific method make us unhappy? A client's belief in God, for instance, might well strengthen his or her happiness and desire for survival. Yet for Ellis's atheism, such a theistic conviction would be scientifically unwarranted. So which criterion of rationality should the client use—scientific verifiability or happiness?

If one begins with the second criterion for rationality, scientific verifiability, it is hard to see how one could demonstrate the claim that it is only rational to believe those things that contribute to survival and happiness. Evans offers an interesting point.

> Suppose, for example, that Ellis's view was countered by someone like Bertrand Russell, who holds that it is only reasonable to accept beliefs which we have good reason to suppose to be true. As Russell understands this view, it implies that a truly rational individual would doggedly cling to what is most true or most likely to be true, even if this were to shorten his life or make him miserable. How would one go about testing the relative merits of Ellis's "evolutionary" view as opposed to Russell's view, using the hypothetico-deductive method?[31]

In a response to Evans's article, Ellis argues that Evans does not fully understand his position. Science is rational, says Ellis, in the sense that it is "more objective, efficient, flexible, and open-minded than nonscientific or anti-scientific methodology."[32] The scientific method, argues Ellis, can be employed to determine whether or not a given behavior increases or decreases a person's level of happiness. Ellis attempts to get around the tension between this happiness versus verifiability criterion by saying that they are related *correlationally*, and not "intrinsically, inherently, or identically."[33]

> Where, then, does science come in? Why does RET use any "scientific" or "empirical" criteria of "rationality"? Not as criteria-in-themselves but as strong *correlates* of the Goals of survival and happiness. For RET hypothesizes—not dogmatizes!—that when humans rigorously stay with unabsolutistic and conditional preferences and desires, they notably *increase* (though not insure) their

chances of fulfilling their basic Goal of a satisfying existence. . . . RET includes a somewhat dualistic view of rationality, with a hedonistic and scientific view that overlap and are correlated but are not identical. It mainly uses survival and happiness as a criteria of rationality—and especially, as criteria for help- ing psychotherapy clients who are clearly unhappy and who therefore come for treatment.[34]

Ellis does concede that sometimes dogmatic beliefs can lead to happiness. Yet in the long run, these beliefs do more harm than good and do not create long-term happiness.

Yet if Ellis uses the criteria of survival and happiness for judging what is rational, then we must quickly ask: *Whose* survival and happiness? Our own individual hap- piness? Our wife or husband's happiness? Our family's happiness? Our children's happiness? The happiness of the poor? The hungry? Unless Ellis assumes, as do many humanistic psychologists, a pre-established world of harmony in which everyone can be happy simultaneously, he needs to consider the ethical quandary of conflict between various pursuits of happiness. A metaphysics of pre-established harmony does not seem to fit Ellis's philosophical framework; remember above that deep metaphors of cosmic indifference rather than harmony seem more con- genial to this thought. So we are left with the dilemma of what to do in the face of conflicting desires for happiness. Ellis wants to appeal to a pragmatic standard. "Personally," he says, "I believe with Richard Rorty that some pragmatic standards of what is 'right' and 'wrong' for a given society can be reasonably established. But I have a hard time . . . validating this view."[35] Yet again the question, "pragmatic for whom?" Ellis does not squarely face the reality of two or more conflicting ethical egoists bumping into each other.

An Atomistic View of Selfhood

Jones and Butman detect another ethical problem in Ellis. Ellis does not believe we humans have a unified, responsible core to our selfhood. The sense of "self" we carry comes from the "coincidental co-occurrence of our own behavior, traits, per- formances, thoughts, memories and so forth."[36] We are simply a stream of thoughts, behaviors, and performances. Borrowing from behaviorism, Ellis does not believe our atomistic behavior patterns are held together by a unified core we can call a "self."

This is why Ellis insists that any attempt to evaluate an entire "self" is hopelessly impossible. We can evaluate a particular behavior, but a human being produces such a multitude of behaviors that evaluation of the whole person is impossible. In this sense, there are only criminal behaviors, not criminals; there are only deceptive actions, not deceitful people. The totality of all our behaviors can never be added up. Consequently, Ellis dislikes the discussion of self-worth or self-esteem. As Jones and Butman indicate, he would prefer that we not make a general judgment about ourselves at all. Any generalization about our ultimate worth is actually irrational, because once again, we can only evaluate specific behavior.

> Thus Ellis's ultimate answer to the self-esteem question is not to evaluate our-
> selves at all. But recognizing the pernicious and irrational human tendency to
> evaluate their whole selves globally (I'm a sinner; look at what I did"), Ellis con-
> cedes that at times it may be more efficient to globally and artificially evaluate
> our whole selves, declare ourselves acceptable and be done with it. He would
> rather that we not grade ourselves at all, but if we are going to grade ourselves
> anyway, let everyone assign themselves A+'s and be happy.[37]

This refusal to evaluate the entire self (because there is ultimately no unifying agent behind all our behavior) brings mixed blessings. On the one hand, it can be used as an argument against any sort of harsh judgment of self or others. No one's entire identity is expressed in a single act, therefore it is irrational to jump from a concrete behavior to an entire indictment of the person. All of us are more than any specific behavior. Further, it is beyond the scope of limited, human rationality to "size up" anyone, including ourselves.

On the other hand, Ellis's atomistic view leaves us with a fragmented self, a self that seems less than a cohesive, responsible agent. It is obviously difficult to hold anyone responsible for their behavior if there is not a choosing, deciding, guiding, cohesive agent behind the behavior.

The Limits of Isolated Reason

While Ellis believes we inevitably struggle with irrationalities, we *do* have the freedom to rise above them. Thus, his approach is Pelagian in that the strongly self-willed person can decide to be rational and move away from crooked thinking. This self-willed change does not necessitate the intervention of therapeutic acceptance or restored relationship. He has little use for Rogers, who believed that we need to *be* accepted before self-acceptance is possible. He would have even more disdain for the Augustinian and Lutheran tradition that, in theological terms, believed we need the grace and acceptance of God before being able to accept and forgive ourselves. In contrast to such views, Ellis argues that we can simply declare ourselves uncon-ditionally acceptable: "Healthy people . . . unconditionally accept themselves because they *choose* to do so, regardless of how well or badly they perform and regardless of how much approval they receive from others."[38] Ellis finds no need for a horizon of grace. Yet we must ask: Is it really possible for us each to accept our-selves in spite of all the condemning voices surrounding us? How can we declare ourselves acceptable when it is our own opinion that is on trial in the first place?

In contrast to Ellis, we suggest that as isolated human beings we are capable of such radical self-doubt that the message of acceptance often cannot reach us. It must be mediated, passed on indirectly, and given concrete form. Many times, the abstract, hypothetical notion of "acceptability" is not very plausible to us. Simply "willing our own acceptance" is not only arduous, but probably impossible.

Ellis, we would argue, has an unrealistic view of an individual's ability to change basic self-perceptions completely on his or her own. All individual thought occurs within what Peter Berger frequently calls social "plausibility structures" (or what Gadamer and Ricoeur called an "effective history") and needs the ongoing community reinforcement for both the formation of the self as well as for its cognitive and emotional support.[39] Ellis believes that all persons have the capacity to be "iron-willed" in maintaining their views in an alien plausibility structure. His maverick approach minimizes the role of community support in maintaining new cognitions.[40]

The larger question then quickly becomes this: Does Ellis adequately appreciate the extent of human vulnerability? It is here that we can see his secularized Pelagianism at work. The human being, through an exercise of will, can not only declare him- or herself acceptable, but can also "stubbornly decide" not to be emotionally disturbed. Yet the deeper issue is whether Ellis, in minimizing human vulnerability, also minimizes the sources of oppression in a person's life? By insisting on a self-cure, does he end up belittling the wound? Put another way, is the injury not "deeper" than reason? Are there emotional wounds we simply cannot "think our way out of," particularly when we are isolated?

Just as Pelagius protested Augustine's understanding of the human will as highly conflicted, corrupted, corporately embedded, and in need of liberation, so Ellis objects to the psychoanalytic understanding that the will is often determined by unconscious, destructive processes. For Pelagius we are free to act righteously if we will just do it; for Ellis, we are free to act healthily if we will just think straight. For neither Pelagius nor Ellis is there a problem of the will's bondage. As we have seen, even the traditional understanding of psychotherapy as a kind of interpersonal acceptance or horizontal grace is denied by Ellis. The human will needs no one's acceptance except its own to overcome obstacles in its determined attempt to live rationally.

In fact, Ellis's model of the therapist is one of a cognitive coach. Yet are there not regions of the psyche that are "deeper" than conscious reason can uncover, areas that will find release more from empathic participation than from cognitive challenge? Ellis's entire framework is built on the assumption that the hidden recesses of the psyche can be fairly easily tapped by conscious reason. In fact, he talks about being able to get to the core irrationalities of a person just by listening to them for a few minutes. Does his approach do justice to the intricate processes of the psyche?

For instance, since human destructiveness or "evil" stem from crooked thinking, Ellis believes this dilemma can be remedied through cognitive restructuring. "Salvation" is strictly a cerebral process. Jones and Butman contrast Ellis's position with a biblical view of evil arising from the human "heart" or what Niebuhr would call our anxiety and our resulting prideful and sensuous efforts to find security without faith in the God. Jones and Butman write, "The heart is surely not synonymous with a thought pattern, because the heart *precedes* the thought pattern. Thus a Christianized RET cannot look at the heart as a belief system; the heart must be more. This casts doubt on the most fundamental aspects of RET understanding of rationality."[41]

Jones and Butman go on to say that just as cognitive processes influence emotions, so emotional processes may indeed affect cognitions. The relationship between thoughts and feelings is reciprocal. Thus, the dynamic and client-centered therapy emphasis on the primacy of affect may offer a corrective to a one-sidedness in the strict cognitive models. Clearly, Ellis's theory of emotions has not convinced everyone in academic psychology circles. Theories of emotion may well be more complex than he allows.

Ellis's Critique of Religious Faith

For Ellis, religion is hopelessly detrimental to mental health. For instance, the entire Christian enterprise, in his mind, deflates self-direction, encourages dependence on an illusory deity and church authority, decreases a willingness to think on one's own, and encourages masochistic self-sacrifice in the name of agape.[42] It retreats from the real problems of human existence, outlaws tolerance, cannot stomach ambiguity, childishly demands certainty, and promotes dogmatism rather than scientific reasoning. Unable to accept themselves, religious people make their self-evaluations dependent upon a superstitious deity or the members of their religious community.

Ellis has maintained a reputation for being rather "hard" on people of faith. Yet we would argue that his criticism of faith, while pretending to emerge from the objective voice of reason, emerges from another faith—a faith that contains its own vision of the ideal self, its own ethical horizon, and its own dogma about the ultimate context of human life. Psychologist Paul Watson, who analyzes the contemporary psychologies in ways similar to our approach, agrees: "The RET promotion of what seems to be a transcultural ideal self, its confidence in the ability to discover purely empirical foundations for a sustainable social life, and its advocacy of an essentially Stoic form of rationality all suggest a form of commitment, a kind of faith that criticizes religion from within a very particular ideological surround."[43]

To further illustrate this point, Watson examines Ellis's position on the Christian notion of sin. Ellis is quite negative concerning the merits of this doctrine. "The concept of sin," says Ellis, "is so humanly inhumane that it would be difficult to conceive a more pernicious technique for keeping mankind moral."[44] For Ellis, sin is tied to self-blaming, which promotes self-preoccupation and an inability to function. Yet Watson's point is that Ellis extracts the notion of sin from its own context or "ideological surround" and ethnocentrically pulls it into his own framework. Put differently, Ellis's conceptual world strips the Christian understanding of sin from its "intra-ideological meaning."[45] By extracting the notion of sin and placing it under his own particular umbrella of meaning, Ellis can then associate it exclusively with neurotic guilt and see it as an abominable notion. Given this transplantation of sin from its own ideological surround, it is no wonder Ellis can say, "The concept of sin is the most direct and indirect cause of virtually all neurotic disturbance. The sooner psychotherapists forthrightly begin to attack it the better their patients will be."[46] Ellis describes his understanding of sin.

> For one thing, guilt and self-blame induce the individual to bow nauseatingly low to some arbitrary external authority, which in the last analysis is always some hypothetical deity; and such worship renders him proportionately less self-sufficient and self-confident. Secondly, the concept of guilt inevitably leads to the unsupportable sister concept of self-sacrifice for and dependency upon others—which is the antithesis of true mental health. Thirdly, guilty individuals tend to focus incessantly on past delinquencies and crimes rather than on present and future constructive behavior. Fourthly, it is psychophysically impossible for a person to concentrate adequately on changing his moral actions for the better when he is obsessively focused upon blaming himself for his past and present misdeeds. Fifthly, the states of anxiety created in an individual by his self-blaming tendencies induce concomitant breakdown states in which he cannot think clearly of anything, least of all constructive changes in himself.[47]

We could spend pages critiquing this passage from the perspective of the critical hermeneutic approach to psychology informing this book. Rather than always seeing "external authority" as "arbitrary," Gadamer would suggest that we see some of the religious classics as formulating humane and enriching images of the human; this is an authority that contains wisdom. That is why these classics endure with people returning to them time and again. One also should note that when Ellis speaks of "changing . . . actions for the better" he reveals his own system of value judgments with their potential for being arbitrary and even invoking guilt.

Yet clearly, a full Christian understanding of sin cannot be grasped apart from its relationship to grace—an insight that Ellis misses. The idea of sin is not designed to perpetuate guilt reactions, but to indicate how we have fallen short of a God-inspired potential. It need not create debilitating emotions and excessive self-preoccupation when placed inside this larger framework of grace. In fact, it is the very unconditional grace and acceptance of God that many persons claim releases their guilt and shame *so that they are then able to look at their sin.* According to Watson, ripping sin-language out of its grace-infused "ideological surround" (what we would call its narrative vision and metaphors) is not fair to the best of the Christian tradition, which is "Good News" and not self-berating news.[48]

Of course the possibility that clients may have a genuine sense of guilt because they have fallen short of the potential for which they have been divinely called is immediately dismissed in Ellis's atheistic ideological surround. Consequently, guilt is instantly "psychologized" and perceived as most unhealthy.

Aaron Beck: Anxiety, Primal Thinking, and Egocentric Bias

Along with Ellis, Jones and Butman also evaluate the related perspective of cognitive-behavioral therapy. They indicate that the cognitive-behavioral therapies differ somewhat from both strict behavior therapies and rational emotive therapy. They depart from behaviorism in that (a) they believe that some human behavior is caused by internal or mental events, and (b) they believe the internal, mental processes of humans are not adequately explained by the learning processes of animal behavior. In turn, they differ from rational-emotive therapy in that they are "more well integrated into the overall discipline of psychology, more scientific in their formulation, less dogmatic and more well researched."[49]

While several figures have been important in this school of thought, the work of psychiatrist Aaron Beck has been crucial. Beck shares with Albert Ellis a view of human fulfillment as the capacity to nonreactively reason in the midst of potentially stressful circumstances. Cerebral control is the cornerstone of an effective life. The possibility of reason being flooded by emotion, losing its balance, and engaging in cognitive distortions is ever-present. This tendency does not result simply from social and familial factors. For Beck, human beings must struggle with their own evolutionary heritage of primal, survival thinking. What was at one time essential for human survival has now become an obstacle for harmonious social living and calm reason. As we have seen, Ellis argues that we are "hard wired" for both rational and irrational tendencies from birth throughout life. Beck extends this analysis to include insights from evolutionary psychology, insights that help us understand our exaggerated, primal thinking as part of the highly threatening circumstances in our evolutionary history. His major statement of this problem is his *Prisoners of Hate: The Cognitive Basis of Anger, Hostility, and Violence* (1999).[50] Unfortunately, this work had not been produced at the time Jones and Butman analyzed the cognitive-behavioral therapies. We will give it careful attention.

Beck believes the primary enemy of healthy living is an overreaction to psychological threats. In the face of such a threat, anxiety, if not interrupted, pushes us into a predictable pattern of excessively egocentric, rigid, and hostile thinking. We interpret the world out of a disproportionate fear for our own safety—be it physical or psychological. Quick, premature assessments push us into all-or-nothing thinking dominated by an egocentric bias. This emotional reasoning replaces the higher functions of rationality. Anxiety-intoxicated reaction eliminates our ability to respond. Beck writes,

> The intrusion of the more primitive coding system produces a skewing of information processing. This "cognitive shift" introduces a systematic bias into the interpretations and inferences in various psychopathological conditions. . . . In terms of cognitive processing, individuals experience psychological distress when they perceive a situation as threatening to their vital interests. At such times, there is a functional impairment in normal cognitive processing: Perceptions and interpretations of events become highly selective, egocentric, and rigid. The person has a decreased ability to "turn off" distorted thinking and self-corrective perceptions, to concentrate, to recall, or reason. Corrective functions, which allow reality testing and refinement of global conceptualizations, are weakened.[51]

Beck indirectly invites us to take a more tolerant view of our egocentric bias as he describes it as a necessary part of our evolutionary survival. He argues that an egocentric outlook is "discernible throughout the animal kingdom and is apparently embedded in our genes."[52] Both self-protection and self-promotion are obviously necessary for survival. Yet Beck goes on to say that anxiety can push this protective self-concern into an inordinately defensive, antagonistic tendency if it is not "balanced by such social traits as love, empathy, and altruism, the capacity for which is also represented in our genome."[53] Beck seems unaware of how close he is in these statements to Reinhold Niebuhr's understanding of the relation between anxiety and sin. Both Niebuhr and Beck agree that appropriate attention to self-survival can quickly become self-preoccupation. In turn, this self-preoccupation blocks our ability to focus and think creatively. Beck, as we see below, continues at the naturalistic level of analysis, never injecting the concepts of human freedom and responsibility that, as Niebuhr teaches, transform this primitive and indeed useful natural reactivity into something exaggerated and overdetermined for which we are, as humans, finally responsible.

Thus, for Beck, hostility emerges largely from an anxiety-provoked thinking disorder.

> As part of our survival heritage, we are very much aware of events that could have a detrimental effect on our own well-being and personal interests. We are sensitive to actions that suggest a put-down, imposition, or interference. . . . The tendency to over-interpret situations in terms of our own frame of reference is an expression of the "egocentric perspective." When we are under stress or feel threatened, our self-centered thinking becomes accentuated, and at the same time the area of our concern expands to irrelevant or remotely relevant events. Out of the tapestry of the multiple patterns contributing to another person's behavior, we select a single strand that may affect us personally.[54]

The movement goes from (a) constructing the facts in our own favor, to (b) exaggerating a transgression, to (c) attributing malice to the opposition.[55]

Beck believes that these primitive thinking patterns were helpful and adaptive under prehistoric conditions in which survival depended upon quick, almost instantaneous reactions to threats or danger. Rapidly identifying an enemy was an important part of survival. As Beck puts it, "A single false negative (misidentifying an enemy as a friend) would have been fatal."[56] It was essential to immediately categorize others as threatening or nonthreatening. One's life depended on it. There were no gray areas. The thinking was global, crude, and hypervigilant, but necessary for survival.

The survival advantages of primal thinking, however, are matched with some disadvantages. As we anxiously reduce the data around us into a few crude categories, we overlook much information. We exaggerate certain features of the situation. We take details out of their context, interpret those details self-centeredly, and make sweeping generalizations. "Consequently, the thinking is unbalanced: it may be satisfactory for true life-or-death emergencies, but it is disruptive to the smooth functioning of everyday life and to the solution of normal interpersonal problems."[57]

Beck thinks it is possible to identify a unified structure in primal thinking that accounts for much of humanity's anger, hostility, prejudice, and bigotry. Further, this process is the same at both the individual and the group level.

> No matter what the external causes of antagonistic behavior, the same internal or psychological mechanisms are generally involved in its arousal and expression. And as with destructive interpersonal action, cognitive distortions incite anger and prompt the hostile behavior. Thus, unwarranted personal attacks that arise from prejudice, bigotry, ethnocentrism, or military invasion involve the primal thinking apparatus: absolute categorical cognition, on the one hand, and obliviousness to the human intensity of the victims, on the other.[58]

Regardless of the various factors involved in helping trigger a hostile reaction, the cognitive pattern is the same. The pattern usually moves from (a) perception of a threat to ourselves or the values we hold as sacred, to (b) escalation of anxiety, which pushes us into a primal mode of all-or-nothing thinking, to (c) an automatic preparation for attack in order to defend ourselves or our values, to (d) a crowding out of other human qualities such as empathy and perspective-taking, and to (e) the elimination of the kind of creative thinking for which we are capable in less anxious moments. This cognitive process is similar to Freud's ego defenses: while the maneuvers may have been originally necessary for our survival, we have learned them "too well" and they block a deeper analysis of our situation.

Borrowing from the work of Sam Keen, Beck describes how anxiety pushes us from seeing differences in others to constructing enemies.[59] First, we lump all members of the opposition together so that they lose their identities as unique individuals. Second, we view all opposing persons as interchangeable, and hence, disposable. Third, we dehumanize the opposition by stripping them of human qualities for which we might feel some empathy or compassion, thus turning them into inanimate objects. Fourth, we "demonize" the opposition by making them the very embodiment of evil. Killing them is then no longer optional; they *must* be exterminated. Fifth, we connect all abstract notions of evil to the enemy so that our hatred and desire to destroy them is sustained. Sixth, we constantly emphasize the manner in which this evil enemy threatens our very being. And seventh, we attack the projected image but kill real people.[60]

> Primitive mechanisms for processing information, retained from our evolutionary experience, prejudice our judgments about people who differ from us. Cognitive biases may also lead us to indiscriminately attribute malice to anyone whose actions or beliefs conflict with ours. As the vise of our cognitive apparatus tightens, we tend to squeeze these people into the Enemy category: the angry spouse, the member of a religious or racial minority, the outspoken

political revolutionary. It becomes increasingly difficult to observe others reflectively, objectively, and with perspective.[61]

After reviewing the violence associated with Western religious traditions and concluding that both the Bible and the Koran promote dualistic thinking by dividing the world into absolute categories of good and evil, Beck goes on to ask whether psychology can help.

> It is evident that the institutions of religion have, at best, succeeded only partially in solving the problem of either individual or mass violence. What does the understanding of the psychology of the individual have to offer? Formulating the psychological factors that lead to violence can provide the framework for understanding anger, hostility, and violence. This framework, in turn, can suggest strategies to people for dealing with their hostile reactions as well as provide a basis for conflict resolution between groups and states.[62]

Greater self-understanding can eliminate or greatly reduce violence.

Beck further suggests that our self-serving, egoistic attitudes only tell one side of the story. We are also equipped through our evolutionary history to be affectionate, kind, and empathic. "Thus, we manifest our basic ambivalence—self-indulgence, self-adulation, and selfishness in one situation, and self-sacrifice, humility, and generosity in another."[63] Human beings are both prosocial and antisocial at the same time.[64]

More than Cognition?

The key factor for Beck, as we saw in Ellis, is an optimism about humanity's capacity to move from *recognizing* faulty thinking to *arresting* and *changing* it. By understanding the manner in which our thinking apparatus works, we can challenge and transform it. All the ills in human behavior can be traced back to anxious, distorted thinking. Thus, evil is ultimately due to our "frightened cognitions."

We would argue, via Niebuhr, that the anxiety that produces irrational thinking is a manifestation of distrust in our Source. Stated differently, Beck is describing the cognitive manifestation of what Niebuhr meant by original sin. This is an inevitable, though not necessary, process whereby our anxious awareness activates cognitive distortion. Following Niebuhr, we suggest that the vision of calm reason is only ultimately possible with a faith in the providence of God.

Also, the question must be raised as to whether exaggerated thinking in the face of anxiety tells the full tale of human destruction and evil. Beck is helpful in showing us how egocentric bias emerges when we are threatened. Yet faulty thinking in the face of stress does not get to the depths of self-deception. Beck makes the transition of anxious into nonanxious thought look a little too easy. In his world, clear thinking gets rid of evil. Sin is primarily a cerebral problem, a matter of distorted cognition. But surely there are other times in which egocentricity guides human thought even when anxiety has not triggered exaggerated thinking. An ongoing ontological anxiety, which is part of our juxtaposition of nature and spirit, makes egocentricity a temptation even when things appear "calm." Stated more directly, we can sin when we're composed as well as when we're nervous.

In the same way that the humanistic psychotherapies assume that we will act in a constructive manner once our basic needs are met, so Beck seems to assume that we will act in constructive ways once we are thinking rationally. Again, he appears to believe that cleaning up our cognitive processes will produce ethical behavior. While the humanistic therapies argue that ethical behavior will automatically result when we are connected to the actualizing tendency, Beck comes close to saying that ethical behavior will automatically result when we are connected to our rational capacities.

According to L. Rebecca Propst, Beck's contention that individuals have the capacity to rise above their own behavior and thought processes as they internally dialogue and argue with themselves is reminiscent of Niebuhr's understanding of the *imago dei*.[65] The self-transcendence inherent in this dialogue, for Niebuhr, is part of the essence of being human. Similarly, says Probst, "this seems to receive direct expression in cognitive therapy's control models, which postulate that self-control and self-efficacy, the essence of mental health, are achieved when the individual becomes aware of self-statements and becomes able to stand back from them and argue with them."[66]

In Niebuhr's view, however, we are always in dialogue with ourselves, our neighbors, and God.[67] Beck's naturalistic ontology does not address this third level of dialogue. From a Niebuhrian perspective, this leaves Beck unable to analyze the ultimate context of alienation with self and others. Self-estrangement is rooted in a larger reality—an estrangement from our Source. Niebuhr would argue that the dialogue with self, while important, cannot heal this larger context of alienation. Reason, alone, cannot "cure" the human condition. Stated more directly, we cannot "talk ourselves out of" this larger context of estrangement and anxiety. Cognitive therapy can be extremely helpful in eliminating a multitude of mental distortions about everyday events in our lives. It can help with depression, some forms of anxiety, and a host of other psychological problems. But its philosophical framework is not large enough to engage the ultimate questions of human existence. Niebuhr contends that "the self distinguishes itself by a yearning for the ultimate."[68] He further adds that if we miss this characteristic, "we have failed to define the total anatomy of human selfhood."[69]

Again, reason cannot ultimately resolve the self's preoccupation with its own security and power, even when it detaches from itself in transcendent self-evaluation. Even during this time of detachment, according to Niebuhr, the self is still unduly focused on its own concerns: "The self is, in fact, more, rather than less, inclined to be concerned with itself when it detaches itself from a situation and views it from a transcendent position. . . . The self, in short, could use reason to justify its ends as well as to judge them, and there [is] evidently no power in reason to limit the desires and ambitions of men."[70] For Niebuhr, reason alone cannot emancipate the self's bondage to its own interests. Cognitive therapy, in spite of its usefulness in dealing with emotional distress, cannot unlock the door of self-preoccupation. While more could be said about Beck's calm confidence in the face of ontological anxiety, we will reserve it for the end of this chapter because our critique of Beck also applies to Ellis and Bowen.

Murray Bowen and Nonreactivity

Murray Bowen, a psychoanalytically trained psychiatrist and perhaps the most important theorist in family systems therapy, shares a culture of calm reason with Ellis and Beck. As we shall see, Bowen identifies the primary enemy of mental health as anxious reactivity. This reactivity results from a failure at "differentiation," a process that necessitates a poised, rational response to the emotional processes surrounding us. Differentiation in one's family-of-origin is particularly difficult because of the recurrent emotional patterns that have been operative in families through multiple generations. Yet, as we shall see, the vision of human fulfillment in Bowen is the nonanxious, nonreactionary self who reasons clearly in the face of stress. "In Bowen's system the hallmark of the well adjusted person is rational objectivity and individuality. A differentiated person is able to separate thinking from feeling."[71] The healthy person is first and foremost a self-regulated person. Autonomy, for Bowen, involves a high degree of independence in thought and action while maintaining a connection and investment in others. Like Ellis and Beck, Bowen sees nonreactive cognition as salvific for the human predicament.

As Nichols and Schwartz contend, "to this day Bowen's theory is the most thoughtful and thoroughgoing system of ideas family therapy has produced."[72] Bowen began his clinical training at the Menninger clinic in 1946, where he focused on mother-child symbiosis. It was here that he began to formulate his major construct, the "differentiation of the self," which refers to the ongoing process of self-regulation in the face of anxiety and reactivity. Then in the mid-fifties, Bowen moved to the National Institute for Mental Health, where he further expanded his study of mother-child symbiosis and constructed the notion of "triangulation" (the natural tendency to bring a third party into a conflict between two people, particularly for purposes of ventilation) in family systems. At the end of the 1950s Bowen left NIMH and joined the faculty of Georgetown University Medical School, where he remained until his death in 1990. He wrote very little, and his theory is known primarily through his close associates and interpreters, Michael Kerr and Rabbi Edwin Friedman.

Throughout his career, Bowen was strongly theoretical in his orientation. He believed that the majority of mental health professionals were entirely too caught up in the narrow preoccupation with techniques or therapeutic maneuvers. Instead, they needed to grasp the importance of having a theory about the family system. Effective therapists need to (a) have a strong understanding of the multigenerational nature of family process, (b) have worked on their own differentiation issues with their families-of-origin, and (c) maintain a high level of differentiation as they work with families in order to avoid the many invitations to join a family's anxiety and reactivity. In other words, they must not be pulled or "sucked into" the system.

Bowen's family system theory was part of a new orientation in mental health treatment. The major emphasis was on the family, rather than strictly on individuals within the family. This dramatically parted company with the standard treatments of individual pathology in most forms of psychotherapy. Rather than highlighting the unconscious or individual psychopathology, the target of clinical pursuits was the interpersonal dynamics that shape family systems and, in turn, impact individuals. We get to the individual *through* the family. The system takes on a life of its own. It is governed by rules, which are often not explicitly stated but which bind individual members. Thus, an analysis of the family's interpersonal communication, explicit and implicit rules, and relationship dynamics is the focus of family therapy.

Much of family therapy, according to Jones and Butman, emerged from two important sources: (a) general systems theory in biology, and (b) cybernetics in computer science. "System thinkers dislike analyzing and reducing phenomena to their most basic elements (reductionism or atomism); they prefer studying the complexities of organizational structures. And they are especially curious about patterns of communication and control in troubled individuals and their extended families."[73] A system is a "group of interconnected or interrelated parts which mutually interact across time."[74] Systems are characterized by wholeness, meaning that the sum is greater than its parts. They are also characterized by interrelatedness, or the fact that all parts impact each other. All systems have boundaries that distinguish one sub-system from another. Systems tend to be either open or closed to varying degrees. Closed systems are rigid and incapable of genuine response. They can only *react*; they cannot *respond*.

General systems theory emerged in the late 1940s and early 1950s as technological advancements made it possible to build mechanical models with properties very similar to the human brain.[75] "All living systems are complex in terms of their allegiances, coalitions and relationships. Ideally, they are fluid rather than static, continually evolving as developmental crises and challenges are faced and dealt with in an adaptive and healthy manner."[76] Thus general systems theory is concerned with understanding the structural and functional rules of a particular system. It is especially interested in a system's information processing, ways of adapting to changing circumstances, and manner of organizing and maintaining itself.[77] Information concerning the results of past performance are processed in order to shape future behavior, a process called "self-corrective feedback." The scientific name assigned to the investigation of this "feedback" is cybernetics. According to Herta A. Guttman, this includes "the study of self-regulation, self-reproduction, adaptation, information processing and storage, and goal-oriented behavior."[78]

Bowen and Kerr insist, however, that the Bowenian system is *not* based on the concepts in general systems theory.[79] While we may safely say that the family operates in ways that are *similar* to the dynamics of a humanly constructed physical system, the family system is a *natural* system.

> The existence of natural systems does not even depend on the human's being aware of them. The principles that govern a natural system are written in nature and not created by the human brain. The solar system, the ant colony, the tides, the cell, the family of *homo erectus*, are all natural systems. The human family system sprung from the evolutionary process and not from the human brain. We did not create it.[80]

Bowen's theory of self-differentiation, his central concept, is rooted in a metaphor from cellular biology. Cell division is healthy and necessary for the survival of the organism. It is crucial that the differentiating cell become autonomous by essentially saying to its cell-of-origin, "I am not you!"[81] In fact, it is cancerous cells that cannot divide in a healthy manner but can only duplicate themselves. This replication becomes toxic for the system. Healthy cells are able to autonomously divide while maintaining an ability to stay connected to other cells. Stated simply, the purpose of cell division is not isolation.

Bowen argues that humans face two counterbalancing life forces: individuality and togetherness, or aloneness and belonging. These dual needs must be balanced, and anxiety always tempts us to move toward one direction at the exclusion of the other. Too much togetherness or undifferentiated "we-ness" with others can produce positive fusion. Positive fusion involves an anxious attachment to another in which we must agree with them because differences are perceived as highly threatening. Interestingly, however, Bowen also talks a great deal about negative fusion. This involves compulsive disagreement and rebellion from another, a necessary defiance often confused with freedom. The only way one can feel emancipated is to defy the position of another, no matter what that position is. The problem is that these rebellious persons are still indirectly controlled in the sense that they "must" do the opposite of what they believe is another's position. Having to fight is as enslaving as having to agree. Either way, the possibility of self-regulation is lost.

If fusion is a danger on one side, "emotional cut-off" is a danger on the other. In this reaction, engulfment fears trigger such anxiety that freedom is sought through aloneness. Consequently, distance is the only interpersonal solution. By denying one's needs for others and trying to find refuge in being alone, the needs for closeness and togetherness are lost.

Thus, both separation anxiety and incorporation anxiety in families-of-origin can set the stage for relationship difficulties throughout life.

> One of the major observations to come out of the "mother-child symbiosis" research was the observation of repetitive relationship patterns: alternating cycles of closeness and distance, exquisitely sensitive to shifts in emotional

tension within either mother or child, or the relationship between them. Separation anxiety coupled with incorporation anxiety was believed to be the underlying dynamic. From these observations, Bowen focused on the notion of anxious attachment, a pathological form of attachment driven by anxiety that subverted reason and self-control. Anxious attachment is the opposite of "functional attachment," which is a central aspect of differentiation.[82]

Differentiation, then, is the lifelong task of separating from one's family-of-origin without completely disconnecting from them. Differentiation involves "living life from the inside out," operating with a sense of balance and centeredness, and knowing where one's own identity ends and another begins. It involves being clear about one's own belief system, taking "I" positions, being responsible only for oneself while being responsive to others, and balancing the two fundamental human drives of separateness and togetherness. Put another way, it is about maintaining integrity.

It is crucial to understand that differentiation is an intrapsychic, as well as an interpersonal, process. Intrapsychic differentiation is the ability to separate feelings from thinking. It involves the capacity to rise above strong emotion and suspend action until one has analyzed a situation. It does not assume that the strength of one's feelings accurately reflects reality. Put simply, it consults reason before acting. Intrapsychic differentiation, then, is an ability to recognize nonshamingly one's own emotions while distinguishing them from a rational assessment of what is occurring. Like Ellis and Beck, Bowen knows that the knee-jerk reactivity of one's emotional life can sabotage autonomy and diminish one's ability to maturely respond. "Undifferentiated people hardly distinguish thought from feelings; their intellects are so flooded with feelings that they are almost incapable of objective thinking. Their lives are governed by an acceleration of feelings from those around them, either blindly adhered to or angrily rejected."[83] Transcending one's emotions does not mean ignoring them. Nor does it mean becoming cold, aloof and indifferent toward life. It *does* mean being able to resist reactivity. We can respond to anxious circumstances without getting "pulled into" the circuit of anxiety. Differentiation involves the ability to "think things through," maintaining self-governance even when those around us are emotionally out-of-control. Bowen was quite sober about the difficulty of sustaining this process. It is a lifelong task that is never mastered. Probably the most for which we can realistically hope is to act in a differentiated manner seventy percent of the time.

It is also crucial to understand that differentiation should never be confused with an isolated independence. This is why, according to Bowen expert Rabbi Edwin Friedman, it is dangerous to equate the words "differentiation" with "autonomy." Autonomy does not always necessitate a relational component. For Bowen, differentiation necessitates staying connected.

> Obviously, differentiation has its origin in the biological notion that cells can have no identity, purpose, or distinctiveness until they have separated from—

that is, left—their progenitors (differentiation is a prerequisite to specialization even if one is ultimately going to fuse to accomplish one's purpose). But also implicit in this biological metaphor or homologue is the idea that such self has little meaning if the cell cannot connect. In its simplest terms, therefore, differentiation is the capacity to be one's own integrated aggregate-of-cells person while still belonging to, or being able to relate to, a larger colony. As already indicated, such a biological metaphor also has ramifications for thinking and the conduct of therapy since the incapacity to achieve some balance in the self-togetherness struggle will tend to create a style of thinking that shows up in either/or, all-or-nothing, black-and-white conceptualizations and, eventually, family cutoffs.[84]

Again, the enemy of differentiation is reactivity. Emotional systems indeed react, and *reactivity needs reactivity*. In other words, an undifferentiated family system is counting on its anxious reactivity to cause one to react in turn. When the pattern of reactivity is halted, the possibility of change can occur. This is why Bowen insisted that the best thing we can do for our families, as well as for ourselves, is to work on our own tendencies toward reactivity.

Interestingly, Bowen's understanding of anxiety and reactivity in the family system are consistent with what we know about the functions of various regions of the brain. Bowen's theory is often connected to the work of neurologist Paul MacLean and his discussion of the "triune brain."[85] The survival response of the human organism is located in the brainstem, or what is called the "reptilian brain," which we share with lizards, snakes, crocodiles, and so on. The emotional response of the brain is located in the limbic system that we share, at a much more developed level, with other mammals such as dogs, cats, and horses. Both of these brain "layers" operate without premeditation. They comprise only about fifteen percent of the entire brain.

The remaining eighty-five percent of the brain is located in the cerebral hemispheres. It is here in the neocortex that analyzing, reflecting, symbolizing, and creative thinking occur. The neocortex provides the arena in which we find new ways to cope, new strategies for improving our lives.

When we experience strong anxiety, we often automatically react out of the lower brain functions. Steinke lists the following as symptoms of this anxiety-induced "take over" by the lower brains: "impulse overwhelms intention; instinct sweeps aside imagination; reflexive behavior closes off reflective thought; defensive postures block out defined positions; and emotional reactivity limits clearly determined direction."[86] Again, anxiety pushes us into the lower, more primitive regions of the brain (mammalian and reptilian regions), rather than in the neocortex, where we can engage in higher thought forms and more creative activities. What Bowenian Edwin Friedman calls "reptilian regressions" are automatic, nonimaginative, survival moves. Anxiety has kicked us out of the neocortex and down into the lower parts of the brain where instinctual survival is dominant. The task is to lower the anxiety and get back in the frontal lobes where self-differentiated action can take place.

> At the onset of threat, self-preservation has more relevance for survival than self-awareness. Long before we could ever talk or think, we called on automatic processes for survival. We call on them again and again. Besides, they act faster than the thinking processes. When we are anxious, we act before we think. The Automatic Pilot joins forces with the House of Emotion and dominates. In a reptilian regression our behavior is not mediated through the neocortex. Anxious, we are apt to lose objectivity and civility. We are in a position to be neither responsible nor loving. Reason and love are best served in time of calm. . . . In periods of intense anxiety, what is most needed is what is most unavailable—the capacity to be imaginative.[87]

Moderate amounts of anxiety are helpful in that they motivate and mobilize our capacity for change. If, however, this anxiety rises above a motivating capacity, as it frequently does, our own thought processes become very narrowed and self-defeating. Flooded with anxiety, we lose our ability to think with calm deliberation (neocortex activity).

> We are therefore less self-choosing and self-directing. We have less capacity to distinguish between thought and feeling. Anxiety throws us into a state of emotional survival. We are less capable of hearing and seeing without coloring what we observe to fit our feelings. When feelings take over, distortion and misconceptions occur. Even when we "intellectualize" or "hide" our feelings, anxiety is at the helm of life. It is a situation of feelings controlling self.[88]

However, the great foe of self-differentiation is not so much *acute* anxiety as *chronic* anxiety. Acute anxiety is time-limited, intense, and a vehicle of change. In fact, Bowenians typically attempt to turn chronic anxiety into acute anxiety. Emotional pain accomplishes this most of the time. For Bowen, this is why it is so important *not* to pull others out of their pain. "Pain rescue" only allows acute anxiety to turn back into chronic anxiety, as it pulls persons back into the same dysfunctional patterns that keep them prisoners.

But how, specifically, do we lower our anxiety and make progress toward self-differentiation? If we are looking for techniques or detailed guidelines, Bowen will frustrate us. He suggests that we place ourselves in situations of anxiety and work on maintaining our sense of self. This means being loyal to the person we are, taking full responsibility for our actions, not allowing ourselves to get "caught up" in the reactivity of others, and attempting to stay relatively calm in the face of family chaos. This necessitates both giving up our attempts to control other family members and relating to them without fusion, rebellion, or emotional cut-off. For Bowen this involves "having the courage to engage emotionally intense situations repeatedly and to tolerate the anxiety and internal emotional reactivity associated with trying to become more of a self, an anxiety of progression rather than regression."[89] This capacity to control our anxiety pivots on our ability to distinguish our reason from our feelings. We need to respond out of our understanding and not out of our affect. Notice, however, that Bowen's view of understanding is much flatter than the view of understanding in Gadamer, Ricoeur, and hermeneutic philosophy. Understanding for them always entails reflection on our effective history as it conditions our emotions; for Bowen, understanding seems to settle directly on our so-called primitive emotions themselves, unqualified by culture, history, and the classics that provide the ideals for our emotions. From the perspective of hermeneutic philosophy, Bowen's understanding short-circuits the hermeneutic circle that makes for true understanding. Nonetheless, to Bowen's credit, he sees the task of understanding ourselves as a lifetime process. We make gradual gains each time we control our anxiety level inside a circuit of reactivity. Also, simply understanding the emotional dynamics of a family system helps prepare the way for differentiated action. And fortunately, if one member of a family reduces his or her anxiety, the overall system itself becomes a little less anxious as well.

In some ways, the Bowenian emphasis on the multigenerational connectedness of family pathology offers a way of understanding the transmission of "original sin." Unresolved psychological issues "handed to us" in our own families-of-origin get "passed on" to our children, who in turn pass their own unresolved issues onto their children. A genogram study quickly reveals that our system's issues are larger than our own individual psyches. Systems can easily assign roles for individual members to play. These roles may well be necessary for a dysfunctional system to continue, yet they may be quite unhealthy for the individual playing them. Children can sometimes "carry" the pathologies of their parents, particularly when the parents refuse to acknowledge their own faults and take responsibility for their lives. Clearly, Bowen has helped us understand how "the sins of the fathers are visited upon the third and forth generation."

Yet there is also a danger here. Some have pointed toward the possibility of the individual getting "lost in the system" in family therapy.[90] Originally working very hard to eliminate scapegoating and pathologizing of an individual family member, perhaps some of the family therapies have pushed a systems emphasis at the expense of individual responsibility? Jones and Butman believe they have. While they applaud a movement away from the radical individualism of some schools of traditional therapy, they believe family therapy can come dangerously close to a "collectivist view of persons."[91] This view sees individuals as merely a product of familial interaction. Personal identity is viewed as simply a product of social interaction. The important reality is the system, and the particular issues of the individual are treated as mere symptoms of this larger systemic problem. Jones and Butman fear that extreme forms of this collectivist mentality eliminate the internal processes and developmental histories of individuals.

> We object to the loss of respect for individuality evident in the more strategic and structural models of family therapy. The most striking and salient characteristics of an individual are at risk of being replaced by the global and sometimes generic characteristics of family systems. It seems ironic to make this criticism, in that we have roundly criticized many other therapy systems for their rank individualism, but family therapy in some instances swings too far in

the other extreme. . . . Systemic thinking, although it is a refreshing alternative paradigm for creating working models of personality, psychopathology, and psychotherapy, tends to blur those qualities that make us more distinctive (i.e., our potential to be active agents engaged in a quest for meaning and significance). Responsible persons who make choices are surely more than the sum product of external social forces.[92]

Jones and Butman further argue that many of the core assumptions—and we would add "deep metaphors"—of systemic therapies are deterministic, mechanistic, and perhaps even reductionistic. This bears some similarities to Skinnerian behaviorism. For Skinner there are only "bad" environments, not "bad" people; for some family therapies, there are only "dysfunctional" families, not "dysfunctional" people. Again, the implicit assumption appears to be that individuals do not have the internal resources to rise above the family. Ethical responsibility from this perspective is most problematic.

Interestingly, Richardson, Fowers, and Guignon argue the exact opposite point.[93] They believe that while family therapy may *appear* to be more relationally oriented and less individualistic, it has in fact accepted and promoted the notion that individual fulfillment is the primary purpose of life. The central function of family life is to nurture the capacity for individual autonomy. The nuclear family serves as a private retreat from the larger community, a place where self-fulfillment is encouraged. The family therapies have frequently conveyed negative views of both the extended family's meddling and the larger community's tensions. The goal of the family is not to connect members with the social world and its larger moral context, but to avoid the pressures and larger issues tied up with social living. Stated kindly, the modern nuclear family is too individualistic in its orientation; stated more critically, it fosters narcissism and emotional self-containment.

This ideology of individualism marks a shift from the more corporate orientation of nineteenth-century family life.[94] This corporate model was much more concerned with the emotional well-being of the family even though this may have necessitated self-sacrifice for individual members. Today, "the family is increasingly seen as the sphere within which individual needs and desires are to be satisfied."[95] Richardson, Fowers, and Guignon make the following observation about family therapies:

> For all their merit, they may exemplify a subtle, uncritical version of contemporary family ideology with its endorsement of the emotionally private family empowered for the purpose of promoting individual well-being. . . . Thus, with some recent exceptions, family therapy seems to have rather single-mindedly promoted the privacy of the nuclear family, as much through inattention to the embeddedness of the family in a larger social network as through the negative evaluation of extended family and community meddling. This conceptual neglect of the *healthy* social embeddedness of families is curiously contrary to system theory and may well indicate the power of the contemporary ideology of the family in shaping family therapy theory.[96]

Richardson, Fowers, and Guignon believe that family therapy must balance an emphasis on individual rights with a renewed sense of social embeddedness. Even the very focus on the individual is strongly influenced by a larger cultural and ethical vision that fosters a solitary mind-set. Family therapists need to be more aware of the underlying ideologies that inform and shape their work.

We would suggest, however, that Bowen's theory does a better job than most family therapy models in avoiding the extremes of a collectivist and an individualist perspective. It escapes the impersonal nature of some deterministic system theories by stressing the importance of self-differentiation. On the other hand, it avoids some of the pitfalls of radical individualism by emphasizing that relationality is a primary ingredient of differentiation. Bowen does not support a self-contained autonomy. In fact, one of his most frequent points is that differentiation involves a separate relationship with each member of one's extended, not just nuclear, family. Just as Erikson argued that identity-formation is important for intimacy, Bowen argues that self-definition, or differentiation, is important for connectedness. Without the capacity to connect and invest in others, one is *not* differentiated.

Bowen's theory of self-differentiation also places responsibility on each individual to take care of his or her own emotional health. This is often misunderstood because Bowen encourages family members to carefully investigate the emotional dynamics of their system and grasp the family influence on their self-defeating behavior. He insists that each member, no matter how troubled their family system, take full responsibility for his or her own healing and recovery process. The idea that Bowen encourages a "blaming of mom and dad for all of one's emotional problems" is a severe distortion of Bowen's claim. Yet to get "unhooked" from the system's dysfunctional pattern, we have to understand the role we've played. From this awareness, we can move toward self-responsibility and emotional health.

To conclude this discussion as to whether collectivism or individualism is the closet ethic of Bowen, we want to add this. The difficulty with Bowen is his failure to clearly distinguish the biologistic language of differentiation and connectedness found in his systems theory from a more properly articulated moral language of differentiation and relatedness, i.e., a language of mutuality and equal regard. Because the two languages contaminate each other and because there is no clear differentiation between his mechanistic deep metaphors and his more properly moral language, his implicit ethic is unstable, swinging one moment toward collectivity and another toward good old standard American individualism.

Conclusion: What about Ontological Anxiety?

Ellis, Beck, and Bowen have a high view of our ability to tame our anxiety. But we must ask, as we did the humanistic psychologies, whether or not this includes ontological anxiety. This anxiety does not arise merely from family reactivity, irrationally exaggerated cognitions, or primal thinking in the face of threat. This anxiety can emerge when environmental stressors are quite sedate. Ellis, Beck, and Bowen believe that the key to a fulfilling life is regaining self-control. They make the significant assumption that this regaining of control is possible. Yet do they adequately appreciate the anxiety that emerges from realizing we cannot possibly have ultimate control over our lives? This is the anxiety of Kierkegaard, an anxiety growing out of the very structures of finitude.

We agree with Niebuhr that, ultimately, the attempt to eliminate our own anxiety usually creates even more self-preoccupied anxiety. The desire for security easily becomes greedy. It escalates toward another denial of the insecurity built into the human condition. The final remedy for anxiety is trust, not control. As Niebuhr puts it, "faith in the providence of God is a necessity of freedom because, without it, the anxiety of freedom tempts man to seek a self-sufficiency and self-mastery incompatible with his dependence upon forces which he does not control."[97] Smooth, unperturbed, nonreactive living is a nice goal. Whether or not we can achieve it without a trust in the Source of our lives is another question. We would suggest that the Judeo-Christian tradition points toward an important wisdom in its emphasis that this type of nonanxious self-control is beyond the boundaries of finitude. As we have said, trying to eliminate anxiety can bring on its own anxiety. Attempts at control become more and more self-preoccupying, often turning us away from the tasks of living and narrowing our focus to our own nonreactivity. Self-monitoring easily becomes self-absorption. The ultimate antidote to ontological anxiety is more related to trust than self-mastery. Anxiety, as the precondition of destructive behavior, is too powerful without it.

Psychology's Relationship with Religion: Toward an Intramural Discussion

In this concluding chapter, we engage the debate about the relation of psychology and theology as this has emerged in evangelical Protestant circles. But we pursue this conversation not just to have an in-house dispute between different branches of Protestantism. The issues are much deeper. At stake is the thesis that the image of the human ensconced in the classics of the Jewish and Christian traditions offer an invaluable—in fact, essential—narrative envelope for the more detailed empirical and clinical work of the modern psychologies. We address this evangelical discussion because at least some of these authors implicitly hold that hypothesis as well, although they develop it in ways different from our own approach. In passing through this conversation we hope to emerge with a message not only for the Christian religion but for the public and scientific pursuit of psychological studies.

During the 1990s, theoretical work about the relation of psychology and theology was more robust in evangelical circles than mainline Protestant circles. *Religious Thought and the Modern Psychologies* was read and discussed in conservative Protestant intellectual circles, often, we are happy to say, with appreciation. Yet, it was also perceived and sometimes criticized as a liberal Protestant position. Increasingly, however, such labels as liberal and conservative are both misleading and irrelevant. In the pages that follow, our work will simultaneously appear as both more to the left and more to the right of some of the so-called evangelical authors whom we will review. In other words, the discussion within these circles and between them and the position of this book is complex. Strange bedfellows will emerge; from some angles of vision, our so-called liberal perspective will seem to have the most in common with some of the allegedly more conservative models for relating psychology and Christian theology. In other ways, that will not be the case.

Our thesis is this: When the hermeneutic model for relating psychology and Christian thought is rightly perceived and employed, it will help order the different positions within evangelical circles. It also will help order the difference between our position and these so-called conservatives. And finally, it will aid in making sense of the differences between all of the so-called Christian-theological theoreticians of psychology, liberal or conservative, and contemporary allegedly secular understandings. The hermeneutic view that conceives psychology as the study of the mental and behavioral processes connected with practical moral wisdom helps locate, along a continuum, the competing perspectives for relating psychology to theology reviewed in this chapter.

In a very important article in the *American Psychologist*, Stanton L. Jones identifies what he believes to be a constructive relationship between religion and the science and profession of psychology.[1] Jones's article, both similar to our efforts and to some extent influenced by our position,[2] seeks to demonstrate that much of psychology's refusal to take religion seriously has been based on an outdated philosophy of science, a perspective steeped in positivism. Jones believes the dialogue between psychology and religion has frequently been reduced to a monologue in which psychology does all the talking. This one-directional relationship has occurred in three ways: (a) the development of the psychology of religion in which religious experience is studied scientifically, (b) the use of psychological and mental health resources for pastoral counseling and religious education, and (c) the employment of psychological findings to critique and modify religious constructs.[3] An underlying assumption seems to have been that while religion has very little to offer psychology, religion can serve as an interesting object of psychological study.

Psychology's view of religion has often been a part of a more classic division of religion and science. Jones points toward Ian Barbour's explanation of why science and religion are often viewed as separate and incompatible. First, it is often assumed that science rests on facts while religion rests on faith. Second, scientific claims are thought to be verifiable or falsifiable while religious claims are not. And third, the criteria for choosing between scientific findings are clear while the standards for choosing between religious claims are ambiguous and highly subjective.[4] Further, says Jones, many scientists believe that religion only raises questions about meaning, significance, ethics, and ultimate value. Consequently, it makes no factual claims on reality whatsoever.

Jones disagrees with this division. In fact, it is precisely the "cognitive and declarative dimension" in which Jones is interested.[5] Similar to our own analysis, Jones believes that every religion offers "content claims" on (a) the nature of the universe, (b) what constitutes ultimate reality, (c) the nature of human beings, (d) the place of humanity in the ultimate scheme of things, and (e) the nature of morality.[6]

Again, for Jones, the problem with much of religious dialogue with psychology is that it is out of date. In other words, it still operates on the assumptions derived from logical positivism and does not work with a more informed philosophy of science. The logical positivist view of science asserts that (a) scientific knowledge is grounded in empirical facts that are "uninterpreted, indubitable, and fixed in meaning,"[7] (b) theories are induced or deduced from these value-free facts, (c) these theories are rejected or maintained completely on the basis of their ability to "survive experimental tests,"[8] and (d) science progresses through a gradual accumulation of these "facts."

According to Jones, positivist science has been dying since the 1950s. In its place, postpositivistic science argues that all data is theory-laden. In other words, there are selective processes, biases, and expectations in our "findings." Most simply, we often "find" what we are looking for. Scientists, however hard they may try, cannot approach data without prior beliefs and prejudices. Then Jones adds something that is entirely consistent with hermeneutic philosophy's more positive view of the role of pre-understandings in shaping cognition. He writes, "Without preorienting conceptions of some sort, we cannot perceive data at all."[9] It is simply not true that scientists inductively wait, after scrutinizing data, to commit themselves to a particular theory. Scientists, says Jones, usually believe in their theories before they put them to the test.[10] While Jones admits that Thomas Kuhn may have exaggerated the radical nature of paradigm shifts in the history of science, Kuhn's point that science does not represent a slow accumulation of bare facts is quite accurate. No matter how dedicated we may be to strict empirical science, we come out of an ideological home world that pushes certain questions and neglects others. We are human investigators, not robots.

Jones recognizes that there are times when science and religion seem to function quite differently. This is especially true when religion is struggling to grasp and describe God or ultimate reality and science works with a very small piece of laboratory data. Yet eventually, science will inevitably ask deeper questions.

> Science has goals that transcend the mundane description of discrete empirical reality, and religion often has inspiration of saying something about the empirical aspects of human reality . . . Despite their many differences, scientific and religious attempts at understanding are both exercises of human rationality that are shaped by our preorienting assumptions, are accountable to human experience, are influenced by the human communities of which we are a part, and are attempting to understand aspects of our experienced realities. They are different, but there is not an unbridgeable chasm between the two.[11]

The primary area of interaction between psychology and religion is when psychology takes on the larger task of defining what it means to be healthy, fulfilled, mature, or fully functional. This can be especially seen in the areas of personality theory and psychotherapy. Hardly a neutral technology, psychotherapy is inherently prescriptive and has a definite image of the good life.

Further, argues Jones, most of us have been lay psychologists all our lives. In other words, we have absorbed, as part of our pre-theoretical world, assumptions about what is normal, healthy, and mature. Stated differently, we "bring more" to the study of psychology than we bring to the study of chemistry or physics.

Jones further asks whether this means that psychology is less of a science than the harder sciences. Three factors seem to prompt a "yes" to this question: (a) psychology is a relatively new scientific discipline, (b) psychology is "stuck" with studying a complex, irreducible, often inaccessible subject—human beings, and (c) the likelihood of bringing implicit assumptions into this study is far greater than in the study of some other scientific disciplines. Those assumptions about the human condition, argues Jones, are likely to have been influenced directly or indirectly by some dimension of religious thought.

> The explicit incorporation of values and worldviews into the scientific process will not necessarily result in a loss of objectivity or methodological rigor. What is new about this proposal is not the incorporation of assumptions into the process, but rather the proposal that psychological scientists and practitioners be more explicit about interaction of religious beliefs and psychology. If scientists, especially psychologists, are operating out of worldview assumptions that include the religious, and if the influence of such factors is inevitable, then the advancement of the scientific enterprise would be facilitated by making those beliefs explicitly available for public inspection and discourse.[12]

Jones thus concludes his article by suggesting that psychology should give more attention to the philosophical, ethical, and religious issues that form the background of clinical practice. As he puts it, "A substantial fraction of coursework in graduate programs in applied psychology should be devoted to religious traditions, religious and moral dimensions of professional practice, and the philosophical and theological parentage of contemporary systems of thought."[13] Also, says Jones, we need greater honesty among therapists about the value-ladenness of the mental health enterprise. Pretentious notions of value neutrality need to be exposed as hiding implicit ideological assumptions.

Obviously, much of Jones's argument is in fundamental agreement with our position. We have maintained that the primary task of psychology is hermeneutical. Jones makes no reference to hermeneutical philosophy or the contributions of Gadamer, Ricoeur, Bernstein, and others. But his argument, in many respects, reflects that point of view and would have profited had hermeneutic philosophy been more explicitly invoked. Psychology, he argues, involves the deliberate explication, analysis, and interpretation of our inherited culturally and historically shaped images of the human condition. All of us belong to a pre-theoretical community of discourse. As Peter Berger might say, a worldview dangles from every conversation.[14] Human experience is never studied "in the raw." Instead, it is always linguistically and historically mediated experience. In psychological efforts we attempt to gain some "distance" from this experience, as Ricoeur might say, but the very need for distancing already shows that we have been somewhat saturated by a tradition.[15]

Elsewhere, one of us has defined religion as a "narrative or metaphorical representation of the ultimate context of reality and its associated worldview, rituals, and ethics."[16] To qualify as religious, a phenomenon therefore needs (a) a narrative or metaphor of ultimacy, (b) a worldview that understands human life in its ultimate context, (c) rituals, and (d) an ethical system. These four factors must be held together by an identifiable community of celebration. Religion is at bottom a "faith in the way things are" that goes beyond sense impression and narrowly empirical description.

Are we saying that all clinical psychologies are secretly full-blown religions in disguise? No. Instead, we have argued that modern psychologies are frequently quasi religions with faith assumptions about the ultimate context of our lives and the goals of human fulfillment. As such, these psychologies inevitably cross over into matters that are also important to religion. Again, there is nothing inappropriate about this crossover *as long as* these psychologies self-consciously understand that they are not speaking as "pure scientists," but have instead entered the arena of philosophical hermeneutics.

Also, we have not called for an explicitly religious psychology, but instead, a religiously informed philosophical anthropology.[17] Being explicit about our own philosophical assumptions brings about far greater possibility of honest dialogue than pretending that we have no such assumptions or that we have achieved a place of complete neutrality.

Similar to Jones, we have argued that contemporary psychology needs to do its research and practice *in dialogue* with a broader religiously informed philosophical anthropology, informed by the deeper metaphors embedded in the Western religious tradition. It is these classic images of human nature and fulfillment that continue to inform what Gadamer frequently called our "effective history." Indeed, classic texts and monuments live on in our current experience whether we are consciously aware of it or not. They have become part of the pre-theoretical symbolic world out of which we live our lives.

The Tension between Mainliners and Evangelicals

An unfortunate reality in psychology's dialogue with religion is that Protestant mainliners and evangelicals often do not pay much attention to each other. While the disciplines of systematic, biblical, and philosophical theology show signs of an increased dialogue, the psychology/theology discussion could benefit from ecumenical encouragement.

Less worried about embracing psychology as a source of help in the healing enterprise, the psychology/theology discussion within mainline traditions has generally concentrated less than evangelicals on the philosophical or methodological problems of relating theology to psychology. Evangelicals, on the other hand, have energetically engaged the methodological concerns since the early 1970s. The emergence of Fuller Theological Seminary's Graduate Program in Psychology in 1964, along with the birth of Rosemead School of Psychology in 1970, helped stimulate part of this discussion. In 1973, the *Journal of Psychology and Theology* emerged as a forum for sharing and debating ideas about theology's relationship to psychology. A little later, in 1982, the Christian Association of Psychological Studies (CAPS) began its own publication, the *Journal of Psychology and Christianity*, which has also offered an arena in which "psycho-theology," as it is sometimes called, and the methodological issues of integration could be discussed.

Not all within evangelical circles have welcomed these attempts to integrate theology and psychology. The resisters represent what is often called the "anti-psychology" movement. In 1970, Jay Adams published *Competent to Counsel*, which most evangelicals have seen as an unfortunate fundamentalist withdrawal from a new and promising dialogue.[18] For Adams, however, engaging secular psychotherapies and personality theories inevitably contaminates biblical authority, which is the *only* source necessary for counseling. Over three decades later, this "Nouthetic Counseling" movement, as it is called, seems not to have lost its radical anti-psychology demeanor. A spin-off of the group, the International Association of Biblical Counselors, appears to be less inflammatory in its language, yet still believes that Scripture alone is sufficient for counsel. David Powlison, perhaps the most frequently identified leader of Biblical Counseling, is certainly willing to engage other evangelicals about their integration projects. Yet he believes that the secular psychotherapies are so steeped in anti-Christian assumptions that open dialogue with them is dangerous due to psychology's contaminating influence. Even a glance at Powlison's writing, however, shows a level of intellectual reflection that was not present in his predecessors.[19] While Powlison's view still seems extreme, even to most evangelicals, his voice is a welcomed relief from some of the dialogue-damaging crusades of previous anti-psychology voices.

So why do evangelicals and mainliners not pay much attention to each other? What suspicions between these two groups create tension and roadblocks to dialogue?

Some mainliners would perhaps argue that evangelicals have not adequately appreciated the depth psychologies and their understanding of the unconscious factors that affect human reasoning. Still clinging to a form of positivism embedded in Protestant Scholasticism, the evangelical preoccupation with propositional truth hinders a deeper, often symbolic, understanding of both Scripture and the human psyche. Scriptural verifiability replaces the positivist understanding of empirical verifiability. This preoccupation with correct doctrine naturally leads evangelicals to over-prize cognitive approaches to therapy while neglecting the insights of the neo-Freudian and humanistic models.

Thus, mainliners may argue that they make better therapists than evangelicals because they recognize the depths and complexity of psychological processes. This gives them both keener insight into the dynamics of sin and a greater compassion for the human dilemma. Out of this understanding of the layers of human complexity, they are able to be less judgmental with clients.

In turn, evangelicals might respond that mainliners have lost their "nose" for detecting the "add on" material to many of the clinical psychologies. In other words, mainliners often fail to recognize the implicit assumptions in secular therapies that are at odds with the Judeo-Christian tradition. Overly enthusiastic about new forms of healing, many mainliners have uncritically accommodated Christianity to the newest form of therapeutic salvation. Evangelicals fear that the distinctiveness of the Christian message is lost. Eric Johnson and Stanton Jones in their *Psychology and Christianity* (2000) provide a very useful summary of the evangelical debate. They describe what evangelicals consider to be liberal theology's excessive accommodation and uncritical embrace of the clinical psychologies:

> Generally speaking, however, liberal Protestants who had been shaped by and supportive of some of the themes of modernism in practice seemed to view the relation of faith and psychology as largely one-directional. They saw modern

psychology as aiding in a reconstruction of the faith along the lines suggested by modern values (greater individualism, softened personal morality, reason/ science as more authoritative than biblical revelation) (cf. Oden, 1984). This general orientation has continued to the present (e.g., Browning, 1966, 1987; Capps, 1990; Howe, 1995), with greater sophistication and more willingness to critique mainstream psychology (e.g., Browning, 1987) but still with a greater openness to contemporary values and thought and a greater skepticism toward the Bible than seems compatible with historic Christianity.[20]

While it may be true that this "general orientation has continued to the present," as Johnson and Jones indicate, many within a more "liberal" perspective have indeed tried to reclaim the uniqueness of their theological roots within pastoral care. This statement also overlooks the extent to which evangelicals have themselves used the work of mainline theologians in their own efforts to orient their work on the relation of psychology and theology, especially the work of Thomas Oden and, as we have already indicated, *Religious Thought and the Modern Psychologies*.[21] Also, many mainliners have blown a whistle on themselves and their uncritical psychological indulgences. The American Association of Pastoral Counselors, the Society of Pastoral Theology, and the Society of Practical Theology, all of which are dominantly mainline and liberal groups, attest in recent years to a greater focus on theological identity. Suggesting that mainliners have not recognized some of their earlier extravagances with psychology is like saying that evangelicals have still not taken psychology seriously. Neither is true.

Nevertheless, evangelicals may argue that they are better philosophers and academic psychologists than mainliners because (a) they recognize the hidden, often competing, philosophical assumptions inherent in secular therapies, and (b) they are more interested in the results of empirical research than are mainliners. Persons such as Donald McKay, Malcolm Jeeves, and David Myers are examples of evangelicals who have done quite well in the more scientifically oriented dimensions of psychology.

The analytic psychiatrist, Carl Jung, whom we have already investigated, offers a specific example of some of the differences between many mainline and evangelical approaches to psychology's relationship with religion. Jung has been frequently embraced by liberal and mainline pastoral theologians who believe he offers a marvelous framework for interpreting psycho-spiritual issues. Jung's emphasis on moving beyond the ego into the higher reaches of the Self, his insistence on embracing our own shadows, his invitation to individuation, his accent on the archetypes, the collective unconscious, and the importance of myth can all be viewed as an extremely helpful alternative to Freud's negative view of religion. In fact, one can find a far richer investigation of Jung in most divinity schools and theological seminaries than one can find in graduate psychology departments.

While mainliners and liberals may express an enthusiasm about Jung, evangelicals often think that he provides a good example of excessive accommodation to a psychological perspective, an accommodation that ends up minimizing, and in some cases eliminating, a particular Christian voice. For instance, Christ becomes a symbol of the higher Self. Each of us is on a heroic journey as we take up our own particular cross just as Christ carried his. Christ's death and resurrection become symbols for the death of the ego and the resurrection of the Higher Self. Our task is to follow Jesus, not in the sense that he is our Lord, but only in the sense that he offers a good model of ego transcendence. Any specific role that Jesus might have played in the world's redemption, any understanding of Christ as a unique disclosure of divine love, is enveloped in a different paradigm that ends up reducing theological affirmations to psychological processes. According to many evangelicals, this is precisely the kind of theological abandonment that frequently occurs in religion's dialogue with psychotherapy.

Thus, evangelicals and mainliners differ in their willingness to risk dialogue with various therapies. Mainliners tend to meet secular therapies as dialogue partners that should be taken seriously at each of the five dimensions of practical moral thinking—even the higher levels of moral principles, deep metaphors, and implicit narratives about the meaning of life. They believe that real dialogue does not take place if one side invokes an epistemological privilege that is unearned. The psychologies cannot dismiss the relevance of implicit moral values and worldviews as if they were not present or do not really count. But Christian theology cannot invoke the correction of psychology's deep metaphors and narratives without giving further reasons why theistic metaphors are more adequate to experience than the mechanistic, harmonistic, dualistic, or blind selection metaphors of many of the modern psychological systems. Chapter six of this book, in which we advance critical reasons for the greater adequacy of theistic metaphors, doubtless makes many evangelical nervous. The kind of critical or apologetic theology called for in this chapter is not widely practiced in evangelical circles. But we believe that the romance that many evangelicals today have with the modern social sciences requires this level of critical dialogue. We do not believe that the issues between psychology and theology at this level of practical thinking can be rightly settled by simply announcing that these modern disciplines do not conform to the eyes of faith and that, of course, the eyes of faith are always right. The two of us acknowledge that our thinking begins in faith, but it is as well a faith that submits to critical reflection—a critical reflection that we recommend to both the *faith of the modern psychologies and the faith of those who call themselves Christians*. We recommend this attitude to our evangelical colleagues, not just to settle intramural differences between different wings of the Christian tradition but to better argue, and more publicly argue, the case for the relevance of Christianity to the disciplines of contemporary psychology.

Or, to say it even more pointedly, evangelicals tend to enter the dialogue with the conviction that Scripture provides an epistemologically privileged starting point. This claim is entirely appropriate from the standpoint of faith. Some such beginning point is also recognized as inevitable from the perspective of hermeneutic philosophy; if thought does not begin with one set of pre-understandings (one kind of faith), it begins with another. The question is, can we honestly retain these pre-understandings—our faith—unless we are ready to submit them to certain tests? Both liberals and conservatives must begin in faith if they are to call themselves Christians. The difference between them is that so-called liberals should be more open to being tested, even at the higher levels of practical wisdom, i.e., their views of the ultimate context of experience. Evangelicals are much more likely to begin with the firm conviction that their particular interpretation of revelation provides the final word about the human condition and then dismiss, without dialogue or critical assessment, all worldviews and ethics that do not themselves adhere to this initial stance.

Some of the differences here are clearly connected to different views of the nature of God's revelation. Generally speaking, evangelicals value special revelation (as propositionally revealed through Scripture) over general revelation, which recognizes God at work in natural processes throughout God's creation. Psychotherapy is clearly one of those natural instances in which God's healing could be seen to be at work as part of God's general revelation. On the other hand, some evangelicals, most notably David Myers, invoke general revelation as a theological justification for trusting the results of scientific psychology. In both cases—special or general revelation—evangelicals are likely to see cognitive truth as the model of the kind of truth that revelation manifests. Truth as practical truth—truth as practical wisdom that consists of metaphysical assumptions as well as concrete moral application—seems less prominent in their understanding of either special or general revelation.

Also, evangelicals may claim that liberals still gravitate toward an overly optimistic view of human potential. They may further argue that a realistic appraisal of the twentieth century promotes a strong doctrine of sin, not a belief in human innocence and goodness. In fact, some conservative evangelicals make strange bedfellows with strict Freudians in their assessment of the human condition. While it is generally true that evangelicals have not been heavily influenced by the psychoanalytic tradition, many Calvinistic evangelicals and orthodox Freudians share a view of humanity's rather depraved existence. Put another way, some evangelicals like Freud's pessimistic view of the human instincts and believe it is an accurate estimation of fallen humanity after Adam's essential goodness was lost.

We have instead agreed with William James and Reinhold Niebuhr in their views concerning the human instincts. Unlike Freud, James and Niebuhr do not see our basic human instincts as inherently destructive or out-of-control. Instead, both argued that there is some order and regularity within the instincts just as there is order and regularity within our spiritual capacity for self-transcendence. Niebuhr, in fact, was able to argue that our freedom is still intact enough to potentially trust God. Yet overwhelmed by anxiety, we recoil in distrust and place our own strategies at the center of our existence.

Niebuhr is able to articulate this understanding only if he reads the Adamic story nonliterally. Many evangelicals still approach the biblical account of the fall in terms of a historical-causal explanation. Once they do this, then Freud's morbid and hopeless account of our instincts seems compatible with their own negative view of the human condition. Read thusly, only Adam as literal, historical person had genuine freedom. After his fall, his descendants are born into a world that is inherently evil. Unless we are prepared to say, along with Augustine, that all of us somehow mysteriously chose along with Adam, and that Adam's loss of freedom is passed on to us genetically, then it's hard to understand how we are each responsible for our condition. Let us state this issue more sharply: The literalization of the Adamic story undermines the very freedom that makes human decision meaningful. Sin must not be interpreted to result from our biological makeup. If we are indeed "hard wired" to sin, then talk of freedom is meaningless. We don't simply enter a sinful world; we *are* sinful for simply showing up! Augustine may have championed the notion of created goodness in his fight with the Manichaeans, but for all practical purposes, Adam's descendants *are* born in an evil, Manichaean world. Embodied existence itself is sinful, corrupt existence. The Genesis account is therefore reduced from a powerful story about the corruption of existential freedom to an unfortunate hunt for sin's historical first cause.

Disputes within Evangelical Circles

In their *Psychology and Christianity,* Jones and Johnson asked four leading but divergent representatives within evangelical circles to provide an overview of their position and respond to each other.[22] The four positions, representing the dominant ones on the evangelical playing field, are identified as the "levels of analysis" position, represented by well-known social psychologist David Myers; the "integrationist" perspective represented by clinical psychologist and popular author Gary Collins; the "Christian psychology" position represented by philosophical psychologist Robert Roberts; and the Biblical Counseling position, represented by David Powlison. These four positions constitute an excellent case study of the issues at stake in the dialogue between psychology and theology. It is our belief that the hermeneutic understanding of the relation between theology and psychology can help make sense of the rather striking divergences between the four allegedly evangelical thinkers.

We especially are interested in examining how this evangelical conversation has dealt with what we have called "metaphors of ultimacy" in clinical psychology. What contribution does this discussion provide our own efforts? In order to probe this potential donation, perhaps we should look into the disagreements among evangelicals concerning the value of both scientific and clinical psychology.

A helpful way to get at this issue is to look at the controversy surrounding David Myers, esteemed scholar in both evangelical and social psychology circles, as well as the author of one of the most widely read introductory psychology texts. An excursion into the evangelical responses to Myers will help us better understand their views of clinical psychology's relationship to Christian theology.

To repeat, our own argument has been that clinical psychologies should not be chastised for maintaining metaphors of ultimacy, but only be challenged to make those metaphors explicit and be more prepared to defend them. By doing this, any pretense of being "purely" or "narrowly" scientific would be lost; they would be forced to recognize that such justifications will lead them into the fields of metaphysics and ethics. Further, we believe that it is inevitable that clinical psychologies eventually deal with these issues of life's ultimate context, our moral obligation, and our level of needs. The reason, again, is that these clinical visions attempt to account for the patterns, dynamics, and processes of human life. They cannot be held captive to a narrow empiricism that employs only limited, observable, and quantifiable data. Their questions and scope are larger than this. Put simply, we don't care that the clinical psychologies represent a religious outlook; we just want them to be self-conscious and fully accountable about doing so. Some of them may indeed offer a more adequate religious outlook than others, and they certainly have every right to talk about ethical concerns. We just ask that they take off the "hard science" hat while they do so.

Stances within evangelical circles appear to boil down to four positions: (a) scientific psychology may be embraced as one among several valid "levels of explanation," but we should be suspicious of clinical psychology (Myers); (b) we may cautiously relate and "integrate" all psychology to Christian thought, which is the final arbiter of all truth (Collins); (c) secular psychology is so infused with ideology that we must develop a full "Christian psychology" before we begin any sort of discussion (Roberts); and (d) we must avoid secular psychotherapy and develop a "Christian counseling" that is judged by the standards of scripture alone (Powlison).

Myers's "Levels of Analysis" and His Evangelical Critics

Following the physicist Richard Bube, David Myers and Malcolm Jeeves argue that there should not be a conflict between psychology and theology because each discipline functions at a different level of analysis.[23] Various levels of analysis investigate different "layers" of reality. Physics, chemistry, biology, psychology, social psychology, sociology, political science, literature, philosophy, and theology all ask different kinds of questions, and consequently, their boundaries should not be blurred.[24] Each level is accessible through the particular methods unique to that discipline.

> Which of the various perspectives is pertinent all depends on what you want to talk about. Take romantic love, for example. A physiologist might describe love as a state of arousal. A social psychologist would examine how various characteristics and conditions—good looks, similarity of the partners, sheer repeated exposure to one another—enhance the emotion of love. A poet would express the sublime experience that love can sometimes be. A theologian might describe love as the God-given goal of human relationships.[25]

Because love can be described at many different levels, we need not assume that any *one* level has a monopoly on the analysis business. Again, each level asks different questions and brings with it different methodologies by which to investigate its topic. Reducing a phenomenon to "nothing but" the explanation offered by a particular level of analysis creates unnecessary debate and misunderstanding. Yet this can happen in several directions. While it may be more common to reduce philosophical, literary, or theological explanations to physiological processes, it is also possible to reverse the reduction: physiological processes are "nothing but" ideas, the movement of the spirit, and so on. Myers believes there is room for both.

Myers is clearly a research psychologist. Most evangelical scholars concerned about the dialogue between psychology and religion are clinical psychologists and counselors. Myers is not very interested in the traditional clinical/theological tendency to relate a concept from personality theory such as Rogerian incongruence to the Christian notion of sin, or the Jungian notion of individuation to Christian spirituality. Instead, he wants to demonstrate the continuities between exciting new discoveries in scientific psychology and ancient wisdom. Thus, though he, himself, is a social psychologist, he is very energetic about neuroscience, cognitive science, behavior genetics, molecular genetics, and evolutionary psychology.

Traditionally, there has been little debate about the "hard" areas of psychology (brain physiology, visual perception, animal learning, and so on) and Christian theology. The controversial areas have been more related to personality theory and psychotherapy, where larger questions about motivation, purpose, human fulfillment, and the nature of human relationships inevitably arise. But for Myers, psychology has no business dealing with the ultimate questions of our lives. It is clearly out of its depth in these pursuits. In Myers's mind, expecting scientific psychology to offer its students guidance for the meaning of their lives and reasons for their existence is like "criticizing bowling for not being aerobic exercise or like criticizing biology for not being internal medicine."[26]

Myers believes that many of the Christian critiques of psychology are aimed at a very outdated mode of psychology, one that is not taken seriously in most academic psychology departments. He makes frequent reference to today's standard introductory psychology textbooks to demonstrate that scientific psychology has moved far beyond what many consider to be the current issues of psychology. Myers points approvingly toward the fact that most standard psychology texts refer to what he calls the "long-dead" personality theorists such as Freud, Jung, and Rogers in merely one or two paragraphs.[27] Myers is in a position to know such things, having himself written what is undoubtedly one of the most widely used introductory psychology texts.[28]

Yet this comment is most confusing. For if we turn away from an introductory text to a personality theory text, these "long-dead" people are quickly resurrected. Do they not occupy a legitimate place in psychology as well? Surely in every psychology department, personality theory is taught. This course may not offer the empirical tidiness of a course on brain research, but given the range of its investigation, how could it? Personality theories could not possibly serve up a full portrait of the human psyche based exclusively on the manipulation of a small cluster of data-controlled experiments. If personality theories are too "soft" to be useful, then what are clinicians supposed to draw upon when they engage in the practice of helping people with their problems? The latest findings in molecular genetics may not provide clinicians with quite what they need in working with a person's anxiety disorder. Of course these personality theories need to be checked and changed when they overlap with more explicitly scientific psychology and can be empirically falsified. Yet the fact that further empirical research can offer a corrective is no reason to dismiss the current theory. Surely, this would be throwing the baby out with the bathwater.

At times there seems to be an ambiguity in Myers. On the one hand, he does not explicitly rule out personality theory or psychotherapy as a legitimate part of psychology. Yet on the other hand, he seems to relegate these parts of the discipline to a level of analysis distinct from his much-preferred academic and research psychology. Myers knows as well as anyone that the clinical psychologies and personality theories must *of necessity* deal with larger issues than a strict empirical methodology can handle. Do we therefore disengage clinical psychology from its "harder science" associates? Undeniably, most who work in clinical psychology and personality theory will quickly admit that it is not a precise science. In fact, the kind of careful analysis involved in the emergence of personality theory, according to fellow evangelical Robert Roberts, is not unlike the work of philosophical reflection, a point we have made as well throughout this book. Roberts writes,

> the kind of constructs that typically arise out of clinical experience—contestable again—are made on the basis of the kind of careful but not statistically worked up observations that informed an Aristotle, a Chrysippus, a Thomas Aquinas. That conceptions basic to the kind of constructs that distinguish one therapeutic school from another or one personality theory from another are contestable is shown by the diversity and rivalry of those theories.[29]

Evangelical critics point out that while Myers insists that psychology does not purport to answer "ultimate questions," he turns right around and tells us that psychology can help us understand *why* people think, feel, and act the way they do.[30] Does the "why" question never contain or bump into an ultimate horizon? Myers's own work on happiness is often cited as an example of going beyond his own narrow prescription of what should be psychology's focus.

Much of the evangelical argument with Myers seems to be focused on the issue of epistemological authority. Myers is accused of placing all truth under the scrutiny of empirical verification. Comments such as the following both demonstrate Myers's deep respect for the authority of science, and provoke evangelical concern about a possible scientific "imperialism": "If nature does not conform to our presumptions, so much the worse for our presumptions. Disciplined, rigorous inquiry—checking our theories against reality—is part of what it means to love God with our minds."[31] While he explicitly encourages the differing methodologies of philosophy, sociology, or theology, say Myers's critics, these disciplines remain inferior to the empirically verifiable data of the hard sciences. The underlying suggestion is that if psychology is not strongly empirically based, then it is worth little in the world of truth-claims. Other levels of analysis are free to think what they want, but the scientific method delivers in a way that the rest of the levels do not. Again, wouldn't the logic of Myers's analogy place personality theory, psychotherapy, motivation theory, and larger issues of human existence outside the boundaries of scientific psychology? Again, while Myers is critical of what he calls the "sages of the ages" approach to psychology, he often seems to limit psychology so as to exclude many of its traditional areas. For Myers, a "philosophical" approach must find its "corrective" in scientific methodology. For instance, while some philosophical psychologists celebrate the insights of Aristotle, they fail to mention that Aristotle believed the human mind to be in the heart, which scientific psychology obviously now knows to be false.[32]

It is precisely at this point that some of Myers evangelical associates fear a "creeping empiricism" in his work. They are concerned that this will eventually eliminate other perspectives as truth contributors. How long, then, before we can only speak meaningfully about what empirical science has to say?

We suggest that a complete divorce of scientific and clinical psychology may create its own problems. For instance, let's examine Myers's well-known and highly interesting conclusions about how research demonstrates a cross-cultural tendency within human beings to think more highly of ourselves than is warranted. This self-serving cognitive distortion can be observed in our tendencies to take responsibility for our successes while blaming others for our failures; seeing ourselves as more tolerant, fair, and socially skilled than others; having clearly inflated confidence in our own beliefs; justifying our past behaviors; revising our past in self-enhancing ways, and so on. In his fascinating book, *The Inflated Self,* as well as his social psychology text, he documents this widely reported evidence of self-inflation in social psychology.[33] Myers then points toward the connection between this research finding and the traditional Judeo-Christian emphasis on pride as our root problem, the first sin. Contemporary social psychology research confirms that Paul and Augustine were correct in asserting that our major dilemma is thinking more highly of ourselves than we ought. Thus, the widespread diagnosis of low self-esteem, so prominent in popular psychology, is inaccurate. While Myers admits that some people may struggle with low self-esteem, the clear evidence is that our major problem is pride.

Myers, however, exhibits a bit of philosophical naïveté in claiming that empirical work that reveals the self-serving behavior of humans proves the Christian doctrine of sin. This would not be the case unless extra-scientific interpretation were brought to this data that demonstrates that humans do this out of freedom, uncoerced by biological necessity or social conditionedness. Such research could just as easily be used to support a Manichaean view of the intrinsic and unchosen evil of the created world. Maybe we are evil because we were made evil by an evil god or demigod. Myers does not seem to realize the hermeneutic context of his interpretations of the so-called scientific data on our selfishness. Hard science, in his hands, is interpreted by the Christian classics that once shaped his effective history and pre-understandings. But, from the perspective of a hermeneutic interpretation of both theology and psychology, Myers's social-psychological experiments do not so much confirm the Christian doctrine of sin as provide a degree of distanciated evidence that adds to the plausibility of the idea of sin.

But for Myers, scientific psychology, not the speculations of personality theory, gives us the deeper insight into the reality of the over-valued self. Yet it is precisely at this point that Myers's scientific social psychology is called into question, not only by theology, but by methods and perspectives within personality theory and psychotherapy. How did Myers and other social psychologists arrive at this conviction that pride is the primary culprit of the human condition? The answer is through questionnaires, surveys, and brief interviews. Yet how do we know that many of these responses do not engage in compensatory thinking for fears of inadequacy? How do we know that these highly conscious self-affirmations do not serve as a "cover-up" for anxious fears of not being acceptable? It would be misguided to suggest that all these self-evaluations are a simple disguise for deeper problems. Yet it is precisely clinical and personality theory that insists on asking what levels of anxiety, freedom, and self-doubt might be beneath our flattering self-reports. Do these perspectives uncover deeper layers of self-perception and experience than controlled social-science observation and experimentation are able to unearth?

We believe that our hermeneutic model for relating theology and psychology could be helpful for Myers. We think that Myers's high regard for objective scientific psychology would be better understood if it were conceptualized as a moment of distanciation—not absolute objectivity—within his wider religious interpretive interests and commitments. Myers is a respected social psychologist. But, even more deeply, he is a kind of Christian theologian attempting to understand his faith and extend its interpretive power to a variety of contemporary social contexts. There are times, however, when his levels of explanation approach sounds like what philosophers of science call foundationalism. Scientific psychology, he tells us, deals with facts; in saying this, he seems to posit an ideal state of scientific objectivity. Theology and ethics, he tells us, function at different levels of explanation; somehow or other, the objectivity of science, he contends, can help, and sometimes even correct, the value-laden character of theology that itself functions on a different level of explanation. We fear that within this model is really a kind of foundationalism that homologizes all truth to the same level—a level that can be addressed and even corrected by empirical investigation. The concept of practical wisdom, so central to this book, does not reduce all knowledge to either empirical or metaphysical truth. The model of practical wisdom that we have developed in this book holds that both empirical and metaphysical judgments (visions of the ultimate context of experience) contribute to practical wisdom, but in the end it is distinguishable from both of these alternative models of truth.

It is more likely, however, that Myers brings to his role as social psychologist a variety of assumptions, pre-understandings, and questions shaped by his religious heritage. These questions to a considerable extent shape his social psychological interests and interpretations. His theology, as is all theology, is multidimensional, as we have argued on these pages; it contains a narrative and metaphorical level but also a variety of assumptions, colored by these narratives, about both moral truth and the facts of this world. Among these facts are such issues as what we need, what we want, and what we can have and do in light of the realities of our social and natural constraints. Myers rightly uses his social psychology, not so much to question and clarify the deep metaphors and narratives of his faith tradition, but to test and correct the more factual aspects of that tradition that also are a part of his inherited theological beginning point. These more factual aspects involve questions such as whether people empirically and measurably act in ways that theology has traditionally defined as sinful. Myers's science tells him, yes. Do both mothers and fathers on average contribute to their children's well-being, as the tradition has tended to think? Myers's scientific social psychology says, yes. Are parents today as influential as we like to think? The new science tells us, no; peers are often, at least in today's society, more influential. But all of these empirical questions have their meaning, we would contend, with reference to his prior theological commitments when these are understood within the hermeneutic model for relating psychology and theology advanced in this book.

The Issue of Epistemological Privilege

As is often the case, the evangelical discussion revolves around the issue of authority or epistemological privilege in the claims of psychology and theology. The place and authority of Scripture becomes central. What role, exactly, does the Bible play in our attempts to integrate psychology and theology? Gary Collins, the second prominent evangelical reviewed by Johnson and Jones, believes that Myers goes too far in his movement toward a kind of "scientific imperialism" (what we call foundationalism) in which even Scripture is evaluated in terms of its empirical verifiability: "the core issue is whether the Bible is the authoritative Word of God that transforms and becomes the standard against which we evaluate our psychology, or whether psychological science is the standard against which we evaluate our beliefs? I take the former stance. It appears to me that Myers leans toward the latter."[34] As a representative of the "integration" model of relating psychology to theology, Collins wants to maintain a cautious interaction with psychology because he is convinced that most of twentieth-century psychology has secular roots incompatible with a Christian perspective. While he does not believe Christianity should develop its own psychology, as do Robert Roberts and David Powlison, he does believe that a Christian needs to be armed with scriptural authority as a guiding light in all integrational efforts. With this qualification, Christians may enter the jungles of secular psychology and sometimes find things that are most useful.

Differing from Myers's emphasis on research psychology, Collins believes that the crossroads at which Christianity and psychology meet is clinical and applied psychology. It is at this juncture that the nature of human beings, the dilemmas of our condition, theories of motivation, and questions of human fulfillment meet. His integrationist approach is more willing than Myers to criticize psychology, even scientific psychology, especially if it contradicts what appears to be scriptural teaching. And it is always the Bible as a "deposit" of revelation that has this epistemological privilege. Scripture is thus isolated from its associated standards of authority: reason, experience, and tradition.

For Myers, because "all truth is God's truth" we can plow full steam ahead with scientific methods and understand the divinely given network of nature. What are we afraid of? Let's move ahead. Yet for Collins, and particularly for conservatives such as David Powlison—Johnson and Jones's representative of the Biblical Counseling view—it's a little more complicated than this. Put most directly, Powlison does not think that Myers's approach adequately appreciates the noetic consequences of sin: "He joyously holds creation and common grace in view but misses the consistent disorienting effect that fallenness exerts on conceptual systems—and the consistent reorienting effect of redemption."[35] For Powlison, sin has infiltrated all dimensions of our thinking and psychological theorizing is no exception. Therefore, says Powlison, a Christian psychology should guide all of our research. If we leave out the issue of sin and our need for redemption, how can we possibly understand the human condition? In describing "the" Christian psychology, Powlison states the following:

> Our psychology should affect research into *anything*—at minimum affecting our presuppositions and interpretive categories, the criteria by which we weigh the significance of findings, and the implications we draw. For example, without God's realigning Word, it is impossible for human beings to accurately observe and interpret such things as human motivation: conflicting instincts? primary and secondary drives? socio-biological hard-wiring? compensation for low self-esteem? unmet needs from the hierarchy of needs? lusts of the flesh?[36]

Going further, Powlison enlists the support of Calvin in his claim that the "natural person" has no ability to make sense of his or her human desires. Contemporary psychology is disabled because its thinking is poisoned by sin. "Empiricistic methodology offers no reliable corrective to our liability to error, because self-deceiving people design studies, then collect and interpret data."[37] Thus the psychology enterprise is doomed from the start. Please note that this Reformed approach is not simply saying that psychology can tell us nothing of *divine* nature; it can tell us nothing of *human* nature as well. Even parallels between such issues as God's love and Rogerian unconditional positive regard are fallacious, with the latter being a "crude counterfeit" of the former.[38]

So, again, much of the battle here is about epistemological authority. Myers trusts God's revelation in nature and believes that anything we claim about "special" revelation needs to match these findings. His critics believe he is subordinating special revelation (which they equate with Scripture) to scientific knowledge.

In many ways, this is a replay of Reformation issues: How far can the unaided reason be trusted? Myers trusts scientific reason to give us an accurate account of the way things are. He limits the scope of what scientific reason investigates so as to make sure that it does not deal with the ultimate questions of life. People such as Collins enter the integration discussion with a cautious stance, ever aware of the possibilities of being duped. Individuals such as Robert Roberts—Johnson and Jones's representative of the Christian psychology view—believe that the secular psychologies offer nothing short of competing paradigms that challenge Christianity's view of the human condition. His solution is to develop a psychology that relies on Christian resources alone. In his various writings, and especially his essay in *Psychology and Christianity*, he gives suggestive interpretations of the implicit psychology of the Sermon on the Mount and its celebration of the psychology of Christian happiness *(markarois)* and its associated virtues such as being poor in spirit *(ptochoi to pneumati)*, being gentle *(prays)*, and being righteousness *(dikaiosyne)*.[39] Roberts elaborates a psychology of *Christian ideals—the goals of the Christian life*. He also describes a psychology of Christian sin—such characteristics as anger, revenge, lust, adultery, and divorce.[40] Roberts is extremely insightful in insisting that there is something like a Christian psychology and that both theologians and a society informed by Christian ideals must learn to describe it. In this sense, Roberts is taking seriously a major source of what Gadamer and Ricoeur call the classical that has formed and shaped our ideals. Christians in their witness and confession go further than Gadamer and Ricoeur; they call these classics—these ideals—"revelation." Modern psychology, on the other hand, says it is describing human psychology in its *isness*, although as we believe that we have shown, it sneaks ideals and normative values in nonetheless. Our argument has been that modern psychology must take on both responsibilities—to describe both the *isness* and the ideal *telos* of the human psyche. The hermeneutic model makes it possible for modern psychology to critically retrieve the ideals of effective history and yet, at the same time, gain the distance required to refine our understanding of the average empirical regularities of human motivation, thought, and need that we bring to our critically retrieved ideals.

Roberts, who is more of a philosopher than either a clinical or research psychologist, may have a very important point, one that both evangelicals, mainliners, and society as a whole should take with great seriousness. Before becoming preoccupied with describing and explaining the *isness* of our empirical psyches, we should come to understand the psychologies implicit in our religious and philosophical classics. In fact, careful reading of Roberts demonstrates he has almost as much interest in the philosophical psychologies of Aristotle, the Stoics, and Aquinas as he does the implicit psychologies found in the Sermon on the Mount or in the letters of Paul. In fact, what first appears as a conservative argument in Roberts conceals a radical liberal agenda. Roberts implies something with which we would agree; it is impossible to adequately understand the New Testament without understanding the surrounding psychologies of Roman Hellenism with which the New Testament writers both interacted and absorbed and yet amended. It is also impossible to understand

Paul without understanding the Stoics, Augustine without understanding neo-Platonism, Aquinas without understanding Aristotle, and even Luther without understanding the medieval nominalists. Philosophy, philosophical psychology, and today the modern psychologies provide insights into more general theories of action that Christian understandings—yes, Christian psychology, if you will—adds to, reorients, and redirects. As Ricoeur would say, these psychologies provide insight into the archaeology of common human motivations and actions that our various teleologies, including the goals of the Christian life, qualify and redirect. But Ricoeur would add, and we do as well, that we cannot know the full meaning of our ideals, goals, and images of fulfillment unless we also understand the regularities of human experience that our teleologies transform.

The modern psychologies of today, as did the ancient philosophical psychologies, give us insight into these regularities and archaeologies. To this extent, we agree with Myers's desire to retain the distanciating moments of both the modern scientific *and* the modern clinical psychologies; we have, however, more confidence than Myers that the latter contain such moments. But our hermeneutic philosophy leads us to have sympathies with Roberts and his claim that our encounter with the distanciating ambitions of the modern psychologies can best be pursued within careful attention to the religious classics that have shaped our effective histories. However, from our perspective, both Collins and Powlison seem to bring the raw edge of faith too directly and immediately into the dialogue between psychology and theology. This is entirely appropriate for the confessional context of the inner life of the witnessing church. But for the public dialogue between psychology and the Christian faith, a more philosophical stance is required. We hold that this public dialogue is best pursued when the witness of faith is expressed in the outlines of a theologically informed philosophical anthropology that reminds professional psychology of the fullness of the human, critiques this psychology (as we have in this book) when it lapses into matters of faith and morals, and both informs and constrains the research agenda of both the narrowly scientific and the clinical psychologies. This statement explains the importance of the theologically oriented philosophical anthropologies argued for throughout this book. Time and again, it seems to us, our evangelical colleagues confuse the rhythms and spontaneities of the confessing church with the requirements of public dialogue and critique. In the end, we believe that both our appreciation for and criticism of the modern psychologies exceeds that of our evangelical friends. This is why, as we suggested above, the traditional categories of liberal and conservative, mainline and evangelical, are for the most part irrelevant on the issue of the relation of Christian faith and theology to the modern psychologies.

Roberts believes that only after we have reclaimed the classic psychologies of the faith can Christians think about a dialogue with secular psychology. Here we have sympathies with Roberts. But we resist the more radical suspicions of Powlison when he asserts that any form of integration will inevitably end with a blend that cannot be trusted.

Developing Two Types of Psychology

As we have seen, Myers believes that it is a mistake to "throw in the towel" on our attempts to build a scientifically objective psychology. He enlists the support of British neuropsychologist Donald McKay in arguing that all "ideological psychologies," even Christian ones, need to be rejected. McKay's position is that the Christian in psychology has a vocational calling to

> "tell it like it is," knowing that the Author is at our elbow, a silent judge of the accuracy with which we claim to describe the world He has created. In this sense our goal is objective, value-free knowledge. If our limitations, both intellectual and moral, predictably limit our achievement of this ideal, this is something not to be glorified in but to be acknowledged in a spirit of repentance. Any idea that it could justify a dismissal of the ideal of value-free knowledge as a "myth" would be irrational—and as irreligious—as to dismiss the idea of *righteousness* as a "myth" on the ground that we can never perfectly attain that.[41]

For McKay and Myers, our call is to read the data of nature as reliably as we can, eliminating as much tainting ideology as is humanly possible. The fact that as thinking, feeling, subjective researchers we will not arrive at a "purely objective truth" should not cause us to abandon the task. Recognizing some of the pretensions of the Enlightenment does not mean that we quit investigating. It just means that science should be a humbler enterprise, always careful about extrapolating grand theories from its data.

While we believe that Myers's tendency toward foundationalism does not adequately grasp the importance of the pre-understandings we bring to data, we salute his attempt to sharpen this moment of distanciation within the interpretive process. By all means, let us make an attempt in empirical psychology to be as unbiased as we can. We contend that in the world of psychology there is room for both a rigorous scientific approach and a larger, critical-philosophical and hermeneutic approach.

Scientific psychology will always be focused on a smaller range of observable and controllable data and it can serve to check and test theology at the level of its empirical remarks. Its contributions at this level are crucial since theology necessarily will need to relate its visional and moral dimensions to some description of the empirical. Yet scientific psychology needs to maintain a certain epistemic humility as it engages in the tasks of focused analysis. As we have tried to argue throughout this book, every scientist brings a horizon of assumptions to his or her work. These orienting assumptions make understanding possible. Without them, we would have no context out of which to focus and select particular data to study. Also, the scientific questions eventually will move into larger questions of interpretation, meaning, and ethics. When scientific psychology becomes intoxicated with its Enlightenment belief that it has achieved a timeless, ahistorical standpoint on the whole of reality (the visional, the obligational, or even the empirical), then it needs to be "sobered" by a critical, philosophically oriented psychology that questions its epistemological framework and implicit assumptions. The task of a larger, critical psychology will be to help scientific psychology understand the philosophical matrix out of which it operates (often, positivism), as well as the normative claims it sometimes makes. The task of scientific psychology, on the other hand, will be to provide a very important, and corrective, empirical check (moment of distanciation) on the empirical assumptions of common sense, philosophy, and theology. Held together, these two approaches can avoid the modernist pretensions of "pure" objectivity, along with the rampant subjectivism sometimes typical of postmodernity.

Evangelicals and Postmodernity: Mixed Blessings

At times the tables should perhaps be turned on Myers's evangelical critics. This is particularly true in reference to their celebration of the postmodern implications for science. Science, they say, is definitely theory-laden as it selects, distorts, and frequently fabricates facts. Even at the highly experimental level of psychology, a theory decides what to pay attention to, what to bring into focus, and what to ignore. These qualities clearly get in the way of any pretense at "objectivity," which is never humanly possible. Interestingly, right-wing evangelicals at this point make strange bedfellows with Marxists, feminists, and others who focus on the tainted and corrupting nature of ideology.

However, to be consistent, evangelicals must not excuse their own theorizing efforts. Sometimes they forget that theological thought is as limited, finite, and partially distorted as any other thought. They cannot claim an island of epistemological certainty in the otherwise turbulent waters of postmodernity. For instance, some evangelical authors have no problems identifying psychology's diversity, particularly in clinical psychology. Yet when it comes to the issue of "the" Christian faith, they ignore the most empirical fact around: Diversity flourishes there as well! Robert Roberts, for instance, insists upon speaking in the plural about "psychologies" while he speaks only in the singular about theology. Yet even within the world of evangelical theology alone, there are a variety of perspectives. For instance, consider the difference of opinion about theology's relationship to psychology at Fuller and Westminster Theological Seminaries. Further, it does not help that all these groups appeal to an infallible authority in the Scriptures because it is the same human thought, "corrupted by sin," according to their own estimation, that pushes them to select, distort, modify, and pay attention to certain biblical passages that support their highly theory-laden approach to the Scripture. Put directly, if they want to kick out positivist science, then they need to relinquish their positivist view of scriptural authority. They are stuck with the hermeneutical problem just like everyone else. It is entirely justifiable to begin with the attestations of faith and entirely acceptable to expose and critique the moral religious dimensions of the modern psychologies, as we have done throughout this book. But if evangelicals want to bring faith into a public dialogue and critique of the modern psychologies, they must take on the additional responsibility of giving publicly articulate reasons and justifications for the power and adequacy of the Christian faith to provide frameworks and direction to these disciplines. This additional responsibility the evangelical community has so far declined to accept. They prefer to trump their opponents with appeals to faith.

Some Concluding Thoughts

Throughout this book, we have tried to steer a course between Enlightenment foundationalism and postmodern relativism. Like our confessional, narrative, and cultural-linguistic friends, we believe that all thought begins in faith-assumptions. We agree that no one starts the investigative or interpretive process with a clean slate. We bring inherited assumptions to whatever we interpret. Without these assumptions, as orienting frameworks, experience would be impossible to understand. Rather than trying to eliminate these orienting assumptions, we can use them constructively to advance conversation. As one of us recently heard a friend humorously say, "There is no such thing as an immaculate perception." All of us have been parented and saturated by traditions. We agree that any Enlightenment pretense of complete objectivity or any foundationalist claim to absolute certainty must be rigorously challenged. We approach the classic texts of the Western tradition *having already been shaped by those texts.*

This book has argued that a major part of the pre-understanding we bring to our experience has been shaped, whether consciously or unconsciously, by the religio-ethical dimensions of Western experience. As we have seen, some of our allies in the hermeneutical approach have not fully appreciated the important role of religion in shaping our effective histories. In contrast to this, we have argued that at the edge of social scientific theories, regardless of how secular they may claim to be, are theologies that enter into the descriptive moment. Religious traditions occupy a major role in the classics and monuments that have informed our consciousness. Even when we have consciously rejected particular doctrines of faith traditions, those horizons of understanding have a way of sneaking back into the picture as they shape our assumptions about human needs, fulfillment, obligation, and the ultimate context of our lives. Beneath even the most practical activity is a hidden world of theories and assumptions.

So yes, we all begin in faith. And yes, this confessional starting point cannot be universally, certainly, and unequivocally validated. Our world is indeed pluralistic and we need to grieve and let go of the Enlightenment hope for a neutral starting point and universal agreement on a common theory. Nevertheless, we part company with a strictly confessional approach that believes that simply declaring our narrative should be the end of the story. Confessional language is wonderfully important in our religious communities. However, we daily move out of those communities and into public arenas that require further conversation. The fact that we will not be able to provide that public conversation with certain, absolute answers does not mean that we should stop talking. While absolute reasons are out of our grasp, there is still a place for providing *good reasons* for our perspective. Apologetics can lose its grandiosity and yet still be important. Surely there is a middle ground between complete rational proof and fideism. This moment of distanciation, this time of self-critical reflection and the offering of reasons, occurs within a larger conversation and interpretive process. As David Tracy has reminded us, the point of conversation is not arguing, although a genuine conversation may well have a submoment in which argument is crucial.[42] Without an advancement of some public reasons for what we believe, a conversation cannot take place at all. We then give up the hope of our faith-perspective "making sense" outside the walls of our confessional community.

Following Tracy, we have argued that a revised correlational model needs to contrast both the questions and answers of a faith-tradition with the questions and answers of contemporary perspectives. It is not enough, via Tillich, to match Judeo-Christian answers to the existential questions of our age. A mutually critical correlation of perspectives is necessary. And a revised correlational approach is only possible if we accept our obligation to provide validity claims. It is here that we are in agreement with Richard Bernstein:

> For although all claims to truth are fallible and open to criticism, they still require validation—validation that can be realized only through offering the best reasons and arguments that can be given in support of them—reasons and arguments that are themselves embedded in the practices that have developed in the course of history. We never escape from the obligation of seeking to validate claims to truth through argumentation and opening ourselves to the criticism of others.[43]

Again, the key is to remember that offering our validity claims is part of a larger hermeneutic process. *While we distance ourselves from our pre-understanding, we do not forget that we* have *a pre-understanding.* We can distance ourselves from our traditions without alienating ourselves from those traditions. The constant reminder of our own pre-understanding will help prevent us from falling back into some form of foundationalism that claims to have eliminated all pre-understandings.

Throughout this book, we have used Reinhold Niebuhr as an example of the kind of critically reflective thinking and distanciation we advocate. Niebuhr clearly understood, as well as anyone, the historical and social locatedness of all human thought. He also realized the dangers of intellectual pride and its conviction that we have grasped the final truth with total clarity. Yet Niebuhr fully engaged in the more modest goal of showing the relevance of the traditional Christian understanding of original sin for a contemporary understanding of the human condition. Was everyone convinced? Of course not. Did he make a powerful case for the relevance of a notion that many thought to be long dead? Indeed he did. Niebuhr did not shy away from contrasting a Judeo-Christian understanding of the human dilemma

with other models. He moved outside of strictly confessional language and publicly argued that Judeo-Christian insights into the human condition made a great
deal of sense. He began in faith but also provided highly plausible arguments for
his position.

We believe that just because the apologetic task can sometimes fall back into an
Enlightenment foundationalism, which attempts to "prove" all its convictions
before a neutral bar of reason, does not mean that all validity defenses are therefore
misguided. Apologetics becomes grandiose insofar as it forgets that it is a submoment within a broader process of interpretation and conversation. Enlightenment-
intoxicated apologetics develops amnesia about its own pre-understanding and the
prejudices that go along with that. Making validity claims is never the end of the
conversation. It is simply a part of it. And the point is to advance the conversation,
not supply irrefutable arguments.

Notes

Preface to the Second Edition

1. William Doherty, *Soul Searching: Why Psychotherapy Must Promote Moral Responsibility* (New York: Basic Books, 1995).

2. Ellen Hermans, *The Romance of American Psychology* (Berkeley: University of California Press, 1995).

3. Philip Cushman, *Constructing the Self, Constructing America* (Cambridge, Mass.: Perseus, 1995).

4. Frank C. Richardson, Blaine J. Fowers, and Charles B. Guignon, *Re-envisioning Psychology* (San Franciso: Jossey-Bass, 1999).

5. Hans-Georg Gadamer, *Truth and Method*, ed. Garrett Barden and John Cumming (New York: Crossroad, 1982).

6. Don S. Browning, *A Fundamental Practical Theology: Descriptive and Strategic Proposals* (Minneapolis: Fortress Press, 1991).

7. Paul Ricoeur, *Hermeneutics and the Human Sciences: Essays on Language, Action, and Interpretation*, ed. and trans. John B. Thompson (New York: Cambridge University Press, 1981), 61.

1. Faith and the Modern Psychologies

1. For a discussion of the question of evidence in clinical psychology, see Erik Erikson, "The Nature of Clinical Evidence," in *Insight and Responsibility* (New York: Norton, 1964), 49–80.

2. Malcolm Jeeves, *Psychology and Christianity: The View Both Ways* (Leicester: Inter-Varsity, 1976), 27.

3. Don S. Browning, *Pluralism and Personality: William James and Some Contemporary Cultures of Psychology* (Lewisburg, Pa.: Bucknell University Press, 1980).

4. For a useful introduction to this school of psychology, see Harry Guntrip, *Psychoanalytic Theory, Therapy, and the Self* (New York: Basic, 1971). For a more advanced review, see Jay R. Greenberg and Stephen Mitchell, *Object Relations in Psychoanalytic Theory* (Cambridge, Mass.: Harvard University Press, 1983).

5. Ludwig Wittgenstein, *Philosophical Investigations* (Oxford: Blackwell, 1963). For excellent applications of Wittgenstein's perspective to an understanding of the social sciences, see R. S. Peters, *The Concept of Motivation* (London: Routledge and Kegan Paul, 1958), and Peter Winch, *The Idea of a Social Science and Its Relation to Philosophy* (London: Routledge and Kegan Paul, 1980).

6. Ian Barbour, *Myths, Models, and Paradigms* (New York: Harper & Row, 1974), 5.

7. Ibid., 34.

8. Heinz Kohut, "Introspection, Empathy, and Psychoanalysis: An Examination of the Relationship between Mode of Observation and Theory," in *The Search for the Self* (New York: International Universities Press, 1978), 205–33.

9. In grouping these psychologists and philosophers together, I am doing so because of the similarities they have in emphasizing the importance of life themes and narratives as a mode of psychological interpretation. See Henry Murray, *Explorations in Personality* (New York: Oxford University Press, 1938); Erik Erikson, *Insight and Responsibility,* 49–80; Robert Lifton, *History and Human Survival* (New York: Vintage, 1971); Heinz Kohut, *The Analysis of the Self* (New York: International Universities Press, 1971); Donald Spence, *Narrative Truth and Historical Truth* (New York: Norton, 1982); Paul Ricoeur, *Freud and Philosophy* (New Haven: Yale University Press, 1970); William Barrett and Daniel Yankelovich, *Ego and Instinct* (New York: Random House, 1977); Rom Harré and P. F. Secord, *Explanation of Social Behavior* (Totowa, N.J.: Littlefield, Adams, 1973).

10. For an introduction to Dilthey's view of hermeneutics and his place in the history of *Geisteswissenschaften,* see Richard Palmer, *Hermeneutics: Interpretation Theory in Schleiermacher, Dilthey, Heidegger, and Gadamer* (Evanston, Ill.: Northwestern University Press, 1969).

11. Hans-Georg Gadamer, *Truth and Method* (New York: Crossroad, 1982). The first English edition was published by Sheed and Ward in 1975.

12. Richard Bernstein, *Beyond Objectivism and Relativism* (Philadelphia: University of Pennsylvania Press, 1983).

13. Robert Bellah, Richard Madsen, William Sullivan, Ann Swidler, and Steven Tipton, *Habits of the Heart: Individualism and Commitment in American Life* (Berkeley: University of California Press, 1985).

14. Gadamer, *Truth and Method,* 267.

15. Ibid., 235–37.

16. Ibid., 331–32.

17. Ibid.

18. Ibid., 275, 289.

19. Paul Ricoeur, *Hermeneutics and the Human Sciences,* ed. and trans. John B. Thompson (Cambridge: Cambridge University Press, 1981), 60.

20. Cushman, *Constructing the Self, Constructing America,* 6–7; and Frank C. Richardson, Blaine J. Fowers, and Charles B. Guignon, *Re-Envisioning Psychology: Moral Dimensions of Theory and Practice* (San Francisco: Jossey-Bass, 1999), 107.

21. Gadamer, *Truth and Method,* 255–56.

22. Bellah et al., *Habits of the Heart,* 28–29.

23. Ibid., 301.

24. Cushman, *Constructing the Self, Constructing America,* 22; Richardson et al., *Re-envisioning Psychology,* 11–12.

25. Richardson et al., *Re-envisioning Psychology,* 17.

26. Ricoeur, *Hermeneutics and the Human Sciences,* 60–61.

27. These five dimensions were first developed in Don S. Browning's *Religious Ethics and Pastoral Care* (Philadelphia: Fortress Press, 1983), 53–71. They have since been elaborated at length in Browning's *A Fundamental Practical Theology* (Minneapolis: Fortress Press, 1991).

28. Habermas's four validity claims are similar but different than my five dimensions and serve different purposes. But both sets of categories are derived through a reconstructive empirical procedure. For more on Habermas on this issue, see his *Moral Consciousness and Communicative Action* (Cambridge, Mass.: MIT Press, 1990), 32.

29. William Frankena, *Ethics* (Englewood Cliffs, N.J.: Prentice-Hall, 1973); John Rawls, *A Theory of Justice* (Cambridge, Mass.: Harvard University Press, 1971); Stephen Toulmin, *An Examination of the Place of Reason in Ethics* (Cambridge: Cambridge University Press, 1950).

30. Frankena, *Ethics*, 65.

31. Ibid., 10, 14, 65.

32. Ibid., 65; Alan Gewirth, "Rights and Virtues," *Analyse & Kritik* 6 (1984): 28–48.

33. Of the many works of Stanley Hauerwas, the most substantive is *A Community of Character* (South Bend, Ind.: University of Notre Dame Press, 1982); for the philosophical counterpart to this position, see Alasdair MacIntyre, *After Virtue* (South Bend, Ind.: University of Notre Dame Press, 1981).

34. Paul Tillich, *Systematic Theology*, 3 vols. (Chicago: University of Chicago Press, 1951–63), 1:18–19.

35. Reinhold Niebuhr, *The Self and the Dramas of History* (New York: Scribner's, 1955), 128.

36. Jeeves, *Psychology and Christianity*, 18.

37. David Myers, *The Human Puzzle* (San Francisco: Harper & Row, 1978), 11–18.

38. Seward Hiltner, *Preface to Pastoral Theology* (Nashville: Abingdon-Cokesbury, 1958), 221–22; Daniel Day Williams, "Truth in a Theological Perspective," *Journal of Religion* 28 (October 1948), 242–54.

39. William James, *Essays in Radical Empiricism* (Cambridge, Mass.: Harvard University Press, 1976), 21–44; Alfred North Whitehead, *Process and Reality* (New York: Harper & Row, 1960), 238–54.

40. David Tracy, *Blessed Rage for Order* (New York: Seabury, 1975), 32–34.

41. Tillich, *Systematic Theology*, 1:61.

42. Paul Tillich, *Theology of Culture* (New York: Oxford University Press, 1959), 112–26.

43. David Tracy, "The Foundations of Practical Theology," in *Practical Theology*, ed. Don S. Browning (San Francisco: Harper & Row, 1983), 63.

44. See Don S. Browning, "Introduction" and "Pastoral Theology in a Pluralistic Age," in *Practical Theology*, 1–20, 187–202; also Don S. Browning, "Toward a Practical Theology of Care," *Union Seminary Quarterly Review* 36 (Winter 1981): 159–72; and idem, *Religious Ethics and Pastoral Care*.

2. Vision and Obligation in Christian Anthropology

1. George Lakoff and Mark Johnson, *Metaphors We Live By* (Chicago: University of Chicago Press, 1980), 3.

2. Ibid., 5.

3. Barbour, *Myths, Models, and Paradigms* (New York: Harper & Row, 1974), 12.

4. Max Black, *Models and Metaphors* (Ithaca, N.Y.: Cornell University Press, 1962).

5. Paul Ricoeur, "Metaphor and the Problem of Hermeneutics," in *Hermeneutics and the Human Sciences*, ed. and trans. John B. Thompson (Cambridge: Cambridge University Press, 1981), 170.

6. Ricoeur, "Metaphor and the Problem of Hermeneutics," 180.

7. Sallie McFague, *Metaphorical Theology: Models of God in Religious Language* (Philadelphia: Fortress Press, 1982), 35.

8. Ibid.

9. Reinhold Niebuhr, *The Nature and Destiny of Man: A Christian Interpretation*, 2 vols. (New York: Scribner's, 1941–43), 1:123.

10. Don S. Browning, *Generative Man: Psychoanalytic Perspectives* (Philadelphia: Westminster, 1973), 147.

11. Niebuhr, *The Nature and Destiny of Man*, 1:21–25, 123.

12. Ibid., 1:3.

13. Ibid., 1:152–53.

14. St. Augustine, *The Confessions of St. Augustine* (New York: New American Library, 1963), 10.8.

15. Niebuhr, *The Nature and Destiny of Man,* 1:27.

16. Ibid., 1:28.

17. Ibid., 1:181–84.

18. Niebuhr, *The Nature and Destiny of Man,* 2:84–85.

19. Ibid., 2:69, 81.

20. Ibid., 2:74, 82–84.

21. William James, *Principles of Psychology,* 2 vols. (New York: Dover, 1950), 1:291–96, 329.

22. For a discussion of the relation of James's phenomenology to his functionalism, see Don S. Browning, *Pluralism and Personality: William James and Some Contemporary Cultures of Psychology* (Lewisburg, Pa.: Bucknell University Press, 1980), 64–86.

23. Paul Ricoeur, *Freedom and Nature: The Voluntary and the Involuntary,* trans. Erazim V. Kohak (Evanston, Ill.: Northwestern University Press, 1966), xvii.

24. Paul Ricoeur, *Fallible Man,* trans. Charles Kilbley (Chicago: Regnery, 1965), 26–56.

25. Paul Ricoeur, *The Symbolism of Evil,* trans. Emerson Buchanan (New York: Harper & Row, 1967); idem, *Freud and Philosophy,* trans. Denis Savage (New Haven: Yale University Press, 1970).

26. Jean-Paul Sartre, *Being and Nothingness,* trans. Hazel Barnes (New York: Citadel, 1964).

27. William James, *The Will to Believe* (New York: Dover, 1956), 9; idem, *Principles of Psychology,* 2:486–88.

28. Ricoeur, *Freedom and Nature,* xv.

29. Ibid.

30. James, *Principles of Psychology,* 1:224–91. For additional discussions of James's phenomenology, see Bruce Wilshire, *William James and Phenomenology* (Bloomington: Indiana University Press, 1968); Richard Stevens, *James and Husserl: The Foundations of Meaning* (The Hague: Martinus Nijhoff, 1974); Hans Linschoten, *On the Way towards a Phenomenological Psychology* (Pittsburgh: Duquesne University Press, 1968); John Wild, *The Radical Empiricism of William James* (New York: Anchor, 1970).

31. Frank C. Richardson, Blaine J. Fowers, and Charles B. Guignon, *Re-Envisioning Psychology: Moral Dimensions of Theory and Practice* (San Francisco: Jossey-Bass, 1999), 230.

32. Max Weber, *The Protestant Ethic and the Spirit of Capitalism,* trans. Talcott Parsons (New York: Scribner's, 1958), 27, 47–48.

33. Philip Rieff, *Freud: The Mind of the Moralist* (Chicago: University of Chicago Press, 1979), 329–57; idem, *The Triumph of the Therapeutic* (New York: Harper & Row, 1966), 1–47.

3. Metaphors, Models, and Morality in Freud

1. Philip Rieff, *The Triumph of the Therapeutic* (New York: Harper & Row, 1966), 26–27, 40–41, 58–59.

2. Discussion of Freud is still relevant. Although his impact on psychology and psychotherapy may be declining, he still shaped many of the basic terms of the fields and still is the major influence, for good or ill, on the entire mental health field's understanding of religion. See the excellent work on this issue by David Larson, "Systematic Analysis of Research

on Religious Variables in Four Major Psychiatric Journals, 1978–1982," *American Journal of Psychiatry* 143/3 (March 1986): 329–34.

3. Brooks Holifield, *A History of Pastoral Care in America* (Nashville: Abingdon, 1983), 194–95, 212–13, 246–48.

4. Ian Barbour, *Myths, Models, and Paradigms* (New York: Harper & Row, 1974), 43.

5. Sallie McFague, *Metaphorical Theology: Models of God in Religious Language* (Philadelphia: Fortress Press, 1982), 67.

6. Barbour, *Myths, Models, and Paradigms*, 49.

7. Sigmund Freud, *New Introductory Lectures*, trans. W. J. H. Sprott (New York: Norton, 1960), 216.

8. Ibid., 248.

9. Ibid., 217.

10. Frank J. Sulloway, *Freud: Biologist of the Mind* (New York: Basic, 1979), 14.

11. Sigmund Freud, "The Neuro-Psychoses of Defense," *Standard Edition of the Complete Works of Sigmund Freud* (London: Hogarth, 1962), 3:60–61.

12. Sigmund Freud, "Formulations regarding the Two Principles in Mental Functioning," *General Psychological Theory*, ed. Philip Rieff (New York: Collier, 1963), 21–22.

13. Sigmund Freud, "Project for a Scientific Psychology," in *The Origins of Psychoanalysis* (New York: Basic, 1954).

14. Ernest Jones, *The Life and Work of Sigmund Freud* (New York: Basic, 1955), 2:3; Erik Erikson, *Insight and Responsibility* (New York: Norton, 1964), 42; Paul Ricoeur, *Freud and Philosophy* (New Haven: Yale University Press, 1970), 87–88.

15. Sigmund Freud, *Beyond the Pleasure Principle*, trans. James Strachey (New York: Bantam, 1963), 105.

16. Reinhold Niebuhr, "Human Creativity and Self-Concern in Freud's Thought," in *Freud and the Twentieth Century*, ed. Benjamin Nelson (Gloucester, Mass.: Peter Smith, 1974), 260.

17. Ibid., 270.

18. Reinhold Niebuhr, *The Self and the Dramas of History* (New York: Scribner's, 1955), 8.

19. Ibid., 270.

20. Freud, *New Introductory Lectures*, 104.

21. Niebuhr, *The Self and the Dramas of History*, 10.

22. Ibid., 9.

23. Ricoeur, *Freud and Philosophy*, 61.

24. Ibid., 116.

25. Ibid., 387.

26. Ibid., 432.

27. Philip Rieff, *Freud: The Mind of the Moralist* (Chicago: University of Chicago Press, 1979), 143.

28. S. Freud, "The Unconscious," *Standard Edition*, 14:186.

29. Freud, *New Introductory Lectures*, 131.

30. Freud, *Beyond the Pleasure Principle*, 70–81; idem, *The Ego and the Id*, trans. Joan Riviere (London: Hogarth, 1957), 54–68; idem, *New Introductory Lectures*, 137–52.

31. Freud, *Beyond the Pleasure Principle*, 70–81.

32. Freud, *The Ego and the Id*, 56.

33. Sulloway, *Freud*, 395–99.

34. Freud, *Beyond the Pleasure Principle*, 98.

35. Ibid., 70–71.

36. Ibid., 79.

37. Lee Yearley, "Freud as Critic and Creator of Cosmogonies and Their Ethics," in *Cosmogony and Ethical Order,* ed. Robin Lovin and Frank Reynolds (Chicago: University of Chicago Press, 1985), 404–9.

38. Freud, *New Introductory Lectures,* 217.

39. For discussion of positivism in psychology, see Malcolm Jeeves, *Psychology and Christianity: The View Both Ways* (Leicester: Inter-Varsity, 1976), 39; Edward Sampson, *Justice and the Critique of Pure Psychology* (New York: Plenum, 1983), 73–75; Russell Keat, *The Politics of Social Theory: Habermas, Freud, and the Critique of Positivism* (Chicago: University of Chicago Press, 1981), 12–37.

40. Tillich, *Systematic Theology,* 3 vols. (Chicago: University of Chicago Press, 1951–63), 1:4–5, 7–8.

41. S. Freud, "Analysis Terminable and Interminable," in *Therapy and Technique,* ed. Philip Rieff (New York: Collier, 1963), 264.

42. Freud, *Beyond the Pleasure Principle,* 80.

43. Yearley, "Freud as Creator and Critic," 408.

44. Reinhold Niebuhr, *The Nature and Destiny of Man: A Christian Interpretation,* 2 vols. (New York: Scribner's, 1941–43), 1:27.

45. Ibid., 28.

46. William James, *Principles of Psychology,* 2 vols. (New York: Dover, 1950), 2:383–441; Don S. Browning, *Pluralism and Personality: William James and Some Contemporary Cultures of Psychology* (Lewisburg, Pa.: Bucknell University Press, 1980), 156–78.

47. Harry Harlow, "William James and Instinct Theory," in *William James: Unfinished Business* (Washington, D.C.: American Psychological Association, 1969), 21.

48. Sigmund Freud, *Civilization and Its Discontents,* trans. James Strachey (New York: Norton, 1961), 44.

49. Ibid., 56.

50. William Frankena, *Ethics* (Englewood Cliffs, N.J.: Prentice-Hall, 1973), 15.

51. Ernest Wallwork, "Thou Shalt Love Thy Neighbor as Thyself: The Freudian Critique," *Journal of Religious Ethics* 10 (Fall 1982): 269.

52. Freud, *Civilization and Its Discontents,* 55.

53. Ibid., 56.

54. Gilbert Harman, *The Nature of Morality* (Oxford: Oxford University Press, 1977), 143.

55. Wallwork, "Thou Shalt Love Thy Neighbor as Thyself," 266.

56. Ibid.

57. Ibid., 277.

58. S. Freud, *Group Psychology and the Analysis of the Ego,* trans. James Strachey (New York: Bantam, 1960), 86.

59. Wallwork, "Thou Shalt Love Thy Neighbor as Thyself," 285–86.

60. Ibid., 279.

61. Ibid., 286.

62. Freud, *Civilization and Its Discontents,* 67.

63. Ibid., 57.

64. Ibid., 58.

65. Ibid., 57.

66. Barbour, *Myths, Models, and Paradigms,* 49.

67. Mircea Eliade, *Myths, Dreams, and Mysteries,* trans. Philip Mairet (New York: Harper & Row, 1960), 23–26.

68. Niebuhr, "Human Creativity and Self-Concern in Freud's Thought," 263–65.

69. Ibid., 274.

70. Niebuhr, *Self and the Dramas of History,* 128.

71. Niebuhr, *The Nature and Destiny of Man,* 1:182.

72. Ibid.

73. Ibid., 182–83.

74. Niebuhr, *The Nature and Destiny of Man,* 2:69.

75. Ibid., 254.

76. Ibid., 68–69.

77. Ibid., 69.

78. Ibid., 68–69.

79. Ibid., 70–76.

80. Ibid., 82.

81. Ibid., 84.

82. Victor Furnish, "Neighbor Love in the New Testament," *The Journal of Religious Ethics* 10 (Fall 1982): 322.

83. Ibid.

84. Niebuhr, *The Nature and Destiny of Man,* 2:98–99.

85. Ricoeur, *Freud and Philosophy,* 469–83.

4. Self-Actualization and Harmony in Humanistic Psychology

1. For an excellent critique of the origins and moral logic of the values clarification movement, see Johannes van der Ven, *Formation of the Moral Self* (Grand Rapids: Eerdmans, 1998), 256.

2. Rieff, *The Triumph of the Therapeutic,* 31–32.

3. Ibid., 232–61.

4. Ibid., 30.

5. Norman O. Brown, *Life against Death* (New York: Viking, 1959); Herbert Marcuse, *Eros and Civilization* (Boston: Beacon, 1955).

6. Paul Vitz, *Psychology as Religion: The Cult of Self-Worship* (Grand Rapids: Eerdmans, 1977), 17–18.

7. Daniel Yankelovich, *New Rules: Searching for Self-Fulfillment in a World Turned Upside Down* (New York: Random House, 1981), xviii, 85–106.

8. Ibid., 49–54.

9. Ibid., 235.

10. Robert Bellah, Richard Madsen, William Sullivan, Ann Swidler, and Steven Tipton, *Habits of the Heart: Individualism and Commitment in American Life* (Berkeley: University of California Press, 1985), 32–35, 47, 48–50; Robert C. Fuller, *Americans and the Unconscious* (New York: Oxford University Press, 1986).

11. Bellah et al., *Habits of the Heart,* 46–51.

12. Ibid., 47.

13. Frank C. Richardson, Blaine J. Fowers, and Charles B. Guignon, *Re-Envisioning Psychology: Moral Dimensions of Theory and Practice* (San Francisco: Jossey-Bass, 1999), 48.

14. Brooks Holifield, *A History of Pastoral Care in America* (Nashville: Abingdon, 1983), 222.

15. Ibid., 223–24.

16. Don S. Browning, *Pluralism and Personality: William James and Some Contemporary Cultures of Psychology* (Lewisburg, Pa.: Bucknell University Press, 1980), 195–210.

17. Holifield, *A History of Pastoral Care in America,* 288–94.

18. Don S. Browning, *Atonement and Psychotherapy* (Philadelphia: Westminster, 1966); Thomas C. Oden, *Kerygma and Counseling* (Philadelphia: Westminster, 1966).

19. James Lynwood Walker, *Body and Soul: Gestalt Therapy and Religious Experience* (Nashville: Abingdon, 1971).

20. See especially Seward Hiltner, *Pastoral Counseling* (Nashville: Abingdon-Cokesbury, 1958).

21. Carl Rogers, *Client-Centered Therapy* (Boston: Houghton Mifflin, 1951), 487.

22. Ibid., 489.

23. Ibid., 490.

24. Kurt Goldstein, *The Organism: A Holistic Approach to Biology Derived from Pathological Data in Man* (Boston: Beacon, 1963), 197.

25. Ibid.

26. Abraham Maslow, *Motivation and Personality* (New York: Harper & Brothers, 1954), 124.

27. Abraham Maslow, *Toward a Psychology of Being* (New York: Van Nostrand, 1962), 147.

28. Ibid.

29. Ibid., 145.

30. Frederick S. Perls, Ralph F. Hefferline, and Paul Goodman, *Gestalt Therapy: Excitement and Growth in the Human Personality* (New York: Dell, 1951), 11.

31. Browning, *Pluralism and Personality,* 196–98.

32. Ibid., 196.

33. Carl R. Rogers, *On Becoming a Person: A Therapist's View of Psychotherapy* (Boston: Houghton Mifflin, 1961), 118.

34. Ibid., 189.

35. Maslow, *Motivation and Personality,* 340.

36. Maslow, *Toward a Psychology of Being,* 145.

37. Frederick S. Perls, "Morality, Ego Boundary, and Aggression," *Complex* (Winter 1954): 51.

38. Isaac Franck, "Self-Realization as Ethical Norm: A Critique," *Philosophical Forum* (Fall 1977): 9.

39. Ibid.

40. Ibid.

41. Ibid., 19.

42. Ibid., 20.

43. William Frankena, *Ethics* (Englewood Cliffs, N.J.: Prentice-Hall, 1973), 14.

44. Paul Ricoeur, *Oneself as Another* (Chicago: University of Chicago Press, 1992), 171; Martha Nussbaum, *Women and Human Development: The Capabilities Approach* (Cambridge: Cambridge University Press, 2000), 13.

45. Ricoeur, *Oneself as Another,* 206; Nussbaum, *Women and Human Development,* 96–101.

46. Frankena, *Ethics,* 18.

47. Ibid.

48. Immanuel Kant, *Foundations for the Metaphysics of Morals,* trans. Lewis White Beck (New York: Bobbs-Merrill, 1959), 18.

49. Kurt Baier, *The Moral Point of View* (New York: Random House, 1965); R. M. Hare, *The Language of Morals* (New York: Oxford University Press, 1964).

50. Frankena, *Ethics*, 19.

51. Ibid.

52. David Norton, *Personal Destinies: A Philosophy of Ethical Individualism* (Princeton, N.J.: Princeton University Press, 1976), ix.

53. Ibid., 20, 129–30.

54. Ibid., 4.

55. Ibid., 15, 360.

56. Ibid., 306–9.

57. Ibid., 275–358.

58. Richardson, Fowers, and Guignon, *Re-envisioning Psychology*, 73.

59. Rogers, *On Becoming a Person*, 177.

60. Ibid., 178.

61. Ibid.

62. Fuller, *Americans and the Unconscious*.

63. Abraham Maslow, *The Further Reaches of Human Nature* (New York: Viking, 1971), 209.

64. Abraham Maslow, *Eupsychian Management* (Homewood, Ill.: Dorsey, 1965), 103.

65. Ibid., 11.

66. Maslow, *Toward a Psychology of Being*, 76.

67. Ibid., 76–77.

68. Ibid., 77.

69. Niebuhr, *The Nature and Destiny of Man: A Christian Interpretation*, 2 vols. (New York: Scribner's, 1941–43), 1:27.

70. Ibid.

71. Ibid., 103.

72. Ibid., 135.

73. Ibid., 178.

74. Ibid., 178–79.

75. Søren Kierkegaard, *The Concept of Dread*, trans. Walter Lowrie (Princeton, N.J.: Princeton University Press, 1957), 38.

76. Niebuhr, *The Nature and Destiny of Man*, 1:179.

77. Ibid., 182-83.

78. William James, *Principles of Psychology*, 2 vols. (New York: Dover, 1950), 2:393.

79. Ibid.

80. Anna Freud, "The Concept of Developmental Lines," in *Psychoanalytic Study of the Child* (New York: International Universities Press, 1963), 245–65.

81. John E. Gedo and Arnold Goldberg, *Models of the Mind: A Psychoanalytic Theory* (Chicago: University of Chicago Press, 1973), 7.

82. Edward O. Wilson, *On Human Nature* (Cambridge, Mass.: Harvard University Press, 1978), 60.

83. Niebuhr, *The Nature and Destiny of Man*, 1:126, 134–36.

84. Ibid., 1:135–36.

85. William James, "A Pluralistic Mystic," *Hibbert Journal* 8 (July 1910): 739–59.

86. Victor Turner, *The Ritual Process* (Chicago: Aldine, 1969), 94; Arnold Van Gennep, *The Rites of Passage* (Chicago: University of Chicago Press, 1969), 11.

87. Jerome Frank, *Persuasion and Healing* (New York: Schocken, 1974), 27–30.

88. For application of Turner's categories to contemporary therapy, see Don Browning, *The Moral Context of Pastoral Care* (Philadelphia: Westminster, 1976), 33–37.

89. Johannes van der Ven, *Formation of the Moral Self* (Grand Rapids: Eerdmans, 1998).

90. Arnold Green, "Social Values and Psychotherapy," *Journal of Personality* 14 (1945–46): 34–35.

5. Husbandry and the Common Good in Skinner

1. B. F. Skinner, *Walden Two* (New York: Macmillan, 1976), 261.

2. For statements on their views of hermeneutics, see David Tracy, *The Analogical Imagination* (New York: Crossroad, 1981), 124–53; for Paul Ricoeur, see "The Task of Hermeneutics," in *Hermeneutics and the Human Sciences,* ed. and trans. John B. Thompson (Cambridge: Cambridge University Press, 1981), 43–62.

3. Skinner, *Walden Two,* 96.

4. Ibid.

5. Ibid., 106.

6. For an interesting philosophical critique of Skinner, see Paul Ricoeur, "A Critique of B. F. Skinner's 'Beyond Freedom and Dignity,'" *Philosophy Today* 17 (Summer 1973): 166–75.

7. Skinner, *Walden Two,* 261.

8. B. F. Skinner, *Science and Human Behavior* (New York: Free Press, 1953), 73.

9. Ibid.

10. B. F. Skinner, *Beyond Freedom and Dignity* (New York: Bantam, 1972), 57.

11. Ibid., 32-33; Skinner, *Science and Human Behavior,* 93–106.

12. Skinner, *Walden Two,* v.

13. B. F. Skinner, *About Behaviorism* (London: Jonathan Cape, 1974), 205.

14. B. F. Skinner, *Cumulative Record* (New York: Appleton-Century-Crofts, 1961), 353.

15. Skinner, *Beyond Freedom and Dignity,* 14.

16. Ibid., 123.

17. Sallie McFague, *Metaphorical Theology: Models of God in Religious Language* (Philadelphia: Fortress Press, 1982), 83; Ian Barbour, *Myths, Models, and Paradigms* (New York: Harper & Row, 1974), 158.

18. McFague, *Metaphorical Theology,* 84.

19. Charles Darwin, *The Origin of Species by Means of Natural Selection,* 6th ed. (New York: Appleton, 1929), 35.

20. Ibid., 294.

21. Ibid., 304.

22. Ibid., 306.

23. Paul Tillich, "The Two Types of Philosophy of Religion," in *Theology of Culture* (New York: Oxford University Press, 1959), 10–29.

24. Skinner, *Beyond Freedom and Dignity,* 19.

25. William James, "Remarks on Spencer's Definition of Mind as Correspondence," in *Collected Essays and Reviews* (New York: Russell and Russell, 1969), 44.

26. William James, *Principles of Psychology,* 2 vols. (New York: Dover, 1950), 2:624–28.

27. Skinner, *Beyond Freedom and Dignity,* 106.

28. Ibid., 107.

29. Ibid.

30. Ibid., 109.

31. Ibid., 110.

32. Skinner seems unaware of the arguments in moral philosophy against building ethical arguments on naturalistic statements pertaining to what *is* a factual state of affairs. Most

of these arguments would apply to Skinner's views on the relation of contingencies of reinforcement to ethics. See William Frankena, *Ethics* (Englewood Cliffs, N.J.: Prentice-Hall, 1973), 99.

33. James, *Principles of Psychology,* 2:661–69; idem, *The Will to Believe* (New York: Dover, 1956), 187.

34. James, *Principles of Psychology,* 2:675.

35. Skinner, *Beyond Freedom and Dignity,* 106.

36. Skinner, *Walden Two,* 123.

37. Ibid., 252.

38. Skinner, *About Behaviorism,* 205.

39. Ibid., 206.

40. Frankena, *Ethics,* 34.

41. Skinner, *Beyond Freedom and Dignity,* 129–30.

42. For a critique of utilitarianism, see Frankena, *Ethics,* 41–43; Alan Donagan, *The Theory of Morality* (Chicago: University of Chicago Press, 1977), 192–209; Frederick G. Reamer, *Ethical Dilemmas in Social Service* (New York: Columbia University Press, 1982), 21–23.

43. John Rawls, *A Theory of Justice* (Cambridge, Mass.: Harvard University Press, 1971), 4–17.

44. Skinner, *Walden Two,* 264.

45. Rawls, *A Theory of Justice,* 433.

46. Reinhold Niebuhr, *The Nature and Destiny of Man: A Christian Interpretation,* 2 vols. (New York: Scribner's, 1941–43), 2:264.

47. Skinner, *Beyond Freedom and Dignity,* 47.

48. Ibid., 48.

49. Ibid., 106.

50. B. F. Skinner, *Particulars of My Life* (New York: Knopf, 1976), 76.

51. Ibid.

52. Ibid., 149–52.

53. Daniel B. Shea, "B. F. Skinner: The Puritan Within," *The Virginia Quarterly Review* 1 (Summer 1974), 416–37.

54. B. F. Skinner, *A Matter of Consequences* (New York: Knopf, 1983), 402–3.

55. Ibid.

56. Ibid.

57. Niebuhr, *The Nature and Destiny of Man,* 1:50.

58. Ibid., 184.

59. Ibid., 188–89.

60. Reinhold Niebuhr, *An Interpretation of Christian Ethics* (New York: Meridian, 1958), 148.

61. Ibid.

62. Niebuhr, *The Nature and Destiny of Man,* 2:59.

63. James, *Principles of Psychology,* 1:124.

64. William James, *Talks to Teachers on Psychology and to Students on Some of Life's Ideals* (New York: Dover, 1962), 34–35.

6. Making Judgments about Deep Metaphors and Obligations

1. Mircea Eliade, *Myths, Dreams, and Mysteries,* trans. Philip Mairet (New York: Harper & Row, 1960), 23–26.

2. Carl Jung, *Symbols of Transformation,* vol. 5 of *Collected Works,* 21 vols., ed. Herbert Read, Michael Fordham, and Gerhard Adler, trans. R. F. C. Hull (Princeton, N.J.: Princeton University Press, 1953–92), 380.

3. William James, *The Will to Believe* (New York: Dover, 1956), 116.

4. Stephen Toulmin, *The Return to Cosmology* (Berkeley: University of California Press, 1982), 70.

5. Ibid.

6. Ibid., 56.

7. Sigmund Freud, *Beyond the Pleasure Principle,* trans. James Strachey (New York: Bantam, 1963), 80.

8. Stuart McLean, "Metaphor Theory and Faith Development," unpub. ms.

9. David Norton, *Personal Destinies: A Philosophy of Ethical Individualism* (Princeton, N.J.: Princeton University Press, 1976), 78–79.

10 Peter Homans, *Theology after Freud* (Indianapolis: Bobbs-Merrill, 1970), 170–82.

11. Jürgen Habermas, *Knowledge and Human Interests,* trans. Jeremy J. Shapiro (Boston: Beacon, 1968); for an extension of the Frankfurt School into the domain of psychology, see Edward Sampson, *Justice and the Critique of Pure Psychology* (New York: Plenum, 1983).

12. Norma Haan, Robert Bellah, et al., eds., *Social Science as Moral Inquiry* (New York: Columbia University Press, 1983).

13. Immanuel Kant, *Foundations of the Metaphysics of Morals* (New York: Bobbs-Merrill, 1959), 18.

14. For Habermas's use of a procedural and intersubjective restatement of Kant's categorical imperative, see Jürgen Habermas, *Communication and the Evolution of Society* (Boston: Beacon, 1979), 90.

15. Paul Ricoeur, *Oneself as Another* (Chicago: University of Chicago Press, 1992), 206.

16. Jürgen Habermas, "Interpretive Social Science vs. Hermeneuticism," in *Social Science as Moral Inquiry,* 251–70.

17. See Russell Keat's call for two models of the social sciences in his *The Politics of Social Theory: Habermas, Freud, and the Critique of Positivism* (Chicago: University of Chicago Press, 1981), 38–65.

18. Most of the metaphysical positions I have listed here are in the so-called process philosophy tradition of metaphysics, which is represented by: William James, *A Pluralistic Universe* (New York: Dutton, 1971); Alfred North Whitehead, *Process and Reality* (New York: Harper & Brothers, 1960); Charles Hartshorne, *The Divine Relativity* (New Haven, Conn.: Yale University Press, 1948); Schubert M. Ogden, *The Reality of God* (New York: Harper & Row, 1964); Robert C. Neville, *God the Creator* (Chicago: University of Chicago Press, 1968).

19. Stephen Toulmin, *The Return to Cosmology: Postmodern Science and the Theology of Nature* (Berkeley: University of California Press, 1982), 261–74, outlines how the psychotherapeutic psychologies and the modern ecological disciplines are functioning to spin out two different cosmologies. One he calls the white philosophy; it is associated with the modern psychotherapies, is reminiscent of Epicureanism, and emphasizes detachment and psychological interiority. The other he calls the green philosophy and is reminiscent of ancient Stoicism. It is associated with the modern ecological movement and emphasizes fittedness to the order of nature. From this perspective, Freud is clearly closer to the Epicurean or white philosophy. On the other hand, Erikson would be a good example of what Toulmin is calling the green philosophy with its Stoic and ecological overtones.

20. William James, *The Varieties of Religious Experience* (New York: Doubleday, 1978), 37.

21. James, *A Pluralistic Universe*, 125–26. James's metaphysical enterprise can be seen in his contention that "the only material we have at our disposal for making a picture of the whole world is supplied by various portions of that world of which we have already had experience."

22. Ian Barbour, *Myths, Models, and Paradigms* (New York: Harper & Row, 1974), 143.

23. Sallie McFague, *Metaphorical Theology: Models of God in Religious Language* (Philadelphia: Fortress Press, 1982), 137–44.

24. Barbour, *Myths, Models, and Paradigms*, 143.

25. Ibid., 107–8.

26. Thomas Kuhn, *The Structure of Scientific Revolutions* (Chicago: University of Chicago Press, 1970), 43–52.

27. Barbour, *Myths, Models, and Paradigms*, 104.

28. Kuhn, *The Structure of Scientific Revolutions*, 43–52.

29. Barbour, *Myths, Models, and Paradigms*, 112–18. Barbour takes a critical realist position on the question of the relation of concepts in science and religion to reality. The critical realist believes that although concepts never completely capture the realities to which they refer (as naïve realism would), their relation is neither simply arbitrary nor instrumental. The critical realist believes that concepts "deal with only restricted aspects of events. . . . The critical realist," Barbour writes, "makes only a tentative commitment to the existence of entities something like those portrayed in the model" (47).

30. Lawrence Kohlberg, *The Philosophy of Moral Development: Moral Stages and the Idea of Justice*, Essays on Moral Development, vol. 1 (San Francisco: Harper & Row, 1981), 197.

31. Ibid.

32. The Oxford moral philosopher Basil Mitchell's argument is useful here. He argued for the analogy between Kant's categorical imperative and the Christian principle of neighbor-love. He also contended that the grounding of Christian neighbor-love in the status of humans as children of God made in the *imago Dei* gave it the deeper and more profound justification. This was his way of showing the importance of background beliefs—what this book calls visions and narratives—to otherwise highly similar principles of obligation. See his *Morality, Religious and Secular: The Dilemma of the Traditional Conscience* (New York: Oxford University Press, 1980), 154.

33. William Frankena, *Ethics* (Englewood Cliffs, N.J.: Prentice-Hall, 1973), 29.

34. William James, *The Meaning of Truth* (Ann Arbor: University of Michigan Press, 1970), 227.

35. James, *A Pluralistic Universe*, 165–284.

36. Paul Ricoeur, *Freud and Philosophy* (New Haven, Conn.: Yale University Press, 1970), 477–524.

37. Charles W. Kegley and Robert W. Bretall, *Reinhold Niebuhr: His Religious, Social, and Political Thought* (New York: Macmillan, 1961), 10.

38. Reinhold Niebuhr, *The Nature and Destiny of Man: A Christian Interpretation*, 2 vols. (New York: Scribner's, 1941–43), 2:71.

39. Hartshorne, *The Divine Relativity*, 1–22.

40. James, *A Pluralistic Universe*, 268–70.

41. Ibid., 275.

42. H. Richard Niebuhr, *The Responsible Self* (New York: Harper & Row, 1963), 30.

43. Ibid., 31.

44. Sigmund Freud, *Civilization and Its Discontents*, trans. James Strachey (New York: Norton, 1961), 57.

45. Heinz Kohut, *The Restoration of the Self* (New York: International Universities Press, 1977), 45; John E. Gedo and Arnold Goldberg, *Models of the Mind: A Psychoanalytic Theory* (Chicago: University of Chicago Press, 1973), 73–101.

46. Carl Rogers, "Reinhold Niebuhr's *Self and the Dramas of History*," *Pastoral Psychology* 9 (June 1958): 17.

47. Ibid.

48. Ibid.

49. Niebuhr, *The Nature and Destiny of Man*, 1:191.

50. Ibid., 203.

51. Paul Ricoeur, *The Symbolism of Evil*, trans. Emerson Buchanan (New York: Harper & Row, 1967), 151–57.

52. Niebuhr, *The Nature and Destiny of Man*, 2:68.

53. Ibid.

54. Immanuel Kant, *Religion within the Limits of Reason Alone*, trans. Theodore Greene and Hoyt H. Hudson (New York: Harper & Brothers, 1959), 42; idem, *Foundations of the Metaphysics of Morals*, 11–43.

55. Niebuhr, *The Nature and Destiny of Man*, 2:88.

56. Ibid., 89.

57. Ibid., 88.

58. Ibid., 82.

59. Ibid., 84.

60. Ibid.

61. Anders Nygren, *Agape and Eros*, trans. Philip S. Watson (Philadelphia: Westminster, 1953), 44.

62. Ibid., 734.

63. Ibid., 735.

64. Martin D'Arcy, *The Mind and Heart of Love, Lion and Unicorn: A Study in Eros and Agape*, rev. ed. (New York: Meridian, 1959); Robert Johann, *The Meaning of Love: An Essay towards a Metaphysics of Intersubjectivity* (Westminster, Md.: Newman, 1955).

65. Daniel Day Williams, *The Spirit and the Forms of Love* (New York: Harper & Row, 1968).

66. Louis Janssens, "Norms and Priorities in a Love Ethics," *Louvain Studies* 6 (Spring 1977): 219.

67. Ibid., 219.

68. Ibid.

69. Ibid., 220.

70. Gene Outka, *Agape: An Ethical Analysis* (New Haven, Conn.: Yale University Press, 1972), 290–91.

71. Outka, *Agape*, 56.

72. Janssens, "Norms and Priorities in a Love Ethics," 228.

73. Ibid., 228.

74. Ibid.

75. Victor Furnish, "Neighbor Love in the New Testament," *The Journal of Religious Ethics* 10 (Fall 1982): 227.

76. Reginald Fuller, "The Double Commandment of Love," in *Essays on the Love Commandment*, ed. Reginald Fuller (Philadelphia: Fortress Press, 1975), 51.

77. Furnish, "Neighbor Love in the New Testament," 329.

78. Ibid.

79. Ibid., 332.

80. Luise Schottroff, "Non-Violence and the Love of One's Enemies," in *Essays on the Love Commandment*, 23.

81. Frankena, *Ethics*, 9–10.

82. Janssens, "Norms and Priorities in a Love Ethics," 210.

83. Ibid., 212.

84. See particularly Judith Vaughan's insightful study *Sociality, Ethics, and Social Change: A Critical Appraisal of Reinhold Niebuhr's Ethics in the Light of Rosemary Radford Ruether's Works* (New York: University Press of America, 1983); and also Judith Plaskow, *Sex, Sin and Grace: Women's Experience and the Theologies of Reinhold Niebuhr and Paul Tillich* (Lanham, Md.: University Press of America, 1980).

7. Creation and Self-Realization in Jung

1. For an up-to-date summary of the claims of evolutionary psychology, see David Buss, *Evolutionary Psychology: The New Science of the Mind* (Boston: Allyn and Bacon, 1999).

2. Philip Rieff, *The Triumph of the Therapeutic* (New York: Harper & Row, 1966), 109.

3. Ibid., 122.

4. Victor Turner, "Body, Brain, and Culture," *Zygon* 18 (September 1983): 241.

5. Anthony Stevens, *Archetypes: A Natural History of the Self* (New York: Morrow, 1982), 17.

6. Ibid.

7. Frank J. Sulloway, *Freud: Biologist of the Mind* (New York: Basic, 1979), 4. Before Sulloway, Ernest Jones also referred to Freud as the "Darwin of the mind."

8. Stevens, *Archetypes*, 17.

9. Ibid.

10. Representative works of these scientists are Konrad Lorenz, *On Aggression*, trans. Margorie Wilson (New York: Bantam, 1970); Niko Tinbergen, *The Study of Instinct* (London: Oxford University Press, 1951); Robin Fox, *Encounter with Anthropology* (London: Peregrine, 1975).

11. For representative works see Heinz Hartmann, *Essays on Ego Psychology* (New York: International Universities Press, 1964); David Rapaport, ed., *Organization and Pathology of Thought* (New York: Columbia University Press, 1951); and Erik Erikson, *Childhood and Society* (New York: Norton, 1950).

12. W. R. D. Fairbairn, *An Object Relations Theory of the Personality* (New York: Basic, 1952); Harry Guntrip, *Psychoanalytic Theory, Therapy, and the Self* (New York: Basic, 1971); Donald Winnicott, *Playing and Reality* (New York: Penguin, 1980).

13. Stevens, *Archetypes*, 64–67, 90.

14. Carl Jung, *Memories, Dreams, Reflections*, ed. Aniela Jaffe and trans. Richard and Clara Winston (New York: Pantheon, 1963), 3.

15. Ibid., 222.

16. James Olney, *Metaphors of Self* (Princeton, N.J.: Princeton University Press, 1972), 87.

17. Carl Jung, *Collected Works* (henceforth referred to as *CW*), 21 vols., ed. Herbert Read, Michael Fordham, and Gerhard Adler, trans. R. F. C. Hull (Princeton, N.J.: Princeton University Press, 1953–92), 11:78.

18. Ibid.

19. As quoted in Olney, *Metaphors of Self,* 107. A slightly different version can be found in Jung, *Psychological Types, CW* 6:253.

20. Jung, *CW* 8:184.

21. Jung, *Memories, Dreams, Reflections*, 45.

22. William James, *Principles of Psychology*, 2 vols. (New York: Dover, 1950), 2:390.

23. Ibid., 2:393.

24. Ibid.

25. Jung, "On Psychic Energy," *CW* 8:10.

26. Jung, "The Theory of Psychoanalysis," *CW* 4:181.

27. Jung, "Instinct and the Unconscious," *CW* 8:135–36.

28. Jung, *CW* 8:203.

29. Jung, *CW* 9.1:226.

30. Jung, *CW* 5:420.

31. Jung, *CW* 8:440; 11:223.

32. For the concept of diagnosis in Paul Ricoeur, see his *Freedom and Nature* (Evanston, Ill.: Northwestern University Press, 1966), 87–88; also see his *Freud and Philosophy* (New Haven: Yale University Press, 1970), 436–37.

33. Morton Kelsey, *Christo-Psychology* (New York: Crossroad, 1982); James Hillman, *Re-Visioning Psychology* (New York: Harper & Row, 1975).

34. In *Re-Visioning Psychology* Hillman seems to undermine any degree of free and responsible moral deliberation, something that Jung himself never completely does, when he writes, "Rather than looking at myths morally, archetypal psychology looks at moralities mythically" (179). Hillman seems to have collapsed any differentiation between consciousness and the archetypes when he writes that "in our choices and decisions we are always reflecting mythic stances" (ibid.).

35. John Bowlby, *Attachment and Loss*, vol. 1, *Attachment* (New York: Basic, 1969); and vol. 2, *Separation* (New York: Basic, 1973).

36. Stevens, *Archetypes*, 3.

37. Ibid., 27-28.

38. Ibid., 17.

39. Ibid., 73.

40. Ibid.

41. Roger Sperry and J. Levy-Agresti, "Differential Perceptual Capacities in Major and Minor Hemispheres," *Proceedings of the National Academy of Sciences* 61 (1968): 11–51.

42. Ernest Rossi, "The Cerebral Hemisphere in Analytic Psychology," *Journal of Analytic Psychology* 22 (January 1977): 39.

43. Ibid.

44. Ibid., 42–44.

45. Ibid., 45.

46. Stevens, *Archetypes*, 263; J. P. Henry, "Comment," *Journal of Analytic Psychology* 22 (January 1977): 53.

47. Stevens, *Archetypes*, 264–65.

48. Ibid., 265.

49. Ibid., 267–68.

50. Ibid., 272.

51. Ibid.

52. David Norton, *Personal Destinies: A Philosophy of Ethical Individualism* (Princeton, N.J.: Princeton University Press, 1976), 3, 4, 161–62.

53. Stevens, *Archetypes*, 66.

54. Ibid.

55. Ibid., 64.

56. Ibid., 141.

57. Ibid., 141–42.

58. Jung, *CW* 7:171.

59. Ibid., 172.

60. Ibid.

61. Ibid., 108.

62. Ibid.

63. Jung, *CW* 9.1:187.

64. Jung, *CW* 7:219.

65. Jung, *CW* 5:246–48.

66. Jung, *CW* 7:232.

67. Jolan Jacobi, *The Psychology of C. G. Jung* (London: Kegan Paul, Trench, Trubner, 1942), 119.

68. Jung, *CW* 16:261.

69. Jung, *CW* 10:301.

70. Jung, *CW* 11:341.

71. Ibid., 340.

72. Ibid.

73. Ibid., 341–42.

74. William Frankena, *Ethics* (Englewood Cliffs, N.J.: Prentice-Hall, 1973), 19.

75. Jung, *CW* 7:217.

76. Jung, *CW* 9.1:284–85.

77. Jung, *CW* 7:65.

78. Jung, *CW* 9.2:266.

79. Victor White, *God and the Unconscious* (New York: World, 1961), 18.

80. Jung, *CW* 11:168.

81. Ibid.

82. Ibid., 173.

83. Ibid., 372.

84. Ibid., 376.

85. Ibid., 415.

86. Ibid., 461.

87. Ibid., 78.

88. Jung, *Memories, Dreams, Reflections,* 329.

89. Jung, *CW* 11:365.

90. Ibid., 385.

91. Ibid., 457.

92. Stevens, *Archetypes,* 216.

93. Ibid., 227.

94. Ibid., 240.

95. H. L. Philp, *Jung and the Problem of Evil* (London: Salisbury Square, 1958), 32.

96. Ibid., 32-33.

97. Ibid., 34.

98. Ibid.

99. Paul Ricoeur, *The Symbolism of Evil,* trans. Emerson Buchanan (New York: Harper & Row, 1967), 213.

100. Ibid.

101. Ibid., 173–80.

102. Ibid., 283.

103. Ibid.

104. Ibid., 242.

105. Jung, *CW* 11:367–77.

106. Ricoeur, *The Symbolism of Evil*, 321.

107. Reinhold Niebuhr, *The Nature and Destiny of Man: A Christian Interpretation*, 2 vols. (New York: Scribner's, 1941–43), 1:168.

8. Generativity and Care in Erikson and Kohut

1. Don S. Browning, *Generative Man: Psychoanalytic Perspectives* (Philadelphia: Westminster, 1973), 21–22.

2. Ibid., 216.

3. Heinz Hartmann, *Essays on Ego Psychology* (New York: International Universities Press, 1964), xii, 192, 231.

4. Erik Erikson, *Identity, Youth, and Crisis* (New York: Norton, 1968), 208–9.

5. Ibid.

6. Heinz Kohut, *The Analysis of the Self* (New York: International Universities Press, 1971), xii.

7. Erik Erikson, *Identity and the Life Cycle* (New York: International Universities Press, 1959), 149.

8. Kohut, *The Analysis of the Self*, 240–45; Erikson, *Identity and the Life Cycle*, 122–33.

9. Heinz Kohut, *The Restoration of the Self* (New York: International Universities Press, 1977), 273–80.

10. Hartmann, *Essays on Ego Psychology*, x, 293–94.

11. Heinz Kohut, *The Search for the Self* (New York: International Universities Press, 1978), 208.

12. John E. Gedo and Arnold Goldberg, *Models of the Mind: A Psychoanalytic Theory* (Chicago: University of Chicago Press, 1973), 64.

13. William James, *Principles of Psychology*, 2 vols. (New York: Dover, 1950), 1:224–91; George Herbert Mead, *Mind, Self, and Society* (Chicago: University of Chicago Press, 1934), 4–5.

14. Jay R. Greenberg and Stephen Mitchell, *Object Relations in Psychoanalytic Theory* (Cambridge, Mass.: Harvard University Press, 1983), 95–98.

15. Erik Erikson, *Childhood and Society* (New York: Norton, 1963), 261.

16. Erikson, *Identity and the Life Cycle*, 149.

17. Erikson, *Insight and Responsibility* (New York: Norton, 1964), 231.

18. Browning, *Generative Man*, 153–54.

19. Erikson, *Insight and Responsibility*, 154.

20. Ibid., 93, 124–30; idem, *Childhood and Society*, 263; idem, *Young Man Luther* (New York: Norton, 1962), 177–78.

21. Erik Erikson, *The Life Cycle Completed* (New York: Norton, 1982), 74.

22. Kohut, *The Analysis of the Self*, xv.

23. Ibid., 118.

24. Kohut, *The Restoration of the Self*, 99.

25. Erikson, *Young Man Luther*, 208.

26. Kohut, *The Analysis of the Self*, 26.

27. Kohut, *The Restoration of the Self,* 45; Heinz Kohut, *How Does Analysis Cure?* (Chicago: University of Chicago Press, 1984), 52.

28. Kohut, *The Analysis of the Self,* 27.

29. Heinz Kohut, "The Disorders of the Self and Their Treatment: An Outline," *International Journal of Psychoanalysis* 59, 4 (1978): 414.

30. Ibid.

31. Reinhold Niebuhr, , *The Nature and Destiny of Man: A Christian Interpretation,* 2 vols. (New York: Scribner's, 1941–43), 1:3.

32. Ibid., 150.

33. Niebuhr, *The Self and the Dramas of History* (New York: Scribner's, 1955), 88.

34. H. Richard Niebuhr, *The Responsible Self* (New York: Harper & Row, 1963), 71.

35. Niebuhr, *The Self and the Dramas of History,* 28.

36. Ibid., 30.

37. Ibid., 35.

38. Ibid., 129.

39. Niebuhr, *The Nature and Destiny of Man,* 2:vii.

40. Kohut, *The Restoration of the Self,* 83.

41. Ibid., 133; idem, *How Does Analysis Cure?* 10. Here Kohut speaks not of a "blue print" but of a "nuclear program of action" and a "creative-productive potential."

42. Kohut, *The Restoration of the Self,* 241.

43. Erikson, *Identity, Youth, and Crisis,* 218.

44. Erikson, *Identity and the Life Cycle,* 116.

45. Kohut, *The Restoration of the Self,* 30–32.

46. Heinz Kohut, "Introspection and Empathy in Psychoanalysis," in *The Search for the Self,* 231.

47. Peter Homans, *Theology after Freud* (Indianapolis: Bobbs-Merrill, 1970), 90.

48. Kohut, *The Restoration of the Self,* 89; idem, *The Analysis of the Self,* 152–53.

49. Erikson, *Young Man Luther,* 111–12.

50. Erikson, *Childhood and Society,* 267.

51. Erikson, *The Life Cycle Completed,* 67.

52. Erikson, *Childhood and Society,* 267; idem, *Identity, Youth, and Crisis,* 138.

53. Erikson, *Insight and Responsibility,* 131.

54. Erikson, *Identity, Youth, and Crisis,* 138.

55. Erikson, *Insight and Responsibility,* 130.

56. Ibid., 131.

57. Erikson, *Identity, Youth, and Crisis,* 138.

58. Erikson, *Insight and Responsibility,* 130.

59. Kohut, *The Restoration of the Self,* 114.

60. Ibid., 40.

61. Kohut, "Introspection, Empathy, and the Semi-Circle of Mental Health," *International Journal of Psychoanalysis* 63 (1982): 403.

62. Kohut, *How Does Analysis Cure?* 12.

63. Kohut, *The Restoration of the Self,* 237.

64. Kohut, "The Semi-Circle of Mental Health," 401.

65. Ibid., 402.

66. Ibid., 403.

67. Ibid., 404.

68. Edward O. Wilson, *On Human Nature* (Cambridge, Mass.: Harvard University Press, 1978), 149–67; for additional perspectives on this point of view see Richard Dawkins, *The Selfish Gene* (Oxford: Oxford University Press, 1976); George C. Williams, *Adaptation and Natural Selection* (Princeton, N.J.: Princeton University Press, 1966).

69. Erikson, *Insight and Responsibility,* 131.

70. Ibid., 219–43.

71. Ibid., 233.

72. Louis Janssens, "Norms and Priorities in a Love Ethics," *Louvain Studies* 6 (Spring 1977): 229.

73. Erikson, *Insight and Responsibility,* 231.

74. Ibid., 233.

75. Ibid., 239.

76. Erik Erikson, *Gandhi's Truth* (New York: Norton, 1969), 412.

77. Ibid.

78. Janssens, "Norms and Priorities in a Love Ethics," 229.

79. Ibid.

80. Ibid.

81. William Barrett and Daniel Yankelovich, *Ego and Instinct* (New York: Random House, 1977), 386–409.

82. Erikson, *Childhood and Society,* 249.

83. Ibid.

84. Ibid., 250.

85. Ibid., 251.

86. Erikson, *Insight and Responsibility,* 116.

87. Erikson, *Youth, Identity, and Crisis,* 96.

88. Ibid., 106.

89. David Rapaport, "A Historical Survey of Psychoanalytic Ego Psychology," in Erikson, *Identity and the Life Cycle,* 15.

90. Erikson, *Childhood and Society,* 69.

91. Ibid.

92. Erikson, *Insight and Responsibility,* 152.

93. Erikson, *Childhood and Society,* 16.

94. Kohut, *The Analysis of the Self,* 299.

95. Ibid., 307.

96. Kohut, *The Restoration of the Self,* 222.

9. Psychology and Society: Toward a Critical Psychological Theory

1. Edward Sampson, *Justice and the Critique of Pure Psychology* (New York: Plenum, 1983), 49.

2. Ibid.

3. Ibid., 47.

4. For a general introduction to this school, see Raymond Geuss, *The Idea of a Critical Theory: Habermas and the Frankfurt School* (Cambridge: Harvard University Press, 1981).

5. The work of Erich Fromm was often criticized by American psychology for its lack of clinical relevance. Although there might be some truth to this criticism, in view of the fact that Fromm did indeed attempt to make clinical contributions upon occasion, on the whole the American psychological establishment failed to grasp the meaning of his work within the

context of the broader critical program of the Frankfurt School. Little attention was paid to his more specifically social writings such as *The Sane Society* (New York: Rinehart, 1955) and *Marx's Concept of Man* (New York: Ungar, 1965).

6. Erich Fromm, *Beyond the Chains of Illusion: My Encounter with Marx and Freud* (New York: Simon & Schuster, 1962).

7. Kenneth J. Gergen, *Toward Transformation in Social Knowledge* (New York: Springer-Verlag, 1982); and John M. Broughton, "Piaget's Structural Developmental Psychology," *Human Development* 24 (1981): 382–411.

8. From the beginning of his research on moral development, Kohlberg has been clear that to pursue such research requires prepsychological philosophical definitional work on the meaning of the moral. Some commentators have criticized him for his inclinations toward Kantian formulations. But regardless of this point, he shares with those more self-consciously associated with critical theory the impulse to precede his empirical work with critical philosophical analyses of the domain he wishes to clarify with his empirical research. See his *The Philosophy of Moral Development: Moral Stages and the Idea of Justice*, Essays on Moral Development, vol. 1 (San Francisco: Harper & Row, 1981).

9. Russell Keat, *The Politics of Social Theory: Habermas, Freud, and the Critique of Positivism* (Chicago: University of Chicago Press, 1981), 11.

10. Norma Haan, Robert Bellah, et al., eds., *Social Science as Moral Inquiry* (New York: Columbia University Press, 1983), 1–16.

11. Robert Bellah, Richard Madsen, William Sullivan, Ann Swidler, and Steven Tipton, *Habits of the Heart: Individualism and Commitment in American Life* (Berkeley: University of California Press, 1985), 297–307.

12. Keat, *The Politics of Social Theory,* 78–86, 133–67.

13. For an interesting discussion of the issues between the philosophical hermeneuticians and Habermas, see Paul Ricoeur's "Ethics and Culture: Habermas and Gadamer in Dialogue," *Philosophy Today* (Summer 1973): 153–66.

10. Reason and Reactivity in Ellis, Beck, and Bowen

1. Stanton L. Jones and Richard E. Butman, *Modern Psychotherapies: A Christian Appraisal* (Downers Grove, Ill.: InterVarsity, 1991).

2. Ibid., 9.

3. Albert Ellis, *New Approaches to Psychotherapy Techniques* (Brandon, Vt.: Journal of Clinical Psychology Monograph Supplement, 1955).

4. Note that Albert Ellis has changed the name of Rational-Emotive Therapy to Rational-Emotive Behavioral Therapy. His reasons for doing this, along with a re-statement of his views in the light of postmodernism can be found in his *New Directions for Rational Emotive Behavior Therapy: Overcoming Destructive Beliefs, Feelings, and Behaviors* (New York: Prometheus, 2001). Since most of the references used in our book are to RET rather than REBT, we have maintained the older name.

5. Ellis, *New Directions,* 13.

6. Albert Ellis, *Reason and Emotion in Psychotherapy* (Secaucus, N.J.: Citadel, 1962), 36.

7. Ibid., 335.

8. Albert Ellis, *How to Stubbornly Refuse to Make Yourself Miserable about Anything—Yes, Anything!* (Secaucus, N.J.: Lyle Stuart, 1988), 13.

9. Ellis, *Reason and Emotion in Psychotherapy,* 121.

10. Ibid., 123–24.

11. Ellis, *How to Stubbornly Refuse*, 48.

12. Ibid., 34.

13. Jones and Butman, *Modern Psychotherapies*, 175.

14. Ibid., 181.

15. Ibid., 175.

16. Edwin Schur, *The Awareness Trap: Self-Absorption Instead of Social Change* (New York: McGraw-Hill, 1976).

17. Ibid.

18. S. A. Rigazio-DiGilio, A. E. Ivey, and D. C. Locke, "Continuing the Post-Modern Dialogue: Enhancing and Contextualizing Multiple Voices," *Journal of Mental Health Counseling* 19 (1997): 233–55.

19. Terry D. Cooper, "Karl Marx and Group Therapy: An Old Warning about a New Phenomenon," *Counseling and Value* 29 (October 1984): 22–26.

20. Ellis, *New Directions*, 52.

22. Ibid., 52.

23. Ellis, *How to Stubbornly Refuse*, 23.

24. Quoted in Jones and Butman, *Modern Psychologies*, 185.

25. Ibid.

26. Frank C. Richardson, Blaine J. Fowers, and Charles B. Guignon, *Re-Envisioning Psychology: Moral Dimensions of Theory and Practice* (San Francisco: Jossey-Bass, 1999), 68.

27. C. Stephen Evans, "Albert Ellis' Conception of Rationality: How Reasonable Is Rational-Emotive Therapy?" *Review of Existential Psychology and Psychiatry* 14:2, 3 (1984–1985): 129–39.

28. Albert Ellis et al., *RET: Handbook of Rational-Emotive Therapy* (New York: Springer, 1977), 15.

29. Evans, "Albert Ellis' Conception of Rationality," 141–42.

30. Albert Ellis, "Rational Emotive Behavior Therapy," in *Current Psychotherapies*, ed. Raymond J. Corsini and Danny Wedding, 5th ed. (Itasca, Ill.: Peacock, 1995).

31. Evans, "Albert Ellis' Conception of Rationality," 131.

23. Ibid., 132.

32. Albert Ellis, "Yes, How Reasonable Is Rational-Emotive Therapy (RET)?" *Review of Existential Psychology and Psychiatry* 14:2, 3 (1984–1985): 135–39.

33. Ibid., 135.

34. Ibid., 136–38.

35. Ellis, *New Directions*, 52–53.

36. Jones and Butman, *Modern Psychotherapies*, 175.

37. Ibid., 176.

38. Albert Ellis, *The Case against Religion: A Psychotherapist's View* (Austin: American Atheist Press, 1980), 37.

39. Peter Berger, *The Sacred Canopy: Elements of a Sociological Theory of Religion* (New York: Doubleday, 1967).

40. See Terry D. Cooper, "The Plausibility of a New Self: Self-Esteem from a Sociology of Knowledge Perspective," *Counseling and Values* 35:1 (October 1990): 31–38.

41. Jones and Butman, *Modern Psychotherapies*, 183.

42. Ellis, *The Case against Religion*.

43. Paul J. Watson, "Changing the Religious Self and the Problem of Rationality," in *Changing the Self: Philosophies, Techniques, and Experiences*, ed. T. Brinthaupt, R. Lipka, and P. Richard (Albany: State University of New York Press, 1994). Watson, too, has built on—yet

extended in his own way—the basic insights and methodology of *Religious Thought and the Modern Psychologies*. In this essay, he opens with the words "Psychotherapeutic attempts to change the religious self must simply occur as an encounter between client and therapist. Yes, as Browning (1987) notes, they also represent 'a cultural problematic of great general significance' (p. 2). The difficulty is that both religion and the modern psychologies 'provide concepts and technologies for the ordering of the interior life' (Browning, 2), and like moral philosophies generally (MacIntyre, 1981, 50–51), clinical psychologies begin with some definition of 'fallen' or pathological forms of 'human nature,' specify some *telos* or goal toward which the individual should strive, and then employ the practical reasoning and experience of therapy to move a client from the former to the latter condition. In short, 'significant portions of the modern psychologies, and especially the clinical psychologies, are actually instances of religio-ethical thinking.'" After an extensive philosophical discussion, and his own analysis of Ellis, he concludes with another reference to *Religious Thought and the Modern Psychologies* by writing "some social scientific definition of the ideal self could be accepted as the 'objective' and universal criterion of adjustment, but such definitions now seem based upon non-empirical assumptions very much like those of religion. They are 'instances of religio-ethical thinking (Browning, 1987, 8), and an excessive confidence in the social sciences could betray an ethnocentrism.'" Rather than speaking of visions, deep metaphors, and principles of obligation, Watson gets to much the same thing with the idea of "ideological surround." See Watson's "Changing the Religious Self and the Problem of Rationality," 109, 133.

44. Ellis, *Reason and Emotion in Psychotherapy*, 142.

45. Watson, "Changing the Religious Self," 124.

46. Ellis, *Reason and Emotion in Psychotherapy*, 146.

47. Ibid., 138–39.

48. Watson, "Changing the Religious Self," 125–26.

49. Jones and Butman, *Modern Psychotherapies*, 198.

50. Aaron T. Beck, *Prisoners of Hate: The Cognitive Basis of Anger, Hostility, and Violence* (New York: Perennial, 1999).

51. Aaron T. Beck and Marjorie Weisher in Arthur Freeman et al., *A Comprehensive Handbook of Cognitive Therapy* (New York: Plenum, 1989), 23.

52. Ibid., 6.

53. Ibid., 6.

54. Ibid., 26.

55. Ibid., chap. 2.

56. Ibid., 38.

57. Ibid., 73.

58. Ibid., 15.

59. See Sam Keen, *Faces of the Enemy: Reflections of the Hostile Imagination* (San Francisco: HarperSanFrancisco, 1986).

60. Beck, *Prisoners of Hate*, 15–17.

61. Ibid., 30–31.

62. Ibid., 21–22.

63. Ibid., 35.

64. Ibid., 39.

65. L. Rebecca Propst, "Cognitive Psychology and Psychotherapy," in Rodney Hunter, ed., *Dictionary of Pastoral Care and Counseling* (Nashville: Abingdon, 1990), 188–90.

66. Ibid., 189.

67. Reinhold Niebuhr, *The Self and the Dramas of History* (New York: Scribner's, 1955), 4.

68. Ibid., 5.

69. Ibid.

70. Ibid., 17–18.

71. Michael Nichols and Richard C. Schwartz, *Family Therapy: Concepts and Methods* (Boston: Allyn and Bacon, 1998), 150.

72. Ibid., 44.

73. Jones and Butman, *Modern Psychotherapies,* 351.

74. Ibid., 351.

75. Herta A. Guttman, "Systems Theory, Cybernetics, and Epistemology," in *Handbook of Family Therapy,* vol. 2, ed. Alan S. Gurman and David P. Kniskern (Bristol, Pa.: Brunner/Mazel, 1991), 41.

76. Jones and Butman, *Modern Psychologies,* 351.

77. Guttman, "Systems Theory, Cybernetics, and Epistemology," 41.

78. Ibid., 41.

79. Michael E. Kerr and Murray Bowen, *Family Evaluation: An Approach Based on Bowen Theory* (New York: Norton, 1988), 24.

80. Ibid.

81. We borrow this phrase from Lawrence Matthews, a Bowenian pastoral counselor, who led a Bowen workshop at the 1998 American Association of Pastoral Counselors Convention.

82. Nichols and Schwartz, *Family Therapy,* 142.

83. Ibid., 144.

84. Edwin H. Friedman, "Bowen Theory and Therapy," in *Handbook of Family Therapy,* vol. 2, ed. Alan S. Gurman and David P. Kniskern (Bristol, Pa.: Brunner/Mazel, 1991), 141.

85. Paul McLean, "Brain Evolution Related to Family, Play, and the Isolation Call," *Archives of General Psychiatry* 42 (1985) 405–17; also, for a brief overview, see Peter L. Steinke, *How Your Church Family Works: Understanding Congregations as Emotional Systems* (Washington D.C.: Alban Institute, 1994), chap. 2.

86. Steinke, *How Your Church Family Works,* 18.

87. Ibid., 18.

88. Ibid., 29–30.

89. Kerr and Bowen, *Family Evaluation,* 130–31.

90. Michael Nichols, *The Self in the System: Expanding the Limits of Family Therapy* (New York: Brunner/Mazel, 1987).

91. Jones and Butman, *Modern Psychotherapies,* 361.

92. Ibid., 363.

93. Richardson, Fowers, and Guignon, *Re-Envisioning Psychology.*

94. Ibid., 76.

95. Ibid.

96. Ibid., 82–83.

97. Reinhold Niebuhr, *The Nature and Destiny of Man,* vol. 1 (New York: Scribner's, 1964), 271.

11. Psychology's Relationship with Religion:
Toward an Intramural Discussion

1. Stanton L. Jones, "A Constructive Relationship for Religion with the Science and Profession of Psychology: Perhaps the Boldest Model Yet," *American Psychologist* (March 1994): 184–99.

2. Jones's article is a major breakthrough in the discussion of the relation of psychology and religion and demonstrates both creativity and uniqueness. To call attention that *Religious Thought and the Modern Psychologies* was quoted several times in the article is designed not to detract from its uniqueness but to reveal part of the reason we rely on it to advance our argument.

3. Ibid., 184–85.

4. Ibid.

5. Ibid.

6. Ibid.

7. Ibid.

8. Ibid.

9. Ibid.

10. Ibid., 187.

11. Ibid., 189–90.

12. Ibid., 193.

13. Ibid., 196.

14. Peter Berger, *The Sacred Canopy: Elements of a Sociological Theory of Religion* (New York: Doubleday, 1967).

15. Don S. Browning, "Can Psychology Escape Religion? Should It?" *International Journal for the Psychology of Religion,* 7/1 (1997): 1–21.

16. Ibid., 3.

17. Ibid., 8–10.

18. Jay E. Adams, *Competent to Counsel: Introduction to Nouthetic Counseling* (Grand Rapids: Ministry Resources Library, 1970).

19. See, for instance, his "A Biblical Counseling View," in Eric L. Johnson and Stanton L. Jones, eds., *Psychology and Christianity: Four Views* (Downers Grove, Ill.: InterVarsity, 2000).

20. Ibid., 33.

21. In addition to the extensive use of our work in Jones and Butman's *Modern Psychotherapies,* the work of Thomas Oden is frequently and appreciatively invoked as well.

22. Ibid.

23. Richard Bube, *The Human Quest: A New Look at Science and the Christian Faith* (Waco, Tex.: Word, 1971); David G. Myers and Malcolm A. Jeeves, *Psychology through the Eyes of Faith,* rev. ed. (San Francisco: HarperSanFrancisco, 2002).

24. Myers and Jeeves, *Psychology through the Eyes of Faith,* 8.

25. Ibid., 8–9.

26. Johnson and Jones, *Psychology and Christianity,* 131.

27. Ibid., 226–27.

28. David G. Myers, *Psychology,* 6th ed. (New York: Worth, 2001).

29. Johnson and Jones, *Christianity and Psychology,* 152.

30. Ibid., 97.

31. Ibid., 55.

32. Ibid., 181.

33. David G. Myers, *The Inflated Self: Human Illusions and the Biblical Call to Hope* (New York: Seabury, 1980); *Social Psychology* (New York: McGraw-Hill, 1996).

34. Johnson and Jones, *Christianity and Psychology,* 86.

35. Ibid., 97.

36. Ibid., 193–94.

37. Ibid., 98.

38. Ibid., 98.

39. Ibid., 160.

40. Ibid., 161.

41. Quoted in Myers and Jeeves, *Psychology through the Eyes of Faith,* 15.

42. David Tracy, *Plurality and Ambiguity* (San Francisco: Harper & Row, 1987), 28–31.

43. Richard J. Bernstein, *Beyond Objectivism and Relativism: Science, Hermeneutics, and Praxis* (Philadelphia: University of Pennsylvania Press, 1983), 168.

Index

Adaptive responses. *See* Natural selection

Adorno, Theodor, 112, 213

Agape, 14, 27–28, 47, 50, 52–56, 82, 124, 126, 130–34, 135, 138–41, 215, 228, 229. *See also* Love; Niebuhr, Niebuhr; Self-sacrifice

Aggression, 26, 46, 48, 50, 52, 64, 85, 125, 170, 173, 174, 175, 197, 198, 208, 231, 232–33

Altruism. *See* Other-regard

Animal husbandry. *See* Skinner, B. F.

Anthropology
  Christian, 23–28, 32, 44, 76–81, 93, 102, 103, 115, 245
  moral, viii, 23, 25, 26, 28–30, 37, 45, 178, 234, 245, 247–49, 250, 253, 254, 259, 262, 263. *See also* Niebuhr, Reinhold; Skinner, B. F.

Anxiety, 15, 23, 27, 41, 51, 52, 76–80, 93, 99, 102–3, 123, 128–30, 142, 179, 183, 194, 195, 207, 221, 223, 227, 229–33, 235–44, 253, 259

Aquinas, Thomas (Saint), 92, 114, 257, 262–63

Archetypes. *See* Jung, Carl

Aristotle, 25, 70, 86, 92, 117, 134, 198, 257, 262–63

Augustine, Saint, 23, 25, 29, 51, 55, 77, 128, 134, 135, 151, 153, 171, 207, 226, 227, 254, 258, 263

Autonomy, 30, 61, 63, 93, 95, 99, 105, 153, 174, 185, 202, 203, 235, 238, 242, 243

Barbour, Ian, 5–6, 22, 34, 49, 51, 90, 110, 116, 117, 205, 246, 281 n.29

Barrett, William, 6, 204

Barth, Karl, 28, 42

Beck, Aaron, 3, 4, 13, 14, 31, 217, 229–35, 238, 243–44
  cognitive-behavioral therapy of, 229–35

and egocentric bias, theory of, 229–33
and primal thinking in the face of anxiety, 229–234. *See also* Survival

Behaviorism. *See* Skinner, B. F.

Bellah, Robert, 7, 10, 59–60, 214

Berger, Peter, 227, 248

Bernstein, Richard, ix, 7, 248, 267

Bible, 13, 23, 25, 29, 38, 55, 77, 86, 128, 131, 133, 135, 138–40, 178–80, 217, 233, 249, 250, 252, 253, 260–62, 265

Biology. *See* Human nature; Natural selection; Nature

Black, Max, 22, 34, 205

Bowen, Murray, 3, 4, 13, 14, 31, 217, 234–44
  and anxiety and reactivity, understanding of, 235–43
  and differentiation, theory of, 235–43
  and emotional cut-off, concept of, 237, 240
  family systems therapy of, 217, 235–43
  and fusion, negative and positive, theory of, 237
  and nonreactivity, theory of, 235–43
  and self-regulation, concept of, 235, 236, 237, 238, 244

Bowlby, John, 147, 155

Brown, Norman O., 58, 181

Buber, Martin, 188, 191

Bultmann, Rudolph, 28, 54

Butman, Richard, xi, 217, 219–20, 222, 225, 227, 228, 229, 230, 236, 241–42

Capitalism, 77, 210–13

Care, 100, 142, 183, 195, 196, 198, 199–202, 206. *See also* "Cultures" of modern psychology

Caritas, 134, 135, 140, 163, 183, 202. *See also* Love

Catholicism, xiii, 1, 34, 127, 134, 135–38, 175, 202